Relational Economics and Organization Governance

This interdisciplinary book series examines recent developments concerning the "relational view" in economics. While the relational research perspective primarily has roots in philosophy, sociology and economic geography, this series offers contributions to the relational view from such diverse fields as institutional and organisational economics, management, organisational theory, and mathematics. Focusing on a relational approach to contracts and governance, leadership, rents, global cooperation, intersectoral cooperation and civil society, the series welcomes theoretical and empirical research on relational structures in market theory, institutional and organisational economics, the resource-based view of the firm, organisational studies, behavioural economics and economic sociology. Within this range of fields, researchers are invited to contribute to the further development of a relational view in economics.

Jacob Dahl Rendtorff • Lukas Belser
Jessica Geraldo Schwengber
Editors

Advances in Relational Economics

Theoretical, Methodological, Philosophical and Empirical Foundations

Springer

Editors
Jacob Dahl Rendtorff
Social Sciences and Business, Hus 25.1
Roskilde University
Roskilde, Denmark

Lukas Belser
Zeppelin University
Friedrichshafen, Germany

Jessica Geraldo Schwengber
Zeppelin University
Friedrichshafen, Germany

ISSN 2662-9852 ISSN 2662-9860 (electronic)
Relational Economics and Organization Governance
ISBN 978-3-031-75724-2 ISBN 978-3-031-75725-9 (eBook)
https://doi.org/10.1007/978-3-031-75725-9

This Springer imprint is published by the registered company Springer Nature Switzerland AG
The registered company address is: Gewerbestrasse 11, 6330 Cham, Switzerland

Contents

Introduction: The Relational View on Economics – Challenges to a New Paradigm 1
Jacob Dahl Rendtorff

Part I Relational Nature of the Firm

Dynamic Network Models in Relational Theory of the Firm 13
Josef Wieland and Tetiana Unkovska

A Relational View on Organization Ontology: Insights from Methodological Relationism, Process Philosophy, and Critical Realism 47
Jessica Geraldo Schwengber

The Nature of the Firm as Corporate Actor: Relational Economics and the Challenges of Legal Personhood 63
Marc C. Hübscher

Part II Relational Management and Leadership

Stakeholder Management and Relational Economics. Towards Just and Sustainable Business Practices 95
Jacob Dahl Rendtorff

Cooperative Economics and Management and Abolitionist Relationality 119
Jerome Nikolai Warren

Understanding Barriers to Relational Contracting: Exploring Challenges and Solutions 147
Tim Cummins

Leadership as a Temporal Abstraction: A Conceptual Reflection 157
Willem Fourie

Part III Relational Philosophy

Relational Process Atomism: Epistemological and Methodological Considerations on the Metaphysics of Transactions 171
Michael Schramm

A Dynamic Relational Ontology and Its Implications for Epistemology 187
Gil Santos

Relational and Transactional Rationalities in Chinese Thought and Social Practice 213
Matthias Niedenführ

Editors and Contributors

About the Editors

Jacob Dahl Rendtorff is a Professor of philosophy of management and business ethics at the Department of Business and Social Sciences, Roskilde University, Denmark. Rendtorff's research has a broad perspective on organization theory, management, responsibility, ethics and legitimacy of business firms and corporations, corporate social responsibility, business ethics, and philosophy of law.

Lukas Belser is a doctoral researcher at the Chair of Institutional Economics at Zeppelin University. His research focuses on strategy and governance in network organizations. He also focuses on performance measurement and intangible assets. Belser holds a bachelor's degree in political science and a master's degree in general management.

Jessica Geraldo Schwengber is a post-doctoral researcher at the Chair of Institutional Economics at Zeppelin University, project manager of the Transcultural Caravan Network, and managing director of the Leadership Excellence Institute Zeppelin (LEIZ). Her research interest lies in organization theory, relational economics, and transcultural management. Jessica Geraldo Schwengber holds a bachelor's and a master's in economics from University of Roma Tor Vergata (Italy) and a PhD from Zeppelin University (Germany).

Contributors

Tim Cummins University of Leeds, Leeds, UK

Willem Fourie Department of Business Management, University of Pretoria, Pretoria, South Africa

Marc C. Hübscher University of Ulm, Ulm, Germany

Matthias Niedenführ Zeppelin University, Friedrichshafen, Germany

Jacob Dahl Rendtorff Roskilde University, Roskilde, Denmark

Gil Santos Departamento de História e Filosofia das Ciências, Faculdade de Ciências da Universidade de Lisboa, Lisbon, Portugal

Michael Schramm University of Hohenheim, Hohenheim, Germany

Jessica Geraldo Schwengber Zeppelin University, Friedrichshafen, Germany

Tetiana Unkovska University of Basel, Basel, Switzerland

Jerome Nikolai Warren Académie Royale des Sciences, des Lettres et des Beaux-Arts de Belgique, Brussels, Belgium

Josef Wieland Leadership Excellence Institute Zeppelin (LEIZ), Zeppelin University, Friedrichshafen, Germany

Introduction: The Relational View on Economics – Challenges to a New Paradigm

Jacob Dahl Rendtorff

Abstract This chapter presents an introduction and an overview of the chapters in the book which were presented at the third conference on Relational Economics on "The Relational View on Economics—Challenges to a New Paradigm" in Roskilde, Denmark from September 28 to September 29, 2023. The conference was organized as a fruitful partnership between the Leadership Excellence Institute Zeppelin at Zeppelin University, Germany, and the Department of Social Sciences and Business at Roskilde University, Denmark. The chapter gives on this basis an outline of the topics of discussion on Relational Economics which were developed at the third conference on Relational Economics. The chapter presents the intentions of the third conference on Relational Economics with focus on the critical challenges to the new paradigm of economic theory to continue the discussions and reflections of the international research project on Relational Economics. The introduction gives an overview of the interdisciplinary, epistemological, and methodological aims of this conference on Relational Economics.

Keywords Relational economics · Introduction · Interdisciplinary · Methodology · Conferences

The third conference on Relational Economics on "The Relational View on Economics—Challenges to a New Paradigm" took place at the Department of Social Sciences and Business at Roskilde University in Denmark from September 28 to September 29, 2023. The conference was organized as a fruitful partnership between Zeppelin University, Germany, and the Department of Social Sciences and Business at Roskilde University, Denmark. This conference followed up on the first international conference on Relational Economics which took place at Zeppelin University in Friedrichshafen in 2018. And it also continued the discussions of the second conference on Relational Economics that was held at the ESSEC Campus in Paris,

J. D. Rendtorff (✉)
Roskilde University, Roskilde, Denmark
e-mail: jacrendt@ruc.dk

J. D. Rendtorff et al. (eds.), *Advances in Relational Economics*, Relational Economics and Organization Governance,
https://doi.org/10.1007/978-3-031-75725-9_1

Cergy, with the title "Cooperating in Value-Creating Networks—A Relational View" (Rendtorff, 2024a). It was the intention of the third conference on Relational Economics, with its focus on the critical challenges to the new paradigm of economic theory, to continue the discussions and reflections of the international research project on Relational Economics. The aim of the conference was to develop the interdisciplinary, epistemological, and methodological reflections on Relational Economics following up on the previous conferences and continue research within the framework of the Relational Manifesto which focuses on the relation between economics and organizational governance (Wieland, 1989, 1993, 1996, 1999, 2005, 2013, 2014, 2020).

Having established the relational view on economics as an important research paradigm, it was the aim of the third conference on Relational Economics to ask questions about the possibilities and limits of this approach through questions concerning the relational view on the economy as an important new paradigm of economic thinking. In this book, we present the most important papers and essays that were presented at the conference as a part of the mutual research project on Relational Economics. The papers for the conference followed up on the earlier reflections on Relational Economics as an effort to understand economic and social value creation in the networks of relations between different stakeholders in society in the framework of national and global interactions between different actors. The relational view focuses on the dynamics of governance in relation to current economic and social actors (Wieland, 2020). In this perspective, the conference continued to engage leading international scholars in relation to reflections on the paradigm of Relational Economics in their respective fields of research.

The starting point of the conference was that a relational view on economics underlines the complexity and dynamism of modern-day economy and society. In such a view, social and economic values are created in non-linear transactions in dynamic processes of regio-global cooperative networks. In the empirical world, this calls for new forms of relational business models and governance mechanisms to interlink resources from stakeholders from different economic and social systems.

In this view of Relational Economics, economy is, by its very nature, dynamic and a relational phenomenon characterized by the impact of interactive links between different system logics, network effects, and their governance. To find resilient and innovative practical solutions for these issues, the willingness and ability to cooperate is key. It is therefore a field of genuine transdisciplinary research and academic discourse. The aim of the conference was to contribute to this process and to facilitate cross-disciplinary discussion about the current socio-economic challenges currently shared in a networked reality (Wieland, 1989, 1993, 1996, 1999, 2005, 2013, 2014, 2020).

To this end, the contributions presented at the conference from the fields of economics, business administration, organizational theory, complexity theory, evolutionary economics, relational sociology, political science, and philosophy were both theoretical and empirical. The conference had more than 25 participants and a few occasional local spectators from different countries and different disciplinary backgrounds who contributed to foster interdisciplinary discussion and an intensive exchange of ideas.

In this setting, the first part of the conference concentrated on methodological individualism vs. relationism. Key issues of discussion were atomistic vs. relational epistemology, including discussions of relational rationality, complexity theory, and the role of analytical sociology in the relational paradigm of the economy. The second part of the conference focused on intangible assets and accounting, including relational accounting, knowledge management, EU taxonomies on sustainability, and creating shared value in Europe. The third part of the conference included discussion of alternatives to capitalism with a focus on relational economy and society. Key topics for further investigation included relational approaches to the economy, cooperative economics, stakeholder capitalism, and network theory. Finally, in the fourth part of the conference, speakers concentrated on the challenges of developing a relational theory of the firm. Important topics of discussion in this context were relational rents and costs, including cultural and intercultural management, relational organizational learning, and organizational resilience.

The choice of Roskilde University for developing the new paradigm of Relational Economics can be considered a very good fit since the project of Relational Economics is built on a new approach to economics that corresponds very well to a socially engaged vision of the economy. This is also the case with Roskilde University which, since its establishment in 1972, has focused on problem-oriented learning in research and teaching. This is combined with interdisciplinary thinking as an important mindset and scientific and academic approach. Roskilde University is based on participant-directed project work in groups, based on case study-oriented learning with a focus on the social relevance of teaching and research. In economics and business, this also implies an interdisciplinary and problem-oriented approach, which provides an excellent basis for Relational Economics. In a way, Roskilde University can be said to have been attempting to develop the relational paradigm since the first students were enrolled in 1972. The focus on problem-oriented, interdisciplinary, and participant-directed project work, also called problem-oriented project learning (PPL) in economics provided a relational view on economic science and thought, thereby placing economics at the center of critical social theory.

In the 1970s, students were very left wing and they wanted economics and business to be critical social sciences contributing to social transformation toward justice and equality in society. Later, in the 1980s, the teaching methods of Roskilde University contributed to the education of very good candidates that were highly sought-after in private business and public administration. The interdisciplinary and problem-oriented approach had contributed to this education of very competent professionals. In a survey in 1988—by a major newspaper—Roskilde University was rated number one among universities by businesses in Denmark. Today, during many changes, the core pedagogical principles and values of research and teaching have nevertheless been maintained and this provides an excellent basis for Relational Economics, where different economic and social science approaches are combined across different academic fields.

In particular, regarding research and teaching in ethics, responsibility, and legitimacy of business and corporations, the relational view is important for developing ethical reflections in business (Rendtorff, 2009a, b, 2011, 2020). This is also the case for ethics and moral challenges in more general contexts in Europe (Rendtorff, 1998, 2014a, b). Research in ethics, responsibility, and legitimacy of business requires philosophy of management and philosophical reflections in economics. In particular, this is the case with regard to personal and organizational integrity (Rendtorff, 2015, 2024b). From this perspective, the relational approach is increasingly important (Rendtorff, 2013a, b, c, d, 2017a, b, 2019a, b, 2020). There is a close connection between the relational view on economics and ethics, ethical economy, and stakeholder management (Bonnafous-Boucher & Rendtorff, 2016; Rendtorff & Bonnafous-Boucher, 2023). Thus, it was as part of the critical evaluation of Relational Economics that this approach to economic thought could learn a lot from Roskilde University, regarding the teaching of economics and business administration and leadership in an international perspective.

With this perspective, the conference established a close connection between Relational Economics and postwar theory of international relations with a focus on global interdependence and institutionalization of social cooperation in the international community. As a discipline of international relations, Relational Economics includes integration of international economics in the debates about the different schools of international relations. Relational Economics has an international dimension since economic relations include political and cultural interactions between societies in the international community. The paradox of the economic market is that it is not independent, but that it is always integrated into cultural, social, and political institutions in the international community.

Integrated into the international community, the market economy can be understood as a series of relational transactions between stakeholders who are situated in different political, social, and cultural contexts. Relational Economics takes place in the social cultural space of globalization, and relational economic interactions are built on the social and cultural interactions between stakeholders in the international community.

It was also the aim of the conference to search for the deeper ontological foundations of the relational view. Seen from the perspective of the philosophy of physics, the concept of relationality is important to investigate. From Newton to Bohr and Heisenberg, relations and relationality are important topics to investigate as deep ontological concepts. The study of the paradigm of Relational Economics becomes a question of the ontology of economics or business metaphysics. While Newton's universe of classical physics can be seen as universe construction and building blocks, a universe of things, quantum physics can be conceived as a universe of events and relations. While the classical paradigm of physics can be said to be based on substantial knowledge, the modern worldview is aware that knowledge is limited. Truth is not objective: it is not a fundamental object of inquiry since relations, time, and movement replace the classical outlook of physics. Following this modern physics from Bohr and Einstein, the concepts of Relational

Economics are integrated into the metaphysics of process philosophy with a focus on events and transactions as focal points of relational interactions.

From the point of view of such a relational ontology of transactions, social ontology follows the principle of transactions as the key to understanding relational interactions. With these ontological lenses, the paradigm of Relational Economics presupposes an ontological pluralism based on processes and events. In this relational ontology, every entity is an object and event, based on relations between systems (Rendtorff, 2013a, b, c, d). As a social theory, Relational Economics presupposes a dynamic relational ontology, presupposing a holism where there is an integrated relation between parts and the whole. In this sense, there is an integration of the different dimensions of economic interaction where organizations function as open systems rather than machines and closed systems. The relational economic business paradigm is based on this integration of parts and whole in this dynamic development of the management paradigm of Relational Economics.

Thus, following Josef Wieland, the relational paradigm defends a network-based and integrative view of the firm. This ontological view precedes the famous business scholar Michael Porter's activity-based view of the firm. Porter's ambitious proposal to make a business model out of the activity view of the firm does not take sufficiently into account the importance of relations for business. Indeed, creating shared value could be reinterpreted from the point of view of Relational Economics (Rendtorff, 2017b; Wieland, 2017). Here, the resource and capability view of the firm is closer to the relational view, since the firm's value chain, propositions, and market segments are built on relations. According to the relational view, we should not understand the firm's relations as a value chain, but rather as a network. Resource and capability network theory needs to be more receptive to the importance of the web of relations that constitute the activities of the firm in the relational web of interactions with society and other firms. From the relational perspective, it is important to conceive the business model of interactions between firms as a system of interdependent activities performed by focal firms in interaction with other firms and political and social actors. In this way, the ontology of Relational Economics implies a transactional business model, where market share and profitability are determined by relations and interactions in networks. Following such a conception, the relational business model implies a strong criticism of a neoclassical view of the firm. The relational view insists that the "image of atomistic actors competing for profit against each other in an impersonal marketplace is increasingly inadequate in a world in which the firms are embedded" in social and cultural contexts.

From this perspective, the relational thought of Josef Wieland emphasizes that the point of view of a relational business model following Relational Economics fundamentally implies a social network and institutional perspective. The relational paradigm of economics includes the following key dimensions: (1) multiple stakeholders; (2) boundary spanning activity with fluid boundaries of the network of economics; (3) shared value creation (tangible and intangible) for all stakeholders; (4) exploiting of business opportunities; (4) structure dependency (membership aspect, including identity, status, resources, and access); (5) inimitable and substitutable network for value creation; (6) not maximizing profit, but maximizing opportunities; and (7) focusing on the importance of structures and identities of actors. On this basis, the new relational paradigm proposes the relational business model as a construction of a unifying idea.

In this business model, the firm is understood as a relational event, where finding new stakeholders helps to create new business opportunities. Therefore, there is a close connection between Relational Economics and stakeholder theory. Stakeholder management and stakeholder identification contribute to the development of the relational business model. Governmental law and different government stakeholders contribute to the development of the firm's relations to relevant stakeholders in the company. In this context, investments should be understood in the perspective of a combination between stakeholder management, management of value chains, and understanding of the interactive and social and cultural aspects of relational transactions. The relational paradigm of the business firm emphasizes that interactions and relations are definitive for the role and positions of company stakeholders. Different stakeholders may transform into different relations in the web of interactions that constitute the relational economy. Suppliers may be customers, and customers may transform into stakeholders of the employees. Different stakeholders are involved in different transactions where different relational spaces have an impact on the formation of the business model of the firm.

In this context, challenges to the relational paradigm include the integration of sustainability in the development of the relational business model. Moreover, there is the need to define a clear preference for dealing with different stakeholders in the management and solution of conflicts and other interactions. The relational paradigm needs to develop models for understanding and defining management tasks in relational interactions. This includes models for prioritizing and identifying the most important stakeholders, and Wieland emphasizes that transcultural competencies are essential for developing the management of the relational business model. Moreover, it is important to consider transcultural competencies as important general competencies in the management of the transcultural competencies as general competencies that are necessary to form relations in business and economics. In this context, the development of business targets and strategy, as well as leadership approaches and realization of good business, is important to contribute to developing the organization and growth of the firm based on the relational business strategy.

Following up on stakeholder management and the relational business model, relational contracting is an important part of the relational business paradigm. Research into and management of relational contracting makes relational contracting and contract relations an important part of the development of relational economic thinking in business. Relational contracting is important for developing sustainability and social responsibility in economics because relational contracting is based not only on formal and legal contracts but also on a broader relational conception of contracting. As the relational paradigm develops out of the transaction cost paradigm, there is a strong focus on contracting in the relational approach to economics. However, contracts are not only understood as formal contracts but also as boundary objects for operations in business. While some contracts are relational and other contracts are transactional, it can still be argued that all contracts include a fundamental relational dimension. Contracts in relational contracting are involved in a process where contracts contribute to managing uncertainty and delivering economic benefit for the development of the organization.

Accordingly, management of contracts constitutes a framework for relational application. In this sense, it is important to use the contract as an instrument for relational management to develop organizational governance to address uncertainty in the management of the organization. Contracts can then be defined as an important part of the relational business model development.

The papers in this book can be seen to discuss different dimensions of these approaches to Relational Economics. Indeed, relational contracting is key to understanding the functions of relations in different forms of economic actions. Relational contracting can be considered as a part of economic action that is defined by transaction cost economics, which can be considered as an important predecessor for Relational Economics. Transactional contracting implies close collaborative relations with stakeholders with a focus on fairness in the transactions. Accordingly, transactional contracting also provides the foundations for understanding the challenges of ethics and equity in contractual relations in the environment of the firm.

Moreover, leadership of contractors and stakeholders may be considered an important part of the development of the paradigm of Relational Economics. In the relational perspective, leadership is about establishing relations with the internal and external stakeholders in the firm and its environment. From the point of view of Relational Economics, leadership involves the capacity to deal with processes and events. Relational leadership is concrete and context-based, and relational leadership includes continuous concern for the fluidity of the moment in leadership. This implies that leadership as a contextual and temporal concept is fundamentally relational as a processual event in the organization.

Regarding the theory of the firm and the nature of the firm as a corporate actor, Relational Economics can be considered as a challenge to the traditional concepts and theories of legal personhood (Rendtorff, 2009a). While mainstream theories of the firm regard the business organization as an instrument to maximize shareholder value, based on profits and increasing market value, the relational concept of the firm considers the value creation of the firm as emerging out of cooperation and relational networks. Seen from the relational perspective, shared value creation in networks is essential for the economic development of the firm. In this perspective, the firm in Relational Economics can be considered as a social institution or social matrix based on shared value creation in social networks. This is the foundation for Wieland's development of institutional and transaction economics into a relational theory of the firm, based on social interaction, governance, and networks (Wieland, 1989, 1993, 1996, 1999, 2005, 2013, 2014, 2020).

In this sense, Relational Economics presupposes a dynamic social ontology with a specific relational epistemology. Such an ontology considers ontological categories as mutually related and interdependent. In ontology, it is not a substance that is essential but rather the relational ontological categories, where the firm is constituted in the social interaction between different relational categories. The epistemological dimension of this ontology is based on social perceptions of the world, where relational categories are formed through the intentionality structures of the human mind. The epistemological dimensions of this relational paradigm are applied in the formation of human knowledge of the firm in relational networks.

From the ontological perspective, Relational Economics combines transactions with events and processes. Here, Relational Economics can be combined with the famous British philosopher Whitehead's process philosophy, which regards the world as continuously changing. Closely linked to this, it is possible to propose the epistemological perspective of Relational Economics as process thinking, presupposing the view of the world as relations between parts, where the atoms of the relational networks are linked to each other through the relational transactions of interaction in the relational networks. Relational Economics is dynamic process thinking, based on the view of the world as changing in an evolutionary process with interactions between relational systems.

Thus, a relational view on the ontology of organizations may combine elements from methodological relationism, process philosophy, and critical realism. A relational ontology of the firm does not consider essences and substances as primary in the theory of the firm. The relational view on organizations presupposes an anti-substantialist methodological individualism that combines process philosophy with analysis of relations and networks of firms. This does not exclude a critical realist view of the firm, but in order to understand the ontology of the firm, it is necessary to focus on the constitution of social interactions in which the firm takes part.

The stakeholder perspective on organizations can here easily be reinterpreted as a part of the relational view on the firm. Stakeholder management can be said to deal with the internal and external relations of the firm, embedding the firm in society. Stakeholders are those groups who affect or are affected by the corporation to contribute to the sustainability of the firm. Stakeholder management is here a contribution to the leadership and strategic management of the firm. Stakeholder theory forms the bridge between Relational Economics and institutional theory and transaction cost economics, since it demonstrates how the firm is linked to stakeholders through informal and formal contractual obligations. Stakeholder management is open to a relational definition of the objectives and the goals of the firm, linking Relational Economics to a framework for relational governance and leadership of the firm. With the relational view, stakeholder thinking finds strong integration in economic theory and economic reflections.

Thus, the relational view on the firm implies the conception of the firm as being built on dynamic network models. Going back to the classical conception of the firm in the theory of the firm by Ronald Coase in 1937, the theoretical program of Relational Economics takes up the classical question of why firms exist. Relational Economics regards the firm as a web of relations, built into social institutions and processes. The relational view regards interactions between firms and markets as constituted through processes and networks. With this, Relational Economics integrates transaction cost economics and institutional economics with a social conception of the value creation of firms on economic markets. The relational view on the firm permits one to develop a new deeper understanding of the firm and economic interaction in complex, cultural and intercultural, and international contexts of interaction between business organizations in global society.

In this context, Relational Economics can be proposed as a vision of cooperative economics, including other alternative forms of economic organizations such as social enterprises or cooperative enterprises. Relational Economics draws on the experience of social enterprises and community economics to understand the social ties in the cooperation between business and society. Cooperative economics implies a vision of long-term operations in business organizations aiming at contributing to the public good of society including shared value creation between businesses, public organizations, and NGOs. Economic contracts contribute to the social good of society, and in this sense, there is an important moral and ethical dimension to the perspective of Relational Economics as a vision of economics and society based on egalitarian concepts of social cooperation for justice and the common good.

References

Bonnafous-Boucher, M., & Rendtorff, J. D. (2016). *Stakeholder theory: A model for strategic management* (Springer briefs in ethics). Springer Science+Business Media.

Rendtorff, J. D. (1998). The second international conference about bioethics and biolaw: European principles in bioethics and biolaw. *Medicine, Health Care, and Philosophy, 1*(3), 271–274.

Rendtorff, J. D. (2009a). *Responsibility, ethics and legitimacy of corporations*. Copenhagen Business School Press.

Rendtorff, J. D. (2009b). Basic ethical principles applied to service industries. *Service Industries Journal, 29*(1), 9–19.

Rendtorff, J. D. (2011). Institutionalization of corporate ethics and social responsibility programs in firms. In K. Buhmann, L. Roseberry, & M. Morsing (Eds.), *Corporate social and human rights responsibilities: Global, legal and management perspectives* (pp. 244–266). Palgrave Macmillan.

Rendtorff, J. D. (2013a). Basic concepts of philosophy of management and corporations. In C. Luetge (Ed.), *Handbook of the philosophical foundations of business ethics* (pp. 1361–1386). Springer Science+Business Media.

Rendtorff, J. D. (2013b). Philosophical theories of management and corporations. In C. Luetge (Ed.), *Handbook of the philosophical foundations of business ethics* (pp. 1409–1432). Springer Science+Business Media.

Rendtorff, J. D. (2013c). Recent debates in philosophy of management. In C. Luetge (Ed.), *Handbook of the philosophical foundations of business ethics* (pp. 1433–1457). Springer Science+Business Media.

Rendtorff, J. D. (2013d). The history of the philosophy of management and corporations. In C. Luetge (Ed.), *Handbook of the philosophical foundations of business ethics* (pp. 1387–1408). Springer Science+Business Media.

Rendtorff, J. D. (2014a). Risk management, banality of evil and moral blindness in organizations and corporations. In C. Luetge & J. Jauernig (Eds.), *Business ethics and risk management* (Ethical economy, Vol. 43, pp. 45–70). Springer Science+Business Media.

Rendtorff, J. D. (2014b). European perspectives. In H. A. M. J. ten Have & B. Gordijn (Eds.), *Handbook of global bioethics* (pp. 293–310). Springer Science+Business Media.

Rendtorff, J. D. (2015). Business ethics, strategy, and organizational integrity: The importance of integrity as a basic principle of business ethics that contributes to better economic performance. In *Handbook of research on business ethics and corporate responsibilities* (pp. 91–105). IGI-Global.

Rendtorff, J. D. (2017a). *Cosmopolitan business ethics: Towards a global ethos of management* (Finance, governance and sustainability: challenges to theory and practice series). Routledge.

Rendtorff, J. D. (2017b). Creating shared value as institutionalization of ethical responsibilities of the business corporation as a good corporate citizen in society. In J. Wieland (Ed.), *Creating shared value: Concepts, experience, criticism* (Ethical economy, Vol. 52, pp. 119–139). Springer.

Rendtorff, J. D. (2019a). *Philosophy of management and sustainability: Rethinking business ethics and social responsibility in sustainable development*. Emerald Group Publishing.

Rendtorff, J. D. (2019b). Sustainable development goals and progressive business models for economic transformation. *Local Economy, 34*(6), 510–524.

Rendtorff, J. D. (2020). The concept of business legitimacy: Learnings from Suchman. In J. Rendtorff (Ed.), *Handbook of business legitimacy: Responsibility, ethics and society*. Springer.

Rendtorff, J. D., & Bonnafous-Boucher, M. (Eds.). (2023). *Encyclopedia of stakeholder management* (Elgar encyclopedias in business and management series). Edward Elgar Publishing.

Rendtorff, J. D. (2024a). The new ethical values of the relational market economy: Value change in the private business world and the movement towards sustainable development goals. In J. Wieland, S. Linder, J. G. Schwengber, & A. Zicari (Eds.), *Cooperation in value-creating networks: Relational perspectives on governing social and economic value creation in the 21st century* (pp. 21–36). Springer.

Rendtorff, J. D. (2024b). Organisational integrity, citizenship, and legitimacy. In M. Kaptein (Ed.), *Research handbook on organisational integrity* (pp. 497–510). Edward Elgar Publishing.

Wieland, J. (1989). *Die Entdeckung der Ökonomie: Kategorien, Gegenstandsbereiche und Rationalitätstypen der Ökonomie an ihrem Ursprung*. Haupt.

Wieland, J. (1993). *Formen der Institutionalisierung von Moral in der Unternehmung: Die amerikanische Business-Ethics-Bewegung: Why and how they do it*. Haupt.

Wieland, J. (1996). *Ökonomische Organisation, Allokation und Status*. Mohr (Siebeck).

Wieland, J. (1999). *Die Ethik der Governance* (Metropolis-Reihe “Studien zur Governanceethik,” Vol. 1, 5th ed., 2007). Metropolis.

Wieland, J. (2005). *Normativität und Governance* (Metropolis-Reihe “Studien zur Governanceethik,” Vol. 3). Metropolis.

Wieland, J. (2013). *Shared value durch Stakeholder Governance* (Gemeinsam mit Andreas E. H. Heck). Metropolis.

Wieland, J. (2014). Governance ethics: Global value creation, economic organization and normativity. In *Ethical economy. Studies in economic ethics and philosophy*. Springer.

Wieland, J. (Ed.). (2017). *Creating shared value: Concepts, experience, criticism* (Ethical economy, Vol. 52). Springer.

Wieland, J. (2020). *Relational economics: A political economy. Relational economics and organization governance*. Springer.

Jacob Dahl Rendtorff is a professor of philosophy of management and business ethics at the Department of Business and Social Sciences, Roskilde University, Denmark. Rendtorff’s research has a broad perspective on organization theory, management, responsibility, ethics and legitimacy of business firms and corporations, corporate social responsibility, business ethics, and philosophy of law.

Part I
Relational Nature of the Firm

Dynamic Network Models in Relational Theory of the Firm

Josef Wieland and Tetiana Unkovska

Abstract This chapter explores the dynamic network models within the framework of the Relational Theory of the Firm, proposing a paradigm shift from traditional microeconomic and transaction cost economics towards a relational and network-oriented perspective. Building on Ronald Coase's foundational questions about the existence and nature of firms, we delve into the complex relational networks that significantly influence modern firms' development and functioning. This study introduces the concept of relational networks, where firms act as nodes within intricate webs of stakeholders, emphasising non-linear network effects, self-reinforcing mechanisms and synergetic phenomena. We present a methodological approach grounded in complexity, non-linearity and synergy to model firm dynamics in relational networks. This chapter outlines a comprehensive conceptual framework, including the conception of complex networks, network effects and non-linear dynamics, culminating in a dynamic benefit function for firms within these networks. This function integrates the firm's operational, financial and relational dimensions, highlighting the impact of bilateral interactions and network synergies on overall firm performance. This chapter proposes the relational network equilibrium as a state where the dynamic benefit function is maximised, accounting for the firm's integrated role within the network. We discuss the implications of network connectivity, coverage and synergetic effects on firm behaviour, introducing the concepts of Cooperation Rent and functional invariants as critical elements in understanding relational network dynamics. Our research paves the way for future studies on modelling the non-linear dynamics and synergetic effects in relational networks, emphasising the need for interdisciplinary approaches and advanced mathematical tools. This paradigm shift offers a fresh lens to view the nature of

J. Wieland (✉)
Leadership Excellence Institute Zeppelin (LEIZ), Zeppelin University,
Friedrichshafen, Germany
e-mail: josef.wieland@zu.de

T. Unkovska
University of Basel, Basel, Switzerland
e-mail: unkovska@yahoo.com.ua

J. D. Rendtorff et al. (eds.), *Advances in Relational Economics*, Relational Economics and Organization Governance,
https://doi.org/10.1007/978-3-031-75725-9_2

the firm and the firm's development in the global business landscape, providing actionable insights for economic and financial governance practices.

Keywords Relational theory of the firm · Dynamic network models · Non-linear network effects · Synergetic phenomena · Relational networks · Cooperational Rent · Network synergies · Relational network equilibrium

1 Introduction

Ronald Coase in his work "*The Nature of the Firm*" in 1937 posed deep fundamental questions that still motivate researchers today. Why do firms exist, what is the nature of the firm as an institutional phenomenon, how do they work in reality and what determines the limits of their growth? If market mechanisms ensure the most efficient allocation of resources in the economy, then why do firms—the strict hierarchical structures, "islands of administrative socialism" in the ocean of market relations—exist? If hierarchical structures (firms) are better mechanisms of resource allocation than the market, why hasn't the whole market economy gradually turned into one huge firm? What is the institutional nature of the interactions between firms and markets?

The search for answers to these groundbreaking questions led to the development of alternative theories of the firm, to a deeper understanding of the nature of the firm and to the development of transaction cost economics (TCE). TCE allowed "the black box" of transaction costs, which had not been investigated before by standard economics, to be opened so as to obtain bright insights about the nature of the firm and to formulate a viable hypothesis that the existence of the firm and the limits of its growth are determined by the purpose of transaction cost minimisation. This was a theoretical and empirical breakthrough in understanding the behaviour of firms, because price theoretical explanations of the firm did not provide a fruitful understanding of its nature and of the mechanisms of its functioning. They did not reveal the phenomena of complex relational network effects, which largely determine the firms' development in the modern world. Non-linear network effects both within the firm and in the external environment fundamentally change many established views. Therefore, a new profound level of understanding of the firm's nature and of the logic of its development based on the Relational Economics paradigm is required.

The Relational Economics paradigm considers the firm as a governance structure of complex relational network of a firm's stakeholders. Firm is one of the nodes (actors) in this heterogeneous network that is immersed in the external environment, which also is a network of complex networks. This conceptual view determines our methodological approaches to modelling the firm into the paradigm of the Relational Theory of the Firm. This new paradigm encompasses understanding relational networks and absorbs deep insights into interdisciplinary research and philosophy of complex dynamic processes. It allows us to take a fresh look at the nature of the firm and understand the underlying engines of modern global business and the world economy.

In our view, these perspectives are promising, as a new research approach can be a bridge connecting the theory of the firm with the great stratum of human knowledge gained by various sciences in the exciting fields of complex networks and synergetic phenomena. We agree with Nobel Prize winner Ilya Prigogine, father of the theory of dissipative structures, who wrote that the development of science is not identical to the steady unfolding of scientific disciplines, each of which is subdivided into watertight sections (2018). On the contrary, the convergence of different problems and viewpoints contributes to the unsealing of the formed sections and cubbyholes and to the effective "intermingling" of scientific culture. Turning points in the development of science have consequences that go beyond pure science and affect the entire intellectual atmosphere (Prigozhin & Stengers, 2018).

The Relational Theory of the Firm is a new, complex and intriguing field of research, requiring specialised modelling techniques to fully grasp its ideas and apply them to the practice of economic and financial governance. This chapter delves into our methodological approaches to modelling the firm and applying these approaches to develop practical network models based on a relational view of economics.

2 Methodological and Conceptual Approach to Modelling in the Relational Theory of the Firm

2.1 Conception of a Complex Network

The complex network is a key conception for modelling a broad class of systems with the complex network structure. They have been investigated in different areas of human knowledge, including physics, chemistry, biology, biophysics, neurobiology, geology, climate change and environmental sustainability, information technologies and artificial intelligence, and social and economic sciences. Networks of many interacting agents demonstrate different architectures, dynamics and very rich phenomenology. Complex network theory is a rapidly developing science based on tremendous progress that has already been achieved. A huge body of research in modelling social-economic and financial complex networks has already been developed. That research has brought new insights and, at the same time, raised new questions about the behaviour of firms in complex networks. The dynamic relational network processes within the firm and in its external environment demonstrate non-linear network effects, self-enforcing mechanisms and synergetic phenomena that are typical for the world of complex networks.

The classical microeconomic models of the firm and TCE don't cover the needs of modelling development of the firm as dynamic processes in complex networks. We need adaptation and application of complex network methodology for modelling the firm into the framework of the Relational Theory.

The conceptual foundation of complex network methodology combines two core interdisciplinary categories: complex systems and networks.

A complex system is a set of many interconnected and interacting elements or subsystems that is considered as a whole organism. The evolution of the complex system conception is present in a vast stratum of research in thermodynamics, statistical physics, cybernetics, information technology, theory of dissipative structures, synergetics, general theory of complex systems and others. Statistical physics and thermodynamics, including pioneering works by Maxwell, Boltzmann, Gibbs and other prominent scientists, made a fundamental contribution to understanding complex systems and connections between the behaviour of a large number of particles at the micro level and the emergence of a macroscopic phenomenon.

The next breakthrough was made by the works of Prigogine et al. (1977), Prigogine (1978, 1980), Nicolis and Prigogine (1989), and Haken (1973). They developed the new paradigm of non-linear thinking and complex systems methodology on an interdisciplinary basis. Further significant steps were made by establishing the special Santa Fe Institute for systematically studying complexity (Arthur, 2010, Arthur et al., 2020, Krakauer 2024).

Now complex systems methodology is a rapidly growing interdisciplinary area of human knowledge that is used by many fundamental and applied sciences, including economics and finance. Social and economic research in this area is developing intensively and includes, among many others, works by Arthur (1999, 2015, 2021) and Axtell (2007).

There are three inter-related fundamental categories underlying the concept of complex systems—complexity, non-linearity and synergy (or emergent property of complex systems).

2.2 Complexity

Complexity is a fundamental property of nature that permeates all the universe from microscopic particles to space-scale systems. Complexity is a very productive frame of thinking for research on any scale of natural or artificial systems, including the neural network of the human brain, human-created micro- and macro-level socio-economic systems, particularly relational networks of interacting economic agents (Amit, 1989; Biggiero & Magnuszewki, 2023; Hopfield, 1982, 1984; Hopfield & Tank, 1985).

There is still no clear and universal definition of complexity. A general conceptual view of the complexity phenomenon exists and specifies in applying to systems of different nature. This doesn't mean a mechanical transfer of process understanding from one field of science to another; rather, it indicates a new level of understanding the "universality-specificity" dichotomy. The comprehension of general universal principles does not replace specific knowledge about concrete complex systems. But they allow us to see the right direction of research and stimulate the discovery of new properties and non-obvious underlying regularities in the behaviour of specific complex systems, in particular, firms from the perspectives of Relational Economics.

Complexity has two important aspects:

- Consisting of many interacting and inter-related components
- Difficulties in understanding, in other words, requiring a large amount of information for its description

These two aspects are the basis for two quantitative approaches to assessing the degree of a system's complexity: structural and informational.

The information approach to complexity is based on the assessment of the quantity of information needed to describe the system. In particular, one of the information metrics of complexity is the quantity of information (I) for complex system description, calculated by the formula

$$I = \log_2 \Omega,$$

where Ω is the number of possible states of the system.

The structural approach to complexity is based on the study of the set of the system's elements and the structure of their inter-relationships, called the topology of the system. The concept of a complex network is used for modelling the topology of a complex system, for studying its properties and their influence on the system's dynamics. Complex network theory is a rapidly developing science with a powerful mathematical apparatus of graph theory and complex systems methodology. Recent well-known works in these fields include Albert and Barabási (2000, 2002), Barrat et al. (2008) and many other books and research papers.

2.3 Conception of Network and Network Effects

Conception of network and methodology of network modelling are based on the well-developed mathematical theory of graphs.

A graph (network) is a set of nodes (also called vertices, points or actors) connected by threads (also called edges or links):

$$G = (V, Z)$$

where $V = \{V_i; i = \overline{1,n}\}$*—the set of nodes, and* $Z = \{Z_{ij}; i = \overline{1,n}; j = \overline{1,n}\}$*—the set of threads between* V_i *and* V_j*.*

Adjacency matrix $A = (A_{ij}), i = \overline{1,n}; j = \overline{1,n}\}$ of the network $G = (V, Z)$ is a structural matrix that characterises the topology of the network:

$$A_{ij} = \begin{cases} 1, \text{if there is thread } Z_{ij} \text{ between } V_i \text{ and } V_j; \\ 0, \text{if there isn't thread } Z_{ij} \text{ between } V_i \text{ and } V_j. \end{cases}$$

When we consider the strength of connections between nodes, in other words, the weights of connections, we speak about a weighted network with quantitative measures described by the matrix of weights W:

$$W = (W_{ij}),$$

$$i = \overline{1, n}; j = \overline{1, n},$$

where W_{ij} is the weight of connection between V_i and V_j.

There are fundamental conceptions of network density, connectivity, centrality and betweenness, heterogeneity, cluster coefficients, topological overlap and network dynamic characteristics that developed in complex network theory. There is a vast body of books and research papers in the field of complex network theory, including its applications in economics and finance. The paradigm of the Relational Theory of the Firm opens up bright perspectives for using this huge body of human knowledge in complex network methodology for modelling the firm's functioning and development.

There are many books and research papers considering different types of network effects in firms' development, particularly Biggiero and Magnuszewski (2021), Biggiero et al. (2016), Rohlfs (1974) and others, where these pioneering authors articulated and modelled the network effects in the economy on a micro and macro level.

There are different types of non-linear network effects, which the dynamics of the firm's development demonstrates.

One type of such phenomena from the group of the demand-side is network effects in price dynamics, which does not obey the classical equations of microeconomics. This is the dependence of the prices of the goods or services in relational networks on the number of consumers and network participants who use it. For instance, this is the case of price dynamics of communication services, Internet, software applications, phones, computers, currencies, services of network platforms, and other goods and services connected with interactions of network participants. These network effects were described by Metcalfe (Hendler & Golbeck, 2008)—the value of a network asset is proportional to the square of the number of its users:

$$p \approx \frac{n^2}{2},$$

where p is the value of the asset to users; n is the number of network users.

The second type of network effects for firms is the effect of network scale economies or increasing returns. For instance, a taxi firm such as Uber is a relational network that includes managers, cars with drivers and clients that need trip services. If the taxi firm increases the number of cars and drivers in a city, and improves the network of relational transaction structure, it could increase the number of trips on a larger scale by connecting cars to customers more quickly. This network effect gives rise to additional value and extra returns to the firm because of its relational network nature. It is an example of a *synergy effect*, where multiple interactions between nodes result in a combined effect that is larger than the simple sum of their separate effects.

The third type of network effects for firms is cost advantage effects. We describe these in more detail in the following paragraph with practical network models.

The next type of network effects for the firms is non-linear effects of innovative clusters. Innovation clusters are the type of relational networks that generate a series of powerful network effects on both the demand- and supply-sides: from cost savings for firms and increased efficiency in implementing innovative ideas to diffusion of innovations and technology, as well as explosive synergy effects for the entire innovative cluster.

The network effect of innovation diffusion theory started its popularity from the groundwork of Rogers' (2003) *Diffusion of Innovations* that was first published in 1962. He determined five key elements that influence the spread of innovations: the innovation itself, the network of adopters, relational and communication channels (in essence, *relational networks*), time and social system. The core of diffusion paradigm is in inter-relationships between innovation decision-making process, relational networks for communication and knowledge exchange, an S-shaped rate of adoption, and personal, economic and social characteristics of various adopters' categories (in fact, it is a set of relational network node states, which we introduce in Relational Theory of the Firm) that was developed by Valente (1995), Valente and Rogers (1995) and others.

In general, the structure of the firm's relational networks has a deep impact on the qualitative and quantitative parameters of network effects. The Relational Theory of the Firm permits us to form a wide systematic picture of the relational network effects for the firm and fill the gap existing in classical microeconomic and transaction cost theories. For this purpose, we need to consider the next fundamental methodological conceptions—non-linearity of complex networks and synergy.

2.4 Non-linearity of Complex Networks

Non-linear thinking is radically different from thinking in linear categories. Non-linearity is a fundamental feature of complex systems that manifests itself in a huge variety of phenomena, including synergetic and network effects, spontaneous synchronisation, self-reinforcing cycles, uncontrolled self-organisation and the spontaneous emergence of new ordered structures within the system. These phenomena underlie the origin of life, the functioning of the brain and the whole living organism, and the natural and socio-economic phenomena. Non-linearity is a fundamental feature of real economic systems, including the firm as a governance structure in complex relational networks. Its dynamics cannot be modelled and predicted by using only linear methods. So, we need a deep understanding of the essence of non-linearity and of why it is so different from linearity.

The deep watershed between linear and non-linear dynamics is vividly described by Danilov (2006). He wrote that the world of non-linear regularities, as well as the world of non-linear phenomena behind it, is frightening, conquering and irresistibly alluring with its inexhaustible variety. Variability and exuberance of forms reign supreme here. What accurately captures and conveys the characteristic features of one class of non-linear functions says nothing about even the simplest features of the non-linear functions of another class. The same non-linear function responds differently to the equal increments of the independent variable depending on what value of the independent variable the increment is given. Non-linear functions contrast with linear ones by their almost complete "insensitivity" to changes in some values of the independent variable and their great sensitivity to changes in other values of the independent variable. Any linear function responds to change in the independent variable with the same change in its value for any values of the variable. This is where the line of demarcation between the world of linear and non-linear phenomena is drawn (Danilov, 2006, 208).

The mathematical models of physics have, at one time, passed its painful evolution from linear to non-linear methods. Physicists in the past believed that it is the linear theory that gives the main part of an infinite series of consecutive approximations to the truth, and non-linearity was assigned a small role of a correction that does not change the essence of conclusions. The linear mathematical apparatus was an indispensable element of their mathematical culture, "entered the flesh and blood, acquired almost tangible forms in the series of bright physical ideas and images of entities, allowing physicists, bypassing the burdens of difficult analysis, to intuitively foresee the answer" (Danilov, 2006, 208). However, according to Mandelshtam (1972) in his *Lectures on the Theory of Oscillations*, those who hoped that the linear mathematical apparatus could be adapted to solve new non-linear problems were disappointed—the linear mathematical apparatus rejected the alien tissue of non-linear supplements. Artificial linearisation was ineffective, in the most cases taught nothing and sometimes was extremely harmful.

Many prominent scientists wrote about the need to develop non-linear complex systems thinking in social and economic sciences. As Prigogine and Stengers (2018) wrote, it is no coincidence that the term introduced in MTI, "counterintuitive", has become quite firmly established. It reflects the habit of linear thinking and the collision with unpredictable reality that behaves non-linearly. The example given by Conrad Hal Waddington is illustrative: a slum clearance programme, instead of improving the situation, makes it worse. New buildings built to replace demolished ones attract more people to the neighbourhood, but if no employment is provided, they continue to be poor, and their housing becomes even more overcrowded. As Prigogine wrote, we are trained to think in terms of linear causality, but now we need a new "means of thinking".

In our opinion, it is no accident that the phenomena of extra-rapid economic growth (what is called an "economic miracle" in some countries) or abrupt financial collapses are still considered as unpredictable. Economic science today has reached a high level of maturity that actualises the necessity of transition to non-linear complex systems thinking, which physics, chemistry and biology once passed through. At present, researchers of complex economic systems follow the way of solving non-linear problems "piece by piece", using systems' individual particularities. This is quite a good approach to gain experience in non-linear modelling, which other sciences have also passed through, but it should not remain as a strategic highway of methodological development. Non-linear complex network economics at the micro and macro levels should achieve internal integrity. As with the emergence of non-linear physics, it is necessary to create a non-linear culture of economic thinking, including reliable mathematical models and economic concepts adequate to new tasks, to develop non-linear intuition, necessary where the intuition developed on linear tasks turns out to be unsuitable. And the most significant category of non-linear thinking, which we need in the Relational Economics perspective, is the concept of synergy.

Synergy (or emergent properties of complex systems). The phenomenon of synergy is closely related to conceptions of complexity, networks and non-linearity. The term synergy comes from the Attic Greek word συνεργία (synergia) from συνεργός (synergos), meaning "working together". Synergy means the holistic effect of the interactions and coherent collective behaviour of the complex system's inter-related parts. This effect is much greater than the simple sum of the results of each part. The synergy effects of inter-relations and interactions of the system's elements manifest themselves in powerful collective phenomena at the macroscopic level. It is a manifestation of Aristotle's philosophy, who said "The whole is more than the sum of its parts". Synergy is the pillar of a methodological bridge between the massive behaviour of elements at the micro level, which appears chaotic, and the surprising macroscopic phenomena, which sometimes seem unpredictable.

In the seminal works by the physicist Haken (1973, 1983, 1987, 1988), he defined synergetics as a new science of cooperative phenomena in complex systems. Haken built a comprehensive methodological and conceptual structure for the analysis of cooperative phenomena in physics and chemistry, and suggested directions of its applications to biology and the social sciences. He made a great contribution to chaos theory and self-organisation and gave new insights into understanding cooperative self-ordering in complex systems dynamics.

Synergy is a synonym for the conception of emergence, often encountered in research into complex systems. Emergency is understood as the property of a system, irreducible to the properties of its parts. Emergency arises due to the coherent collective behaviour of the system's elements and endogenous generating non-linear macroscopic effects. These effects can appear as a local or global emergency in a system. A local emergence arises when coherent behaviour occurs in a small part of the system, and global emergence is a result of coherent behaviour of elements that covers the whole system. Inter-relationships between local and global emergency in complex systems are a very promising issue that gives many insights for understanding synergy phenomena.

A classic example of global emergency (synergy) in neurobiology is the phenomenon of the content-addressed memory in complex neural networks of the human brain. The famous and intensively cited paper of Hopfield (1982) with his Hopfield model and the concept of network attractors was a significant breakthrough not only in understanding synergy phenomena in the human brain but also in the development of the methodology for modelling synergetic effects in complex neural networks. Hopfield gave new insights into guiding principles of complex network behaviour and developed the fruitful conception of network attractors. We will discuss and use this conception in the next paragraph.

There are many well-known examples of synergy effects in different complex networks in social life and economy. A vast body of scientific literature is focused on these studies by Axelrod (1997).

From the perspective of the Relational Theory of the Firm, it is very important to research coherent behaviour of elements and synergetic collective effects that arise at the level of the whole relational network. The synergetic bridge between the dynamics of nodes at the micro level, their collective behaviour and macroscopic phenomena at the level of whole relational network provides an understanding of the new relational network's capabilities.

From our point of view, the collective phenomenon of synergy arising at the level of whole relational networks is the main source of emergence of Cooperational Rent (Wieland, 2020; Wieland et al., 2022). Cooperational Rent is a fundamental synergetic property of relational networks that keeps the elements of the networks together. This process is non-linear—the cooperative behaviour and coherent dynamics of the nodes in the relational network lead to the growth of Cooperational Rent; on the other side, the increase in cooperative rents leads to additional revenues for each node and an intensified cooperative behaviour that keeps the network together.

The synergetic phenomenon of Cooperational Rent is a manifestation of the underlying microscopic processes of the node's relational transactions and system-forming basis for the development of the firm as a governing structure in the relational network of its stakeholders.

The relational networks' synergetic property of Cooperational Rent can arise through different mechanisms. Some of these mechanisms (without calling its results Cooperational Rent) have been studied from a variety of perspectives in many research papers. Some of these mechanisms are as follows:

1. Receiving additional benefits for a whole relational network because of filling structural holes. There is a vast body of research papers, including Burt (1992), and Snijders et al. (2010) focused on structural holes and benefits of filling them for some nodes and for the whole network.

   They found several types of benefit:

   - Information benefits in three forms (access, timing and referrals).
   - Control benefits, including control of assets such as sharing equipment, brands, technologies, human capital or knowledge.
   - Development of innovations and others. It is considered in Ahuja (2000) and Balkundi et al. (2009).

Structural hole theory has now evolved into a rapidly developing branch of complex network science. We can use these novelties in the development of the Relational Theory of the Firm.

2. Mechanism of "resources effect" that enhances organisations' resource endowment and optimises the utility of resources.
3. Creation of economies of scale; notable nodes of the network can share R&D, technologies, procurement, production, operations, marketing plans, distribution channels, unified management and sales strategies.
4. Mechanism of using the effectiveness of relational transactions to cross the barriers of ineffective relationships, thereby establishing a "build-govern" network position to innovative development.
5. Reduction of internal and external total costs, including transaction costs.
6. Mechanism of getting additional financial benefits through new access to debt resources and increasing financial leverage for stimulating growth of net profit and earning per share (EPS), tax savings and cash flow optimisation.
7. Synergetic effects in economic systems connected with mechanisms of non-linear feedback loops and self-enforcing mechanisms. As written in Dobusch and Schüßler (2012), and Sydow et al. (2009), most researchers agree that the self-reinforcing mechanisms include five main effects: cooperation effects, coordination effects, complementarity effects, expectation effects and investment and learning effects. These mechanisms have been described both at the micro level of organisations and at the meso level of technological fields and industries.

We introduce a specific function of synergetic effect (Syn $(G(t))$) in our network model of the firm for generalisation and quantification of these mechanisms and modelling the process of generating Cooperational Rent. We describe it in more detail in the part of the chapter focused on modelling the firm.

Summarising this paragraph, we briefly considered the essence of four methodological pillars for modelling in the framework of the Relational Theory of the Firm—complexity, complex network systems, non-linearity and synergy.

The next methodological puzzle that we need to consider before modelling the firm from the perspective of the relational view is the concept of equilibrium and its generalisation for non-linear complex networks—the dynamical network attractor.

3 Resolution of Methodological Paradoxes in the Concept of Equilibrium: Functional Invariant and Dynamical Network Attractors

3.1 Introduction to the New Concept of an Economic System's Functional Invariant

The concept of equilibrium is a fundamental category of economic theory and underlies the research of all scientific schools describing the behaviour of economic systems at the macro and micro levels. Thinking in terms of equilibrium permeates the entire structure of economic knowledge at the paradigm level. Practically, no study of economic processes can avoid the category of equilibrium or related concepts.

At the same time, the question of the deep meaning and fundamental essence of the equilibrium state of an economic system remains insufficiently investigated. Due to the fact that the substantive meaning of the term "equilibrium" seems intuitively obvious and is often interpreted differently depending on the context and level of (macro- or micro)economic systems, there are many different definitions of the term equilibrium.

In classical macroeconomics, the understanding of equilibrium corresponds to the Marshallian concept of market equilibrium, considered as obvious: the market reaches equilibrium when demand equals supply (1). The price at which this equality is fulfilled is the equilibrium price:

$$\begin{aligned} D &= f(p); S = g(p); \\ D\ (p^*) &= S(p^*), \end{aligned} \tag{1}$$

where p^* is the equilibrium price in the market; $S = g(p)$ is the supply function dependent on price p; and $D = f(p)$ is the demand function that reflects consumers' behaviour dependent on the market price.

In later works by authors including John R Hicks and Paul A. Samuelson, who do not consider Eq. (1) as self-evident, the understanding of the origin of this equation was deepened. These authors came to the conclusion that the equilibrium state described by Eq. (1) should be considered as the limit of the trial-and-error process of the price adjustment mechanism, the dynamics of which is described by the equation:

$$\frac{dp}{dt} = h\ (t) \cdot [S(p) - D(p)] \tag{2}$$

$$\frac{dh}{dt} < 0, \quad h(0) = 0,$$

where $\frac{dp}{dt}$ is the rate of price change, and $\frac{dh}{dt}$ is the rate of change of function $h(t)$, which describes the process of adjusting the price to the changes in relationships between demand and supply.

Equation (2) describes the law of supply and demand: prices rise when demand exceeds supply and falls in the opposite case. Equations (1) and (2) together define a dynamic process in which demand, supply and price change in accordance with this law and, if the process is stable, reach some equilibrium level. When the functions $S(p)$, $D(p)$, $p(t)$ reach their equilibrium levels, the influences that cause their changes disappear.

The concept of equilibrium of an economic system at the micro level has a different meaning. In classical microeconomics, the equilibrium of a firm (or bank, consumer, household) is understood as achieving the maximum of its utility function and is modelled as the solution of an optimisation problem under given constraints.

Thus, there is a fundamental difference in understanding the concept of equilibrium for the economic system at the macro and micro levels. The equilibrium of the macrosystem, unlike the system at the micro level, is achieved due to the spontaneous market mechanism of interaction and balancing of oppositely directed economic forces and is not associated with the process of subjective goal setting. The cases of such states are market equilibria, Keynes' (2018) equilibrium of the unemployment rate and national income, partial and general market equilibrium, etc. In contrast, the achievement of equilibrium by the economic system at the micro-level (firms) is based on the goal-oriented activity of a specific management subsystem. In this case, the management goal is understood as the achievement by the system of the utility function maximum value, i.e., some special state that contributes to its preservation, adaptation to external conditions, functioning and development in accordance with the criteria of the governing body.

This conceptual gap reveals insufficient attention paid to the universal essence of equilibrium of an economic system of any kind and level. George Stigler, in his famous work *Perfect Competition, Historically Contemplated* (1957), articulated the fundamental problem of economic theory, which consists in the insufficient attention of researchers to the precise definition of the terms used, the validity of the underlying assumptions and the existence of implicit assumptions that are implied from the context. He concluded that such logical gaps in the foundations of theory can lead to contradictory and paradoxical conclusions, the validity of which requires further analysis. To overcome this methodological problem, Stigler formulated the basic requirements that determine the analytical value and the necessary level of rigour of introduced economic concepts. He wrote that a concept introduced with satisfactory clarity, that is, with as much clarity as the state of the science allows, must define a model that can be used by professionals in a wide variety of theoretical investigations so that there is no need to discuss the foundations of science in every extension or application of the theory. The definition should encapsulate the core essence of the phenomenon being examined to ensure that theoretical predictions are empirically reliable.

In our opinion, the most profound essential definition of equilibrium, which meets the requirements formulated by Stigler, is the definition given by Fritz Machlup in his prominent works *Equilibrium and Disequilibrium: Misplaced Concreteness and Disguised Politics* (1958), and *Essays on Economic Semantics* (1963). He defines equilibrium as "a constellation of selected inter-related variables so adjusted to one another that no inherent tendency to change prevails in the model which they constitute". Chiang and Wainwright (2005), in their seminal book *Fundamental Methods of Mathematical Economics*, mitigate the methodological gap between micro- and macro-equilibrium by using Machlup's definition and introducing the terms of *non-goal equilibrium* for the macro level and *goal equilibrium* for the micro level. This is a fruitful line of thinking, based on which we have tried to develop Machlup's definition of equilibrium and give it the universal mathematical form of functional invariant. From this form, all other definitions of equilibrium at both macro and micro levels follow as special cases for specific applications. We develop here T. Unkovska's initial idea published in her book *Financial Equilibrium of the Firm* (1997).

Based on the requirements to the definitions formulated by Stigler, to develop a meaningful universal definition of equilibrium of an economic system in mathematical form, it is necessary to identify the essential characteristics of the equilibrium state, formulate its generalised systemic understanding and then analyse its specific manifestations for economic systems of different types. For this purpose, let us turn to the concepts of teleonomy and goal determination for economic systems.

The problems of a teleonomic goal determination of the behaviour of systems of various classes are the subject of extensive literature in philosophy, thermodynamics, statistical physics and the general theory of complex systems, in particular, Prigogine (1978, 1980) and Haken (1983, 1987, 1988).

The methodological approaches developed in this context allow us to use a generalised understanding of purpose and teleonomic description to study economic systems of various types.

The *system-wide understanding of the goal* of any system consists in understanding it as a specific form of interaction that allows us to find a certain directionality of processes and their conditionality by the final state. In this case, we are not talking about conscious goals set by governing subjects, but about their analogues, objective in nature. In this sense, purposefulness and goal orientation is a qualitative certainty of existence and development of the system and manifests itself in the appropriate directionality of this development. Goal determination of the system is its determination by the final state, which means that some future state of the system is specified by its initial conditions and internal mechanism of evolution. This mechanism determines the directionality in the behaviour of the system, the manifestation of which is the behaviour of the system with an explicitly expressed "special state"—the state of equilibrium. In this sense, the purposefulness of the system is its endeavour to overcome the deviation from some special ("final") state, called the goal. Since this special state is determined by the system itself, by its internal structure and by the nature of inter-relations of internal forces, the area of stability of the system with respect to this state is its area of goal orientation.

In this area, changes in the system states are invariant with respect to the goal in the sense that the system movement retains the specified striving to overcome the mismatch with the goal. In the process of changes, the system evaluates its states for compliance with the goal. In this case, the evaluation is understood as an objective process of revealing the degree of discrepancy between some state of the system and the goal as its special state in the emerging purposeful reaction to the discrepancy. Such an assessment, in turn, determines the selection of system states in the process of its movement.

According to a famous quote by Max Planck, taken from his *Eight Lectures on Theoretical Physics*, "Nature prefers the more probable states to the less probable because in nature processes take place in the direction of greater probability" (1915, 35). The second principle of thermodynamics about the irreversible increase in entropy means that the system is approaching a state that irresistibly "attracts" it, preferable to others—a state from which the system will not leave "willingly". Prigogine wrote that in the case of a closed system, equilibrium acts as an attracting set, or an attractor for non-equilibrium states (1980, 8). Having reached this attractor set, the system only fluctuates around the *attractor, which can be considered as a generalised dynamical equilibrium of the system*. The equilibrium of a macroscopic system is the result of statistical compensation of the activity of microscopic elements and the manifestation of system's emergent properties (synergy).

Considering the economic system from these system-wide positions, one can notice a deep universal quality of macro- and micro-level systems: their dynamics is determined by the striving for some special final state—a generalised equilibrium state (in the case of non-linear systems, this is the state of a dynamic attractor). At the same time, the mechanisms of achieving equilibrium at the macro and micro levels are fundamentally different. The mechanism of price adjustment of the competitive market provides its movement to the state of equilibrium due to the realisation of the principle of the system's self-regulation with negative feedback. There is a double negation: the discrepancy between the real state and the goal state generates changes in the system, which, step by step, compensate for the discrepancy with the goal.

That is, the goal-oriented behaviour of the macroeconomic system implements the philosophical principle of Hegel's dialectics—the principle of double negation. It is embodied in practice in Le Chatelier's (1891) principle of feedback, formulated for systems of any nature.

The mechanism of achieving equilibrium at the micro level is based on the goal-oriented activity of the governing subsystem and its utility function maximisation. In other words, goal orientation at the market level is implemented due to the objective process of mutual adjustment of internal forces of supply and demand, and goal orientation at the firm level due to the activation of motivational mechanisms of governing subjects and their optimisation behaviour. Despite the difference of these mechanisms, the generalised teleonomic understanding of complex systems gives methodological grounds to see in the goal-oriented behaviour of macro- and micro-level economic systems not just an analogy, but a common type of determination. The movement of an economic system to equilibrium (or attractor in the non-linear case) is a certain invariant, which is "embedded" in the internal structure of an economic system of any level. This allows us to consider the essence of the economic system equilibrium from a unified position and to develop its meaningful definition, which will work both at the macro and at the micro levels and can be modelled by a universal mathematical form—the functional invariant. Let us introduce the definition of a functional invariant (FI) of the economic system as follows. Goal determination of an economic system provides for the existence of some subset of system parameters, the inter-related change of which determines its purposeful movement. Such a set of parameters of the economic system, the change of which determines the goal-directed movement of the system, will be called the functional invariant of the economic system:

$$\mathrm{FI} = \{B\,(t), H_1[B(t)], H_2[B(t)]\},$$

where

$B(t)$ is the basis function of functional invariant.
$H_1[B(t)]$, $H_2[B(t)]$ are the guiding functions of the functional invariant.

The functional invariant includes those parameters of the system that are directly "responsible" for its goal-directed movement due to the interaction of counteracting economic forces and their mutual adaptation. The structure of the functional invariant includes a parameter with special properties, which is the basic factor of goal orientation. The change of this parameter generates the emergence of two oppositely directed processes in the system. If these processes do not balance each other, the system changes. At the micro level, in particular, an increase in a firm's output, if it is less than the equilibrium value, generates an increase in marginal revenue and a decrease in marginal cost. At the macro level, an increasing price in the market causes a reduction in demand and an upward shift in supply.

When the processes balance each other, the system reaches the final goal-oriented state—the state of equilibrium. The parameter, the change of which causes oppositely directed processes, will be called the *basis function of the functional invariant* $B(t)$, *and* the functions characterising these contradictory processes, which should be balanced in the movement of the system—the *guiding functions of the functional invariant:*

$$H_1[B(t)], H_2[B(t)].$$

For a competitive market for some good, the functional invariant is the set of variables including the *basis function of the functional invariant B*(*t*) *which is the price level*:

$$B(t) = P(t)$$

and *two guiding functions (demand function and supply function* that depend on the price $P(t)$):

$$H_1[B(t)] = D(P(t));\ H_2[B(t)] = S(P(t)),$$
$$\text{that is } FI = \{P(t);\ D(P(t));\ S(P(t))\}.$$

At the level of the firm in its classical microeconomic understanding, the functional invariant includes output volume as a basis function

$$B(t) = Q(t),$$

and two guiding functions—marginal revenue and marginal costs:

$$H_1[B(t)] = MR(Q(t)), H_2[B(t)] = MC(Q(t)),$$
$$\text{that is } FI = \{Q(t), MR(Q(t));\ MC(Q(t))\}.$$

The fundamental property of the functional invariant is that a change of the basis parameter leads to oppositely directed changes of the guiding functions; that is, the following relation is valid:

$$\frac{dH_1(B(t))}{dB} \cdot \frac{dH_2(B(t))}{dB} < 0.$$

We introduce *energy function E for economic system* by equation:

$$E = -\frac{dH_1(B(t))}{dB} \cdot \frac{dH_2(B(t))}{dB} = -v_1 \cdot v_2 > 0.$$

The essence of E is the multiplication of the velocities of the guiding function's changes in relation to the change of the basis function. The minus sign means the contrary directions of the processes described by the guiding functions and, respectively, of the velocities of adjustment processes. We call the function E as economic system's energy of striving for equilibrium. It characterises the energy of economic systems that moves it to the specific system's preferential state—equilibrium or dynamic attractor.

This energy function E depends on the guiding function's properties and their derivatives ($v_1$and v_2):

$$v_1 = \frac{dH_1(B(t))}{dB}; \quad v_2 = \frac{dH_2(B(t))}{dB}.$$

Function E is always positive as the economic system moves towards equilibrium:

$$E > 0$$

In the absence of external disturbing influences, the system movement is determined by the interaction of forces defined by the guiding functions. If, during a certain period of time, the action of these forces balances each other, the variables of the functional invariant reach their limit values and the internal tendency to change them disappears, the economic system reaches a state of equilibrium:

$$FI^* = \{B^*, H_1^*, H_2^*\},$$

$$\frac{dB^*}{dt} = 0; \quad \frac{dH_1(B^*)}{dt} = 0; \quad \frac{dH_2(B^*)}{dt} = 0.$$

These introduced concepts allow us to give a general definition of equilibrium for economic systems of different types: the equilibrium state of an economic system is a state in which the variables of its functional invariant are constant in time and remain unchanged in the absence of perturbing influences of the external environment.

The values of the functional invariant variables for the system in the equilibrium state FI^* are called their equilibrium values, and the relationship linking these equilibrium values is called the equation of state of the system:

$$F\left(B^*(t), H_1^*(t), H_2^*(t)\right) = 0.$$

For example, the equation of market equilibrium state is given by

$$F\left(B^*(t), H_1^*(t), H_2^*(t)\right) = F\left(p^*(t), S^*(t), D^*(t)\right) =$$
$$= \frac{dp}{dt} = h(t) \cdot [S(p) - D(p)] = 0.$$

The process of an economic system's relaxation is the process of its transition from a non-equilibrium to an equilibrium state. The relaxation period is the time interval during which this transition takes place. If we consider a process running in an economic system with a speed much slower than the relaxation speed, at any stage of which the variables of the functional invariant have time to equilibrate, it represents a chain of equilibrium states. This process, slow enough in relation to the relaxation speed of the system, is called the equilibrium process. The concept of functional invariant is a useful tool for modelling not only static equilibrium states but also transition processes to equilibrium.

In general, the suggested generalised mathematical definition of the equilibrium state for economic systems of any level is not indisputable and complete. It requires further development from the positions of institutional economics, methodology of statics, comparative statics and dynamics. Nevertheless, it is a step forward in clarifying and unifying in mathematical form the essence of equilibrium states for various economic systems of different levels. In addition, the statement of the problem itself is one more reason to think about methodological gaps and paradoxes in the foundations of economic theory and the importance of fundamental theoretical research on micro and macro levels of economy.

To develop a Relational Theory of the Firm, a very important issue is the modelling of the relational network equilibrium and possible network effects that can help to maximise the Cooperational Rent or, on the contrary, to exacerbate systemic risks for the whole network. Therefore, we need to review the methodological assumptions for modelling the considered systems from the perspectives of statics, comparative statics and dynamics. This is the focus of the next paragraph.

4 Methodology of Statics, Comparative Statics and Dynamics in Modelling Equilibrium

From the perspective of time consideration, equilibrium states are studied within the framework of three methodological approaches: statics, comparative statics and dynamics. Depending on this, different types of equilibrium states are distinguished and, accordingly, different modelling approaches are applied. Debates between various scientific schools about the static and dynamic nature of equilibrium models have a long-term and deep character. A detailed review of these debates and current state of modelling methodology in this area is given in the works of Chiang and Wainwright (2005), Markusen (2020), and Rivot and Trautwein (2020).

If the equilibrium state is studied from the perspective of statics or comparative statics, that is its structure and properties are considered without researching dynamic transitions and shifts, it is classified as static equilibrium. When the equilibrium state is investigated from a dynamic perspective and considered as a process running in time, it is said to be a dynamic equilibrium. These three methodological approaches are based on different systems of assumptions, methods and limitations.

In general, the history of science and economics has convincingly proved that a theory is a useful tool for acquiring new knowledge and applying it in practice if there is a clear understanding of the assumptions within which it is true and the boundaries beyond which it does not work. As applied to economics, such a clear awareness of the assumptions and boundaries of theories is of fundamental importance since key decisions are often made on the basis of established and popular economic theories. However, the underlying assumptions and boundaries of their application are not given sufficient attention, so the practical results of these decisions are quite often unexpected and disappointing.

For modelling in the Relational Theory of the Firm, all three methodological approaches are very important as each of them highlights a particular aspect necessary to understand the whole picture. Therefore, we will formulate the assumptions and boundaries of application for each of the three methodological approaches—statics, comparative statics and dynamics.

4.1 *Static Equilibrium Analysis and Modelling*

Static analysis of economic systems is based on the following assumptions:

1. The equilibrium state is attainable.
2. The system is in a state of equilibrium.
3. The parameters of the external environment are given and remain unchanged.
4. Since the equilibrium state can be maintained for any length of time, the time factor is insignificant.

These assumptions allow us to study the structure and properties of static equilibrium of an economic system. However, a too limited system of initial assumptions of statics impedes correct modelling of dynamic processes on their basis. One of the most vulnerable assumptions of statics is the supposition of invariability of external environment parameters. Theoretically, a static long period is a kind of timeless forever period, during which nothing happens except the complete mutual adaptation of the internal parameters of the system.

From this point of view, equilibrium structures are inert and "immortal": once an equilibrium structure is formed, it can be isolated and maintained forever without further interaction with the external environment. The unrealistic assumption of invariability of external factors relates to the infeasibility of the assumption about the attainability of equilibrium as a necessary property of an economic system. Long before a static equilibrium can be achieved, there usually occurs some dynamic change in the basic fundamental factors, which entails quantitative changes in the equilibrium conditions. As a rule, the economic situation is more a case of non-equilibrium movement towards equilibrium than a case of realised static equilibrium. Even if equilibrium is reached, it exists for a very short period, after which changes in the external environment may occur, taking the system out of equilibrium.

Thus, the concept of static equilibrium is a theoretical construct related not so much to reality as to the internal properties of the system that determine the equilibrium values of the variables of its functional invariant. The meaning of the methodology of statics for realist theory is that it provides a basis for predicting the direction of change of an economic system in the equilibrium region. Chiang and Wainwright (2005) express the basic idea of static analysis as follows: static analysis shows us only where the economic system is going. However, it does not answer the question whether it will arrive there and what will happen to it on the way (Chiang & Wainwright, 2005). We must take into account that the fundamental problems of attainability of the equilibrium state, description of phase transitions and changes in the system under the influence of the external environment volatility are outside the framework of the methodology of statics.

4.2 Comparative Statics

Some of the problems related to the limitations of the static approach were solved by the methodology developed by Hicks (1939), Samuelson (1947) and his subsequent researchers, which was called comparative statics. The time factor and instrumental means were introduced into the theoretical scheme, which allowed one equilibrium state of the system to be distinguished from another and also allowed them to be compared. The main question that comparative statics addresses is what the characteristics of the new equilibrium state are relative to the old one. It is thus a more general theory in which the unrealistic assumption of an unchanging external environment is removed. However, the other limitations of static analysis, in particular, the hypothesis of attainability of equilibrium, remain unchanged.

The system of initial preconditions of comparative statics includes the following assumptions.

1. At the initial moment of time, the system is in a given state of equilibrium.
2. When external parameters change, the system moves to a new equilibrium state corresponding to the changed values of external environmental factors.

Based on the concept of functional invariant, the main problem of comparative statics can be formulated as follows: how will the equilibrium values of the variables of the functional invariant of the system change when the environmental parameters change?

In the framework of comparative static analysis methodology, the evolution of an economic system is presented as a sequential series of equilibrium states, the change of which is caused by the variation of environmental factors. The role of time is reduced to the discrete variable, the values of which correspond to the serial indices of the sequence of equilibrium states. The comparative static approach can be used in quantitative and qualitative analyses. The qualitative aspect considers the problem of the direction of changes, while the methods of quantitative analysis allow us to determine their magnitude. Quantitative analysis in this context is a broader category that includes qualitative analysis, since the assessment of changes in parameters at the quantitative level automatically allows us to establish the direction of their changes as well.

The tools of comparative statics include methods for determining the coefficients of change in the equilibrium values of the functional invariant variables in accordance with changes in exogenous parameters. The mathematical basis of these methods is the theory of differential and integral calculus. The methodology of comparative statics allows one to obtain significant information about the properties of the economic system and some features of its behaviour. However, the fundamental problems of principle attainability of the equilibrium state by the system, problems of describing transition processes and their properties, and estimation of relaxation time remain outside the framework of this methodology. The ways of transition of the system to the equilibrium state, as well as situations of instability, when the equilibrium state is fundamentally unattainable, are not considered in comparative statics.

The next stage in the evolution of methodological approaches was economic dynamics.

4.3 Methodology of Economic Dynamics

The field of economic dynamics (Chiang & Wainwright, 2005; Shone, 2012; Stachurski, 2022) includes investigation of transitional and non-linear processes, issues of attainability of equilibrium and analysis of its stability, non-equilibrium processes, dynamic attractors and synergetic phenomena. Dynamic analysis fills a serious methodological gap left by statics and comparative statics. Within the framework of the economic dynamics methodology, special attention focuses on the possibility and ways of a system's transition to an equilibrium state or dynamic attractor, transitional processes, which can be equilibrium, fluctuating, oscillatory or self-enforcing that take the system out of equilibrium.

The development of an economic system is considered as a process of its change under the influence of internal and external factors. Time is one of the fundamental factors in dynamic models. This approach allows one to escape from static assumptions about the invariability of the external environment, the assumption of mandatory attainability of the equilibrium state and the infinite stay in it. The methodology of economic dynamics assumes that differential equations can be developed based on the properties of the system. When it is possible, the integration of these differential equations permits the trajectories of the system development to be obtained and, given the initial conditions and external parameters, permits its behaviour to be described with a certain degree of accuracy. Also, one of the significant concepts of mathematical tools in modelling dynamic systems and non-linear dynamic processes is the concept of the attractor. Usually, an attractor is defined as a set of states towards which a system tends to evolve for a wide variety of starting conditions of the system. There are different types of attractors: fixed point, finite number of points, limit cycle, limit torus and strange attractor. They have been widely studied by various sciences (Bonotto & Uzal, 2024, Buescu, 1997a, b, Carvalho et al., 2012, Chekroun et al., 2011, Hopfield, 1982, 1984; Hopfield & Tank, 1985) including complex systems theory, and contain a great potential for modelling in Relational Economics, including the Relational Theory of the Firm. The role of network topology in attractor formation is a critical area of research that can lead to a greater understanding of the dynamics of complex relational networks. The network topology has an impact on the system's behaviour and on the formation of attractors that correspond to different states. Further research in this area may help shed more light on the underlying mechanisms and develop new strategies for governing complex relational networks.

To summarise the methodological section, it should be concluded that the evolution of theoretical concepts and modelling tools in economic science reflects the desire of researchers to overcome the static initial principles at an increasingly higher level: from statics to comparative statics, then to dynamics, non-linear dynamics and the theory of complex networks, non-equilibrium processes and synergetics. The variety of modelling methods within these approaches, together with the suggested general concept of equilibrium of an economic system based on a functional invariant, allows for a comprehensive approach to modelling in Relational Economics and the Relational Theory of the Firm.

5 Dynamic Network Model of the Firm in Relational Theory

As we wrote before, the Relational Theory of the Firm considers the firm as an actor in a complex relational network of stakeholders.

We therefore model the firm as an agent, which is one of the nodes $V_i, i=\overline{1,n}$ in complex network $G = (V, Z, W)$, where $V=\{V_i; i=\overline{1,n}\}$ is the set of nodes (different stakeholders with their polycontextual account balances), $Z=\{Z_{ij}; i=\overline{1,n}; j=\overline{1,\mathrm{n}}\}$ is the set of threads between nodes V_i and V_j, and

$W=\{W_{ij}; i=\overline{1,n}; j=\overline{1,n}\}$ is the set of weights that reflects the strength of connection between nodes V_i and V_j. So, we say about the weighted complex network, where W_{ij} is the weight of connection between V_i and V_j.

We consider the volumes of relational assets $(\mathrm{RA}_{ij}), i=\overline{1,n}; j=\overline{1,n}$, between nodes as weights of their connections in the relational network. The matrix RA is the matrix of relational assets between stakeholders V_i and V_j:

$$W=(W_{ij})=(\mathrm{RA}_{ij})=\begin{pmatrix} \mathrm{RA}_{11} & \cdots & \mathrm{RA}_{1n} \\ \vdots & \ddots & \vdots \\ \mathrm{RA}_{n1} & \cdots & \mathrm{RA}_{nn} \end{pmatrix}.$$

Relational assets were formed under the influence of network agents' investment in the relational network development and cooperation by their expenditure on relational costs (RC). Therefore, the matrix of relational assets (RA_{ij}) of the whole stakeholders' network $G=(V,Z,W)$ is a function F_1 of the RC matrix that we call *function of investment in relational network*:

$$W=\mathrm{RA}=F_1\ (\mathrm{RC}), \text{or}$$

$$(W_{ij})=(\mathrm{RA}_{ij})=F_1(\mathrm{RC}_{ij}), \forall i,j,\ \ i=\overline{1,n}; j=\overline{1,n}$$

For $RC_{ij}=0$, $F_1(RC_{ij})=0$.

It means if some elements of the matrix (RC_{ij}) are equal to 0, that is $\mathrm{RC}_{ij}=0$, it means that V_i node doesn't invest resources in cooperation with the node V_j. This causes cooperation between these nodes to collapse.

$$\mathrm{RA}=(\mathrm{RA}_{ij})=\begin{pmatrix} \mathrm{RA}_{11} & \cdots & \mathrm{RA}_{1n} \\ \vdots & \ddots & \vdots \\ \mathrm{RA}_{n1} & \cdots & \mathrm{RA}_{nn} \end{pmatrix}=\begin{pmatrix} F_1(\mathrm{RC}_{11}) & \cdots & F_1(\mathrm{RC}_{1n}) \\ \vdots & \ddots & \vdots \\ F_1(\mathrm{RC}_{n1}) & \cdots & F_1(\mathrm{RC}_{nn}) \end{pmatrix}.$$

The general topology of the relational network $G=(V,Z,W)$ is described by an *adjacency matrix A:*

$A=\{(A_{ij}), i=\overline{1,n}; j=\overline{1,n}\}$ of the network $G=(V,Z,W)$ is a structural matrix that characterises the topology of the network:

$$A_{ij}=\begin{cases} 1, & \text{if there is thread } Z_{ij} \text{ between } V_i \text{ and } V_j; \\ 0, & \text{if there isn't thread } \mathrm{Z}_{ij}\text{between } \mathrm{V_i} \text{ and } \mathrm{V_j}. \end{cases}$$

As usually observed in complex network literature, the simplest index to measure the *influence of nodes is the degree of nodes* $\deg(V_i)$. The degree value of a node is the number of edges of a node. The more neighbouring nodes are connected to a node, the more important the node is.

For analysis of the topology of the relational network $G=(V,Z,W)$, we can use a Laplacian matrix of the network

$$L = D - A,$$

where D is the degree matrix of the relational network, and A is the adjacency matrix; deg (V_i) is a degree of the nodes V_i, $\forall i = \overline{1, n}$

$$D_{ij} = \begin{cases} \deg(V_i), \text{if } i = j \\ 0, \quad\quad \text{if } i \neq j \end{cases},$$

$$D = \begin{pmatrix} \deg\,(V_1) & 0\cdots & 0 \\ \vdots & \ddots & \vdots \\ 0 & 0\cdots & \deg\,(V_n) \end{pmatrix}.$$

The elements of the Laplacian matrix are as follows:

$$L_{ij} = \begin{cases} \deg\,(V_i), & \text{if } i = j \\ -1, & \textit{if } i \neq j \text{ and } V_i \text{ is adjacent to } V_j \\ 0, & \textit{if } i \neq j \text{ and } V_i \text{ is not adjacent to } V_j. \end{cases}$$

For instance, for a complete relational network, the Laplacian matrix is given by

$$L = (L_{ij}) = \begin{pmatrix} \deg(\,V_1) - 1 & -1 & \cdots & -1 \\ \vdots & & \ddots & \vdots \\ -1 & -1 & -1 \quad \cdots & \deg(V_n) \end{pmatrix}.$$

The eigenvalues of L that are called the Laplacian eigenvalues are all real and non-negative (Mohar et al. 1991): they are contained in the interval $[0, \min \{n, 2\ D_{\max}\}]$, where $D_{\max}$ is the maximum degree of $G = (V, Z, W)$.

The set of all Laplacian eigenvalues that is the Laplacian spectrum of the network $G = (V, Z, W)$ is given by

$$\lambda_n = 0 \leq \lambda_{n-1} \leq \lambda_{n-1} \leq \lambda_{n-1} \leq \ldots \leq \lambda_2 \leq \lambda_1.$$

The second smallest eigenvalue is $\lambda_{n-1} \geq 0$ which characterises *connectivity of the relational network.*

Two distinct nodes V_i and V_j in relational network $G = (V, Z, W)$ are connected if there exists a (V_i, V_j)—path in G. The network is connected if all pairs of distinct nodes are connected. Most real relational networks are not completely connected; they are characterised by some degree of connectivity. *Relational network connectivity* is a significant indicator that has a large impact on network productivity and effectiveness. There are several rates of network connectivity in the complex network literature (Banwari, 2022). Besides the second smallest Laplacian eigenvalue as a connectivity indicator, which we noticed before, there are also the Beta Index (β) and Gamma Index (γ) of network connectivity.

The Beta Index (β) introduced by Kansky (1963) is the simplest form of connectivity measure. It gives the average ratio of the number of edges per node, which is linkage intensity:

$$\beta = \frac{z}{v},$$

where z is the number of edges, and v is the number of nodes.

The Gamma Index (γ) is a ratio between the number of nodes and the maximum possible number of edges in a network, in which $v > 2$. It is defined as

$$\gamma = \frac{v}{3\,(v-2)}.$$

All these indicators are useful for analysing network connectivity, and we can calculate all of them in practical tasks.

We will denote the *relational network connectivity* parameter (measured in one way or another) in our model as Con (G).

The second significant parameter of the relational network is an index of *Network Coverage* that means the maximum radius of network action. We denote it as Cover (G). Increasing Con (G) and Cover (G) means that the significance of links and nodes in the relational network is higher. As noticed in the research papers of Nijkamp and Reggiani (1995), Ogura et al. (2019) and Zhang et al. (2023), the measures network connectivity and coverage are essential in investment-oriented networks. These factors increase the productivity of links and nodes, which are essentially based on network externalities. Increasing marginal benefits will be expected if the network capacity grows with direct benefit to the users but without extra payment by the beneficiaries. So, indicators of network connectivity and network coverage are essential for the network's synergy.

We have introduced the necessary notations and definitions, and now, we can develop the model of the firm.

Let U be a K-dimensional vector space of dynamic vectors, $\overrightarrow{S_i\,(t)} = (S_{ik}(t)),\ \forall k = \overline{1,K}$, of the states of the nodes $V_i, i = \overline{1,n}$ in relational network at the moment of t:

$$\overrightarrow{S_i\,(t)} = \begin{pmatrix} S_{i1}(t) \\ S_{i2}(t) \\ S_{i3}(t) \\ \cdots \\ S_{iK-1}(t) \\ S_{iK}(t) \end{pmatrix}.$$

The matrix $S\,(t) = \left((S_{ik}(t))^T\right)_{i=\overline{1,n};\ k=\overline{1,K}}$ is the matrix of the states of all nodes in the relational network, in other words, the *dynamical matrix of states of the relational networks* of the firm's stakeholders at the moment t:

$$S = \begin{pmatrix} S_{11}\ldots. & S_{1K-1} & S_{1K} \\ \ldots. & \ldots & \ldots \\ S_{n1}\ldots. & S_{nK-1} & S_{nK} \end{pmatrix}.$$

The authors of the article "*Modeling Relational Transactions*" by Wieland et al. (2022) suggested that nodes (agents) in relational networks are constituted by inherent accounts. "These accounts are mapped to, and therefore represent, the specific decision logics of the previously introduced functional systems. They have certain balances that capture the agent's performance within a system. This multi-dimensional accounting approach makes it possible to locate the agent in an n-dimensional (where n represents the number of all existing accounts/organizational systems) vector space, whereas every inscription of the vector that represents an agent is based on a particular set of account balances" (ibid.). We use this idea of representation of the vector of states $\overrightarrow{S_i\ (t)}$ and develop it further in our model.

Now, we introduce a cumulative *dynamic benefit function (DBF)* $F_i\left(\overrightarrow{S_i\ (t)}, u_i(t)\right)$ for each node $V_i, i=\overline{1,n}$ in the relational network $G=(V,Z,W)$, where $\overrightarrow{S_i\ (t)}$ is the vector of V_i state at the moment t, and $u_i(t)$ is the *control function of the node* V_i:

$$F_i\left(\overrightarrow{S_\iota\ (t)}, u_i(t)\right) = P_i\left(\overrightarrow{S_\iota\ (t)}, u_i(t)\right) + \sum_{j=1}^{n} A_{ij}B_{ij}(t) + \sigma_i(t)\cdot Syn\left(G(t)\right) \quad (1)$$

Benefits V_i from its own production activity if it was not in the network

Benefits of the V_i node from bilateral interactions V_i with other nodes

V_i part of benefits from the cumulative Synergy Effects of the whole network **(Cooperational Rent)**

Each of the three terms of the integrated dynamic benefit function $F_i\left(\overrightarrow{S_i\ (t)}, u_i(t)\right)$ has different behaviour and dynamics:

1. $P_i\left(\overrightarrow{S_i\ (t)}, u_i(t)\right)$ is a function of benefits of V_i node from its own production activity if there were no relational network connections (when $A_{ij}=0, \forall j=\bar{1},n$):

$$P_i\left(\overrightarrow{S_i\ (t)}, u_i(t)\right) = (1-\text{tax})\left[\ Y_i(\overrightarrow{S_i\ (t)}, u_i(t)\right)\cdot$$

$$p(t) - C_{\text{OP}}\ \overrightarrow{(S_i\ (t), u_i(t))} - C_{\text{FIN}}\ \overrightarrow{(S_i\ (t), u_i(t))}] - C_{\text{TR}}\ \overrightarrow{(S_i\ (t), u_i(t))},$$

where $Y_i\left(\overrightarrow{S_i\ (t)}, u_i(t)\right)$ is a Cobb – Douglas production function with autonomous technical progress for a node V_i:

$$Y_i(\overrightarrow{S_i\ (t)}, u_i(t)) = \alpha_0 K_i(t,u)^{\alpha_1} L_i(t,u)^{\alpha_2} \mathrm{e}^{\varepsilon_i t},$$

where α_0, α_1, α_2 are the coefficients of Cobb – Douglas function (α_1, α_2 elasticity of factors).

$K_i(t, u_i(t))$ is the capital of V_i node at the period t.
$L_i(t, u_i(t))$ is the human capital of V_i node at the period t.
$p_i(t)$ is the price of goods or services that V_i node produces.
$C_{OP}\ (\overrightarrow{S_i\ (t)}, u_i(t))$ is the operational costs of V_i node at the period t.
$C_{FIN}\ (\overrightarrow{S_i\ (t)}, u_i(t))$ is the financial costs for debt repayment at the period t.
tax is the tax rate of the V_i node.
$C_{TR}\ (\overrightarrow{S_i\ (t)}, u_i(t))$ is the transactional costs of V_i node at the period of t.
So, $P\left(\overrightarrow{S_i\ (t)}, u_i(t)\right)$ is net profit of V_i node without consideration of relational network influence.

Two other terms on the right side of Eq. (1) ensure that the network influence is considered. Let's look at these terms in more detail.

2. The second term in Eq. (1) is benefits of the V_i node from its bilateral interactions with other nodes in relational network $G = (V, Z, W)$:

$$\sum\nolimits_{j=1}^{n} A_{ij} B_{ij}(t) = \sum\nolimits_{j=1}^{n} A_{ij}\left[Q_{ij}(t, u_i(t)) - RC_{ij}(t, u_i(t))\right],$$

where (A_{ij}) is the adjacency matrix, $Q_{ij}(t)$ is the gross benefits of V_i node from bilateral interactions with V_j node, $\mathrm{RC}_{ij}(t)$ is the RC of the V_i node for cooperation with V_j node.

3. The third term in the integrated *dynamic benefit function (DBF)* $F_i\left(\overrightarrow{S_i\ (t)}, u_i(t)\right)$ for each node V_i is a share $\sigma_i(t)$ of the cumulative synergetic effects of the whole relational network $G = (V, Z, W)$ at the period of t:

$$\sigma_i(t) \cdot \mathrm{Syn}\ (G(t)).$$

The cumulative synergetic effects Syn ($G(t)$) is the foundation for extra benefits arising for all participants of the whole relational network without additional costs for them—*Cooperational Rent* ($R_{\mathrm{COOP}}(t)$).

The cumulative dynamic benefit function $F_i\left(\overrightarrow{S_i\ (t)}, u_i(t)\right)$ of V_i node is a conceptual and mathematical basis for modelling not only dynamics of each node of the relational network but also the whole process of the relational network functioning and dynamics.

The cumulative dynamic benefit function for the whole relational network is as follows:

$$
\begin{aligned}
&F\left(S(t),\overrightarrow{u(t)}\right)=\sum_{i=1}^{n}F_i\left(\overrightarrow{S_i\ (t)},u_i(t)\right)=\\
&=\sum_{i=1}^{n}P_i\left(\overrightarrow{S_i\ (t)},u_i(t)\right)+\sum_{i=1}^{n}\sum_{j=1}^{n}A_{ij}B_{ij}(t)+Syn\ (G(t),u(t))\ =\\
&=\sum_{i=1}^{n}\left\{(1-\text{tax}_i)\left[\ Y_i(\overrightarrow{S_i\ (t)},u_i(t))-C_{OP}\ \overrightarrow{(S_i\ (t)},u_i(t))-C_{\text{FIN}}\ \overrightarrow{(S_i\ (t)},u_i(t))\right]\right.\\
&\quad-C_{\text{TR}}\ \overrightarrow{(S_i\ (t)},u_i(t))\}+\sum_{i=1}^{n}\sum_{j=1}^{n}A_{ij}[Q_{ij}(t,u_i(t))\\
&\quad-RC_{ij}(t,u_i(t)]+Syn\ (G(t),u_i(t))
\end{aligned}
\tag{4}
$$

These functions (3) and (4) are a mathematical and conceptual basis for modelling dynamics of the firm and the whole relational network in the framework of the Relational Theory of the Firm.

The *relational network equilibrium* is a specific state of relational network $G=(V,Z,W)$, when cumulative benefits, that is a Dynamic Function of Benefits $F\left(S(t),\overrightarrow{u(t)}\right)$, attain maximum value:

$$F\left(S(t),\overrightarrow{u(t)}\right)\ \rightarrow \text{max.}$$

For the set of all possible control function vectors,

$$\overrightarrow{u(t)}=\begin{pmatrix} u_1(t)\\ u_2(t)\\ u_3(t)\\ \cdots\\ u_{n-1}(t)\\ u_n(t.)\end{pmatrix}$$

Let's consider the first term of the dynamic benefit function for the V_i node in more detail.

$$
\begin{aligned}
P_i\left(\overrightarrow{S_i\ (t)},u_i(t)\right)=(1-\text{tax})\left[\ Y_i(\overrightarrow{S_i\ (t)},u_i(t)\right)\cdot p_i(t)-C_{\text{OP}}\ \overrightarrow{(S_i\ (t)},u_i(t))\\
-C_{\text{FIN}}\ \overrightarrow{(S_i\ (t)},u_i(t))]-C_{\text{TR}}\ \overrightarrow{(S_i\ (t)},u_i(t)).
\end{aligned}
$$

This function $P_i\left(\overrightarrow{S_i\ (t)},u_i(t)\right)$ describes the volume of the V_i node net profit after payment of interests on debt, tax liabilities and transaction costs in cases when the firm works without a relational network. In this case, two other terms of Eq. (1) are equal to 0:

$$\sum_{j=1}^{n} A_{ij}B_{ij}(t) = \sum_{j=1}^{n} A_{ij}\left[Q_{ij}(t, u_i(t)) - \mathrm{RC}_{ij}(t, u_i(t)\right] = 0,$$
$$\sigma_i(t) \cdot \mathrm{Syn}\ (G(t)) = 0.$$

In this case, the cumulative dynamic benefit function $F_i\left(\overrightarrow{S_i\ (t)}, u_i(t)\right)$ for the firm (it is isolated V_i node with $A = 0$ in this case) is equal to only first term:

$$F_i\left(\overrightarrow{S_i\ (t)}, u_i(t)\right) = P_i\left(\overrightarrow{S_i\ (t)}, u_i(t)\right) = = (1 - \mathrm{tax})\left[\ Y_i(\overrightarrow{S_i\ (t)}, u_i(t)\right) \cdot$$
$$p_i(t) - C_{OP}\ \overrightarrow{(S_i\ (t)}, u_i(t)) - C_{\mathrm{FIN}}\ \overrightarrow{(S_i\ (t)}, u_i(t))]$$
$$- C_{\mathrm{TR}}\ \overrightarrow{(S_i\ (t)}, u_i(t)).$$

It is a classical microeconomic case with additional consideration of transaction costs. So, the dynamic benefit function can be described by the formula of classical models for the net profit of firms.

If we move to the paradigm of the Relational Theory of the Firm, which considers the firm as an integral part of the relational network, then two additional terms arise in the dynamic benefit function, reflecting the influence of the relational network on the dynamics of total benefits of the firm, including Cooperational Rent.

To explain more clearly the main idea at this stage of research, we can provide an illustrative figure that shows the comparison of a firm's profits in two situations—when it operates autonomously outside the relational network (as in classical microeconomic models), and in the second situation when it is a governance node in the relational network of all the firm's stakeholders (Fig. 1).

The curves TC and TR in Fig. 1 reflect total costs and total returns of the firm, respectively. Total costs in this case do not include RC as in the Relational Theory paradigm. So, according to the classical microeconomic model of the firm, firm's profit, that is the difference between TR and TC, is reflected by the curve P in Fig. 1. The maximum profit corresponds to the maximum value of the difference (TR − TC).

When we move to the Relational Theory paradigm, we must consider additional costs of the firm—its RC. RC has an impact on the curve of the firm's profit: it increases total costs; however, it changes the shape of the profit curve by decreasing transaction costs and generating additional profit by benefits of bilateral relationships in the relational network and the part of Cooperational Rent. The resulting profit is reflected in the figure by the curve (P^{Net}). It can be illustrated in our figure as additional profit through the network effects—it is a "Zone of positive effects of relational network for increasing profit of V_i node" on Fig. 1.

The most interesting and challenging task is further modelling the dynamics of the second and third terms in the integrated function Dynamic Function of Benefits $F_i\left(\overrightarrow{S_i\ (t)}, u_i(t)\right)$—the cumulative benefits of the all nodes V_i from its bilateral interactions with another nodes in the relational network $G = (V, Z, W)$ and the

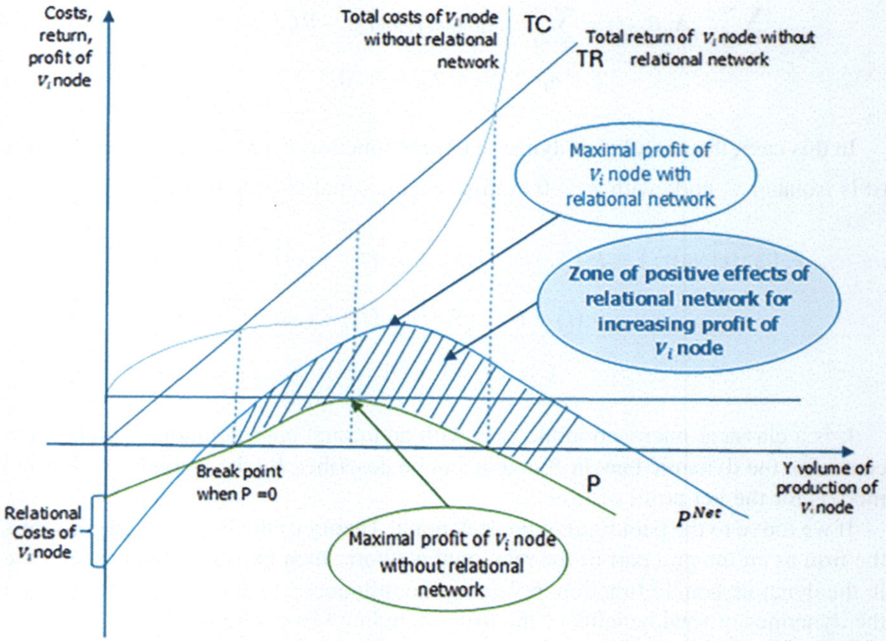

Fig. 1 Profit of the firm (V_i node) with relational network and without it. (Source: developed by the authors)

cumulative synergetic effects Syn $(G(t))$ from the coherent behaviour of the nodes of whole relational network.

These two terms play a fundamental role for the functioning of the firm in a relational network and can significantly change its dynamics, which is the focus of the new paradigm of the Relational Theory of the Firm (Wieland, 2024). For further modelling and a complete description of these two members' dynamics and, consequently, of the firm's network dynamic benefit function, additional research based on the mathematical apparatus of non-linear dynamics and the concept of dynamic attractors is required. The dynamics of the firm includes the action of autocatalytic processes, since the generation of Cooperational Rent stimulates the growth of the firm and its relational assets and, hence, further growth of the whole relational network and the next spiral of increasing Cooperational Rent.

This will be the focus of our future research to further develop the Relational Theory of the Firm.

For now, our results are already a significant step forward in understanding the relational nature of the firm, modelling its dynamics together with the dynamics of the whole relational network. It provides possibilities to develop the simulation models and scenario analysis for applications in practical business governance purposes.

References

Ahuja, G. (2000). Collaboration networks, structural holes, and innovation: A longitudinal study. *Administrative Science Quarterly, 45*(3), S. 425–S. 455. https://doi.org/10.2307/2667105

Albert, R., & Barabási, A.-L. (2000). Dynamics of complex systems: Scaling laws for the period of boolean networks. *Physical Review Letters, 84*(24), 5660–5663. https://doi.org/10.1103/PhysRevLett.84.5660

Albert, R., & Barabási, A.-L. (2002). Statistical mechanics of complex networks. *Reviews of Modern Physics, 74*(1), 47–97. https://doi.org/10.1103/RevModPhys.74.47

Amit, D. J. (1989). *Modeling brain function: The world of attractor neural networks* (1st ed.). Cambridge University Press. Available at http://www.loc.gov/catdir/description/cam023/89015741.html

Arthur, W. B. (1999). Complexity and the economy. *Science, 284*(5411), 107–109. https://doi.org/10.1126/science.284.5411.107

Arthur, W. B. (2010). Complexity, the Santa Fe approach, and non-equilibrium economics. *History of Economic Ideas*. https://doi.org/10.1400/148277

Arthur, W. B. (2015). *Complexity and the economy*. Oxford University Press.

Arthur, W. B. (2021). Foundations of complexity economics. *Nature Reviews. Physics, 3*(2), 136–145. https://doi.org/10.1038/s42254-020-00273-3

Arthur, W. B., Beinhocker, E. D., & Stanger, A. (Eds.). (2020). *Complexity economics. Dialogues of the applied complexity network I: Proceedings of the Santa Fe Institute's 2019 Fall Symposium* (Compass series). The Santa Fe Institute Press.

Axelrod, R. M. (1997). *The complexity of cooperation: Agent-based models of competition and collaboration* (Princeton studies in complexity). Princeton University Press. Available at http://www.jstor.org/stable/10.2307/j.ctt7s951

Axtell, R. L. (2007). What economic agents do: How cognition and interaction lead to emergence and complexity. *The Review of Austrian Economics, 20*(2–3), 105–122. https://doi.org/10.1007/s11138-007-0021-5

Balkundi, P., Wang, L., & Harrison, D. A. (2009). *Bridging the gap: Consequences of structural hole spanning at multiple levels* (Working paper). SUNY Buffalo.

Banwari, L. J. (2022). Measure of connectivity (network) structure: A study. *International Journal of Advanced Research in Commerce, Management & Social Science (IJARCMSS), 5*(04, I), 96–100.

Barrat, A., Barthélemy, M., & Vespignani, A. (2008). *Dynamical processes on complex networks*. Cambridge University Press. Available at http://www.loc.gov/catdir/enhancements/fy0835/2008025427-b.html

Biggiero, L., & Magnuszewski, R. (2021). The general ownership structure of the European aerospace industry: A statistical and network analysis. *Advances in Complex Systems, 24*(05), 2150012. https://doi.org/10.1142/S0219525921500120

Biggiero, L., & Magnuszewski, R. (2023). *Inter-firm networks: Coordination through board and department interlocks* (Relational Economics and Organization Governance). Springer International Publishing. Springer.

Biggiero, L., Angelini, P. P., Basevi, M., Carbonara, N., Mastrogiorgio, A., Pessa, E., et al. (2016). *Relational methodologies and epistemology in economics and management sciences* (Advances in the Finance, Accounting, and Economics (AFAE) book series). Information Science Reference an Imprint of IGI Global.

Bonotto, E. M., & Uzal, J. M. (2024). Global attractors for a class of discrete dynamical systems. *Journal of Dynamics and Differential Equations*. https://doi.org/10.1007/s10884-024-10356-9

Buescu, J. (1997a). Attractors in dynamical systems. In J. Buescu (Ed.), *Exotic attractors: From Liapunov stability to riddled basins* (Springer eBook Collection Mathematics and Statistics, 153, pp. 1–33). Birkhäuser Basel.

Buescu, J. (1997b). *Exotic attractors: From Liapunov stability to riddled basins* (Springer eBook Collection Mathematics and Statistics, 153). Birkhäuser Basel.

Burt, R. S. (1992). *Structural holes: The social structure of competition*. Harvard University Press. Available at https://www.degruyter.com/isbn/9780674029095

Carvalho, A. N., Langa, J. A., & Robinson, J. (2012). *Attractors for infinite-dimensional non-autonomous dynamical systems* (Applied mathematical sciences, Vol. 182). With contributions from J. A. Langa & J. C. Robinson. Springer.

Chekroun, M. D., Simonnet, E., & Ghil, M. (2011). Stochastic climate dynamics: Random attractors and time-dependent invariant measures. *Physica D: Nonlinear Phenomena, 240*(21), 1685–1700. https://doi.org/10.1016/j.physd.2011.06.005

Chiang, A. C., & Wainwright, K. (2005). *Fundamental methods of mathematical economics* (3rd ed., McGraw-Hill international ed., [repr.]). McGraw-Hill.

Coase, R. H. (1937). The nature of the firm. *Economica, 4*(16), 386. https://doi.org/10.2307/2626876

Danilov, Y. A. (2006). *Lectures on nonlinear dynamics*. ComKniga.

Dobusch, L., & Schüßler, E. (2012). Theorizing path dependence: A review of positive feedback mechanisms in technology markets, regional clusters, and organizations. *Industrial and Corporate Change, 22*(3), 617–647. https://doi.org/10.1093/icc/dts029

Haken, H. (1973). *Cooperative phenomena. With contributions from M. Wagner*. Springer Berlin/Heidelberg.

Haken, H. (1983). *Advanced synergetics: Instability hierarchies of self-organizing systems and devices*. Springer-Verlag (Springer Series in Synergetics).

Haken, H. (1987). Synergetics. In F. E. Yates (Ed.), *Self-organizing systems: The emergence of order* (Life science monographs, pp. 417–434). Plenum Press.

Haken, H. (1988). *Information and self-organization: A macroscopic approach to complex systems*. Springer Verlag.

Hendler, J., & Golbeck, J. (2008). Metcalfe's law, Web 2.0, and the semantic web. *Journal of Web Semantics, 6*(1), 14–20. https://doi.org/10.1016/j.websem.2007.11.008

Hicks, J. (1939). *Value and capital: An inquiry into some fundamental principles of economic theory* (Clarendon Paperbacks). Clarendon Press.

Hopfield, J. J. (1982). Neural networks and physical systems with emergent collective computational abilities. *Proceedings of the National Academy of Sciences of the United States of America, 79*(8), 2554–2558. https://doi.org/10.1073/pnas.79.8.2554

Hopfield, J. J. (1984). Neurons with graded response have collective computational properties like those of two-state neurons. *Proceedings of the National Academy of Sciences of the United States of America, 81*(10), 3088–3092. https://doi.org/10.1073/pnas.81.10.3088

Hopfield, J. J., & Tank, D. W. (1985). "Neural" computation of decisions in optimization problems. *Biological Cybernetics, 52*(3), S. 141–S. 152. https://doi.org/10.1007/BF00339943

Kansky, K. (1963). *Structure of transportation networks: Relationships between network geography and regional characteristics. Research Papers, 84*. University of Chigaco, Department of Geography.

Keynes, J. M. (2018). *The general theory of employment, interest, and money*. Springer International Publishing; Imprint Palgrave Macmillan.

Krakauer, D. C. (Ed.). (2024). *Foundational papers in complexity science*. SFI Press.

Le Chatelier, H. (1891). Sur les transformations moléculaires des métaux et leurs conductibilités électriques. *Journal of Physics: Theories and Applications, 10*(1), S. 369–S. 374. https://doi.org/10.1051/jphystap:0189100100036901

Mandelshtam, L. I. (1972). *Lectures in optics, relativity theory and quantum mechanics*. Nauka.

Markusen, J. R. (2020). *Global comparatives statics in general equilibrium: Model building from theoretical foundations*. NBER Working Papers. National Bureau of Economic Research, Inc. (27219). Online verfügbar unter https://ideas.repec.org/p/nbr/nberwo/27219.html zuletzt geprüft am 03.07.2024.

Mohar, B., Alavi, Y., Chartrand, G., Oellermann, O. R., & Schwenk, A. J. (1991). The Laplacian spectrum of graphs. *Graph Theory, Combinatorics and Applications, 2*, S. 871–S. 898.

Nicolis, G., & Prigogine, I. (1989). *Exploring complexity. An introduction*. Freeman.

Nijkamp, P., & Reggiani, A. (1995). *Modeling network synergy: Static and dynamic aspects*. VU University Amsterdam, Faculty of Economics, Business Administration and Econometrics (Serie Research Memoranda, 0049).

Ogura, M., Mei, W., & Sugimoto, K. (2019). Synergistic effects in networked epidemic spreading dynamics. *IEEE Transactions on Circuits and Systems II, 67*(3), S. 496–S. 500. https://doi.org/10.1109/TCSII.2019.2912794

Prigogine, I. (1978): Time, structure, and fluctuations. *Science*, 201 (4358), S. 777–S. 785. https://doi.org/10.1126/science.201.4358.777.

Prigogine, I. (1980). *From being to becoming. Time and complexity in the physical sciences*. Freeman.

Prigogine, I., & Stengers, I. (2018). *Order out of chaos. Man's new dialogue with nature*. Verso (Radical Thinkers).

Prigogine, I., et al. (1977). The evolution of complexity and the laws of nature. In E. Laszlo (Ed.), *Goals in global community. The original background papers for goals for mankind. A report to the Club of Rome*. Pergamon Pr.

Rivot, S., & Trautwein, H.-M. (2020). Macroeconomic statics and dynamics in a historical perspective. *The European Journal of the History of Economic Thought, 27*(4), S. 471–S. 475. https://doi.org/10.1080/09672567.2020.1780750

Rogers, E. M. (2003). *Diffusion of innovations* (Fifth ed.). Free Press. Online verfügbar unter. https://ebookcentral.proquest.com/lib/kxp/detail.action?docID=4935198

Rohlfs, J. (1974). A theory of interdependent demand for a communications service. *The Bell Journal of Economics and Management Science, 5*(1), S. 16. https://doi.org/10.2307/3003090

Samuelson, P. A. (1947). *Foundations of economic analysis* (Vol. 80, Enlarged ed.). Harvard University Press (Harvard economic studies).

Shone, R. (2012). *Economic dynamics. Phase diagrams and their economic application* (1. publ ed.). Cambridge University Press.

Snijders, T. A. B., van de Bunt, G. G., & Steglich, C. E. G. (2010). Introduction to stochastic actor-based models for network dynamics. *Social Networks, 32*(1), S. 44–S. 60. https://doi.org/10.1016/j.socnet.2009.02.004

Stachurski, J. (2022). *Economic dynamics. Theory and computation* (Second ed.). The MIT Press.

Sydow, J., Schreyögg, G., & Koch, J. (2009). Organizational path dependence: Opening the black box. *Academy of Management Review, 34*(4), 689–709. https://doi.org/10.5465/amr.34.4.zok689

Valente, T. W. (1995). *Network models of the diffusion of innovations*. Hampton Press. (Quantitative methods in communication).

Valente, T., & Rogers E. (1995). The origins and development of the diffusion of innovations paradigm as an example of scientific growth. *Science Communication: An Interdisciplinary Social Science Journal, 16*(1995), 238–269.

Wieland, J. (2020). *Relational economics. A political economy* (1st ed. 2020 ed.). Springer International Publishing; Imprint Springer (Springer eBook Collection).

Wieland, J. (2024). *Towards a relational theory of the firm*. Springer Nature.

Wieland, J., von Müller, A., Nikonov, A., Teichert, L., Lehrack, S., & Törner, L. (2022). Modeling relational transactions. In L. Biggiero, D. de Jongh, B. Priddat, J. Wieland, A. Zicari, & D. Fischer (Eds.), *The relational view of economics* (pp. S. 75–S. 96). Springer International Publishing.

Zhang, Z., Zhang, Q., & Li, C. (2023). Do network synergies facilitates the realization of M&a motivation?: From the perspective of network node degree and strength change. *PLoS One, 18*(4), e0284204. https://doi.org/10.1371/journal.pone.0284204

Josef Wieland is Professor of Institutional Economics, Organisational Governance, Integrity Management, and Transcultural Leadership at Zeppelin University in Friedrichshafen and Director of the Leadership Excellence Institute Zeppelin (LEIZ). He is the initiator and president of the German Forum Compliance and Integrity (FCI). He served as the former Chairman of the German Network of Business Ethics (DNWE) and is currently Chairman of DNWE's advisory board. He is a member of the National CSR Forum of the BMAS (German Federal Ministry of Labour and Social Affairs) and serves on the jury for the "CSR Prize" of the German government. He received the Max Weber Prize for Business Ethics of the IW (German Economic Institute) in 1999. In 2004, he received the highly esteemed State Research Prize for Applied Research from the State of Baden-Württemberg, Germany. From 2017 to 2021, he was Vice-President (Research) of Zeppelin University, Friedrichshafen, Germany. In 2024, Josef Wieland has been awarded the distinguished honour to join the International Research Advisory Board of the prestigious Gordon Institute of Business Science (GIBS) at the University of Pretoria in Johannesburg, South Africa.

Tetiana Unkovska, Dr. Sci. in Economics, Kyiv National University of Trade and Economics, wrote her doctorate on Financial Equilibrium of the Firm; she has a Ph.D. in Mathematical Modelling in Economics from Moscow State University of Economics and Information Systems (now a part of the Plekhanov Russian University of Economics) and an M.Sc. in Applied Mathematics from V.N. Karazin Kharkiv National University. She is a renowned researcher in finance and economics. Since 2022, she has been a Research Fellow at St. Gallen University, and since 2023 at the University of Basel, focusing on mathematical economic modelling. She has also been Leading Researcher at the Institute for Economics and Forecasting of the Ukrainian National Academy of Sciences since 2006. Tetiana Unkovska has served as Chief Adviser to the Council of the National Bank of Ukraine for 8 years, specialising in complex financial networks, institutional economics, macroeconomics, monetary policy and financial stability. She is also an Associate Professor in Ukraine and Lecturer in Economic Development, Global Finance, Monetary Policy and Quantitative Methods.

A Relational View on Organization Ontology: Insights from Methodological Relationism, Process Philosophy, and Critical Realism

Jessica Geraldo Schwengber

Abstract This chapter aims to contribute to a relational view of organization ontology. Organization ontology refers to the nature of the organization and to the question "What is the organization?". A relational view of organization ontology in this chapter is built theoretically on three main conceptual blocks. The first is methodological relationism. This is a meta-construct that refuses the primacy of substances. Methodological relationism is therefore anti-substantialist and may allow for a conceptual shift from individualism to relationism in organizational research. The second conceptual block is Whitehead's process philosophy because this chapter adopts the position of relation as processual. The third conceptual block is critical realism and, in particular, the emergent property. Processual relations at a lower (micro) level lead to the emergence of a novel processual entity, namely, the organization. A relational view of organization ontology based on these three conceptual blocks draws on the nature of the organization in the Relational Economics theory view of the organization.

Keywords Organization ontology · Organization theory · Relational economics · Relational thinking · Methodological relationism · Process philosophy · Critical realism

1 Introduction

What is the organization? What does a relational view of the organization imply? These are the questions that this chapter aims to address.

The nature of the organization has already been studied by various scholars. One of the pioneers was Ronald Coase with his essay on the nature of the organization (1937). More recent works have also examined the ontology of the organization (e.g., Seabright & Kurke, 1997; Smith, 2001; Bottazzi & Ferrario, 2005; Fleetwood,

J. G. Schwengber (✉)
Zeppelin University, Friedrichshafen, Germany
e-mail: jessica.schwengber@zu.de

J. D. Rendtorff et al. (eds.), *Advances in Relational Economics*, Relational Economics and Organization Governance,
https://doi.org/10.1007/978-3-031-75725-9_3

2005; Izhar et al., 2013; Hahn & Knight, 2021). This chapter aims to contribute to this stream in the literature. However, this contribution is not only about organization ontology per se but also about the conceptualization of a relational view of organization ontology. In the philosophy of science, different philosophers have adopted and elaborated different ontological positions that have shaped different ways that existence can be conceptualized. This chapter proposes that a relational view of organization ontology is based on the ontological positions of the fluxists, adequatists, and realists, which, in turn, is anchored in process philosophy, methodological relationism, and critical realism.

As for the structure of the chapter, the different ontological positions are first discussed. The aim is to clarify the ontological position in this chapter. While ontological positions are mainly based on philosophical discussions, an inquiry into a relational view of organization ontology may also require clarification of the definition of organization assumed in this chapter. A relational view of organization ontology, as proposed here, is theoretically based on Relational Economics. After these theoretical clarifications, the mainstream organization theories and ontologies are discussed. The discussion argues that such mainstream theories and ontologies may not be well suited to Relational Economics, in which organizations are conceptualized as entities in their own right operating in complex value creation systems. Methodological relationism and process philosophy are then discussed and proposed as a conceptual background for a relational ontology. Following the elaboration of methodological relationism and process philosophy, this chapter discusses how critical realism and the emergent property contribute conceptually to relational ontology. The implications for organization theory are then derived. The chapter concludes with an attempt to answer the question "What is organization in relational terms?" by summarizing the main points discussed.

2 Some Clarification on Ontological Positions

Ontology refers to "what is" the nature of being. It is usually associated with epistemology and methodology. The study of being has a long history in philosophy, and different philosophers have held different ontological positions. Different ontological positions include substantialists versus fluxists and adequatists versus reductionists (Smith, 2012). A further distinction is made between idealist and realist ontologies (Kant, 2014). Substantialists define beings as substance/thing. Fluxists define beings as events or processes. Reductionists privilege a level of existence/reduce being to a level of existence. Adequatists refer to being at different levels of existence and examine the totality of "objects, properties, processes and relations that make up the world on different levels of focus and granularity" (Smith, 2012, p. 48). Idealist ontology assumes that there is no reality apart from human thoughts. Realist ontology, on the other hand, assumes that there is a natural or social reality beyond the human mind (Kant, 2014). The latter distinction can also be made between "foundationalism/objectivist/realism" and "anti-foundationalism/

Table 1 Different ontological positions

Ontological positions	
Fluxist: being as processes/events	*Substantialist:* being as substance/thing
Adequatists: different levels of existence	*Reductionist:* reduction of being to a level of existence
Realistic: natural and social reality beyond thoughts	*Idealistic:* existence as thoughts/mind

Source: Own table based on Smith (2012) and Kant (2014)

constructivist/relativism" (Kant, 2014). While the former assumes that there is an external reality beyond human consciousness, the latter assumes a socially constructed reality. The different ontological positions are summarized in Table 1.

In science, the ontological positions of the researcher influence epistemology and methodology. The former is defined as the theory of knowledge, i.e., what is known. The latter refers to the technique and instruments of scientific investigation. Ontology, epistemology, and methodology need to be aligned (Bracken, 2010), although there is debate in the literature as to which proceeds from which, and some scholars also argue that ontology and epistemology are conflated (see discussion in Kant, 2014). As for this latter claim, in the philosophy of science, ontology and epistemology are studied as two distinct categories. Merging the two would lead to a category mistake (Kant, 2014): "They (epistemology and ontology) are not the same and the one must also not be confused with or reduced to the other" (Kant, 2014, p. 77, own explanation into ()). Reducing ontology to epistemology leads to an epistemic fallacy (Bhaskar, 1998). As for the question of what comes before (either ontology or epistemology), some scholars take the opposite view that epistemology precedes ontology, although traditionally ontology precedes epistemology (Kant, 2014). Other scholars argue that there is no particular direction between epistemology and ontology (ibid.). I take the position that ontology, epistemology, and methodology are distinct concepts, but are inter-related, and that ontological positions precede epistemology and methodology. This means that the way in which being is defined influences the theory of knowledge of being, as well as the techniques and instruments of scientific investigation. Therefore, I call for a clarification of ontological positions, which is/was not always the case in organization studies.

This chapter presents a relational view of organization ontology based on methodological relationism, process philosophy, and critical realism. Process philosophy implies a fluxist ontological position. Methodological relationism is anti-reductionist and therefore, if we consider the distinction as a dichotomy, is closer to adequatism. Critical realism, as the name implies, is based on a (critical) realist position in the sense that it assumes that a social reality (e.g., the organization) is ontologically autonomous and therefore cannot be reduced to human consciousness.

3 Relational Economics as Theoretical Background

In the inquiry into the elaboration of a relational view of organization ontology, after some clarification of the ontological positions, the next step in the argumentation would be to clarify what is meant by organization. Due to an economic/managerial background, organization in this chapter refers to business organizations. The term "organization" instead of "firm" or "corporations" is used because despite having an economic background, the considerations presented can also be extended to other types of organizations such as nongovernmental organizations (NGOs), political parties, etc.

As for the economic theoretical background, this chapter is part of the Relational Economics theory research agenda (Wieland, 2020, 2022; Biggiero et al., 2022). Relational Economics has been influenced by theories such as the institutional economics theory and the theory of the firm. Following scholars such as Commons (1934) and Williamson (2005), in Relational Economics the transaction is the unit of analysis. Stakeholders invest resources and interests in the organization to engage in transactions. In addition to institutional economics and the theory of the firm, Relational Economics has also been influenced by systems theory (e.g., Luhmann, 2013). This influence can be seen in the idea that different stakeholders involved in transactions may operate in different systems (polycontextuality), and have different decision logics (polycontexturality) and different language games (polylinguality). Transactions may then attract multiple logics that need to be relationalized for the completion of transactions. Multicontextual transactions take place in a multifaceted environment of operationally closed, communicatively open, and functionally autonomous systems (Wieland, 2020). Although in multicontextual transactions, business organizations can operate in relation to other systems, business organizations remain coupled with the economic system and specialized in the guiding difference "earning-costs." Relational in Relational Economics term, therefore, means successful relationalization of multiple rationalities and does not therefore merely refer to interpersonal relationships.

In the theory of Relational Economics, the firm (which can be extended to organizations in general) is therefore a nexus of stakeholders' resources and interests. However, the organization is an entity in its own right that exists autonomously from the nexus of stakeholders' resources and interests. If the organization is a distinct entity, it should also be ontologically distinct from the stakeholders and their resources and interests. The application of critical realism as an ontological position in Relational Economics thus contributes to the theoretical specification of the claim that organizations are entities in their own right. While critical realism assumes that social entities (such as the organization) are dependent on human interaction (stakeholders-individuals and/or collective actors), it also assumes that they are ontologically autonomous, namely, separate entities.

Relational Economics also calls for a relational turn in economics. Relational is not understood only as interpersonal relationships, but as a relationalization of the rationalities of the various stakeholders who invest resources and interests in organizational transactions. The organization as an ontologically autonomous entity is thus to be seen as the result of a relationalization process. The assertion that the organization is ontologically autonomous and results from relationalization also means that at least two levels of reality are recognized: the micro level (individuals, individual stakeholders, and their resources and interests, which are real) and the macro level (the organization as an autonomous entity, also real). In this view, Relational Economics is not reductive, as different levels of existence are taken into account. This is in line with methodological relationism, which in contrast to individualism (micro-reduction) and holism (macro-reduction) can be seen as adequatist (no privilege of the micro or macro level but assumption of different levels of existence). In Relational Economics, the different levels (the organization and the stakeholders) are not static, but in a dynamic relational process of continuous mutual transformation. What the organization was, is, and will be is the result of the continuous relationalization of the stakeholders' resources. The organization is in what process philosophy defines as continuous processes of concrescence and transition. Methodological relationalism, process philosophy, and critical realism are further explored below after comparing this view with current organization ontologies.

4 Organization Ontologies and Organization Empirical Reality

Organization in Relational Economics views may require a revision of organization ontology compared to mainstream theories. In mainstream organization theories, the organizational system (the organization) is defined in terms of its components (employees, leaders, managers, etc.). Classical organization theories, such as Weber's (1904/2005) bureaucracy and Taylor's (1919) scientific management of labor, emphasize the Homo economicus and conceptualize organizations as machines that function thanks to a clear division of labor. Neoclassical organization theories, both the human relations school (e.g., Mayo, 1945) and the behavioral school (e.g., Simon, 1947/1976; Simon, 1991; Cyert & March, 1963; Galbraith, 1974), conceptualized organizations as social systems (Oyibo & Gabriel, 2020). Humans were not just Homo economicus, but social beings with bounded rationality and with motivations and needs that go beyond economic ones (Günbayi & Sorm, 2019). Both the classical and the neoclassical theories of the organization emphasize the micro level (micro-reduction) with a focus on employee productivity within delimited organizational boundaries (Bueno & Salapa, 2021). In this context, Scott and Davis (2016) refer to organization theories as substantialist, and it can be added that they are also based on methodological individualism.

Both classical and neoclassical organization theories made an important contribution to explaining the empirical organization reality of their time. For example, classic organization theories were influenced by the challenges of the industrial revolution at the end of the nineteenth century. Neoclassic theories were a response to the criticism of the dehumanization of classic theories and contributed to understanding behavior and productivity beyond economic incentives. Currently, the empirical reality of organizations is characterized by operating in a globalized world and by all the challenges of the twenty-first century. In the twenty-first century, the world is described as a reality consisting of dynamic systems, systems that are bundles of processes (Dombrowski, 2022). This current empirical reality describes an open systems perspective (Scott & Davis, 2016; Oyibo & Gabriel, 2020; Bueno & Salapa, 2021). Organizations can be viewed as open systems because organizations "are capable of self-maintenance on the basis of throughput of resources from the environment" (Scott & Davis, 2016). In Relational Economics term, these resources from the environment come from stakeholders from different systems. Contrary to mainstream organization theories that argue that organizations have to defend themselves from the attacks/risks from the environment, an open systems perspective highlights that those transactions with the environment are essential for the organization's functioning (Scott & Davis, 2016). The essentiality of transactions that attract resources and interests from a bundle of different stakeholders from different systems requires one to look at the organization as a nexus of stakeholders' resources and interests. Mainstream theories, although recognizing the role of the environment, explain organizations by focusing on their internal systems' boundaries (what happens inside the organization). By drawing on systems theory, although the various systems are operationally closed and autonomous, they are communicatively open and therefore interconnected. This interconnection can be observed in networks of value creation. In the value creation process, business organizations are (communicatively) connected not only to other business organizations but also to stakeholders from other systems, such as from civil society and political systems (transactions indeed attract different rationalities). This interconnection is not something that affects only multinational companies as it can also affect small and medium-sized enterprises that limit their activities to a regional or national level. To illustrate this assertion, consider how the Suez blockade in 2021, the COVID-19 pandemic, and the energy crisis resulting from the war in Ukraine have impacted manifold organizations, regardless of size. Davis (2006) compares this interconnectedness to a bowl of oatmeal where "to distinguish between separate organizations is like trying to separate out distinct lumps in a bowl of oatmeal" (Davis, 2006, p. 480). This tendency toward a communicative interconnection between actors of different systems can also be observed in new environmental and human rights regulations, where organizations are held accountable not only for their actions and activities but also for the activities of their partners and for their impact on different stakeholders. This applies, for example, to environmental regulations that hold organizations accountable for environmental impacts and improve the linkages between organizations and external stakeholders at both regional and international levels. Another example is the EU Corporate Sustainability Due Diligence Directive (CSDDD), EU legislation approved in 2024 that aims to protect human rights and the environment in the supply chain and relates business partners in and outside Europe (European Council, 2024). Although these regulations include personal responsibility, in general they refer to corporate responsibility and therefore to a corporate entity distinguished from natural persons. This is in line with a Relational Economics view of the organization as entity in its own right.

This view of organization as a nexus of stakeholders' resources and interest and as an entity in its own right impacts on the ontology of the organization. Classic and neoclassic theories assume socially constructed, cognitive, and substantial/atomistic ontologies. The ontology of social construction assumes that organization is not a real phenomenon that exists in the realm of the real. It does not refer to an extra-linguistic reality (Chia, 2000). Organization does not exist a priori to human intervention. It is a social construction. In cognitive ontology, the agent metaphor is used to explain organizations. The organization is a collection of agents (Boella & van der Torre, 2006).[1]

In the substance/atomistic ontology, organizations develop because individuals have consciously decided to do so. In this cognitive view, the organization is viewed from the characteristics and actions of its individuals. The organization is reduced to the activities of the individuals. Human behavior is autoreferential. Valentinov and Chia (2022) formulate this as follows: "Corporations as macro entities comprising aggregations of discrete autonomous actors." Common to all these ontologies is the focus on the micro level of analysis and the reduction of organizations to the activities of individuals (individualism/micro-reduction).

A view of the organization that is limited to its components (social construction, cognitive and atomistic ontologies) and focuses on the micro level of the internal organizational system would not allow one to capture the dynamic relations in which organizations as distinct actors are involved. Dynamic relations are bundles of processes, which may make processual relational ontology probably the most empirically adequate ontology for organizations in the twenty-first century. It is processual because the organizational system is in continuous relations and relations are dynamic in the sense of continuous transformation. In the words of Dombrowski (2022): "reality is flux and constant transformation, so its static description is only an averaging, a generalization of the dynamic description." A processual relational ontology would be consistent with Chassagnon's (2014) call to see the social reality of organizations "as a complex emergent entity that cannot be reduced to the mere sum of its constitutive components" (ibid., p. 199).

5 Methodological Relationism and Process Philosophy

A relational processual view of organization ontology is firstly based on a methodological shift from individualism to methodological relationism in organization research (Schwengber, 2024). Methodological individualism is a meta-construct

[1] The agent metaphor can be criticized for its anthropomorphizing character, namely, using human attributes to define inanimate beings.

that focuses on the components/parts to explain the system—micro-reduction (Ho & Chiu, 1998; Ritzer & Gindoff, 1992; Subasi, 2020). While some scholars associate relationism with holism (e.g., Overton, 2013), methodological relationism as described here is not synonymous with holism. Whereas in methodological holism, the system defines the parts—macro-reduction (Overton, 2013; Bunge, 2000)—methodological relationism focuses on the relations between the parts of the system and between the parts and the system (Subasi, 2020; Ritzer & Gindoff, 1992; Bunge, 2000). Relationism is located on the continuum between the micro and macro levels (Emirbayer, 1997; Ritzer & Gindoff, 1992). Therefore, relationism reduces phenomena neither to the micro level of explanation (individualism/micro-reduction) nor to the macro level (holism/macro-reduction) (Ritzer & Gindoff, 1992). Methodological relationism is a dynamic relation in which the micro and macro levels change mutually in the relational process.

Methodological relationism as dynamic relations requires further conceptual clarity. There are "relational" (or better interactional) approaches in which relata/substance involved in a relation do not change in the relation; they remain static. This can be the case when individual parts (relata) interact, but in the course of the interaction, they remain static substances that do not change in the interaction process. The relation is external in which the substance remains stable, a separate and isolated substance (von Eschenbach, 2021). This is called an interactional approach (Emirbayer, 1997; Selg & Ventsel, 2020; Selg et al., 2022). A relational approach in which both the micro (parts/relata) and macro (whole/system) change as a result of relationalization is called a transactional approach (Selg & Ventsel, 2020; Emirbayer, 1997), and the relation is transcendental (von Eschenbach, 2021). The transactional approach and transcendental relation are the assumptions of methodological relationism (Schwengber, 2024).

Here, it is argued that such a dynamic relational view may benefit from process philosophy. Alfred N. Whitehead's processual philosophy provides the theoretical background for a processual ontology. Chapter X entitled "Process" in his book "*Process and Reality*" (1927/1978) begins with the generalization "all things flow" (ibid.: p. 208) and then elaborates on the metaphysics of flow/fluency as an antithesis to the metaphysics of substance. Whitehead then distinguishes between two types of flow. The first the scholar called is "concrescence," and the other, "transition." Concrescence is defined as "the process in which the universe of many things acquires an individual unity in a determinate relegation of each item of the 'many' to its subordination in the constitution of the 'novel' one" (Whitehead, 1927/1978, p. 211). Such a "relegation of each item" (namely, concrescence) is defined here as lower level relationalization. Whitehead does not distinguish the "novel thing" from the "concrescence" since the latter is itself the novel thing. There is an actual entity, which is a concrescence and a standpoint for another concrescence. The second "fluency" is transition "from a particular existence to a particular existence" (Whitehead 1927/1978, p. 210). The actual entity is thus always relative, in transition, in creation, in transformation. Whitehead defines process as "the expansion of the universe in respect to actual things" and defines actual entities as "a process proceeding from phase to phase, each phase being the real basis from which its successor proceeds towards the completion of the thing in question" (Whitehead 1927/1978, p. 215). In this processual view, the thing/entity (organization in this chapter) may be in a continuous process of becoming result from continuous relationalization.

The metaphysics of flux/process has been largely ignored in the history of philosophy so that philosophical analysis has focused on static categories (Whitehead, 1927/1978). Processual ontology stands in contrast to this static view (Renault, 2016; Bosi & Malthaner, 2022). A dynamic/processual view would therefore also mean a rejection of substantialism and of the primacy of static substance (the assumption of methodological individualism).[2]

Based on the assumption that relations in which relata/substance do not change are interactional but not processual, relational ontology, as proposed here, also assumes a processual view, as it is dynamic. A process is always relational, as there is no isolated process (Dombrowski, 2022). This is a shift from a substantialist view to dynamic, continuous, and unfolding relations (Emirbayer, 1997; Selg & Ventsel, 2020; Selg et al., 2022). The unit of analysis shifts from substance to processual relations. The relations are transcendental in which, through relationalization, the components of a system mutually transform each other and the system in a relational-processual-transformational emergence (von Eschenbach, 2021; Santos, 2015). It involves a micro-macro relationalization process (Schwengber, 2024). Process ontology is thus characterized by anti-substantialism and relationism (Dombrowski, 2022).

6 Relational Processual Ontology and Critical Realism

By now, it is claimed that organization ontology in Relational Economics requires a processual relational view of the organization. It has been argued that this change requires a shift from methodological individualism to methodological relationism and may be grounded in process philosophy. A shift to relationism would require a focus on dynamic relations between the components (stakeholders and their resources) of the system (the organization). While relational processual ontology allows a shift from a substantial (atomistic, cognitive, and social construction ontologies that explain organizations from the micro level) to a relational view of the organization, critical realism may be useful to further clarify the idea that the organization that results from concrescence is an entity in its own right.

Critical realism was developed by Bhaskar (1978, 1998). Critical realism is based on the assumption that reality is differentiated and stratified. The three realms of reality are empirical, actual, and real. The predominant ontology in organization studies, social construction, for example, reduces (organization) reality to human

[2]For an overview of the differences between substantialism, relationism, and processualism, see Renault (2016).

perception and experience (empirical domain). According to Bhaskar, this reduction of reality to what is known/perceived suffers from anthropocentrism and epistemic fallacy. In opposition to this view, critical realism presupposes intransitive objects of knowledge, namely, objects of knowledge that exist independently of human experience of it. Originally, critical realism mainly referred to natural science. Subsequent scholars, including Bhaskar himself, extended critical realism reasoning to social science. By criticizing anti-naturalistic traditions in social science, Bhaskar (1998) called for an anti-positivist realistic view of social science, in which social phenomena are to be seen as non-natural yet real things. In this sense, critical realism recognizes the ontological reality of social phenomena.

In the view of critical realism, thus, the organization is a non-natural, yet ontologically real, phenomenon. Indeed, in critical realism, the real entity does not only mean material entity as there are different types of reality (material, ideal, artifactual, and social) (Fleetwood, 2005). The organization as an entity in its own right would be a real social entity. Real social entity means that the organization is not (only) material, cannot be touched, and is dependent also on human activity for its existence, but exists independently of "our" identification of it (Fleetwood, 2005). In this view, the micro level (agency) is still important, but the difference from the social construction, agent, and atomistic ontologies is that the existence of the organization is not reduced to the agent/micro level, but to a relationalization at the micro level and between the micro and macro levels. To paraphrase Fleetwood: "to say (. . .) that entities (not only can but do) exist independently of our identification of them does not mean they exist independently of human activity" (Fleetwood, 2005, p. 202). The organization would emerge as a result of a lower level (micro-level) relationalization. Emergence means that the organization depends on relationalization at the lower level, but once emerged, it is distinct from, and ontologically irreducible to the lower (micro) level (Lawson, 2012). It is ontologically irreducible to the lower level because it may possess emergent properties that the elements of the lower level do not possess (Lawson, 2012). This ontologically irreducible emergence is relational in the sense that it is not the properties of the lower level that lead to emergence, but their relationalization (Dombrowski, 2022). This is a processual emergence that results from concrescence and transition, namely, the novel organization that emerges is the result of a dynamic relationalization at the micro level. In this dynamic process, the organization recreates itself and transits from one existence to another in a constantly unfolding process of relationalization. This constant change over time is also called morphogenic (Archer, 1995). On the other hand, the micro level may not remain static neither, but can also change in this process (micro-macro relationalization). In practical terms, this means that while the organization changes, its members (e.g., employees) do not remain static but may change as a result of their relationalization with other members. The micro-macro relationalization means that the system and the parts stick together. In this view, agent and structure interact, and the system and the parts interact, avoiding therefore both macro- and micro-reduction. This process is described in Fig. 1.

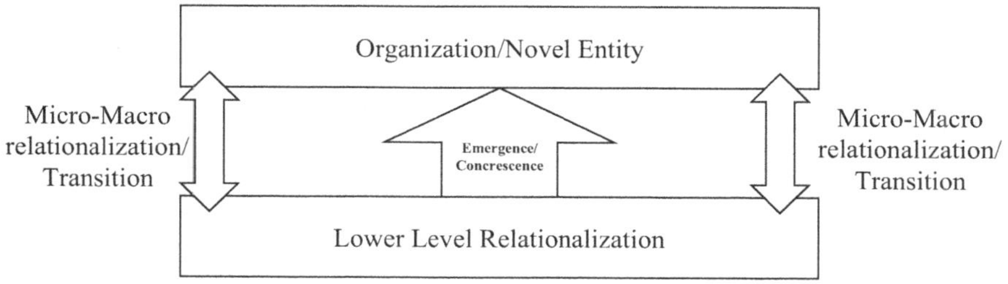

Fig. 1 Emergence. (Source: Adapted from Schwengber (2024))

This emergent property can be seen as an analogy to Popper's concept of the Third World. The organization (Third World) is a nonliving structure that is a product of humans but is autonomous (resulted from emergence/concrescence). Autonomous means that the organization has its own rules and evolves in unexpected ways that are not only predetermined by humans. It is a relational-transformational emergence (Santos, 2015), i.e., a relational process between relata (actors and their resources) that produces the system (the organization), which in turn is ontologically autonomous. The organization is like a bigger formation, also called society in Whitehead's (1927/1978) philosophy, intended as a complex and lasting thing (Schramm, 2022) resulted from the complex joint activities (Emirbayer, 1997) at the lower level.

Emergence, as defined here, is dynamic (processual). It can also be defined as "processual (or dynamical) emergentist" (Dombrowski, 2022). While emergent refers to the radical novelty/ontological autonomy of the higher level that has emerged (the organization), relationalization refers to the dynamic process at the lower level, and the continuous transformation of the organization and its members is the result of relationalization. This dynamic view is based on an ontology of becoming (Renault, 2016) and of continuous transformation/transition, in which patterns of relations are stabilized (Dombrowski, 2022). This stabilization takes place in structures. Even if processes take precedence over structures in processual emergence, there are still structures whose existence depends on the existence of processes. Processes lead to the formation of structures (processual structuralism). Organizations, on the other hand, "are highly organized (complex), functional, multilevel structures" (Dombrowski, 2022). The relationalization can also be viewed as a process of structure formation in the organization (Wieland, 2022).

Organization as a novel entity sounds like a static view of the organization and may therefore sound in antithesis to a relational view. The organization (the entity) is a noun. Weick (1974) argues that organization as a noun is a myth because, according to scholars, "if one looks for an organization one will not find it. What will be found is that there are events, linked together, that transpire within concrete walls and these sequences, their pathways, their timing, are the forms we erroneously make into substance when we talk about an organization" (Weick, 1974: 358). Weick's criticism is based on linguistic grounds of how nouns are used in linguistic-grammatical terms. However, although he criticizes organization as a noun, his definition of organization is processual/relational. When I claim that organization is a novel emergent entity, I mean an entity in the sense that Schoeneborn et al. (2019) have defined as a "processual entity," which creates and recreates (transition from one form of existence to another) through lower level relationalization/concrescence. The actual organization entity that exists in a given moment is what Whitehead defines "an instance of concrescence" (Whitehead 1927/1988), a standpoint for further concrescence/relationalization and therefore transition. Transition depicts the continuous evolution of the organization over time because of relationalization/concrescence (or still morphogenic).

7 Implications for Organizations Reality

It has been stated that the relational view on organization draws on Relational Economics, in which transactions are the units of analysis. In transactions, different stakeholders invest resources and interests. The organization as a nexus of stakeholder resources and interests is an ongoing (processual) concern existing in its transactions (Commons, 1934). If the transaction is the unit of analysis, the lower level relational process takes place at the level of organizational transactions where stakeholders are involved.

To corroborate the coherence of this ontological view of organizations, it suffices to think of any organization. It may consist of human resources (employees, management, leadership, and owners, etc.), material resources (computers, desks, chairs, buildings, etc.), financial resources, cooperation resources, network resources, inter alia; they may be invested in the organization by different stakeholders. These resources are combined (relationalized) for the execution of transactions. However, the organization cannot be reduced to its material existence (e.g., it is not just a building), so it is a social reality. Nor can it be reduced to its employees and managers or individual stakeholders (micro-reduction). The existence of century-old organizations can testify to their existence beyond individuals, although in their lifespan individuals may have contributed to the existence of the organization on certain actual occasions. Contribution is a key concept here, because every component of the system can contribute to its emergence. It is in fact the relationalization (and not the individuals or their single resources) that leads to emergence. It is indeed about relating components (single stakeholders' resources and interests).

The resources and interests of the stakeholders to be relationalized in the organization may come from different stakeholders operating in different systems, for example, investors, NGOs, or communities. The different organizations in different systems can in turn be seen as the result of relationalization at their lower levels. Emergence can thus be generalized to the multiple entities of different systems, which, in turn, can be linked to business organizations in a communicatively open systems perspective. This open systems perspective is depicted in Fig. 2.

The various actors of various social systems (business from economic system, communities for civil society system, government from political system, etc.) are

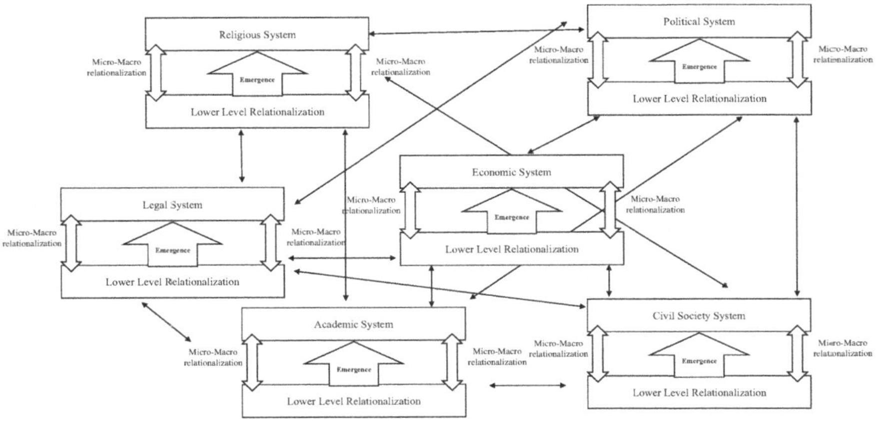

Fig. 2 Open systems. (Source: Own illustration)

thus all the result of the relationalization of lower levels. These different systems (economy, civil society, politic, science, religion, etc.) are autonomous and operationally closed but communicatively connected with each other in an open systems perspective. The (business) organization that emerges from the relationalization of the lower levels is connected to other entities from other systems. This is an open systems view formed by a network of networks in which each system is a network of lower-level components, which is then connected in a broader network.

8 Conclusion

So, what is organization in relational terms? To answer this question, this chapter draws on methodological relationism, process philosophy, and critical realism. Organization in relational terms is firstly anti-substantialist (methodological relationism). It rejects atomistic, social-constructive, and cognitive ontologies in the sense that organization in relational terms is not only individual-centered. Relation is to be understood not merely as an interpersonal relationship but as a relationalization of the resources and interests of organization stakeholders. This relationalization leads to the emergence of the organization. Thus, the organization is an autonomous entity that emerges from a relationalization at a lower level. The emerging organization is distinct from the lower level and is ontologically irreducible to it. It is a novel autonomous entity and therefore ontological real. The organization is the result of concrescence/relationalization. In this dynamic process, the organization is in a continuous transformation, in transition from one existence to another.

The claim that a relational ontology is not individual-centered does not mean neglecting the existence and contribution of individuals to the emergence and continuous transformation of the organization. Rather, it means not reducing organization's existence and its continuous transformation to specific individual actions alone. Organization as autonomous entity means accepting the existence of a (social) reality beyond single human minds.

The organization as an entity in its own right operates in a certain system (e.g., business organization in the economic system). The emergence of the organization as a result of lower level relationalization can be extended to organizations in different systems. The lower level may differ from system to system. Once emerged, organizations of the different systems do not remain in isolation. Although the different systems are operationally closed and functionally autonomous, they are communicatively open. This means that the different organizations of the different systems are communicatively interconnected in an open system.

The theoretical abstract relational view presented in this chapter aims at contributing to explaining the empirical reality in which organizations in the twenty-first century operate, that is, in which organizations as entities are held accountable for their operations in an empirical reality characterized by "a nearly endless series of value chains linking organizations and industries into a network of transactions" (Scott & Davis, 2016, p. 223).

References

Archer, M. S. (1995). *Realist social theory: The morphogenetic approach*. Cambridge University Press.

Bhaskar, R. (1978). *A realist theory of science*. The Harvester Press/Humanities Press.

Bhaskar, R. (1998). *The possibility of naturalism: A philosophical critique of the contemporary human sciences* (3rd ed.). Routledge.

Biggiero, L., de Jongh, D., Priddat, B., Wieland, J., & Zicari, A. (2022). Manifesto for a relational economics. In L. Biggiero, D. de Jongh, B. Priddat, J. Wieland, A. Zicari, & D. Fischer (Eds.), *The relational view of economics: A new research agenda for the study of relational transactions* (pp. 9–13). Springer.

Boella, G., & van der Torre, L. (2006). A foundational ontology of organizations and roles. In M. Baldoni & U. Endriss (Eds.), *Declarative agent languages and technologies IV* (Lecture notes in computer science, Vol. 4327, pp. 78–88). Springer.

Bosi, L., & Malthaner, S. (2022). Processual perspectives. In D. A. Snow, D. Della Porta, D. McAdam, & B. Klandermans (Eds.), *The Wiley Blackwell encyclopedia of social and political movements*. Wiley Blackwell.

Bottazzi, E., & Ferrario, R. (2005). A path to an ontology of organizations. In *Proceedings of the International Workshop on Vocabularies, Ontologies and Rules for The Enterprise (VORTE)* (pp. 9–16).

Bracken, S. (2010). Discussing the importance of ontology and epistemology awareness in practitioner research. *Worcester Journal of Learning and Teaching, 4*.

Bueno, D. C., & Salapa, A. C. (2021). The transformation of organizational theories from classical to contemporary: Analysis in the context of public administration. *Institutional Multidisciplinary Research and Development Journal, 4*, 1–14.

Bunge, M. (2000). Systemism: The alternative to individualism and holism. *The Journal of Socio-Economics, 29*(2), 147–157.

Chassagnon, V. (2014). Toward a social ontology of the firm: Reconstitution, organizing entity, institution, social emergence, and power. *Journal of Business Ethics, 124*(2), 197–208.
Chia, R. (2000). Ontology: Organisation as "world-making". In R. Westwood & S. Clegg (Eds.), *Point/counterpoint: Central debates in organisation theory* (pp. 1–25). Blackwell Publishers.
Coase, R. H. (1937). The nature of the firm. *Economica, 4*(16), 386–405.
Commons, J. R. (1934). *Institutional economics: Its place in political economy*. Macmillan.
Cyert, R. M., & March, J. G. (1963). *A behavioral theory of the firm*. University of Illinois at Urbana-Champaign's Academy for Entrepreneurial Leadership Historical Research Reference in Entrepreneurship.
Davis, R. J. (2006). Firms and environments. In N. J. Smelser & R. Swedberg (Eds.), *The handbook of economic sociology* (pp. 478–502). Princeton University Press/Russell Sage Foundation.
Dombrowski, M. (2022). Processual emergentism. *Erkenntnis*. https://doi.org/10.1007/s10670-022-00539-5
Emirbayer, M. (1997). Manifesto for a relational sociology. *American Journal of Sociology, 103*(2), 281–317.
European Council. (2024). *Corporate sustainability due diligence: Council and Parliament strike deal to protect environment and human rights*. Retrieved January 12, 2024, from https://www.consilium.europa.eu/en/press/press-releases/2023/12/14/corporate-sustainability-due-diligence-council-and-parliament-strike-deal-to-protect-environment-and-human-rights/
Fleetwood, S. (2005). Ontology in organization and management studies: A critical realist perspective. *Organization, 12*(2), 197–222.
Galbraith, J. R. (1974). Organization design: An information processing view. *Interfaces, 4*(3), 28–36.
Günbayi, I., & Sorm, S. (2019). Paradigms in guiding management approaches and theories: Classical, neoclassical, modern, and postmodern theories. *International Journal on New Trends in Education and Their Implications, 10*(2), 39–55.
Hahn, T., & Knight, E. (2021). The ontology of organizational paradox: A quantum approach. *Academy of Management Review, 46*(2), 362.
Ho, D. Y., & Chiu, C. (1998). Collective representations as a metaconstruct: An analysis based on methodological relationism. *Culture & Psychology, 4*(3), 349–369.
Izhar, T. A. T., Torabi, T., Bhatti, M. I., & Liu, F. (2013). Recent developments in the organization goals conformance using ontology. *Expert Systems with Applications, 40*(10), 4252–4267.
Kant, S.-L. (2014). The distinction and relationship between ontology and epistemology: Does it matter? *Politikon: IAPSS Political Science Journal, 24*, 68–85.
Lawson, T. (2012). Ontology and the study of social reality: Emergence, organization, community, power, social relations, corporations, artefacts, and money. *Cambridge Journal of Economics, 36*(2), 345–385.
Luhmann, N. (2013). *Introduction to systems theory*. Polity Press.
Mayo, E. (1945). *The social problems of an industrial civilization*. Harvard University/The Andover Press.
Overton, W. F. (2013). A new paradigm for developmental science: Relationism and relational-developmental systems. *Applied Developmental Science, 17*(2), 94–107.
Oyibo, C. O., & Gabriel, J. M. O. (2020). Evolution of organisation theory: A snapshot. *International Journal of Innovative Research and Development, 9*(9), 221–227.
Renault, E. (2016). Critical theory and processual social ontology. *Journal of Social Ontology, 2*(1), 17–32.
Ritzer, G., & Gindoff, P. (1992). Methodological relationism: Lessons for and from social psychology. *Social Psychological Quarterly, 55*(2), 128–140.
Santos, G. C. (2015). Ontological emergence: How is that possible? Towards a new relational ontology. *Foundations of Science, 20*(4), 429–446.
Schoeneborn, D., Kuhn, T. R., & Kärreman, D. (2019). The communicative constitution of organization, organizing and organizationality. *Organization Studies, 40*(4), 475–496.

Schramm, M. (2022). Relational processes in Whitehead's metaphysics and Commons' economics: The relevance of cosmology for economic theory. In L. Biggiero, D. de Jongh, J. Wieland, A. Zicari, & D. Fischer (Eds.), *The relational view of economics: A new research agenda for the study of relational transactions* (pp. 249–275). Springer.

Schwengber, J. G. (2024). *Organizational learning as relational governance*. Springer.

Scott, W. R., & Davis, G. F. (2016). *Organizations and organizing: Rational, natural, and open system perspectives* (2nd ed.). Routledge.

Seabright, M. A., & Kurke, L. B. (1997). Organizational ontology and the moral status of the corporation. *Business Ethics Quarterly, 7*(4), 91–108.

Selg, P., & Ventsel, A. (2020). *Introducing relational political analysis: Political semiotics as a theory and method*. Palgrave Macmillan.

Selg, P., Klasche, B., & Nõgisto, J. (2022). Wicked problems and sociology: Building a missing bridge through processual relationalism. *International Review of Sociology*. Advance online publication. https://doi.org/10.1080/03906701.2022.2040980.

Simon, H. A. (1976). *Administrative behavior: A study of decision-making processes in administrative organization* (3rd ed.). Free Press.

Simon, H. A. (1991). Bounded rationality and organizational learning. *Organization Science, 2*(1), 125–133.

Smith, D. E. (2001). Texts and the ontology of organizations and institutions. *Studies in Cultures, Organizations and Societies, 7*(2), 159–198.

Smith, B. (2012). Ontology. In G. Hurtado & O. Nudler (Eds.), *The furniture of the world* (pp. 47–68). Rodopi Philosophical Studies (RPS).

Subasi, E. (2020). Society, person, and their connections: A Bhaskarian formulation. *Beytulhikme International Journal of Philosophy, 10*(1), 105–116.

Taylor, F. W. (1919). *The principles of scientific management*. Harper & Brothers Publishers.

Valentinov, V., & Chia, R. (2022). Stakeholder theory: A process-ontological perspective. *Business Ethics, 31*(4), 762–776.

Von Eschenbach, M. E. (2021). Gegenwendige Anverwandlung: Die Bedeutung der Relata im Horizont Relationaler Theorieentwicklung. In M. E. von Eschenbach & O. Schäffter (Eds.), *Denken in wechselseitiger Beziehung* (pp. 187–213). Velbrück Wissenschaft.

Weber, M. (2005). *Economy and society: An outline of interpretive sociology* (G. Roth & C. Wittich, Eds.). University of California Press.

Weick, K. E. (1974). Middle range theories of social systems. *Behavioral Science, 19*(6), 357–367.

Whitehead, A. N. (1978). *Process and reality* (Corrected edition). Free Press.

Wieland, J. (2020). *Relational economics: A political economy*. Springer.

Wieland, J. (2022). Relational economics: Theoretical framework and managerial implications – A short introduction. In L. Biggiero, D. de Jongh, J. Wieland, A. Zicari, & D. Fischer (Eds.), *The relational view of economics: A new research agenda for the study of relational transactions* (pp. 17–41). Springer.

Williamson, O. E. (2005). The economics of governance. *American Economic Review, 95*(2), 1–18.

Jessica Geraldo Schwengber is a postdoctoral researcher at the Chair of Institutional Economics at Zeppelin University, project manager of the Transcultural Caravan Network, and managing director of the Leadership Excellence Institute Zeppelin | LEIZ. Her research interest lies in organization theory, relational economics, and transcultural management. Jessica Geraldo Schwengber holds a bachelor's and a master's in economics from the University of Roma Tor Vergata (Italy) and a PhD from Zeppelin University (Germany).

The Nature of the Firm as Corporate Actor: Relational Economics and the Challenges of Legal Personhood

Marc C. Hübscher

> *Serious analysis of the corporation requires rigorous and comprehensive conceptions of both the corporation and society; and these conceptions must be articulated in comparable, or at least translatable, terms.*
>
> *Lee. E. Preston (1975)*

Abstract The chapter deals with the nature of the firm. The question of the nature of the firm is posed here from the perspective of the firm as a cooperative actor. Based on arguments for a perspective of the firm as a corporate actor, the nature of the firm is the (corporate) intention of the corporate actor to realize shared value creation and therefore to relationalize stakeholders' ability and willingness to cooperate in the process and to enable and ensure it in the form of legitimate governance of stakeholder resources and interests. This perspective requires a distinction between a traditional theory of the firm and a relational (constructivist) theory of the firm. Against the background of this distinction, the understanding of corporate intentionality must be defined, on the one hand, and questions of leadership and the logic of economic action within the firm as well as the consideration and involvement of stakeholders must be redefined, on the other. An alternative theory of the firm is necessary if we do not want to remain at the level of bonobo monkeys in economic theorizing.

Keywords Theory of the firm · Collective intentionality · Cooperate actor · Cooperation · Relational leadership · Stakeholder · Stakeholder governance · Moral responsibility

---

M. C. Hübscher (✉)
University of Ulm, Ulm, Germany
e-mail: MHuebscher@deloitte.de

J. D. Rendtorff et al. (eds.), *Advances in Relational Economics*, Relational Economics and Organization Governance,
https://doi.org/10.1007/978-3-031-75725-9_4

1 Introduction

The firm is a production unit whereby the owners expect to maximize shareholder value in terms of profit and market value by the management. "While this is a caricature of the modern firm, there is no doubt that it is a very useful one" (Hart, 2011, p. 102). But what is the firm? The following considerations deal with the theoretical conception of the firm within relational economics. Relational economics is an economics of cooperation and organization. The focus of interest is on private and societal value creation—shared values in value-creation networks (see Wieland, 2017, 2020), or in a nutshell: "We refer to the strategy and governance that a firm needs in order to achieve this transformation as shared value creation, that is, as the integration of business into the social matrix" (Wieland, 2020, p. 156). In the following, I will focus on a more detailed discussion of cooperation and organization in relational economics. Wieland, and I fully agree with this, updates the old institutional and transactional economics of Commons (2012 [1924], 1990 [1934]) and places the economic organization called the firm at the center of the theory design.[1] The firm is consequently characterized as a functional system and collective actor (see Wieland, 2020, p. 23).[2] While the considerations of the firm as a system and, in particular, as a mode of governance are reasonably argued and very advanced, the position of the firm as a corporate actor is not so derived and is more introduced on an ad hoc basis (see Hübscher, 2019, p. 111). In my opinion, there is still a theoretical gap here, which the following remarks aim to address.[3] The purpose of this chapter is to analyze the firm as a corporate actor in more detail. In particular, the question of cooperation in the process of shared value creation, which is governed by the firm, will play an important role.

In the first step, I will characterize the current state of the idea of the firm in relational economics (part 2). Then, starting from the usual characterization of the firm "as-nexus-of" (see Gindis, 2013), I will emphasize the legal personhood of the firm—or the firm as a legal person—which also forms the basis for further discussions of the corporate actor (part 3). Building on a fundamental distinction between the understanding of the firm in so-called mainstream economics and relational

[1] In relational economics, Wieland (2020: 155–166) combines institutional economics sensu Commons with the process philosophy of A. N. Whitehead (1985 [1927]) in an extremely instructive way, which I cannot discuss here (see Schramm, 2022).

[2] In his explanations, Wieland (2020) mainly speaks of the economic organization as a collective actor. Generally, I will speak here, in my opinion more specifically, of the corporate actor.

[3] For the sake of completeness, it should be noted that there is also a discussion that distinguishes between firm and corporation. "All corporations are firms, but not all firms are corporations" summarizes Hodgson (2015: 205). Robe (2011, 2020), on the other hand, makes a sharp distinction between firm and corporation, according to which the firm characterizes an economic activity and the corporation a legal form. Deakin et al. (2021) show that this view is problematic and also leads to counter-intuitive consequences. This important discussion from a meaning point of view will not concern us further because we understand the firm as a "Legal-Economic Nexus" (Samuels, 2009: 25).

economics (see Biggerio, 2022), I will then emphasize the aspect of corporate intentionality, which is also present in economic organizations. Cooperation and leadership play a particularly important role in the relational understanding of the firm (part 4). Building on this, I will then take up the firm as a network of stakeholder relationships, which already occupies a conceptually prominent position in relational economics framed as stakeholder governance (part 5). The focus will then be on the nature of the firm as a cooperative actor. Some cursory reflections on the (also moral) responsibility of the firm conclude my theoretical proposal for the firm as a cooperative actor in relational economics (part 6). Finally, I will summarize the main arguments for the understanding of the firm in a strong version of the corporate actor (part 7).

2 The Concept of the Firm in Relational Economics

What conceptual role does the firm play in relational economics? Based on the classical distinction between market and organization (see Coase, 1993 [1937]; Williamson, 1975), relational economics makes the economic organization conceptually extraordinarily strong. An organization whose economics, of course, also needs the non-economic prerequisites for carrying out transactions (see Granovetter, 1985; Kreps, 1990; Hodgson, 2013; Gartenberg & Zenger, 2023). Relational economics is a cooperative and organizational economics (see Wieland, 1996, 1998, 2000). It is primarily interested in examining the firm as one, and I would argue the essential, "mechanism of governance" (Williamson, 1996) in the economic Zeitgeist of capitalism and globalization. "Aligning transactions with governance structures in a discriminating way" (Williamson, 1993, p. 90) is an objective of relational economics. "The organization—as a system for processing and allocating different logics, which is to say the enterprise or the organization of another functional system and as a collective actor—is the factual and logical point of reference for relational economics" (Wieland, 2020, p. 23).

Initially, it deals with economic transactions as a basic unit of economic analysis, as the old and also part of the new institutional economics have already seen (see Commons, 1990 [1934]; Williamson, 1985; Wieland, 1996). A transaction can, of course, be described analytically as an economic transaction. However, economy-as-practice is always about embedded transactions, which can be described in principle in different social communication codes, but which, in practice, always take place simultaneously. It is therefore more closely concerned with the organization of relational transactions. And closer to Commons (1990 [1934]) than to Williamson (1985), an economic transaction is relational "if more than two individual or collective actors and polycontextual and polylingual decision logics are constitutive for the conclusion of the transaction" (Wieland, 2020, p. 23). With the economic transaction, society is also always processed, because an economic transaction is never just economic. "Thus, the ultimate unit of activity, which correlates law, economics, and ethics, must contain in itself the three principles of conflict,

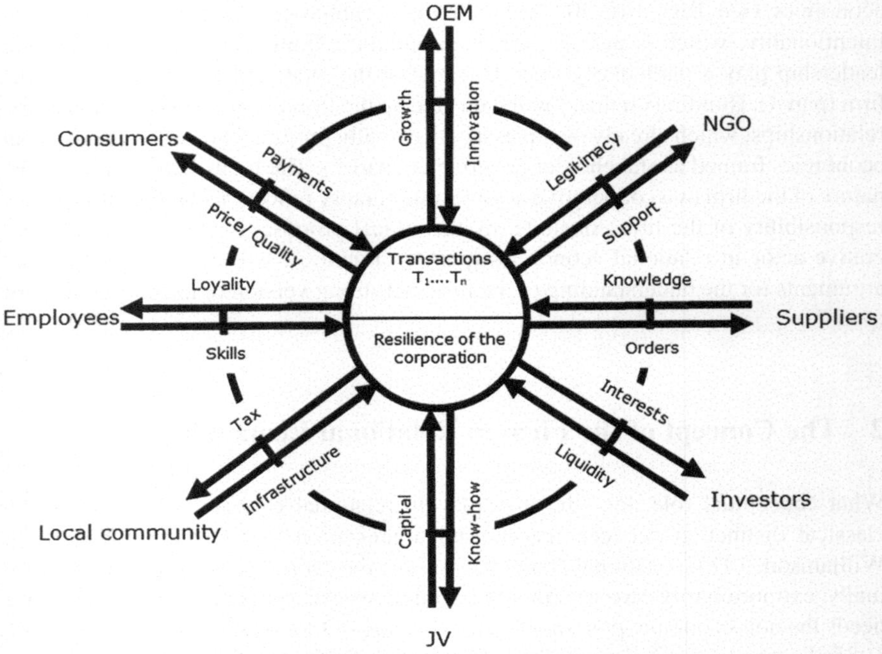

Fig. 1 The firm as a relation of stakeholder resources and interests. (Source: Wieland, 2020: 71)

dependence and order. This unit is a transaction" (Commons, 1990 [1934], p. 58). It is also the relational transaction that allows us to ask about the forms of governance for initiating, executing, and securing transactions. The firm occupies a prominent position empirically, conceptually, and normatively (see Mayer, 2013; Wieland, 2014, 2020; Singer, 2019; Robe, 2020). The "firm as nexus of stakeholders" (Wieland, 2011, p. 225) is not just one but the "Cooperation Project of Society" (Wieland, 2014, p. 121) (see Fig. 1).

"Cooperation is an actor-to-actor relation and a fragile process for the relationalization of societal actors. Markets, organizational charts, and methods are all forms of coordination in which the actors' characteristics are irrelevant. Organizations in their diverse manifestations are examples of forms that enable, require, and delimit cooperation between actors and in which the individual and collective actors' characteristics are significant events" (Wieland, 2020, p. 27). It is about a relational economics of the organization of cooperation projects that is geared towards shared value creation through transactions.

The purpose of the firm is "private and societal value creation" (Wieland, 2020, p. 69) as a "summary measure of the capacity of an organization to create benefits for any and all of its stakeholders over the long term" (Post et al., 2002, p. 45). As an "entity as its own right" (Wieland, 2020, p. 70), the firm is always interested "to ensure its own (theoretically infinite) existence as a form of collective action" (Wieland, 2020, p. 70). As "an organizational form for cooperatively doing business" (Wieland, 2020, p. 70), the firm "consists of the system of relationships" (Coase, 1993 [1937], p. 41) between stakeholders (see Wieland, 2014, pp. 105–120, 2022, pp. 29–39; Schwengber, 2024, pp. 5–8).

In this nexus of stakeholder relations, the firm acts as principal, or if several firms are involved, we are sometimes dealing with multiple "'principal-principal' relationships" (see here and the following Wieland, 2020, pp. 70–76). The stakeholder concept is conceived in strictly economic terms, according to which stakeholders are only those individual or corporate actors who have specifically invested the necessary resources in the cooperation project, in the form and process of the firm. Through these investments, they are also entitled to a share of the (pecuniary or non-pecuniary) rent of cooperation realized with this cooperation project. As the principal of the stakeholders, the firm is essentially the process owner "of relationalizing stakeholder resources" (Wieland, 2020, p. 71), which decides on the form and process of stakeholder governance.

The firm as a nexus of stakeholder relations is already quite well developed in relational economics. In my opinion, the designation of the firm as an entity in its own right, which refers to the characteristics of persons and actors, has not yet gone beyond meaningful allusions and a prominent positioning in relational economics.

3 Beyond "Nexus of": The Case of Legal Personhood

One of the most powerful methodological assumptions in economics is methodological individualism, according to which the economy and society are constitutively attributed to individuals through action (see Neuhäuser & Hübscher, 2010, p. 351; Hodgson, 2013; Hübscher & Neuhäuser, 2021, pp. 222–224). At its core, methodological individualism also determines the theoretical view of how mainstream economics thinks of an economic organization. Although organizational and administration theory has gone through various phases against the background of a stronger practical orientation, it can be said that an economic worldview still prevails today, namely that organizations are means—a kind of input-output black box, a production function—of achieving individual purposes (see Hart, 2011, p. 102; Walker, 2017, pp. 159–160). But can this be used to define the firm?

Let us recall that Coase (1993 [1937], p. 20) understood the firm as a "supersession of the price mechanism." But where does a more or less intelligent input/output correlation get the de facto power to suspend the price system of the market? Coase's answer is the entrepreneur. However, this answer can only be convincing if no reference is made to rights and obligations, but only to the management function within the framework of the value-creation process. In the "modern firm" (Roberts, 2004), however, it is less about the entrepreneur and more about the owners and management (see Berle & Means, 2017 [1932]). This was also recognized by Williamson (1985, p. 318), who identifies the "centrality of management" that makes the difference. But now the description, whether entrepreneur or management, or a definition that describes the firm as a group of individuals or shareholders, overlooks the specific nature of a legally constituted firm, which as a person independently owns assets, concludes contracts, and is ultimately the bearer of rights and obligations (see Hodgson, 2015, p. 208). To the point: the arguments of transaction cost economics are compelling, especially if the firm is understood as a legal person. "Coase and Williamson opened the black box of the firm to inspect its contents. But they forgot about the box itself" (Hodgson, 2015, p. 213).

Grossman and Hart (1986, p. 692) "define the firm as being composed of the assets (e.g., machines, inventories) that it owns" and furthermore the link to human resources is established in that "authority over assets translates into authority over people" (Hart & Moore, 1990, p. 1150). However, Hart, Grossman, and Moore's arguments in favor of the firm do not go any further than the transaction cost economics arguments (see Hodgson, 2015, pp. 221–224). What the entrepreneur or a group of entrepreneurs cannot do, the owner(s) cannot save either. The property-rights approach is of course concerned with ownership and control, but these must be legally secured. Of course, we learn a lot about the idea of property rights, but the approach "says very little about the firm" (Holmström, 1999, p. 87). It is only the legal assignment of personhood that makes a collection of assets into an owning agent, that gives rise to a firm as an entity in its own right, and finally makes the addition "that it owns" (Grossman & Hart, 1986, p. 692) understandable.

However, the effectiveness of the ideology (see Denzau & North, 2000) of not understanding firms themselves as actors but merely in the continuation of the market by other means—an "epiphenomenon of the market" (King et al., 2010, p. 290), for instance—is still clearly evident in the "classic" argumentation of Jensen and Meckling (see Gindis, 2013, 2020). "Viewing the firm as the nexus of a set of contracting relationships among individuals also serves to make it clear that the personalization of the firm implied by asking questions such as 'what should be the objective function of the firm?' or 'does the firm have a social responsibility?' is seriously misleading. The firm is not an individual. It is a legal fiction which serves as a focus for a complex process in which the conflicting objectives of individuals (some of whom may 'represent' other organizations) are brought into equilibrium within a framework of contractual relations. In this sense the 'behavior' of the firm is like the behavior of a market, that is, the outcome of a complex equilibrium process" (Jensen & Meckling, 1976, p. 314).

The clarity and also difficulty with which Jensen and Meckling argue is that they derive personal characteristics from human characteristics (see Gindis, 2013, pp. 128ff.; Gindis, 2020), and from this point of view, there can be no question of organizations being actors or persons. "The corporation is not an individual. It does not feel; it does not choose; it cannot bear the burden of taxes; it cannot bear the costs of regulation; it cannot benefit from tariffs or subsidies. All such actions, of course, can and generally do benefit or harm individuals who have some relationship with the corporation such as investors, employees or customers, but it is literally nonsense to say that the corporation has benefited or is harmed. (...) More to the point, the corporation cannot be socially (or otherwise) responsible! However we end up defining it, the notion of 'being responsible' is a normative concept strictly relevant only to human beings. A corporation can no more be responsible than can a lump of coal" (Meckling & Jensen, 1982, p. 11). Here, however, the baby is being thrown out with the bathwater too hastily.

First of all, we must agree with Dewey (1926, p. 656) as he asked: "What 'person' signifies in popular speech, or in psychology, or in philosophy or morals, would be as irrelevant, to employ an exaggerated simile, as it would be to argue that because a wine is called 'dry', it has the properties of dry solid; or that, because it does not have those properties, wine cannot be possibly 'dry'. Obviously, 'dry' as applied to a particular wine has the kind of meaning which it has when applied to the class of beverages in general. Why should not the same sort of thing hold for the use of 'person' in law?".

The crucial idea, which we can learn quite abstractly from Dewey (1926), is the pragmatist function of meaning. Something counts as something in a context because we assign this meaning to it and not because it is so. This idea was elaborated quite prominently in the speech act-informed social theory of Searle (1995, 2010), who emphasized the constitutive meaningfulness of "'X counts as Y' or 'X counts as Y in context C'" (Searle, 1995, p. 28) for institutional or social facts. This brings us to the second step of the explanation of why the firm is a legal person: X (= the firm) counts as Y (= legal person) (in context C (conclusion of contract)). But while it takes the wine to be described as dry, or the firm to be attributed as a legal person, the question arises as to what it takes to constitute the firm, to found it. The answer is "nothing," except a speech act (see Hübscher, 2011). In other words, a so-called "freestanding Y term" (Smith, 2003, p. 19), which exists "when a status function is created without there being an existing person or object who is counted as the bearer of the status function" (Searle, 2010, p. 20). The legal person is "born" through nothing more than a declarative speech act and also "dies" through nothing more than a declarative speech act that signifies its deletion from the commercial register.

In addition to these socio-ontological references to the logic of the constitution, there are also many arguments from a legal perspective in favor of understanding the firm as a legal person. Blair (2013, pp. 449–454), for example, has distinguished four functions of "corporate personhood." Firstly, asset partitioning (see Hansmann & Kraakman, 2000) refers to the legal construction that company owners are not liable for the debts of the company (limited liability) because the company itself holds ownership of assets and, conversely, the company is not liable for the debts of the owners (see Hansmann & Kraakman, 2000, pp. 810–812; Robe, 2020, pp. 224–225). Secondly, the company is an independent contracting party that not only draws up contracts as "an entity on its own" (Barnard, 1968 [1938], pp. 55ff.) but can also create (intangible) assets, including goodwill, in the successful implementation of contracts. Thirdly, the company is not dependent on individual life expectancies; essentially, it exists indefinitely (hence the so-called perpetuity in company valuation) (see Blair, 2013, p. 448). At least as long as it is not terminated by a declarative speech act. Fourthly, it is the governance structure that recursively constitutes the ability to act in the legal sense: "board governance and entity status complement each other" and "board governance makes it clear who can act for the company" (Blair, 2013, p. 453). If we take the above points together, we see that the firm as a legal person is an "owning agent" (Hodgson, 2015, p. 208). The consequence is that the shareholders do not own the firm; they are merely invested by holding shares in the corporation (see Blair & Stout, 1999; Hansmann & Kraakman, 2000; Spulber, 2009; Robe, 2011; Stout, 2012; Gindis, 2013; Hodgson, 2015).

Clearly, the discussion about a definition of the firm shows the stage of development of the theory (see Hart, 2011, p. 102). Machlup (1967, pp. 27–28) alone distinguished between ten concepts of the firm and saw little hope or sense in finding a consensus here. "I hope there will be no argument about which concept of the firm is the most important or the most useful. Since they serve different purposes, such an argument would be pointless. It would degenerate into childishness" (Machlup, 1967, p. 28). Of course, an understanding of the firm should be problem-oriented (see Machlup, 1967, p. 30), but certainly not arbitrary. In my opinion, it is therefore worth continuing the search for an appropriate definition of the firm. With regard to our discussion, an interesting starting point can be found in Gindis' (2013, p. 208) conclusion: "The firm is neither a coalition of owners nor a collection of assets but a profit-seeking specialized production unit set up for the sale of goods or services, and endowed by law with the capacity to act as a singular legal person."

Admittedly, more could be said about this (see Gindis, 2013), but these essential arguments are sufficient here to assign actor characteristics to economic organizations (see Orts, 2013, pp. 40–51; Hodgson, 2015; Robe, 2020, pp. 220–221). As contracting parties alone, they are obviously held responsible (see Geser, 1990, p. 406; King et al., 2010, p. 294). The social dimension of the company as a corporate actor is, of course, not (only) decided at the legal level, but rather at the level of social interaction and construction processes. Teubner (1987, p. 67), for example, argues, not unexpectedly, strictly in terms of systems theory that the dynamic social reality of the legal entity is characterized by a pulsating sequence of meaningfully interrelated communicative events that constantly reproduce themselves.

King et al. (2010) have presented a meta-theoretical proposal of the organization as a social actor. Their discomfort with organization theory is that, firstly, organizations are spoken to rather than about and, secondly, since Weick (1995), the focus has been on the process of organizing and not on the organization with its "noun-like, enduring, and distinctive qualities of organizations" (King et al., 2010, p. 291). In order to understand the organization as a social, corporate actor, King et al. (2010), like Geser (1990, p. 402), also introduces two criteria: attribution on the one hand and intentionality on the other. We will come back to this.

"An organization is 'a structure composed of positions in relation, not persons in relation' (...). This is applicable to organizations' internal and external relations alike, which involve individual persons, collective persons and societal institutions" (Wieland, 2020, p. 23). The attribution of social issues is based on the recursive relationship between sovereignty and responsibility. Corporate actors are sovereign because they not only decide who are and become members of this organization and who are not, but also because they regulate what the individual may and may not do as an organizational member by means of job descriptions and functions. If organizations decide who may do what and when, then these organizations must also be assigned responsibility because "organizational members' actions are driven not by their preferences but by the members' roles as agents of the organization" (King et al., 2010, p. 294).

4 From Legal Personhood to Corporate Actor

So far, we can state that it does not matter what other attributes are associated with the firm, because an "entity on its own" is created by the socio-ontological construction of legal persons—this is, in a sense, the second part of Gindis' (2013, p. 208) definition of the firm as we have seen. What else it can do or be is a matter for discussion, but it certainly has the right to negotiate and conclude contracts. It can therefore be argued with good reason that the Jensen/Meckling narrative that the firm is only a legal fiction is simply wrong. However, it can be argued that the firm as a business person is artificial or fictional, but nevertheless very real in social ontological terms (see Ortmann, 2010; List & Pettit, 2011, p. 153; Hodgson, 2015, p. 219). In order to move forward from the legal person to the corporate actor, we need something that denotes an actor attribute in an organization. In my opinion, this characteristic is what distinguishes agency, namely the ability to act. In the following, we will conceptually work out some differences that arise against the theoretical background of relational economics in comparison to mainstream economics. We will then summarize important insights into corporate intentionality and finally highlight some consequences of this view for leadership.

4.1 Understanding of the Firm

The ability to act has something to do with intentionality, which an actor has by constitutively attributing it to them. An actor can be good or bad, capable or incapable, professional or amateurish, but this does not change their quality of being an actor. From the description of relational economics (see Biggerio et al., 2022; Biggerio, 2022; Wieland, 2020, 2022), we can see that economic self-evident facts must be thought of differently if we look at the same facts from a different perspective. In the following, we therefore want to distinguish between a firm in the classical economic organizational form of the normative principal-agent theory (see Milgrom & Roberts, 1992), which we will refer to below as the "traditional firm," and an organizational form that is strictly oriented towards cooperation, which we will call the "relational firm."

We have identified a total of eight characteristics that ideally distinguish the traditional from the relational firm (see Table 1). The first four characteristics are quickly summarized for the traditional firm. Firstly, it only understands the language of economics and measures everything in cash flows. Anything that cannot be translated into cash flows is systematically irrelevant. The purpose of the firm is

Table 1 Understanding of the firm—a synopsis

Firm	Traditional	Relational
Coding	monolingual (economic)	polylingual (economic and society)
Objective	profit-maximization (shareholder value)	cooperation rent (shared values)
Focus	shareholder	stakeholder
Logic of Interaction	principal/ agent (strategic)	Partners (communicative)
Collective Intentionality	thin (I-mode)	thick (We-mode)
Shared mental models	recognition of subordination	consent of cooperation
Authority	P-authority (promise to obey)	C-authority (cooperation)
Decision logic	directives	participation

Source: Own table

profit-maximization in terms of profit or market value (see Milgrom & Roberts, 1992, p. 40; Jensen, 2001; Spulber, 2009, p. 69). This value creation is the shareholder value, which of course belongs exclusively to the shareholder (see Friedman, 1970; Rappaport, 2006; BRT, 2019). The normative principal-agent model (see Milgrom & Roberts, 1992; Casadesus-Masanell & Spulber, 2004) is the logic of interaction for the relationship between ownership and control (see Berle & Means, 2017 [1932]) and also within the firm between management and employees (see Alchian & Demsetz, 1972), the application of which is intended to strategically ensure the goal of maximizing shareholder value.

In contrast, relational economics provides a description of the firm, as explained above, which uses a cooperation rent to create shared value from relational transactions, to which all (invested) stakeholders are essentially entitled. If we take this form of cooperation very seriously, then applying the logic of normative principal-agent theory would be harmful, as this theory primarily attempts to coordinate the relations and actions of the firm. Relational leadership, on the other hand, cooperates and relies more on partnering (see Steenkamp et al., 2022, p. 218), which is not a contradiction to authority (see McMahon, 1994).

The other four characteristics have to do with the design of the corporate actor. The classification of the two understandings of the firm also has conceptual consequences as to how collective intentionality can be conceived in the shared mental models (Denzau & North, 2000) and what challenges arise for appropriate leadership of the firm.

4.2 The Idea of Corporate Intentionality

In order to gain some clarity about the discussion on collective intentionality, we will take a look at the philosophical debate. There has long been an intensive debate about the possibility(ies) of collective intentionality. The breadth of this debate could hardly be greater (Schmid & Schweikard, 2009). It ranges from the view that there is no collective intentionality and that every action can be traced back to individual intentions (methodological individualism), to the view that collective intentionality exists precisely when an intention is shared by various individual actors. This is not the place to go through and evaluate the various positions in detail (see Neuhäuser, 2011, pp. 140–152). I will refer directly to Tuomela (2006, pp. 35–41) because he distinguishes between forms of collective intentionality with an I-mode and a We-mode, which I will adopt below as thin and thick forms and characterize in more detail (see Table 2).

I have deliberately chosen a funnel in the illustration because, in my opinion, it is only possible to speak of the possibility of corporative intentionality if the intentions of members of an organization are, firstly, at least related to a formal goal (goal specificity sensu Geser) and, secondly, if the employees are bound by both a formal and an informal structure of the organization. This is achieved through rights and functions of a deontic status according to Searle in generally, especially legally, accepted corporate governance structures and with sometimes significantly deeper, normalized "corporate internal decision structures" (CIDS) (French, 1984). The sovereignty of the organization is recursively constituted by the CIDS through identity and attribution: "organizations regulate" (Duschek et al., 2012). The organization distinguishes between collective and corporate intentionality because there is one more element here compared to collectives, namely the corporation in this case called firm (Orts, 2013; Singer, 2019). This is precisely the idea of corporate intentionality (n + 1), in which the enterprise U (+1) intends that you and I, we (n) as members of the organization, do X. "It is not we who intend that I and you do X," is therefore the formula of corporate intentionality, but "U intends that I and you do X" (Neuhäuser, 2011, p. 154).

The phrase "U intends that ..." (Neuhäuser, 2011, p. 154) can be intentionally very thin or thick. A thin version of corporate intentionality exists when the group member's motivation to act is based on an I-mode reason (IMR), according to which "R is the agent's main private ('non-group') reason for his performing X" (Tuomela, 2006, p. 40). In contrast, we speak of a thick version of corporate intentionality when "Reason R is a group member's motivating We-mode reason (WMR) for performing

Table 2 The idea of corporative intentionality

CI	I – mode (thin)	We – mode (thick)
status	private person	group member
intention	action intention	aim intention
goal	individual	shared
character-ization	"Reason R is a group member's motivating I-mode reason (IMR) for performing an action X if and only if R is the agent's main private ("non-group") reason for his performing X." (Tuomela 2007:40)	"Reason R is a group member's motivating We-mode reason (WMR) for performing an action X if and only if R is the agent's main motivating group ("non-private") reason for his performing X." (Tuomela 2007:40)
mechanism	coordination	"full cooperation" (Cohen 2023)
role	agents	partners

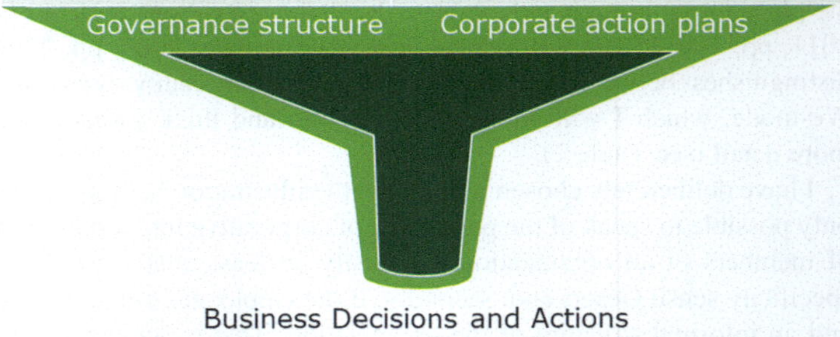

Source: Hübscher (2024)

an action X if and only if R is the agent's main motivating group ('non-private') reason for his performing X" (Tuomela, 2006, p. 40). The thin version of corporate intentionality can ideally be assigned to the traditional understanding of the firm, at least whenever alignment with a common corporate goal is successful. The thick version of corporate intentionality, on the other hand, is based on the relational understanding of the company and thus describes the ideal state in which not only employees but also all other stakeholders involved are motivated by WMR. Finally, we can also describe the thin version as a principal-agent relationship that needs to be coordinated (Milgrom & Roberts, 1992, p. 214), while a thick version of corporate intentionality corresponds to what Cohen (2023, p. 301) has called "fully cooperative."

With this understanding of corporate intentionality, we will see that the distinction between a thin and thick interpretation leads to the result that the organizational assignment of responsibility is inversely proportional to the weakness of corporate intentionality, or more simply: the more intensely the organizational members are motivated by private (individual) reasons to achieve organizational goals, the more it is the (compliance) responsibility of the organization to ensure that the individual ways and means of the organizational members are justifiable. This argument also shows that stakeholder involvement in cooperation for shared value creation must not proceed in a strictly economic manner, because the license to operate must always be justified, which is a normative requirement of society. This normative claim is brought into the firm by the stakeholders and is therefore the subject of the stakeholder dialogue.

Since corporations always have constitutions, the distinction between conjunctive and disjunctive constitutions can also be included in the consideration of the two understandings of the firm (Coleman, 1992). A conjunctive constitution exists when "the beneficiaries of jointly asserted rights are also the possible target actors of jointly created restrictions or demands" (Coleman, 1992, p. 5). Even if Coleman's definition assumes a substantial identity of persons, I believe that the idea of a conjunctive constitution can be linked quite easily to the Republican-liberal idea, where norms should be designed as if the addressees could be authors (the well-known Kantian idea of the Kingdom of Ends); the opposite would then be a disjunctive constitution. While, ideally, conjunctive constitutions are particularly good to think about when there are common goals, in reality, we often have to deal with disjunctive constitutions that separate beneficiaries and target actors, especially in companies according to the traditional understanding. A conjunctive constitutional model, on the other hand, ideally underlies the relational understanding of the firm.

4.3 Leadership and the "Logic" of Decision and Action

A thick version of corporate intentionality and the structure of a conjunctive constitution are neither simply present nor absent but can be created based on what is available to us socioculturally. In essence, the conditions of the possibility of cooperation are at the center of relational leadership (Wieland, 2020, p. 105).

To enable cooperation, the firm as a corporate actor must signal the necessary ability and willingness to cooperate. A value matrix (Wieland, 2014, pp. 161–164) is a suitable form of expression of corporate intentionality, through which the firm makes its values binding for all organizational members, ideally for all cooperation partners. The necessary value statements relate to performance, moral, cooperation, and communication values (Wieland, 2007, p. 100). Notably, cooperation partners learn cooperation through successful cooperation and communication, where the ability and willingness to cooperate come together for the common benefit through shared performance and moral concepts, forming the basis for further cooperation.

In the discussion of relational contract theory, especially in Macneil's work, Wieland (2020, pp. 29–34) identifies various "collective behavioral patterns for successful relational contracts" (Wieland, 2020, p. 32), which can be assigned to

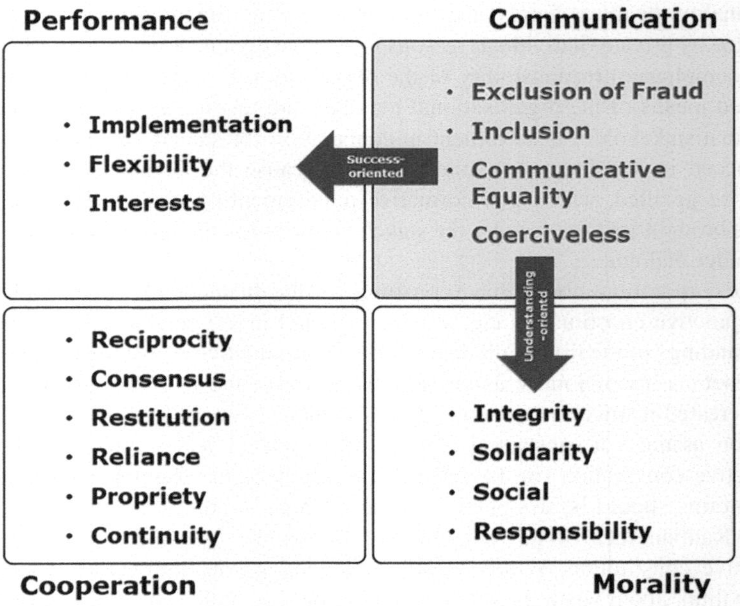

Fig. 2 Value matrix and the "logic" of action. (Source: Modified and adapted from Wieland (2020, p. 33))

the areas of performance, cooperation, and morality (see Fig. 2). However, the field of communication values remains strangely absent from this analysis. Wieland's finding that communication does not appear specifically in relational contract theory according to Macneil is surprising. Communication is of particular importance not only in relational leadership considerations (Cunliffe & Eriksen, 2011; Fairhurst & Connaughton, 2014) but is also explicitly mentioned as a parameter in transaction cost theory for relational exchanges (Artz & Brush, 2000). Although the distinction made there between coercive and non-coercive communication is relevant, it does not go far enough. From a strategic perspective, non-coercive communication reduces asset-specificity risks and negotiation costs (Artz & Brush, 2000, p. 356). Furthermore, there are indications that a well-understood (cooperation) economy should realistically be based on pro-social abilities (Wieland, 2020, p. 34; Hodgson, 2014). This cultural expansion of the actors involved does not introduce a benevolent person into the theory design but assumes that people are neither inherently good nor evil but are made into one or the other through the recursive structuring between actors and institutions (Hodgson, 2004, pp. 30ff.). This also suggests that a purely strategic orientation of cooperation and, beyond that, a pragmatic analysis of "polylingual communication regarding the relations in relational contracts" (Wieland, 2020, p. 34) is insufficient. It needs to be expanded to include an understanding-oriented dimension, a second logic of action: while we can exchange information about performance in a success-oriented way, we can only discuss our morality, or in a first sense, in an understanding-oriented way (Heath, 2003, p. 80).[4] Wieland (2014, p. 162) himself has proposed examples of communication values, but I suggest replacing these with four communication values[5] (see Fig. 2).

These four communication values are not arbitrarily chosen but represent presuppositions (see Habermas, 2005, p. 55) under which one can move in the "logical space of reasons" (Sellars, 1997 [1956], p. 76) or should play the "game of giving and asking for reasons" (Brandom, 2008, p. 112).[6]

The exclusion of fraud implies that cooperation partners must mean what they say. This prerequisite is relevant for both success-oriented and understanding-oriented communication: simply put, I do not trust someone who is deceptive and will not cooperate fully with them. I will return to the presuppositions of inclusion and communicative equality shortly. The precondition of coercivelessness demands thus completes the circle to Relational Contracting Theory and highlights the crucial addition of an understanding-oriented dimension: while the question of coercion is significant in strategic negotiations, communication processes are concerned with coercivelessness. The "unconstrained coercion of the better argument" in the sense of Habermas, aimed at reaching an understanding, differs from setting up an unconstrained argumentation arena for strategic negotiation (Habermas, 1981).

The considerations regarding this differentiation are extensively discussed in the literature on transformational and relational leadership (Bass & Avolio, 1993; Cunliffe & Eriksen, 2011; Fairhurst & Connaughton, 2014; Wieland, 2020). Relational leadership involves "the ability and willingness to fairly pursue the interests of all stakeholders" (Wieland, 2020, p. 110), "dialogue and polyphony" (Cunliffe & Eriksen, 2011, p. 1434), and "responsiveness and responsibility" (Cunliffe & Eriksen, 2011, p. 1438). It also emphasizes "mutual interests and a sense of shared fates and interdependence" (Bass & Avolio, 1993, p. 116).

As we can see, relational leadership requires a different type of leadership than we are usually familiar with from traditional principal-agent theory or transactional leadership. With McMahon (1994) as a reference, I distinguish between different authorities: expert-based (E-authority), promise-to-obey (P-authority), and cooperation-facilitating (C-authority). This instructive distinction helps categorize the concept of relational firms and leadership compared to the traditional understanding of the firm and corresponding transactional leadership. While relational firms correspond to a C-authority, traditional firms can be characterized by a P-authority. Cooperation-enabling leadership is based on "directive-independent reasons," whereas P-authority depends on the reasons of the leader. McMahon

[4] This does not mean that morality is always strategy-free in practice. Morality always has economic consequences, just as economics will always have moral consequences (Wieland, 2007, p. 87).

[5] As examples Wieland (2014: 162) lists "Respect, Belonging, Openness, Transparency, Communication, Willingness to assume risks." Wieland is clearly aware of the difficulty of filling this field in a useful und meaningful way. In Wieland (2020, p. 33), this field remains empty after the discussion of relational contracts.

[6] This "should" is not normatively desirable but pragmatically necessary if understanding and genuine agreement are to be possible (Habermas, 2005, p. 54; Brandom, 2008, p. 110).

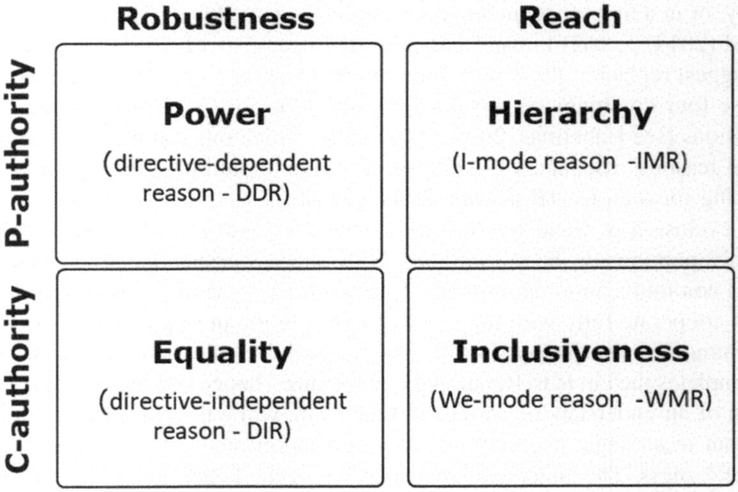

Fig. 3 Reach and robustness of leadership. (Source: Own figure)

(1994) explains, "This is the distinction between what the recipient of a directive would regard herself as having sufficient directive-independent reason to do—that is, what she would regard herself as having sufficient reason to do if the directive in question had not been issued—and what she regards herself as having sufficient directive-dependent reason to do—that is, what she regards herself as having sufficient reason to do given that the directive has been issued" (p. 29).

The strength that an authority can develop can be shown in two dimensions: robustness and reach (McMahon, 1994). While robustness is a function of the variety of situations, reach refers to the number of people who fall under the effect of the authority (see Fig. 3).

The robustness and reach of P-authority are created through power and hierarchy. Weber (1978) describes power as "the probability that one actor within a social relationship will be in a position to carry out his own will despite resistance, regardless of the basis on which this probability rests," which is precisely linked to what we have described as directive-dependent reason (DDR). Furthermore, reach can be linked to hierarchy because it extends as far as the hierarchical structure is organizationally structured. In P-authority as a whole, we can speak of a weak corporate intentionality motivated by IMR (Alchian & Demsetz, 1972). In this respect, we are within the traditional understanding of the company. But how can we imagine the robustness and reach of cooperation-enabling leadership in the relational understanding of the company?

In my opinion, a "fully cooperative" environment requires a broad understanding of participation, which also necessitates full consideration of the communication prerequisites. Hielscher et al. (2014) have identified four criteria for participation, of which the following two are most pertinent: "Inclusiveness of participation: is everybody included or at least represented in the process? Equality of participation:

Can everybody participate in the same way?"[7] (p. 537). While equality is a sign of robustness, which should always be the case if the reasons for authority could also be mine (DIR), reach in cooperation-oriented leadership can be established through a thick version of corporate intentionality (WMR).

These two participation requirements are not only parameters for the robustness and reach of C-authority but also helpful criteria for defining justification as a principle to evaluate norms and actions within stakeholder relations.

Justification should be understood as a principle, not a rule. Justifications "are judgments about what would be permitted by principles that could not reasonably be rejected, by people who were moved to find principles for the general regulation of behavior that others, similarly motivated, could not reasonably reject" (Scanlon, 1998, p. 4). The phrase "could not reasonably reject" constitutes a principle to defend actions and norms as cooperation-related in general (Scanlon, 1998; Forst, 2024).

It is particularly noteworthy that the lower the degree of participation, the higher the demand for clear and transparent justification of business decisions and actions.

5 The Firm as a Relation of Stakeholders

In the previous section, I elaborated on the company as a corporate actor. I identified the development and maintenance of a strong version of corporate intentionality through participation as an essential task of relational leadership. Corporate intentionality constitutively relies on it being shared by all stakeholders or being divisible among them. This is determined by the design of stakeholder governance in terms of process and form.

In the following, we will find the nature of the firm in relational economics in this stakeholder orientation, in order to work out its significance in stakeholder governance in the process and in the form.

5.1 The Nature of the Firm in Relational Economics

So far, I have talked about cooperation and the creation of shared value and have thus suggested that "Redefining the Corporation" (Post et al., 2002) has something to do with the conceptual integration of stakeholders. This arises solely from the fact that cooperation is not only meant intra-organizationally in the relationship between management and employees but has long been positioned inter-organizationally.

---

[7] In addition to inclusiveness and equality, Hielscher et al. (2014, p. 537) also distinguish between the criteria of scope and frequency, which we can neglect here because we believe they are downstream criteria.

As is well known, the question of the quality of cooperation does not end at the boundaries of the firm but extends to society. This brings the stakeholders into consideration in the broadest sense of the word.

Stakeholders are (increasingly) constitutive for the description of the firm (Freeman, 1984; Donaldson & Preston, 1995; Post et al., 2002; Phillips, 2003; Freeman et al., 2010; Freeman et al., 2018; Wieland, 2020; BRT, 2019; Freeman et al., 2020; Schwab, 2021). Thus, we can formulate with Wieland (2020) as follows: The nature of the firm is the (corporate) intention of the corporate actor to relationalize the stakeholders' ability and willingness to cooperate in the process and to enable and ensure it in the form of legitimate governance of stakeholder resources and interests (pp. 70–72). If the company can be described as a nexus of stakeholder relationships, then corporate governance should be geared towards "providing the stakeholders collectively with benefits" (Post et al., 2002, p. 29). From the perspective of the firm as a corporate actor, these benefits have a name: cooperation rent (Wieland, 2014, 2020).

The company as a corporate actor can be the "principal of all stakeholders" (Wieland, 2020, p. 72) and, in turn, be an agent itself as a stakeholder. Stakeholder relationships are fluid and arise and pass as events for the initiation and execution of transactions. The economy is processed (Langlois, 2009) and related through "fluid configurations" (Weber, 1995, pp. 203). Fluid configurations are characterized by the fact that they are event- or transaction-related entities over time that build up problem-solving capacities for private and societal value creation.

5.2 *The Process of Stakeholder Governance*

One of the central questions in the stakeholder approach is who is a stakeholder in the firm. After many years of consideration, Freeman et al. (2020) state: "Stakeholders can be defined as 'any group or individual who can affect or is affected by the achievement of the organization's objectives,' or as 'any group or individual whose continued support is necessary for a company's existence and health'" (p. 9). In our opinion, these definitions are linked to two different perspectives, which have long been known as a strategic and a normative understanding of stakeholders (Donaldson & Preston, 1995, p. 69; Phillips, 2003, p. 118). While one understanding of the enforceability of stakeholder claims determines the legitimacy "to spend time and resources" (Freeman, 1984, p. 45) for justification-driven corporate management, the other understanding assumes that the legitimacy of a claim depends on whether something is at stake for the stakeholder not only functionally, but also normatively. The normative perspective also speaks of a "multi-fiduciary view" (Goodpaster, 1991, p. 323) or of "fiduciary-type obligations" (Donaldson & Dunfee, 1999, p. 237; also Freeman, 1984, p. 249). Wieland (2020) brings a slightly different perspective into play, but one that is certainly compatible with the strategic view, when he understands the contributions of stakeholders as investments in the company, "which the firm, in turn, requires for the completion of its transactions and for its continued existence" (p. 70). These considerations provide us with arguments that help us to concretize the usual distinction between primary and secondary stakeholders (Freeman et al., 2010; Freeman et al., 2020, p. 24). According to Freeman et al. (2018), primary stakeholders are characterized by the fact that they are involved in the company's value-creation process, while the same does not apply to secondary stakeholders (pp. 16–17). Although secondary stakeholders have a legitimate interest in the company's actions, they only have the status of influencers (Freeman et al., 2018). As it is sometimes difficult to distinguish who exactly is involved in the value-creation process, we suggest differentiating stakeholders according to investment commitment and (normative) affectedness. Accordingly:

1. A stakeholder invests in a firm if it provides tangible or intangible resources of an economic or social (e.g., moral, media, and legal) nature and thus makes a contribution to shared value creation (Wieland, 2020, p. 71), or
2. A stakeholder is simply affected if its body, mind, and/or legitimate rights are directly harmed by the corporate action, i.e., a violation of a so-called "hypernorm" (Donaldson & Dunfee, 1999, p. 44). In principle, compliance with hyper-norms can be assumed if there are justifications that cannot reasonably be rejected (Scanlon, 1998, p. 4). This formulation refers to a practical principle of justification (Forst, 2024).

With this distinction, we have introduced a substantive distinction that is not and cannot be clear-cut. It is true that those stakeholders who are invested in a shared value-creation project are always directly affected by the company's actions, but it is not the case that all those who are affected by the company's actions are also invested in the value creation. Even if we operate with a broad concept of investment, not every stakeholder who "is affected by the achievement of organization's objectives" (Freeman, 1984) can also be invested in the organization. Harmonizing mind games that believe they can resolve all conflicting interests in win-win situations (Porter & Kramer, 2011; Pies & Valentinov, 2023, among others) may calm naive minds, but they are not convincing in the complexity of situations. We can therefore state that the degree of impact can go far beyond the level of investment, and it is precisely this excess that is the criterion for the stakeholder who is simply affected.

The identification of stakeholders in principle and the differentiation between invested and simply affected stakeholders is the result of a process that must also generate strategic considerations and normative classifications in order to answer the question of how, and to what extent, these stakeholders can and should be involved in the transaction process.

For this identification, we first propose a governance process based on Wieland (2020, pp. 97–100) in order to then determine the degree of integration of the identified stakeholders in the respective cooperation context of a transaction in a second step on the basis of these results. This governance process for stakeholder identification comprises six steps (see Fig. 4).

The first step is to determine the relevant cooperation context for the respective transaction. By cooperation context, we mean the social space that is spanned by the

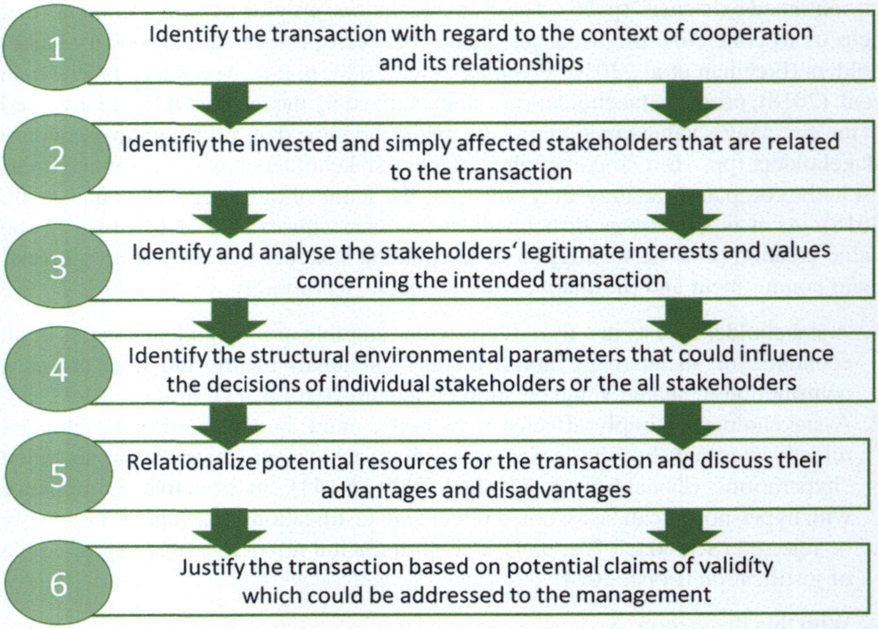

Fig. 4 The process of stakeholder governance. (Sources: Modified and adapted from Wieland (2020: 98))

cooperation requirement itself, the relevant cooperation partners, and the restrictive and enabling environmental parameters.

Once the cooperation context has been determined, the invested and simply affected stakeholders can be identified in a second step. The invested stakeholders are primarily concerned with the resources and capacities that the respective stakeholders can contribute to the successful completion of the transaction. In contrast, the simply affected stakeholders are concerned with the material and normative damage potential that can arise from this transaction. What is the relationship between the terms cooperation partner and stakeholder? For the time being, we can distinguish between them: Every cooperation partner is a stakeholder, but not every stakeholder is a cooperation partner. We will return to this distinction below.

The third step is to gain a clear understanding of the legitimacy of the claims in the form of interests and values that the respective stakeholders associate with this transaction. Legitimacy is undoubtedly a colorful term with admittedly different meanings in sociology and philosophy. We understand legitimacy as a social condition in which something can be regarded as justified if this justification cannot reasonably be rejected (see Scanlon, 1998; Forst, 2024; Hübscher, 2024).

Once the legitimacy of the claims has been assessed and the relevant stakeholders have been identified provisionally but completely, the fourth step is to determine the transaction-relevant environmental parameters that help constitute the cooperation context and can influence the decisions of the stakeholders in different ways.

In the fifth step, the resources and competencies of the invested stakeholders and the risk potential of the simply affected stakeholders are to be related against the background of the social structures and environmental parameters that have an impact on this transaction. Relation here means the creation of a mind-map in which the relationships and interrelationships between investments and affectedness are included in full, but usually not in every detail, and as precisely as possible. This mind-map is then to be evaluated by identifying the advantages and disadvantages of the relationship between affectedness, investment, and cooperation returns.

Since we do not assume the fiction of a harmony of interests and therefore fundamentally expect that transactions cannot always, but rather very rarely, be translated into multiple win-win constellations for all stakeholders, the process contains the final decision to carry out the transaction and a dimension of its practical justification in the sixth and final step. A transaction that has been analyzed in terms of this process of stakeholder governance would always be carried out if this transaction and its seriously considered consequences can be justified generally and reciprocally in the same normative context to which the validity claims of a practical question to corporate governance refer (Hübscher, 2024).

The question of the participation of the identified stakeholders is part of a broad discussion that is also being conducted under the label of "stakeholder democracy" (see Matten & Crane, 2005). Even if we do not consider the term "stakeholder democracy" to be appropriate because it introduces more problems into the discussion than answers, we would like to hold on to a core element that is also, but by no means solely, relevant to democracy, namely the question of stakeholder participation in the governance of transactions (see Hielscher et al., 2014). Once the stakeholders have been identified, the normatively highly relevant question of how far these stakeholders are involved in the entire process must be clarified.

The question of the involvement of cooperation partners is, of course, dependent on the type of firm and the underlying idea of corporate management. If we relate these criteria to the involvement of stakeholders, then we come back to the important characteristics of participation within C-authority: inclusiveness and equality (cf. Hielscher et al., 2014, p. 537).

1. Participation: Can every stakeholder participate directly or vicariously (see Jastram & Berberyan, 2023) in the cooperation project to realize transactions?
2. Equal rights: Can every stakeholder participate in the cooperation project in the same way and with the same quality?

In principle, we maintain that all stakeholders, i.e., invested and simply affected stakeholders, should be directly or indirectly involved in the process of designing, steering and developing the transaction. The extent to which all stakeholders are given equal consideration in the decision-making and control processes seems to us to be the main open and controversial question.

5.3 The Form of Stakeholder Governance

The form of stakeholder governance can ultimately be defined as the combination of the identification and concreteness of the claim (invested vs. simply affected) on the one hand and the degree of participation in the design, steering, and development of the transaction in the dimensions of market, society and planet (see Fig. 5).

The form of stakeholder governance shows a picture that contains the empirical observation that invested stakeholders have a significantly higher degree of participation and co-determination than do stakeholders who are simply affected. What's more, it is actually the case that Planet Earth as a stakeholder (see Fischer-Lescano, 2018; Phillips, 2003) has not even been considered to the same extent in terms of advocacy, let alone on an equal footing.

Stakeholder governance provides the framework for clarifying claims and participation and placing them in a relationship. In normative terms, the claims are initially

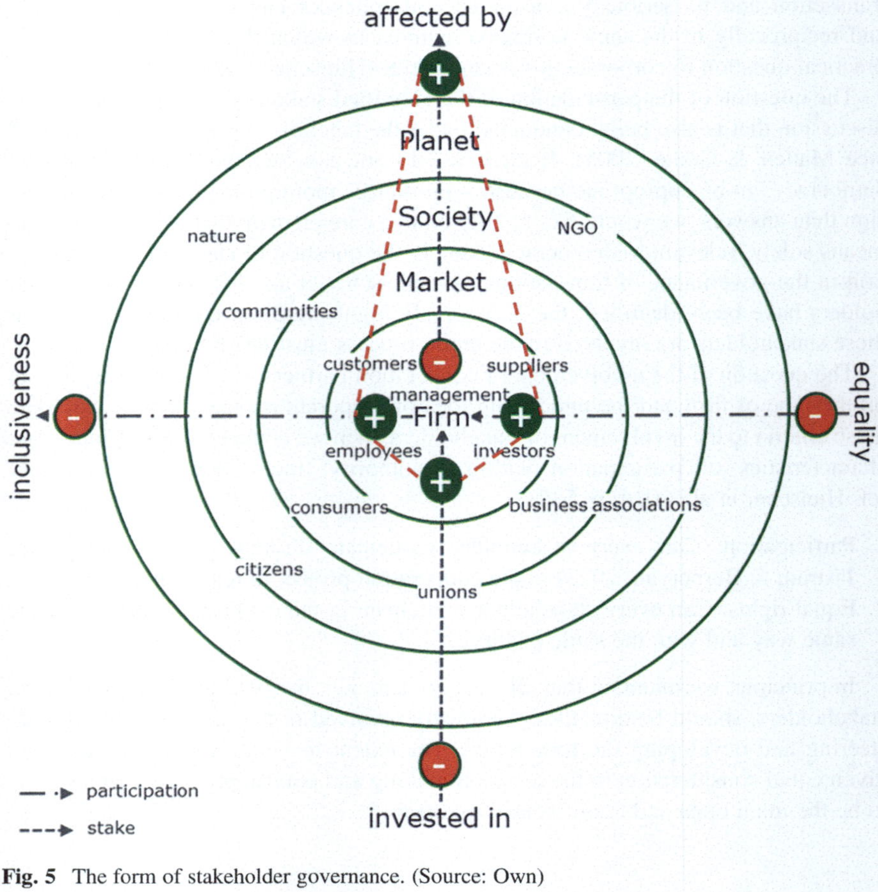

Fig. 5 The form of stakeholder governance. (Source: Own)

of equal importance, so that the aim of stakeholder management should be to consider all stakeholders who seriously deserve this name as a result of the identification phase in the transaction if they, the identified stakeholders, are willing and able to cooperate. At this point, it is repeatedly pointed out with reference to Jensen (2001) that this full consideration leads to a logical problem, because it is impossible to consider *n* demands in an optimization function. This problem can be avoided by following the methodical path of determining a benchmark for corporate management that meets as many demands as possible. In accordance with the idea of shared value creation, the cooperation rent comes onto the radar of the corporate actor.

The cooperation rent is the "unearned income" that the company realizes through the specific bundling of all claims, resources, and skills beyond factor remuneration (cf. Wieland, 2020, pp. 122–127). Of course, the cooperation rent requires cooperation, i.e., the strategy of stakeholder involvement must also be developed as part of stakeholder governance.

We return here to the formulation already introduced that every cooperation partner is a stakeholder, but not every stakeholder is a cooperation partner. Cooperation is a socially inter-subjective phenomenon of reciprocity that simply cannot function on its own. So if a stakeholder is not willing to cooperate and may even be intent on causing harm, then the instruments of interaction need not be the same as in the case of perhaps even unrestricted cooperation, which we even *ideally* assume to be the guiding objective of the stakeholder relationship (see Cohen, 2023, p. 305). The assessment of stakeholders' willingness and ability to cooperate includes a double stakeholder responsibility of the reflexive design of a responsibility architecture. Accordingly, the company is not only responsible for assessing the cooperation behavior of the identified stakeholders and the resulting consequences, but also for the normatively substantiated justification of the questions that (can) naturally arise from the stakeholders even if they were not otherwise involved. The sixth step in the stakeholder governance process is therefore a very important one in practical terms, because it is intended to normatively ensure that the transaction can be justified to all stakeholders in a generally reciprocal manner. Furthermore, it is also important because the comprehensible justifications are a *signal of* the company's own willingness and ability to cooperate.

6 The (Moral) Responsibility of the Firm

So far, I have not yet answered the question of whether companies as corporate actors are also to be understood as moral, and therefore morally responsible, actors. We believe that this question, although it appears quite innocent, is theoretically explosive simply because it fundamentally addresses the conditions for the possibility of corporate social responsibility (CSR; CR). Even if it is generally recognized that the concept of CSR or CR has no really good theoretical basis in all academic and practical debates (see Carroll, 2009; Robe, 2020, pp. 332–335), it remains deeply unsatisfactory if, on the one hand, we talk about a phenomenon such as C

(S)R, but, on the other hand, we do not know whether and, if so, to what extent, the firm itself can be an actor that is fundamentally capable of responsibility. And indeed, the question of the moral responsibility of companies is still extremely controversial today (see Orts & Smith, 2017). Given the current state of the discussion on understanding the firm as a corporate actor, we should ask about the personal characteristics of companies with regard to their capacity for responsibility.

An actor can be described as moral if he possesses freedom of action, foresight, the ability to reflect, and the ability to be affected (see Kettner, 2001, p. 149). In the case of the first three self-explanatory abilities, one can even assume with Geser (1989, p. 220) that the abilities to act responsibly are not only present in corporate actors but are also more pronounced than in individual actors (see Pies, 2001, p. 187; Ortmann, 2010, pp. 80–81). Firstly, corporate actors have more self-responsibility; secondly, they can control the motivation to act; thirdly, they can process more—also normative—complexity; fourthly, they can also act with a high degree of responsibility for consequences, and fifthly and finally, they sometimes also have significant capacities for regulatory responsibility. In short: if individual actors are responsible for these reasons, then corporate actors are not perhaps responsible, but always responsible.

According to Kettner (2001, p. 153), the capacity that also makes responsibility a moral responsibility is "co-concern" as "the complex ability (. . .) to take representatively seriously how (. . .) action activity of A (. . .) in an area for which A is considered responsible (. . .) turns out for the good or bad (. . .) of all beings that count in this respect." I think Kettner's idea can be combined quite well with what List and Pettit (2011, p. 155) have described as "judgmental capacity," namely the ability "for making normative judgments about the options." Can companies make normative judgments, or show some kind of empathy? In order to answer this question, we need to take another look at corporate action. Corporate action is always also a joint action (n + 1), which is in fact carried out by an individual actor as an organizational member on behalf of the company. Corporate involvement then consists of companies using the "reason and intentionality borrowed from their employees to reflect on what is right for them to do" (Neuhäuser, 2011, p. 174). Via corporate governance and CIDS, the results of reflection lead to a corporately mediated, individual self-commitment (see Pies, 2001), according to which an organizational member ultimately acts differently from the individual within the organizational member. The moral (primary) responsibility for a corporate action, therefore, lies with the corporate actor, even if a residual, but downstream, responsibility remains with the individual actor.

However, we should be very careful not to understand corporate actors as moral persons who are understood as "full-fledged members of the moral community, of equal standing with the traditionally acknowledged residents; human beings" (French, 1984, p. 32). The reason is quite simple: moral persons are bound to human dignity (see Neuhäuser, 2011, p. 115) and "human dignity has (. . .) no corporate counterpart" (Kettner, 2001, p. 169). This ultimately leads to the consequence that moral duties, including the moral duty of justification (see Scanlon, 1998; Forst, 2024), are attributed to the company as a moral actor, but no moral rights, which are constitutive of moral persons according to the common interpretation.

7 Concluding Remarks

This chapter focuses on the firm in relational economics. The investigation goes in two directions: on the one hand, the elaboration of the firm as a nexus of stakeholder relations and, on the other hand, the firm as a corporate actor. The focus of this chapter is the firm with its corporate intentionality to be a cooperation partner. Language and communication play a decisive role here, enabling cooperation through participation. Of course, this construction of the firm as a strategic and communicative actor also has consequences for stakeholder governance, for which the firm as an actor is also morally responsible in the sense that it can justify its decisions and actions to its stakeholders. The functional as well as normative challenge of the company as process owner for successful cooperation for the purpose of shared value creation will require further elaboration.

References

Alchian, A. A., & Demsetz, H. (1972). Production, information costs, and economic organization. *The American Economic Review, 62*(5), 777–795.

Artz, K. W., & Brush, T. H. (2000). Asset specificity, uncertainty and relational norms: An examination of coordination costs in collaborative strategic alliances. *Journal of Economic Behavior & Organization, 41*, 337–362.

Barnard, C. I. (1968). *The functions of the executive*. Harvard University Press. (Original work published 1938).

Bass, B. J., & Avolio, B. J. (1993). Transformational leadership and organizational culture. *Public Administration Quarterly, 16*(1), 112–121.

Berle, A. A., & Means, G. C. (2017). *The modern corporation and private property*. Harcourt, Brace and World. (Original work published 1932).

Biggerio, L. (2022). Why we could need a relational economics and why standard economics and its (orthodox) derivations do not help. In L. Biggerio, D. de Jongh, B. P. Priddat, J. Wieland, & A. Zicari (Eds.), *The relational view of economics: A new research agenda for the study of relational transactions* (pp. 43–72). Springer.

Biggerio, L., de Jongh, D., Priddat, B. P., Wieland, J., & Zicari, A. (2022). Manifesto for a relational economics. In L. Biggerio, D. de Jongh, B. P. Priddat, J. Wieland, & A. Zicari (Eds.), *The relational view of economics: A new research agenda for the study of relational transactions* (pp. 9–16). Springer.

Blair, M. M. (2013). The four functions of corporate personhood. In A. Grandori (Ed.), *Handbook of economic organization: Integrating economic and organization theory* (pp. 440–461). Edward Elgar.

Blair, M. M., & Stout, L. A. (1999). A team production theory of corporate law. *Virginia Law Review, 85*(2), 247–328.

Brandom, R. B. (2008). *Between saying & doing: Towards an analytic pragmatism*. Oxford University Press.

BRT. (2019). *Our commitment: Statement on the purpose of a corporation*. Retrieved December 22, 2020, from https://opportunity.businessroundtable.org/ourcommitment/

Carroll, A. B. (2009). A history of corporate social responsibility: Concepts and practices. In A. Crane, A. McWilliams, D. Matten, J. Moon, & D. S. Siegel (Eds.), *The Oxford handbook of corporate social responsibility* (pp. 19–46). Oxford University Press.

Casadesus-Masanell, R., & Spulber, D. F. (2004). *Agency revisited* (Harvard Business School working paper 10-082). https://hbs.edu

Coase, R. H. (1993). The nature of the firm. In O. E. Williamson & S. G. Winter (Eds.), *The nature of the firm: Origins, evolution, and developments* (pp. 18–33). Oxford University Press. (Original work published 1937).

Cohen, M. (2023). Reconstructing the moral logic of the stakeholder approach, and reconsidering the participation requirement. *Philosophy of Management, 22*, 293–308.

Coleman, J. S. (1992). *Grundlagen der Sozialtheorie, Band 2: Körperschaften und die moderne Gesellschaft*. Oldenbourg.

Commons, J. R. (1990). *Institutional economics: Its place in political economy* (Vol. 1). Routledge. (Original work published 1934).

Commons, J. R. (2012). *Legal foundations of capitalism*. Macmillan. (Original work published 1924).

Cunliffe, A. L., & Eriksen, M. (2011). Relational leadership. *Human Relations, 64*(11), 1425–1449.

Deakin, S., Gindis, D., & Hodgson, G. M. (2021). *What is a firm? A reply to Jean-Philippe Robe* (Working paper No. 531). Centre for Business Research, University of Cambridge. https://cbr.cam.ac.uk

Denzau, A. T., & North, D. C. (2000). Shared mental models: Ideologies and institutions. In A. Lupia, M. D. McCubbins, & S. L. Popkin (Eds.), *Elements of reason: Cognition, choice, and the bounds of rationality* (pp. 23–46). Cambridge University Press.

Dewey, J. (1926). The historic background of corporate legal personality. *The Yale Law Journal, 35*(6), 655–667.

Donaldson, T., & Dunfee, T. (1999). *Ties that bind: A social contracts approach to business ethics*. Harvard Business School Press.

Donaldson, T., & Preston, L. E. (1995). The stakeholder theory of the corporation: Concepts, evidence, and implications. *The Academy of Management Review, 20*(1), 65–91.

Duschek, S., Gaitanides, M., Matiaske, W., & Ortmann, G. (Eds.). (2012). *Organisationen regeln: Die Wirkmacht korporativer Akteure*. VS Verlag.

Fairhurst, G. T., & Connaughton, S. L. (2014). Leadership: A communicative perspective. *Leadership, 10*(1), 7–35.

Fischer-Lescano, A. (2018). Natur als Rechtsperson: Konstellationen der Stellvertretung im Recht. *Zeitschrift für Umweltrecht, 2018*, 205–216.

Forst, R. (2024). Welten der Rechtfertigung: Die Diskursethik als kantischer Konstruktivismus. In S. Müller-Dohm, S. Rapic, & T. Wesche (Eds.), *Vernünftige Freiheit: Beiträge zum Spätwerk von Jürgen Habermas* (pp. 238–259). Suhrkamp.

Freeman, R. E. (1984). *Strategic management: A stakeholder approach*. Cambridge University Press.

Freeman, R. E., Harrison, J. S., Wicks, A. C., Parmar, B. L., & De Colle, S. (2010). *Stakeholder theory: The state of the art*. Cambridge University Press.

Freeman, R. E., Harrison, J. S., & Zyglidopoulos, S. (2018). *Stakeholder theory*. Cambridge University Press.

Freeman, R. E., Martin, K. E., & Parmar, B. L. (2020). *The power of and: Responsible business without trade-offs*. Columbia University Press.

French, P. A. (1984). *Collective and corporate responsibility*. Columbia University Press.

Friedman, M. (1970, September 13). The social responsibility of business is to increase its profits. *The New York Times Magazine*. http://www.umich.edu/~thecore/doc/Friedman.pdf

Gartenberg, C., & Zenger, T. (2023). The firm as a subsociety: Purpose, justice, and the theory of the firm. *Organization Science, 34*(5), 1965–1980.

Geser, H. (1989). Interorganisationelle Normkulturen. In M. Haller et al. (Eds.), *Kultur und Gesellschaft* (pp. 211–223). Campus.
Geser, H. (1990). Organisationen als soziale Akteure. *Zeitschrift für Soziologie, 19*(6), 401–417.
Gindis, D. (2013). *The nexus paradox: Legal personality and the theory of the firm* (Doctoral dissertation). https://core.ac.uk/display/16697575
Gindis, D. (2020). On the origins, meaning and influence of Jensen and Meckling's definition of the firm. *Oxford Economic Papers, 72*(4), 966–984.
Goodpaster, K. E. (1991). Business ethics and stakeholder analysis. *Business Ethics Quarterly, 1*(1), 53–73.
Granovetter, M. (1985). Economic action and social structure: The problem of embeddedness. *American Journal of Sociology, 91*(3), 481–510.
Grossman, S. J., & Hart, O. D. (1986). The costs and benefits of ownership: A theory of vertical and lateral integration. *Journal of Political Economy, 94*(4), 691–719.
Habermas, J. (1981). Theorie des kommunikativen Handelns. *Band 1 Handlungsrationalität und gesellschaftliche Rationalisierung*. Frankfurt/Main: Suhrkamp.
Habermas, J. (2005). *Zwischen Naturalismus und Religion: Philosophische Aufsätze*. Suhrkamp.
Hansmann, H., & Kraakman, R. (2000). Organizational law as asset partitioning. *European Economic Review, 44*(4), 807–817.
Hart, O. (2011). Thinking about the firm: A review of Daniel Spulber's the theory of the firm. *Journal of Economic Literature, 49*(1), 101–113. http://www.aeaweb.org/articles.php?doi=10.1257/jel.49.1.10
Hart, O., & Moore, J. (1990). Property rights and the nature of the firm. *The Journal of Political Economy, 98*(6), 1119–1158.
Heath, J. (2003). *Communicative action and rational choice*. MIT Press.
Hielscher, S., Beckmann, M., & Pies, I. (2014). Participation versus consent: Should corporations be run according to democratic principles? *Business Ethics Quarterly, 24*(4), 533–563.
Hodgson, G. M. (2004). *The evolution of institutional economics: Agency, structure and Darwinism in American institutionalism*. Routledge.
Hodgson, G. M. (2013). *From pleasure machines to moral communities: An evolutionary economics without homo oeconomicus*. University of Chicago Press.
Hodgson, G. M. (2014). The evolution of morality and the end of economic man. *Journal of Evolutionary Economics, 24*, 83–106.
Hodgson, G. M. (2015). *Conceptualizing capitalism: Institutions, evolution, future*. University of Chicago Press.
Holmström, B. (1999). The firm as a subeconomy. *Journal of Law, Economics, and Organization, 15*(1), 74–102.
Hübscher, M. C. (2011). Die Firma als Nexus von Referenzpunkten: Institutionen, Identitäten und Sprechakte. In J. Wieland (Ed.), *Die Zukunft der Firma* (pp. 167–193). Metropolis.
Hübscher, M. C. (2019). Rethinking economics: Rezension zu Josef Wieland: Relational economics: Ökonomische Theorie wirtschaftlicher Transaktionen. *Zeitschrift für Wirtschafts- und Unternehmensethik, 20*(1), 108–111.
Hübscher, M. C. (2024). *Konsens versus Rechtfertigung: Integrative Wirtschaftsethik und die Unternehmung als moralischer Akteur*. Forthcoming under review.
Hübscher, M. C., & Neuhäuser, C. (2021). Unternehmen. In L. Heidbrink, H. Schmid, & K. Ziegler (Eds.), *Handbuch Wirtschaftsphilosophie III: Praktische Wirtschaftsphilosophie* (pp. 215–232). Springer.
Jastram, S. M., & Berberyan, Z. (2023). Democratic stakeholder representativeness. *Journal of Public Administration Research and Theory, 33*(2), 1–14.
Jensen, M. C. (2001). *Value maximization, stakeholder theory, and the corporate objective function* (Tuck Business School working paper No. 01-09; Harvard NOM Research paper No. 01-01; Harvard Business School working paper No. 00-058). https://www.sfu.ca/~wainwrig/Econ400/jensen-meckling.pdf

Jensen, M. C., & Meckling, W. H. (1976). Theory of the firm: Managerial behavior, agency costs, and ownership structure. *Journal of Financial Economics, 3*(4), 305–360.
Kettner, M. (2001). Moralische Verantwortung in individueller und kollektiver Form. In J. Wieland (Ed.), *Die moralische Verantwortung kollektiver Akteure* (pp. 146–170). Physica.
King, B. G., Felin, T., & Whetten, D. A. (2010). Finding the organization in organizational theory: A meta-theory of the organization as a social actor. *Organization Science, 21*(1), 290–305.
Kreps, D. M. (1990). Corporate culture and economic theory. In J. E. Alt & K. A. Shepsle (Eds.), *Perspectives on positive political economy* (pp. 90–140). Cambridge University Press.
Langlois, R. N. (Ed.). (2009). *Economics as a process: Essays in the new institutional economics*. Cambridge University Press.
List, C., & Pettit, P. (2011). *Group agency: The possibility, design, and status of corporate agents*. Oxford University Press.
Machlup, F. (1967). Theories of the firm: Marginalist, behavioral, managerial. *The American Economic Review, 57*(1), 1–3.
Matten, D., & Crane, A. (2005). What is stakeholder democracy? *Perspectives and issues. Business Ethics, 14*(1), 6–13.
Mayer, C. (2013). *Firm commitment: Why the corporation is failing us and how to restore trust in it*. Oxford University Press.
McMahon, C. (1994). *Authority and democracy: A general theory of government and management*. Princeton University Press.
Meckling, W. H., & Jensen, M. C. (1982). Reflections on the corporation as a social invention. In R. W. Hansen (Ed.), *Controlling the giant corporation: A symposium* (pp. 33–53). Center for Research in Government Policy and Business. https://delivery.php/ssrn.com
Milgrom, P., & Roberts, J. (1992). *Economics, organization & management*. Prentice-Hall.
Neuhäuser, C. (2011). *Unternehmen als moralische Akteure*. Suhrkamp.
Neuhäuser, C., & Hübscher, M. C. (2010). Unternehmen, ihre (ethische) Governance und Menschenrechte. In B. S. Byrd, J. Hruschka, & J. C. Joerden (Eds.), *Jahrbuch für Recht und Ethik* (Vol. 18, pp. 349–368). Duncker & Humblot.
Ortmann, G. (2010). *Organisation und Moral: Die dunkle Seite*. Velbrück.
Orts, E. W. (2013). *Business persons: A legal theory of the firm*. Oxford University Press.
Orts, E., & Smith, N. C. (Eds.). (2017). *The moral responsibility of firms*. Oxford University Press.
Phillips, R. (2003). *Stakeholder theory and organizational ethics*. Berrett-Koehler.
Pies, I. (2001). Können Unternehmen Verantwortung tragen? – Ein ökonomisches Kooperationsangebot an die philosophische Ethik. In J. Wieland (Ed.), *Die moralische Verantwortung kollektiver Akteure* (pp. 171–200). Physica.
Pies, I., & Valentinov, V. (2023). Trade-offs in stakeholder theory: An ordonomic perspective. *Social Responsibility Journal*. https://www.emerald.com/insight/content/doi/10.1108/SRJ-01-2023-0017
Porter, M. E., & Kramer, M. R. (2011). Creating shared value. *Harvard Business Review, 89*(1/2), 62–77.
Post, J. E., Preston, L. E., & Sachs, S. (2002). *Redefining the corporation: Stakeholder management and organizational wealth*. Stanford University Press.
Preston, L. E. (1975). Corporation and society: The search for a paradigm. *Journal of Economic Literature, 13*(2), 434–453.
Rappaport, A. (2006). Ten ways to create shareholder value. *Harvard Business Review*. https://hbr.org/2006/09/ten-ways-to-create-sharehold
Robe, J.-P. (2011). The legal structure of the firm. *Accounting, Economics and Law, 2*(2), 1–86.
Robe, J.-P. (2020). *Property, power and politics: Why we need to rethink the world power system*. Bristol University Press.
Roberts, J. (2004). *The modern firm: Organizational design for performance and growth*. Oxford University Press.
Samuels, W. (2009). *The legal-economic nexus*. Routledge.
Scanlon, T. M. (1998). *What we owe to each other*. The Belknap Press of Harvard University Press.

Schmid, H. B., & Schweikard, D. P. (Eds.). (2009). *Kollektive Intentionalität: Eine Debatte über die Grundlagen des Sozialen*. Suhrkamp.
Schramm, M. (2022). Relational process in Whitehead's metaphysics and Commons' economics: The relevance of cosmology for economic theory. In L. Biggerio, D. de Jongh, B. P. Priddat, J. Wieland, & A. Zicari (Eds.), *The relational view of economics: A new research agenda for the study of relational transactions* (pp. 249–276). Springer.
Schwab, K. (2021). *Stakeholder capitalism: A global economy that works for progress, people, and planet*. Wiley.
Schwengber, J. G. (2024). *Organizational learning as relational governance*. Springer.
Searle, J. R. (1995). *The construction of social reality*. The Free Press.
Searle, J. R. (2010). *Making the social world: The structure of human civilization*. Oxford University Press.
Sellars, W. (1997). *Empiricism and the philosophy of mind* (R. Rorty, Introduction; R. Brandom, Study Guide). Harvard University Press. (Original work published 1956).
Singer, A. A. (2019). *The form of the firm: A normative political theory of the corporation*. Oxford University Press.
Smith, B. (2003). John Searle: From speech acts to social reality. In B. Smith (Ed.), *John Searle* (pp. 1–33). Cambridge University Press.
Spulber, D. F. (2009). *The theory of the firm: Microeconomics with endogenous entrepreneurs, firms, markets, and organizations*. Cambridge University Press.
Steenkamp, Y., Fischer, D., & de Jongh, D. (2022). Leadership in multi-stakeholder partnerships (MSPs) that address the SDGs: Relational leadership and Ubuntu in dialogue. In L. Biggerio, D. de Jongh, B. P. Priddat, J. Wieland, & A. Zicari (Eds.), *The relational view of economics: A new research agenda for the study of relational transactions* (pp. 213–228). Springer.
Stout, L. (2012). *The shareholder value myth: How putting shareholders first harms investors, corporations, and the public*. Berrett-Koehler Publishers.
Teubner, G. (1987). Unternehmenskorporatismus: New industrial policy und das "Wesen" der juristischen Person. *KritV, 70*, 61–85.
Tuomela, R. (2006). Joint intentions, we-mode, and I-mode. In P. A. French & H. K. Wettstein (Eds.), *Shared intentions and collective responsibility* (pp. 35–58). Blackwell Publishing.
Walker, P. (2017). *The theory of the firm: An overview of the economic mainstream*. Routledge.
Weber, M. (1978). Economy and society (G. Roth & C. Wittich, Trans. & Eds.). University of California Press. (Original work published 1927).
Weber, B. (1995). *Die fluide Organisation: Konzeptionelle Überlegungen für die Gestaltung und das Management von Unternehmen in hochdynamischen Umfeldern*. Haupt.
Weick, K. E. (1995). *Der Prozess des Organisierens*. Suhrkamp.
Whitehead, A. N. (1985). In D. R. Griffin & D. W. Sherburne (Eds.), *Process and reality*. Free Press. (Original work published 1927).
Wieland, J. (1996). *Ökonomische Organisation, Allokation und Status*. Mohr.
Wieland, J. (1998). Kooperationsökonomie: Die Ökonomie der Diversität, Abhängigkeit und Atmosphäre. In G. Wegner & J. Wieland (Eds.), *Formelle und informelle Institutionen der Ökonomie: Genese und Evolution* (pp. 9–33). Metropolis.
Wieland, J. (2000). Die neue Organisationsökonomik: Entwicklung und Probleme der Theorienbildung. In G. Ortmann, J. Sydow, & K. Türk (Eds.), *Theorien der Organisation: Die Rückkehr der Gesellschaft* (2nd ed., pp. 35–66). Metropolis.
Wieland, J. (2007). *Die Ethik der Governance* (5th ed.). Metropolis.
Wieland, J. (2011). The firm as a nexus of stakeholders: Stakeholder management and theory of the firm. In A. Brink (Ed.), *Corporate governance and business ethics* (pp. 225–244). Springer.
Wieland, J. (2014). *Governance ethics: Global value creation, economic organization and normativity*. Springer.

Wieland, J. (2017). Shared value—Theoretical implications, practical challenges. In J. Wieland (Ed.), *Creating shared value: Concepts, experiences, criticism* (pp. 9–26). Springer.
Wieland, J. (2020). *Relational economics: A political economy*. Springer.
Wieland, J. (2022). Relational economics: Theoretical framework and managerial implications – A short introduction. In L. Biggerio, D. de Jongh, B. P. Priddat, J. Wieland, & A. Zicari (Eds.), *The relational view of economics: A new research agenda for the study of relational transactions* (pp. 17–42). Springer.
Williamson, O. E. (1975). *Markets and hierarchies: Analysis and antitrust implications*. Free Press.
Williamson, O. E. (1985). *The economic institutions of capitalism*. Free Press.
Williamson, O. E. (1993). The logic of economic organization. In O. E. Williamson & S. G. Winter (Eds.), *The nature of the firm: Origins, evolution, and development* (pp. 90–116). Oxford University Press.
Williamson, O. E. (1996). *Mechanisms of governance*. Oxford University Press.

Marc C. Hübscher, Prof. Dr., Dipl.-Oec., Dipl.-Handelslehrer, Partner at Deloitte GmbH Wirtschaftsprüfungsgesellschaft and Honorary Professor at the Institute of Sustainable Leadership, University of Ulm, Senior Lecturer at the University of St. Gallen and Göttingen, research areas: Theory of the Firm, Business Ethics, Sustainable Leadership, Critical Theory.

Part II
Relational Management and Leadership

Stakeholder Management and Relational Economics. Towards Just and Sustainable Business Practices

Jacob Dahl Rendtorff

Abstract This chapter proposes a conception of stakeholder management from the perspective of Relational Economics, emphasizing justice based on business ethics and corporate social responsibility (CSR). CSR embodies equity and justice among stakeholders, forming the core of good corporate citizenship. The chapter links corporate social responsibility with sustainable development goals (SDGs), highlighting their importance for business development and ethical stakeholder relations. The concept of Relational Economics views firms as being embedded in social relations, integrating governance, leadership, and management with ethical values and societal responsibilities. Stakeholder management, as envisioned in this framework, supports a new vision of the firm and civil society, promoting decision-making for the common good through reflective judgment. This research explores how Relational Economics and stakeholder theory converge, presenting firms as nexuses of stakeholders and emphasizing the importance of sustainable development in global business practices. The chapter further discusses how stakeholder theory enhances strategic planning by integrating social, cultural, and environmental considerations. It questions traditional economic theories, advocating a more inclusive and ethical approach to business that aligns with global sustainability goals. The study underscores the role of stakeholder management in addressing the complex challenges of sustainability, ethics, and global corporate responsibility, proposing it as essential for the development of just and sustainable business practices.

Keywords Relational economics · Stakeholder management · Corporate social responsibility (CSR) · Sustainable development goals (SDGs) · Business ethics · Corporate governance · Reflective judgment · Social responsibility · Ethical leadership

---

J. D. Rendtorff (✉)
Roskilde University, Roskilde, Denmark
e-mail: jacrendt@ruc.dk

J. D. Rendtorff et al. (eds.), *Advances in Relational Economics*, Relational Economics and Organization Governance,
https://doi.org/10.1007/978-3-031-75725-9_5

1 Introduction

I would like to propose a conception of stakeholder management from the perspective of Relational Economics as a vision of justice based on business ethics and corporate social responsibility (CSR). It can be said that CSR implies equity and justice among the company's stakeholders (Phillips, 2003). This constitutes a normative conception of the stakeholder model and of good corporate citizenship (Zadek, 2001; Rendtorff, 2018, 2024a; Rendtorff & Bonnafous-Boucher, 2023). This is at the center of my argument for a link between CSR, Relational Economics, and stakeholder theory. The idea of sustainable development and sustainable development goals (SDGs) is presented as having fundamental importance for CSR and business development (Elkington, 1999; World Commission, 1987; UN, 2018a, b), and this vision for sustainable development can be analyzed from the perspective of Relational Economics. This relates to the concepts of fairness and justice as the basis for the concrete relationship with stakeholders forming the internal and external relations of the firm with its environment. Subsequently, we can appeal to reflective judgment (Ricœur, 1992) as being at the center of the ethical management of public or private organizations. With this theory of CSR and principles of stakeholder justice in Relational Economics, I follow up on my earlier work on stakeholder theory and CSR (Bonnafous-Boucher & Pesqueux, 2006; Bonnafous-Boucher & Rendtorff, 2013, 2016; Rendtorff & Bonnafous-Boucher, 2023). From this perspective, stakeholder management in Relational Economics contributes to a new vision of the firm and civil society (Bonnafous-Boucher & Pesqueux, 2006). In this context, stakeholder management leads to decision-making for the common good, based on good reflective judgment in the framework of Relational Economics.

2 Stakeholder Management and the Relational View of the Firm

What is the relation between stakeholder theory, stakeholder management, and the relational view of the firm? Relational Economics proposes a concept of governance, leadership, and management that regards the firm as being embedded in social relations (Rendtorff, 2024a, b). Here, Relational Economics combines concepts from Luhmann's systems theory of social and economic systems with insights from transaction cost economics. Moreover, Relational Economics agrees with business ethics research that the firm must deal with challenges of values and morality which cannot be excluded from economic action. Over the years, Relational Economics has developed to become a strong and comprehensive program for understanding the role of business in society (Wieland, 1989, 1993, 1996, 1999, 2005, 2011, 2013, 2014, 2020). Relational Economics insists that the firm is embedded in society as a social system with social and cultural values. The concepts of polycontextuality, polyvalence, and polylinguism in complex societies in

Relational Economics demonstrate how the firm is embedded in a network of shared value creation in social and cultural interaction with different stakeholders in different cultural and social systems surrounding the economic transactions. This embeddedness requires relational and transcultural leadership since the firm operates in different social and cultural contexts. From a global perspective, this relational and transcultural leadership can be combined with cosmopolitan business ethics (Rendtorff, 2018), where globalization requires businesses to assume global and cosmopolitan business responsibilities as global corporate citizens.

With this globalization of the cosmopolitan responsibilities of business firms, relational leadership and governance as stakeholder management must refer to sustainability and sustainable development goals (Rendtorff, 2018, 2020c, 2024a). Global business legitimacy means that firms must operate in relation to these sustainable goals (Rendtorff, 2020a). Moreover, global embeddedness, interculturality, and polycontextuality express the conditions of a political firm where the business corporation has responsibility for human rights and the environment as a global actor that is placed in the social and cultural systems of society. In the following, I propose to situate Relational Economics in the context of the contemporary discussions of business ethics and economic ethics as a conceptualization of new conditions of business legitimacy in contemporary society. The starting point for this approach is to link the philosophy of management with Relational Economics (Rendtorff, 2013a, b, c, d, 2019a, b). I am interested in stakeholder management and stakeholder justice and fairness as the normative ideal for dealing with the firm as a nexus of stakeholders in Relational Economics.

In his theory of Relational Economics, Josef Wieland conceives the firm as a nexus of stakeholders (Wieland, 2011). As a nexus of stakeholders, the firm is situated and embedded in the social context of society. Relational leadership also builds on this idea of the firm as a nexus of stakeholders. This conception of the firm contributes to the integration of stakeholder theory in the institutional theory of the firm, where the firm is regarded as a combination of transaction cost interactions and stakeholder interactions. Leadership theory in the transactional concept of the firm needs to focus on societal and economic value creation not only in relation to shareholders but more broadly to stakeholders and to society. In Wieland's concept of the firm as a nexus of stakeholders, stakeholder management is integrated into corporate governance and business ethics conceived as values-driven and intercultural management which deals with the economic development of the firm.

With this integration of stakeholder theory in Relational Economics, there is a convergence between Wieland's development of Relational Economics and the theory of stakeholder management that I have developed together with Maria Bonnafous-Boucher (Bonnafous-Boucher & Rendtorff, 2013, 2016; Rendtorff & Bonnafous-Boucher, 2023). In a sense, stakeholder theory marks an important renewal of thinking about the firm in complex systems, since it allows for the deconstruction of neoclassical agency theory and concepts of stakeholder primacy of the firm. Therefore, stakeholder theory is an important contribution to the relational view of the firm.

The concept of relation is central to stakeholder theory when we look at the history of the stakeholder concept. In the original Scandinavian concept of the firm from the 1950s onwards, the relational view was central to the understanding of the role of the business firm in society as embedded in social and cultural relations (Bonnafous-Boucher & Rendtorff, 2016; Rendtorff & Bonnafous-Boucher, 2023). The concept of relation also became important in the Stanford definition of the stakeholder firm from 1963 as "those groups that the corporate is dependent on for survival" and in the later definition of stakeholders as those who affect or are affected by the firm. With this, it is evident that stakeholders are defined through their relations to the firm. It was also the concept of relation that became essential in R. Edward Freeman's book on stakeholder management, *Strategic Management: A Stakeholder Approach* (Freeman, 1984). Moreover, the concept of relation also plays an important role in the concept of stakeholder salience when we look at the work on identifying the most important stakeholders of the firm (Mitchell et al., 1997). Furthermore, combining stakeholder management with the concept of corporate social responsibility in relation to the integration of CSR and stakeholder management in the concept of corporate stakeholder responsibility, the stakeholder approach relates to the internal and external environment of the firm focusing on social responsibility in relation to the different stakeholders of the corporation. Here, Relational Economics and stakeholder theory share the important idea that economics is embedded in social relations and that management should be pragmatic regarding integrating concern for civil society in the decision-making of the firm. Stakeholder management is hereby a contribution to the Relational Economics of civil society since the activities of stakeholders are considered as important contributors to civil society.

Thus, strategic planning following stakeholder theory must consider stakeholders as being integrated into society and community. It is necessary to integrate stakeholder management into strategic planning (Ansoff, 1965). Here, stakeholder theory proposes a broad view of strategic planning and criticizes a too limited understanding of strategic planning. The relational concept of stakeholders opens up an understanding of complexity in the strategic management of corporations where management should look at stakeholders as being integrated into the social context of the corporation.

It is in this context that stakeholder theory develops aspects of Relational Economics that have not been considered by economic institutional theory. In *The Economic Institutions of Capitalism*, Williamson rejects that there should be more concern for stakeholders than for shareholders (Williamson, 1995). However, institutional sociology looks differently at this matter (Scott, 2008). This is also the case for DiMaggio and Powell in their analysis of the new institutionalism in sociology (DiMaggio & Powell, 1991). With this approach, institutional theory contributes to situating stakeholder theory in the framework of institutional interaction between organizations. There is an increased institutionalization of ethics and responsibility in management (Rendtorff, 2011). However, there is also an institutional paradox embedded in stakeholder theory and stakeholder management. Kenneth Goodpaster has proposed calling this "the stakeholder paradox" saying that a corporation has fiduciary responsibility for shareholders but at the same time also responsibilities for stakeholders going beyond primary contractual obligations, since stakeholders are embedded in the situational context of the firm (Goodpaster, 1991).

From the perspective of institutional theory and Relational Economics, stakeholder theory can be conceptualized as a global framework for management and corporate governance. In this context, ethical values are essential for shaping stakeholder decisions. There is at the same time a descriptive, prescriptive, and normative frame (an ethical argumentation) for stakeholder management. From the ethical perspective, stakeholder management integrates ethics and economics, and the core of stakeholder management is the relational dimension making the link between business and society.

This means that stakeholder theory should not be considered as a fundamentally new concept of society that requires fundamental changes in the law. Moreover, stakeholder management cannot be regarded as utopian socialism that requires fundamental social change and the creation of a new society with new moral doctrines (Phillips et al., 2003). Stakeholder theory and stakeholder management remain a theory of contemporary organizations that aims at understanding interactions between firms and society.

From this point of view, stakeholders can broadly be defined as (1) those who affect the organization; (2) those who are affected by the organization; (3) those who both affect and are affected by the organization (Freeman, 1984; Bonnafous-Boucher & Rendtorff, 2016). With these broad definitions of stakeholders, it is possible to integrate stakeholder theory with an ethical conception of Relational Economics—a theory of the need for the common good in respect of civil society. Thus, ethical stakeholder management opens the perspective of reflectivity in the firm with a thoughtful extension of the relational point of view. This helps to move beyond moral blindness and lack of moral thinking in organizations (Rendtorff, 2014a, 2020b). This conception of stakeholder management relates and analyzes different forms of interests in relation to one another. Paronamization (extension of perspective) is an important way to open this awareness of the challenges of relationality. This includes prioritization (conscience of complexity), politization (inclusion in decision-making), and finally particularization (conscious understanding).

3 Sustainable Development in the Perspective of Stakeholder Theory

Stakeholder theory can help us define the strategic foundation for sustainable development management based on the triple concern for the triple bottom line and balance of economic, ecological, and social affairs (Elkington, 1999). Relational Economics and stakeholder management receive a new dimension when we use stakeholder management to determine the basis for global sustainable development (Rendtorff, 2019a, b).

When we talk about the triple bottom line, we refer to the fact that companies must not only work with financial profit but must also focus on the social and environmental dimensions of their work. Today, the triple bottom line is closely related to ESG (Environment, Social and Governance) measures which include environmental, social, and governance aspects of companies' activities. Looking for the triple bottom line means focusing on the company's social responsibility in its corporate work.

Historically, there is a close connection between the triple bottom line and the UN's work with sustainability. The UN's concept of sustainable development is based on more than 50 years of work with sustainability. In 1972, the first environmental conference was held under the auspices of the UN. Later, the Brundtland Commission set up by the UN (1987) formulated a strategy for sustainability in the report *Our Common Future: Sustainable Development in International Politics* (World Commission on Environment and Development, 1987). At the environmental conference in Rio in 1992, which marked the 20th anniversary of the UN environmental program, people became aware of the extensive nature of the climate problem. This approach was used by Elkington (1999) in *Cannibals with Forks: The Triple Bottom Line of 21st Century Business* to translate the concept of sustainable development into companies' practical work with the green transition. At the same time, the development from the Millennium Goals (2000) to the SDGs (Sustainable Development Goals) (2015) made it possible for companies to contribute more actively to the green transition through partnerships. The development meant that the whole of society became involved in the global green transition.

The UN's global goals are described in the 2030 strategy with the *Transforming Our World Agenda* from 2015 (United Nations, 2018a). The SDGs combine political goals with visions of economic development and social justice (Hildebrandt, 2016; Sachs, 2012, 2015). In this sense, the SDGs constitute a driving force for local economic development and social change in private companies, Nongovernmental Organizations (NGOs), and public organizations and institutions. Stakeholder management can contribute to determining the possibilities of the world goals to function as a vision and a strategic tool as a basis for economic development and management of private and public businesses, organizations, and institutions. The goal of the UN's global goals is to be an instrument for economic development and regeneration that contributes to economic empowerment and social and political change.

The SDGs are a framework for a new development of stakeholder management and stakeholder thinking with increased focus on business ethics, CSR, and a focus on companies' political and social commitment through the concept of "corporate citizenship," which refers to the fact that companies today must take great responsibility for society (van Zanten & van Tulder, 2018). We are moving from the triple bottom line with a focus on people, the planet, and prosperity to the 17 bottom lines in the world goals, and companies, public organizations, or institutions are required to have visions and values related to the world goals (Rendtorff, 2018, 2019a, b).

The world goals of the *Transforming Our World 2030 Agenda for Sustainable Development* of the UN follow up on the Millennium Development Goals (MDGs) from 2000, which were considered important goals for the world community (United

Nations, 2018a). The SDGs are much more detailed and were adopted by the 193 member states of the UN, building on the UN's previous work on sustainability and involving the wider community, including governments, businesses, NGOs, and civil society.

There are 17 global goals, and they are specified with 169 sub-goals, which together focus on people, the planet, and prosperity (United Nations, 2018a). The private sector, businesses, and public organizations and institutions are essential to realizing the SDG agenda to transform the world by 2030. The UN integrates the global goals with other activities aimed at businesses—including Business for Human Rights, the UN Global Compact, the World Business Council for Sustainable Development, and global initiatives with sustainable reporting—in its efforts to motivate companies to contribute to sustainable development (United Nations, 2018b). The global goals are the focus in the development of a both globally and locally embedded and sustainable economy to deal with global and universal movements of capitalism and growth.

The 17 goals relate to the following topics: (1) No poverty; (2) Zero hunger; (3) Good health and well-being; (4) Quality education; (5) Equality; (6) Clean water and sanitation; (7) Sustainable energy; (8) Decent work and economic growth; (9) Industry, innovation, and infrastructure; (10) Reduced inequalities; (11) Sustainable cities and communities; (12) Responsible consumption and production; (13) Climate action; (14) Life under water; (15) Life in the country; (16) Peace, justice, and strong institutions; and (17) Partnerships for the goals (United Nations, 2018a).

The global goals are very comprehensive and aim at social change in local communities. They cover more than the previous goals of sustainability did in the sense that they add prosperity, peace, and partnerships to people, planet, and profit. The question of companies' global responsibility and stakeholder management for stakeholder justice of the sustainable development goals is closely related to the possibility of developing a new economy that can handle various types of stakeholder challenges, e.g., social justice in the supply chain, respect for the environment, development of more sustainable companies, and consideration for consumers. Stakeholder management and stakeholder thinking are important for democratic decision-making in business and society. Therefore, stakeholder management becomes essential for moving in the direction of sustainable development as proposed by the sustainable development goals (Rendtorff, 2020c).

4 Stakeholder Management as the Foundations of Sustainable Development

Stakeholder management can therefore be used to rethink relevant considerations of business organizations in relation to sustainable development. With stakeholder management from the perspective of Relational Economics, it is possible to move beyond the neoclassical growth mindset based on the company's profit maximization toward an integrated economy (interaction between nature, people, and society). In this context, the EU's policy for green transition can also act as an important regional, national, and international benchmark for the work of business with sustainability. This policy of the green transition can be seen as a follow-up on the European tradition of ethics of human rights and protection of the human person (Rendtorff, 1998, 2014a, b; Rendtorff & Kemp, 2000). It is therefore important to develop a stakeholder model for corporate ethics and responsibility that considers current sustainable development. And it is here that stakeholder management is essential for developing a more sustainable company.

According to this conception of stakeholder theory, ethical principles for stakeholder justice emerge as important values in the dialogue between organizations and stakeholders (Donaldson & Dunfee, 1999). It can be said that the ethical vision of justice is the fundamental goal in stakeholder management. Making decisions according to the theory of business ethics implies a democratic concern. This means that open communication with company stakeholders is constitutive of the values-driven management of the firm (Driscoll & Hoffman, 2000). Realizing the sustainable development goals requires stakeholder management in close communication with relevant stakeholders.

The rationality of stakeholder management is therefore a deliberative rationality (Habermas, 1981). This is the same kind of rationality that we find in the political debate about the common good of society. The head of the company must then be open to the opinions of stakeholders as contributions to the common good of the company. To have universal validity, the normative theory of stakeholders is based on the theory of deliberative communication ethics from the German philosopher Jürgen Habermas (1981). This means respecting the best arguments and treating all dialogue partners with dignity and respect with special concern for the most vulnerable participants in the communicative stakeholder dialogue.

This communicative conception of stakeholder theory begins with a critique of the "shareholder" model of the company (Goodpaster, 1991). But, in fact, from a long-term profit point of view, this can be conceived as a theory which is basically very "pro-shareholder theory," because openness toward all stakeholders ensures greater solidity of the company, as Freeman often says (Freeman, 1984). According to such a conception of the company as constituted by efficiency, rational self-interest, and strategy based solely on individualism cannot ensure the economic growth of the company. Indeed, a pure market economy cannot exist, and the company is always located in a social context with a multitude of different stakeholders (Sen, 1999).

So, the liberal economy of free and fair competition must not only be based on a utilitarian conception of business. Stakeholder theory goes against the conceptions of the neoliberal economist Milton Friedman, for whom the "social responsibility of business is to increase its profits" (Friedman, 1971), because social responsibility implies an openness toward all the company's stakeholders (Wheeler & Sillanpää, 1997, p. 33). We must listen to the company's stakeholders if the company wants to survive in an environment of global competition in society. This is why stakeholder management manifests itself as a response to the expectations of social actors

(McIntosh et al., 1998; Rendtorff, 2018, 2019a, b). Moreover, this is a constitutive fact of the role of the relational dimension in stakeholder theory. And it is on this basis that stakeholder management becomes essential for managing the sustainable development goals.

Consequently, the concept of competitive strategy for industrial analysis by Michael Porter is not sufficient to bring the organization in line with the demand for sustainable development (Porter & Kramer, 2002, 2006, 2011). The concepts of traditional theory are based on an industrial view of the firm's position in society and have not really included the importance of the institutional environment for economic activity (North, 1990). What is important is the rational structure of the internal organization of the company. Michael Porter is particularly interested in the rational structure of the division of labor. It is a monist conception of company governance as a production relationship between management and employees which forgets the complexity of the company's relationships with its social and political environment. In the context of Relational Economics, Porter's concept of "creating shared value" (CSV) is considered to be an important, but not a sufficient, condition for describing the required interaction between business and society. It is therefore that Relational Economics works with "shared value creation" (SVC) as an improvement of Porter's vision of the relation between business and society. With this SVC understands the business corporation as a good citizen in society (Rendtorff, 2017).

We find a conception different from that of Porter in the theory of human resources and in the cultural conception of the company (Schein, 1992). With this we can develop an intercultural concept of SVC: This approach focuses on the needs and relationships between employees and tries to propose common values to integrate individuals into the organization. It is an approach which is aware of the need to find a harmonious relationship with the business environment (Wheeler & Sillanpää, 1997, p. 114). But this approach to organizational theory faces great difficulties in an era where individual employees, clients, and consumers are becoming more aware of their rights.

Therefore, a more complex design of the organization is necessary to understand the relational dimensions of interaction with stakeholders. Stakeholder theory from the perspective of Relational Economics could be based on a cybernetic and systemic conception of the concept of organization (Luhmann, 1979). Organizational systems are in constant interaction and interchange with their environment. To survive, they will have to take into consideration the information provided by the environment. It becomes necessary for the organization to interact with its environment to sense and control its position in the world (Frederick, 1995). This can help an organization to act when it encounters problems or when it is confronted with significant differences from the world around it (Wheeler & Sillanpää, 1997, p. 126).

In this perspective, the theory of stakeholders as constituting the company can be considered as a kind of organizational ecology where the organization—instead of being conceived as a bureaucratic and military entity—is considered as an inclusive company in constant interaction with its environment (Shaw & Barry, 1998). Stakeholders constitute the relational moment of the firm situating and embedding the firm in society (Rendtorff, 2018, 2019a, b, 2024a, b). This interaction contributes to the company's self-perception with a view to ensuring its survival and growth. Dialogue with stakeholders is designed as a learning process with a view to improving the reflexivity of the organization (Paine, 1997). This appears to be a fundamental condition for the organization with a view to learning how we could make progress with the focus on DiMaggio and Powell's "Learning how to Learn" (Wheeler & Sillanpää, 1997, p. 133).

By developing a formalized dialogue with stakeholders, it is possible to engage in a more intense and productive interaction with the business environment. This means that stakeholders are not only strategically defined as subjects and possible causes for corporate benefit or harm. Their interests are evaluated from the perspective of a vision of the common good, implied in the values of the company. Following up on our description of stakeholder concerns, Freeman's definition of stakeholders can illustrate this position: "A stakeholder in an organization is (by definition) any group or individual who can affect or is affected by the achievements of the organization's objectives" (Freeman, 1984). Everyone—even those who are silent—has a right to be listened to and included in the strategic management process. In other words, anyone who is a victim or beneficiary of the organization can be defined as a stakeholder. Stakeholders are any group or individual who stands to benefit from or suffer harm from activities and actions by the corporation, and all those whose rights are violated or respected by the actions of corporations (Freeman, 1999, p. 250).

It is extremely difficult to define the theoretical status of the different stakeholders since their interactive relations are defined in complex stakeholder webs (Freeman, 1984). But firstly, we can distinguish between (1) Voluntary and non-voluntary stakeholders—for example, owners and non-owners; (2) Primary and secondary stakeholders—for example, owners and customers; (3) External and internal stakeholders (e.g., employees and customers). Together, stakeholders form a web of interactive relations that determine the embeddedness of the firm in society.

Yet we can also consider a narrower definition of stakeholders: (1) A stakeholder is any group that is vital to the survival, success, or well-being of the business (2) Or one that helps define the organization, its mission, purpose, or role, and/or (3) Is primarily affected by the organization and its activities. Stakeholders may have different organizational roles in relation to the company and a different position within the company or outside the company. Management by stakeholders is based on the active integration of the different participants in the organization and therefore stakeholder management is an important part of the development of a strong Relational Economics.

This definition is symmetrical and not only strategic because it takes into consideration future changes in the company's strategy, involving duties in relation to new groups of stakeholders, and because it has a relationship to broader policy and strategy of the company. Stakeholders are considered participants in a communicative process of relational interactions which aims to ensure the growing legitimacy of the organization (Ulrich, 1998). It should be emphasized that the company is not an abstract entity but that it is located in a concrete context of duties and responsibilities. So, property rights cannot become a license and a right to ignore respect for the dignity of human persons (Freeman, 1984). Stakeholder management is closely related to the values of respect for the basic ethical principles of concern for human persons and human rights in a cosmopolitan context (Rendtorff, 2018; Rendtorff, 2020c). And therefore, stakeholder management is essential for the contributions of business firms to the realization of the sustainable development goals.

5 Stakeholders and the Recent Directives of the European Union

This use of stakeholder management as foundational for sustainable development can further be applied to the politics and legislative processes by the European Union, which can also be interpreted from the perspective of Relational Economics. Since the establishment of the internal market in 1992, the EU has worked purposefully on corporate responsibility and sustainability. The work on CSR was originally formulated as companies' voluntary contribution to society, which, by virtue of increased legitimacy, would also strengthen competitiveness. Later, CSR is defined as "impact" on society. The EU's new due diligence rules, i.e., the CSRD (Corporate Sustainability Reporting Directive) and CSDDD (Corporate Sustainability Due Diligence Directive) directives from 2023 to 2024, point out the connection between CSR and sustainability in the requirements for corporate ethics and responsibility. With these rules, the EU sharpens the consideration of sustainability as being central to companies' future development in society.

The EU is not only aware of the ethical responsibility with a focus on human rights and social responsibility, but it also highlights the responsibility of aesthetics and creativity for the green transition. Human well-being in body and soul must be the driving force in the green transition. This involves a combination of art, design, and economics. The EU Commission has highlighted the vision of the European Bauhaus as a central creative and artistic vision for the green transition. Concretely, one can mention green innovation in relation to, for example, the development of tasty organic food, trendy textile fashion, smart electric cars, and the idea of rewilding, where you let nature grow into the city. It is important that the company connects to this through creative innovation. It is in this context of a general policy of green transition that we should analyze the recent stakeholder initiative of the EU.

The political and legislative work of the EU on stakeholders and sustainability was inspired by the efforts of the influential UN human rights lawyer John Ruggie to develop business and human rights in the UN (Ruggie, 2013). The Ruggie principles are based on three pillars: protect, respect, and remedy. These principles have been the basis for 31 directives of business and human rights responsibilities. The EU has also continued to work on the texts of "Principes directeurs" of the Organisation for Economic Co-operation and Development (OECD) concerning principles of responsibility for multinational enterprises. Moreover, the ISO (International Standardization Organization) 26000 standards for CSR have been applied to develop the policy of the EU to enforce human rights and sustainability. It is in this context that the EU has developed its regulation on due diligence and stakeholder management of business corporations in reporting and in the supply chain. This regulation follows up on the French law on due diligence (La loi sur la vigilance): this law focuses on risks in relation to the human rights of stakeholders. It is considered by the EU to be the responsibility of corporations to have plans for coping with human rights risk in relation to internal and external stakeholders, including stakeholders in the supply chain.

The European directives are inspired by the French law on due diligence (Loi de la vigilance), (Art. L. 225-102-4.-I.), where the concept of stakeholders is explicitly mentioned with regard to the establishment of a due diligence plan in order to protect human rights. The law introduces the concept of stakeholder in the following sentence: "The plan is intended to be developed in association with society's stakeholders, where appropriate within the framework of multi-party initiatives within sectors or at the territorial level" (Art. L. 225-102-4.-I.). This means that the corporation should include stakeholders to help with the development of due diligence. The process of due diligence should be developed in close collaboration with relevant stakeholders. It will be up to the courts to decide to what extent a corporation follows this requirement. Nevertheless, following up on the French legislation in combination with the human rights principles of the UN, the concept of due diligence by the EU can be said to develop a concept of reasonable due diligence that proposes protection of stakeholders through a due diligence plan that ensures minimization of risk and protection of stakeholders by means of extended social responsibility of business throughout the supply chain. With this, the EU is moving closer to giving stakeholders a precise definition and place in the legal regulations of firms. The firm is not only defined by the shareholders but the EU policy work is moving toward a legal definition of the firm as a part of the relational constituencies of a business organization.

6 Normative Justification of Stakeholder Management

Accordingly, the stakeholder concept enters European directives as a tool to protect vulnerable people throughout the world who are affected by the corporation. This can be seen as the basis for a normative theory of protection of stakeholders. Therefore, it is important to discuss normative stakeholder theory from the perspective of Relational Economics in the following text.

In this context, it is important to distinguish normative theory from a descriptive theory of stakeholder identification (Rendtorff, 2018, 2019a, b). Normative theory concerns the reason why certain people or groups should be taken into consideration by executives and managers who must make decisions. The descriptive theory concerns those who can really count as stakeholders of the company (Mitchell et al., 1997), while normative theory moves beyond description and analyzes criteria for prioritization and selection of viewpoints by specific stakeholders in decision-making.

To establish a normative theory regarding justice in relation to stakeholders, we can ask the question, "How to give priority to different stakeholder demands?". Mitchell, Agle, and Wood attempted to answer this question. They believe that there are three forms of priority logic given to stakeholders that predominate in stakeholder theory: (1) the power of stakeholders to have influence on the company, (2) the legitimacy of the stakeholders' relationship with the company, and (3) the urgency of the requests from the company's stakeholders. With this, they propose the following stakeholder typology which can function as the basis for stakeholder salience: (1) dormant stakeholders (power); discretionary stakeholders (legitimacy); demanding stakeholders (urgency); dominant stakeholders (power/legitimacy); dangerous stakeholders (power/urgency); dependent stakeholders (urgency/legitimacy); definitive stakeholders (power/urgency/legitimacy); non-stakeholders (Mitchell et al., 1997). Thus, the concept of stakeholder salience is defined through the company's relations to the different stakeholders and therefore it presupposes the relational view of the economy.

Many people, groups, and institutions can count as stakeholders (Mitchell et al., 1997, p. 855). From a normative point of view, it is a theory of organizational governance whose goal is the moral integrity of the company (Paine, 1994). More concretely, the following groups could be counted among the stakeholders: "(1) Investors and shareholders, contributing to the economic activity of the company. (2) Managers and executives who are responsible for the daily management of the company. (3) Employees who are responsible for production and who receive their salary from the company. (4) The business partner with whom the company works. (5) The customers who guarantee the existence of the company. (6) The local community which supports and benefits from the company. (7) Civil society including NGOs and community political organizations. (8) The natural environment, including future human generations, nature, and animals, and their representatives among activists of different interest groups and organizations" (Wheeler & Sillanpää, 1997). All these are important stakeholders that must be included in the due diligence plan of the company.

Dialogue with all these stakeholders represents a way of cross-referencing the company's self-perception, but this does not necessarily include the interests of all possible stakeholder groups. It is an infinite process that opens a gradual movement toward the integration of all the interests represented by the different groups.

But we have not yet answered the difficult question of what is important to consider when managers must choose between the interests of different stakeholders (Badaracco Jr., 1997). Freeman's open definition largely leaves companies to define who their stakeholders are. By distinguishing between these different stakeholder concepts, we may be able to define primary and secondary stakeholders, which could help make Freeman's definition more usable for management. In this context, the relationship with basic economic relations as well as the social and political legitimacy of the company have been proposed to define who should be considered the most important stakeholders of the company (Ulrich & Maak, 1997; Rendtorff, 2020a).

Claiming to be a stakeholder does not necessarily imply that you have great power. This is why it is sometimes necessary to focus on stakeholders who claim to have real power rather than those who claim to have an interest in the company. Additionally, the distinction between current and potential stakeholders should be taken into consideration. In this context, we must not forget the importance of sleeping stakeholders. Current stakeholders may be less important than potential stakeholders because potential stakeholders may have much more power and influence over the business. Choosing between different criteria, we could indeed mention power and legitimacy as the most important criteria to define the selection between the different criteria (Mitchell et al., 1997, p. 862). Additionally, from the perspective of the choice theory of selecting the most important stakeholders, we can also mention urgency as an important element for stakeholder identification.

In one sense, legitimacy has to do with power but presupposes a broader definition of power which involves reference to groups or people who are considered to have power in society as such (Rendtorff, 2020a, b). Legitimate stakeholders are considered important to the authority of managerial decision-making. Legitimacy can be defined as a generalized perception or expression of the idea that an organization's actions are desirable or appropriate within a socially constructed system of norms, values, growth, and definitions (Mitchell et al., 1997, p. 867; Rendtorff, 2020a). Urgency is defined as an immediate need for reaction and action. Depending on the urgency, the importance of the different stakeholders can change considerably. Indeed, it is important that the stakeholders are variable, develop, and form with different degrees depending on their context and social development. This may be the cause of the change in the choice of different stakeholders. With this, we can develop a theory of the appropriate choice of relevant stakeholders in managerial decision-making.

7 Principles of Stakeholder Responsibility and Integrity of the Firm

This normative theory of stakeholder management can be proposed as the basis for a concept of stakeholder management for sustainable development taking into account the requirements of the UN and EU. A key idea is here that stakeholder interest converges over time. Ethical stakeholder management implies ethical judgment based on legitimacy. At the same time, stakeholder decision-making is based on communicative action (Habermas). Together these ideas contribute to a stakeholder-based approach to CSR, defined as corporate stakeholder responsibility. Freeman argues in this context for the integration of CSR and stakeholder theory with his theory about how we are supposed to see stakeholder theory as the real foundation for corporate social responsibility. Following Freeman, this means that there cannot be CSR without stakeholder theory.

Freeman's ten principles of stakeholder management are very important here for a relational view of stakeholder management as a contribution to Relational Economics. Freeman's ten stakeholder principles are defined as follows: "1) Stakeholder interests go together over time 2) Stakeholders consist of real people with names and faces and children. People are complex 3) We need solutions to issues that satisfy multiple stakeholders simultaneously 4) We need intensive communication and dialogue with stakeholders—not just those who are friendly 5) We need to have a philosophy of voluntarism, to manage stakeholder relationships ourselves rather than through third parties such as governments 6) We need to generalize the marketing approach 7) Everything that we do serves stakeholders. We never trade off the interests of one versus the other continuously over time 8) We negotiate with primary and secondary stakeholders 9) We constantly monitor and redesign processes to make them better serve our stakeholders 10) We act with purpose that fulfills our commitment to stakeholders. We act with aspiration towards fulfilling our dreams" (Freeman & Velamuri, 2006; Rendtorff, 2009, 2018).

These principles of stakeholder management demonstrate how stakeholder management contributes to the integration of business in society. Nevertheless, stakeholder theory has been criticized for not being able to maintain and create an objective goal of the corporation. Agency theorist Michael Jensen has maintained that stakeholder management provides the corporation with a multitude of goals. This leads to confusion, and, in the end, it makes it very difficult to run a business company. Therefore, Jensen is worried that stakeholder theory cannot have a clear ethical focus. Jensen argues that we have to go back to a "single objective theory" in order to understand the creation of value in the corporation (Jensen, 2002).

Later Jensen proposed integrity as an objective concept and a fact of the positive world of economics and business. It can be argued that it was the encounter with stakeholder theory that led to Jensen emphasizing that morality and ethics are an integrated part of this concept of integrity and quality of life. Jensen pointed at the importance of integrity in mainstream capitalism. He insisted on the connection between integrity and morality, and this was an important modification of his theory (Erhard et al., 2009).

It is interesting that Jensen argues that an objective concept of integrity is different from the ethical and moral concept of integrity as a virtue that was supposed to be subjective and relative to culture. With this positive approach to integrity as an objective fact in the world that can be considered as a workability concept, the author provides an important link between the ontological and ethical concepts of integrity. This contributes to defining an important link between positive economics and ethics and the morality of integrity in business (Erhard & Jensen, 2014).

Jensen insisted that without integrity nothing works, and he provided an important workability concept of integrity, emphasizing the close relation between accountability, promise (stick to your word), truthfulness, honesty, and trustworthiness as not only an important subjective moral virtue, but also as an objective ontological fact of how economic, social, and political systems function in a global world of cosmopolitan morality.

Jensen's critical insistence on the concept of integrity of the firm can be regarded as essential to stakeholder management. But how can integrity be combined with Relational Economics? Maybe, through the focus on wholeness and completeness. The ethical dimension of integrity is essential (Rendtorff, 2015, 2024b). Relations are not isolated but linked to each other in a comprehensive whole. Stakeholder management receives focus with the concept of integrity. Moreover, this is essential in Relational Economics. Therefore, it is important to link stakeholder management with key concepts of justice and fairness in the sense that stakeholder theory provides us with a theory of justice as fairness in organizations.

8 Equity, Justice, and Stakeholder Management

Accordingly, the relationship between corporate stakeholder responsibility, integrity, and the concept of the business corporation as a good citizen in society can be developed using the principle of fairness as the basis for conceptualizing justice and fair relationships with stakeholders (Rawls, 1971). Equity and justice are concrete realizations of the idea of the relationship of corporate social responsibility to stakeholders. In order to define the principles of equity and justice as the basis of relationships with stakeholders, we can mention Robert Philips' book *Stakeholder Theory and Organizational Ethics* (2003). Philips proposes a combination of stakeholder theory and the moral and political theory of John Rawls as the foundation of organizational ethics. The concept of justice as fairness can give us the link between the argument for the ideal concept of business as a good citizen and a republican ethical theory with a concrete definition of social responsibility. In combination with the concept of responsibility, the idea of justice as fairness is the basis for the legitimate treatment of stakeholders. As an ideal of organizational justice, fairness can help us to choose between other normative stakeholders on the one hand and emerging stakeholders or those who are not yet stakeholders on the other hand (Phillips, 2003; Rendtorff, 2018, 2019a, b; Rendtorff & Bonnafous-Boucher, 2023).

We can say that concern with justice should be seen as a way of increasing the common good for stakeholders, which is expressed in the idea of sustainable development (Elkington, 1999). This does not necessarily mean that all stakeholders should be treated in a similar way, but that there should at least be some sort of fairness in the treatment of different stakeholders in decision-making procedures in the business organization. A simplistic and egalitarian conception of justice as fairness is not entirely fair (Phillips, 2003, p. 28). Justice as fairness for stakeholders implies fairness in procedure rather than equality in distribution. I agree with Philips in proposing the argument that radical change in business law is not necessary to apply stakeholder theory in management practice. But I disagree with Philips when he says that the notion of stakeholder should not be interpreted in such a broad way as it is sometimes done in political affairs, for example, when Tony Blair, inspired by

Anthony Giddens, introduced the concept of "Stakeholder Economy" (Phillips, 2003, p. 32). Contrary to what Philips thinks, introducing the concept of stakeholder management as the basis of a theory of good corporate citizenship does not, in my opinion, necessarily result in an abuse of the overly ambiguous stakeholder concept, but rather is an important ideal for political governance.

Stakeholder theory becomes a relational way of accounting for the obligations of different organizations to different agents and constituents of society. From the perspective of Rawls' political philosophy, an organization is conceived as a voluntary association and not as a part of the fundamental structure of society. It is not only the company as such that can be a stakeholder even if the organization can have obligations to social actors which go beyond the obligations to shareholders (Phillips, 2003, p. 38). When we apply these determinations to develop the concept of "justice as fairness," we can make the argument that it, at the organizational level, is possible to apply Rawls' concept of "the original position" and "the veil of ignorance" and the "difference principle" (meaning that inequality is only justified if it is for the benefit of the worst off) (Phillips, 2003, p. 49).

According to Freeman and Rawls, we can say that the moral crux of the stakeholder theory of the firm as a nexus of stakeholders which is deduced from the difference principle is that justice as "fairness" in the organization implies that the constituent stakeholders like shareholders, customers, suppliers, employees, and the local community should be treated fairly, and inequality can only be justified to the extent that it contributes to improving the conditions of the weakest (Freeman, 1999, pp. 409–422). This is a consequence of the corporate citizenship agenda focusing on the social responsibility of the organization as a moral agent (French, 1984). Freeman is correct in proposing the argument that—with the case of the economic market—Rawls' difference principle can have a direct implication for fairness in relation to the fundamental stakeholders of the organization.

This implies that the constituent stakeholders of the organization are part of an original position in which they chose the fundamental principles as well as the principle of difference as the basis of organizational justice such as fairness. This perspective implies that questions of political and moral rights are introduced as a basis for understanding the constituents of the corporation (Ulrich, 1998). In this sense, a difficult question arises as to the justification of the absence of democratic politics in companies. This inequality should be justified as the basis of the difference principle which indicates the need for economic efficiency for the growth and prosperity of society. Yet there is also an argument against the so-called stakeholder paradox which states that an organization cannot have preferential duties to constituents other than shareholders, because this would eliminate the very concept of preferential duty as a result (Goodpaster, 1991; Phillips, 2003, p. 69).

In this sense, the application of the principle of fairness as the basis for fair action in the organization which acts on economic markets can be considered as the concern for "fair play"—a virtue of fair and just action that respects the rules of the game. We can find the concept of "fair play" in John Stuart Mill, who defines it as cooperative conduct with other people which will create new obligations of cooperative conduct and moral responsibility (Phillips, 2003, p. 86). This emerges as an ethical response to the danger of opportunism. According to Philips, the concept of fair play was already present in the early articles of John Rawls where he argued that "fair play" constitutes a request which gives mutual benefit and implies a fair pattern of cooperation in which people allow restrictions of their freedom in order to promote the common good. Under these conditions, it is their duty to cooperate to benefit everyone. We can say that "fair play" implies the responsibility of cooperation toward mutual and equal benefit when the demands of different stakeholders should be taken into consideration (Phillips, 2003, p. 116). Justice as fairness includes a reciprocal obligation to work for mutual benefit, and this constitutes stakeholder management as the foundation of business ethics and corporate social responsibility.

With this theory of justice in stakeholder managements, we can move from stakeholder justice to the contribution of business organizations to sustainable development in relation to the requirements of the UN and the EU. Here, we can define a new relational turn of stakeholder management in which the relational dimension receives increased attention. What we observe is that recent depictions of stakeholder management place the corporation not in the center but rather as a contributor, among others, to the common good. Corporations that no longer place themselves in the center of the stakeholder diagram do not consider themselves as central but focus on the contribution of the corporation to civil society and to community as such—this is the essence of the concept of "good corporate citizenship."

With this we can say that stakeholder management moves toward democracy. But is stakeholder democracy meaningful? How should we define a democratic company? Most private corporations do not operate with democratic inclusion, so how can we meaningfully talk about stakeholder democracy? Public corporations integrate stakeholder democracy and values-driven management, but very often they do not really make it come into reality. Accordingly, stakeholder management needs more attention to the basic dimensions of democracy to really realize the concept of democracy in stakeholder relations.

9 Common Good and Reflective Judgement

On this basis, stakeholder management can be considered as a response to the expectations of corporate citizenship and further as a relational contribution to the common good of society (Zadek, 2001; Rendtorff, 2018, 2019a, b). But stakeholder management is, in addition, legitimate from the perspective of strategic management because stakeholders have legitimate demands that should be treated fairly by organizations (Rendtorff, 2020a, b). This is why stakeholders who do not cooperate directly with companies and who therefore do not have direct normative relationships can be considered as fundamental constituents who have a derivative demand to be taken into consideration (Phillips, 2003, p. 124). So, with Philips, we can say that civil society organizations and the social activists in society can have legitimate expectations if they are representatives of the basic constituents of the company, for example, the employees or the local community (Phillips, 2003, p. 152).

To explain how we can mediate between concerns for different stakeholders we can ultimately emphasize practical reason and judgment as the basis for common action, both for good and just decisions regarding the good life as proposed by the philosopher Paul Ricœur following Aristotle and Immanuel Kant. When considering practical reason, Ricœur makes a combination between Aristotle and Kant (Ricœur, 1987, p. 232; Rendtorff, 2018, 2019a, b). Practical reason ensures respect for the demands of different stakeholders. But because of the possible exceptions to rules and the particularity of the situation, practical wisdom and judgment are demanded as a necessary supplement to practical reason.

Indeed, practical reason is required in exceptional situations of tragic dilemmas where legal rules are difficult to apply. So, to use the theory of judgment in the management of stakeholders, the different faculties of human reason help to mediate between different interests in relation to the ideal of the good life, to the principles of universal morality, and to concrete situations and social decision-making challenges. The Kantian notion of judgment is an effort to mediate between formalist principles and the concrete situations of divergent interests with a view to finding the best and most rational decision. Ricœur defines judgment as a peaceful way of resolving social conflicts, where the individual execution of subjectivist conceptions of justice is replaced by neutral and codified procedures (Ricœur, 1992). General understandings and principles of justice are applied to concrete situations.

This concept of judgment is very important for stakeholder management. Concern for the stakeholder converges over time, as Edward Freeman said. Reflective judgment is essential for the stakeholder issue. Therefore, we can say that the principles of autonomy, dignity, integrity, and vulnerability in the context of stakeholder justice can have great importance and application in business ethics (Rendtorff & Kemp, 2000; Rendtorff, 2017, 2018). In addition, the ideas of sustainable development, responsibility, and justice, but also concern for the community, are not only theoretical visions but also practical measures for social responsibility in stakeholder management (Rendtorff, 2019a, b, c). Judgment is required for reflective thinking about good judgment in Relational Economics. There is much work to be done regarding the application of principles and values from the perspective of reflective judgment. In this sense, ethical principles have great importance in the field of business ethics and in the context of the practice of management by values in Relational Economics.

10 Conclusion

This chapter has discussed stakeholder management and Relational Economics with focus on justice and sustainability in business. It turns out that stakeholder management is an important part of the relational view of the firm as a nexus of stakeholders. Relational Economics considers the firm to be situated and embedded in networks of polycontextuality, polyvalence, and polylinguism in complex societies. Stakeholder management contributes significantly to shared value creation in these complex systems of social interaction. With recent developments of sustainability in the UN and the EU with a focus on CSRD and CSDDD, there has been an increasing need for stakeholder management of the firm as situated in social relations. The sustainable development goals of the United Nations *2030 Transforming our World Agenda* produce a vision for stakeholder management of sustainable business models for the integration of local and global economy. This later became the basis for the EU's work with the green transition and the directives of the CSRD and CSDDD. We can therefore see a general challenge for stakeholder management to deal with stakeholder challenges of due diligence and stakeholder justice with a focus on global goals and sustainability. In this environment of complex social relations, the Relational Economy of stakeholder management is of great significance for the development of a more just and sustainable society.

References

Ansoff, L. (1965). Corporate strategy. In A. C. Martinet (2010), Strategic planning, strategic management, strategic foresight: The seminal work of H. Igor Ansoff. *Technological Forecasting and Social Change, 77*(9), 1485–1487.

Badaracco, J. F., Jr. (1997). *Defining moments: When managers must choose between right and right*. Harvard Business School Press.

Bonnafous-Boucher, M., & Pesqueux, Y. (2006). *Décider avec les parties prenantes. Collection Recherches*. La Découverte.

Bonnafous-Boucher, M., & Rendtorff, J. D. (2013). *Théorie des parties prenantes*. La Découverte. English translation: Rendtorff, J. D. (2013).

Bonnafous-Boucher, M., & Rendtorff, J. D. (2016). *Stakeholder theory. A model for strategic management* (Springer Briefs in Ethics). Springer.

DiMaggio, P. J., & Powell, W. W. (Eds.). (1991). *The new institutionalism and organizational analysis*. University of Chicago Press.

Donaldson, T., & Dunfee, T. W. (1999). *Ties that bind: A social contracts approach to business ethics*. Harvard Business School Press.

Driscoll, D. M., & Hoffman, W. M. (2000). *Ethics matters: How to implement values-driven management*. Centre for Business Ethics, Bentley College.

Elkington, J. (1999). *Cannibals with forks: The triple bottom line of 21st century business*. Capstone.

Erhard, W., & Jensen, M. C. (2014). *Putting integrity into finance: A purely positive approach* (No. w19986). National Bureau of Economic Research.

Erhard, W., Jensen, M. C., & Zaffron, S. (2009). Integrity: A positive model that incorporates the normative phenomena of morality, ethics, and legality. Harvard Business School NOM Working Paper No. 06-11 Barbados Group Working Paper No. 06-03 Simon School Working Paper No. FR 08-05.

Frederick, W. C. (1995). *Values, nature and culture in the American corporation*. Basil Blackwell.

Freeman, R. E. (1984). *Strategic management: A stakeholder approach*. Pitman Publishing.

Freeman, R. E. (1999). The stakeholder corporation. In L. Pincus Hartman (Ed.), *Business ethics* (pp. 137–147). University of Chicago Press.

Freeman, R. E., & Velamuri, S. R. (2006). A new approach to CSR: Company stakeholder responsibility. In A. Kakabadse & M. Morsing (Eds.), *Corporate social responsibility* (pp. 9–23). Palgrave Macmillan. https://doi.org/10.1057/9780230599574_2

French, P. (1984). *Collective and corporate responsibility*. Columbia University Press.

Friedman, M. (1971). The social responsibility of business is to increase its profits. *The New York Times Magazine*.

Goodpaster, K. E. (1991). Business ethics and stakeholder analysis. *Business Ethics Quarterly, 1*(1), 53–73.

Habermas, J. (1981). *Theorie des kommunikativen Handelns I–II*. Suhrkamp Verlag.

Hildebrandt, S. (2016). *Bæredygtig global udvikling: FN's 17 verdensmål i et dansk perspektiv*. Jurist- og Økonomforbundets Forlag.

Jensen, M. C. (2002). Value maximization, stakeholder theory, and the corporate objective function. *Business Ethics Quarterly, 12*(2), 235–256.

Luhmann, N. (1979). *Trust and power: Two essays*. Wiley.

McIntosh, M., Leipziger, D., Jones, K., & Coleman, G. (1998). *Corporate citizenship: Successful strategies for responsible companies*. Financial Times Pitman Publishing.

Mitchell, R. K., Agle, B. R., & Wood, D. J. (1997). Toward a theory of stakeholder identification and salience: Defining the principle of who and what really counts. *Academy of Management Review, 22*(4), 853–886.

North, D. C. (1990). *Institutions, institutional change and economic performance*. Cambridge University Press.

Paine, L. S. (1994). Managing for organizational integrity. *Harvard Business Review, 72*(2), 106–117.

Paine, L. S. (1997). *Cases in leadership, ethics and organizational integrity: A strategic perspective*. Irwin.

Phillips, R. (2003). *Stakeholder theory and organizational ethics*. Berrett-Koehler Publishers.

Phillips, R., Freeman, R. E., & Wicks, A. C. (2003). What stakeholder theory is not. *Business Ethics Quarterly, 13*(4), 479–502.

Porter, M. E., & Kramer, M. R. (2002). The competitive advantage of corporate philanthropy. *Harvard Business Review, 80*(12), 56–68.

Porter, M. E., & Kramer, M. R. (2006). The link between competitive advantage and corporate social responsibility. *Harvard Business Review, 84*(12), 78–92.

Porter, M. E., & Kramer, M. R. (2011). Creating shared value. *Harvard Business Review, 89*(1/2), 62–77.

Rawls, J. (1971). *A theory of justice*. Harvard University Press.

Rendtorff, J. D. (1998). The Second International Conference about Bioethics and Biolaw: European principles in bioethics and biolaw. *Medicine, Health Care and Philosophy, 1*(3), 271–274.

Rendtorff, J. D. (2009). *Responsibility, ethics and legitimacy of corporations*. Copenhagen Business School Press.

Rendtorff, J. D. (2011). Institutionalization of corporate ethics and social responsibility programs in firms. In K. Buhmann, L. Roseberry, & M. Morsing (Eds.), *Corporate social and human rights responsibilities: Global, legal and management perspectives* (pp. 244–266). Palgrave Macmillan.

Rendtorff, J. D. (2013a). Basic concepts of philosophy of management and corporations. In C. Luetge (Ed.), *Handbook of the philosophical foundations of business ethics* (pp. 1361–1386). Springer Science+Business Media.

Rendtorff, J. D. (2013b). Philosophical theories of management and corporations. In C. Luetge (Ed.), *Handbook of the philosophical foundations of business ethics* (pp. 1409–1432). Springer Science+Business Media.

Rendtorff, J. D. (2013c). Recent debates in philosophy of management. In C. Luetge (Ed.), *Handbook of the philosophical foundations of business ethics* (pp. 1433–1457). Springer Science+Business Media.

Rendtorff, J. D. (2013d). The history of the philosophy of management and corporations. In C. Luetge (Ed.), *Handbook of the philosophical foundations of business ethics* (pp. 1387–1408). Springer Science+Business Media.
Rendtorff, J. D. (2014a). Risk management, banality of evil, and moral blindness in organizations and corporations. In C. Luetge & J. Jauernig (Eds.), *Business ethics and risk management* (Vol. 43, pp. 45–70). Springer Science+Business Media.
Rendtorff, J. D. (2014b). European perspectives. In H. A. M. J. ten Have & B. Gordijn (Eds.), *Handbook of global bioethics* (pp. 293–310). Springer Science+Business Media.
Rendtorff, J. D. (2015). Business ethics, strategy, and organizational integrity: The importance of integrity as a basic principle of business ethics that contributes to better economic performance. In *Handbook of research on business ethics and corporate responsibilities* (pp. 91–105). IGI Global.
Rendtorff, J. D. (2017). Creating shared value as institutionalization of ethical responsibilities of the business corporation as a good corporate citizen in society. In J. Wieland (Ed.), *Creating shared value: Concepts, experience, criticism* (Vol. 52, pp. 119–139). Springer. https://doi.org/10.1007/978-3-319-48802-8_7
Rendtorff, J. D. (2018). *Cosmopolitan business ethics: Towards a global ethos of management.* Routledge.
Rendtorff, J. D. (2019a). *Philosophy of management and sustainability: Rethinking business ethics and social responsibility in sustainable development.* Emerald.
Rendtorff, J. D. (2019b). Sustainable development goals and progressive business models for economic transformation. *Local Economy, 34*(6), 510–524.
Rendtorff, J. D. (Ed.). (2020a). *Handbook of business legitimacy: Responsibility, ethics and society.* Springer VS. https://doi.org/10.1007/978-3-319-68845-9
Rendtorff, J. D. (2020b). *Moral blindness in business: A social theory of evil in organizations and institutions.* Palgrave Macmillan.
Rendtorff, J. D. (2020c). Corporate citizenship, stakeholder management, and Sustainable Development Goals (SDGs) in financial institutions and capital markets. *J Capital Markets Stud, 4*(1), 47–59. https://doi.org/10.1108/JCMS-06-2020-0021
Rendtorff, J. D. (2024a). The new ethical values of the relational market economy: Value change in the private business world and the movement towards Sustainable Development Goals in business and economics. In J. Wieland, S. Linder, J. G. Schwengber, & A. Zicari (Eds.), *Cooperation in value-creating networks: Relational perspectives on governing social and economic value creation in the 21st century* (pp. 21–36). Springer. https://doi.org/10.1007/978-3-031-50718-2_2
Rendtorff, J. D. (2024b). Organisational integrity, citizenship, and legitimacy. In M. Kaptein (Ed.), *Research handbook on organisational integrity* (1st ed., pp. 497–510). Edward Elgar Publishing.
Rendtorff, J. D., & Bonnafous-Boucher, M. (Eds.). (2023). *Encyclopedia of stakeholder management* (Elgar Encyclopedias in Business and Management series, 1st ed.). Edward Elgar Publishing. https://doi.org/10.4337/9781800374249.
Rendtorff, J. D., & Kemp, P. (2000). *Basic ethical principles in European bioethics and biolaw.* Center for Ethics and Law.
Ricœur, P. (1987). *Du texte à l'action.* Le Seuil.
Ricœur, P. (1992). *L'acte de juger.* Esprit, juillet 1992.
Ruggie, J. G. (2013). *Just business: Multinational corporations and human rights* (Norton Global Ethics series). W. W. Norton & Company.
Sachs, J. D. (2012). From millennium development goals to sustainable development goals. *The Lancet, 379*(9832), 2206–2211.
Sachs, J. D. (2015). *The age of sustainable development.* Columbia University Press.
Schein, E. H. (1992). *Organizational culture and leadership* (2nd ed.). Jossey-Bass Publishers.
Scott, W. R. (2008). *Institutions and organizations: Ideas and interests.* Sage Publications.
Sen, A. (1999). *Development as freedom.* Harvard University Press.

Shaw, W. H., & Barry, V. (1998). *Moral issues in business* (7th ed.). Wadsworth Publishing Company.

Ulrich, P. (1998). *Integrative Wirtschaftsethik: Grundlagen einer lebensdienlichen Ökonomie* (2nd ed.). Haupt Verlag.

Ulrich, P., & Maak, T. (1997). *Integrative business ethics – A critical approach* (CEMS Business Review, 2, pp. 27–36). Kluwer Academic Publishers.

United Nations. (2018a). *Transforming our world: The 2030 agenda for sustainable development.* https://sustainabledevelopment.un.org/post2015/transformingourworld/publication. Accessed 30 Aug 2018.

United Nations. (2018b). *United Nations global compact.* https://www.unglobalcompact.org/. Accessed 30 Aug 2018.

van Zanten, J. A., & van Tulder, R. (2018). Multinational enterprises and the Sustainable Development Goals: An institutional approach to corporate engagement. *Journal of International Business Policy, 1*(3–4), 208–223.

Wheeler, D., & Sillanpää, M. (1997). *The stakeholder corporation: The Body Shop blueprint for maximizing stakeholder value.* Pitman Publishing.

Wieland, J. (1989). *Die Entdeckung der Ökonomie: Kategorien, Gegenstandsbereiche und Rationalitätstypen der Ökonomie an ihrem Ursprung.* Haupt.

Wieland, J. (1993). *Formen der Institutionalisierung von Moral in der Unternehmung: Die amerikanische Business-Ethics-Bewegung: Why and how they do it.* Haupt.

Wieland, J. (1996). *Ökonomische Organisation, Allokation und Status.* Mohr Siebeck.

Wieland, J. (1999). *Die Ethik der Governance* (Metropolis-Reihe "Studien zur Governanceethik" Band 1, 5th ed.). Metropolis.

Wieland, J. (2005). *Normativität und Governance* (Metropolis-Reihe "Studien zur Governanceethik" Band 3). Metropolis.

Wieland, J. (2011). The firm as a nexus of stakeholders: Stakeholder management and theory of the firm. In A. Brink (Ed.), *Corporate governance and business ethics* (Vol. 39, pp. 143–162). Springer. https://doi.org/10.1007/978-94-007-1588-2_10

Wieland, J. (2013). *Shared value durch stakeholder governance* (with A. E. H. Heck). Metropolis.

Wieland, J. (2014). *Governance ethics: Global value creation, economic organization and normativity* (Ethical economy. Studies in economic ethics and philosophy). Springer.

Wieland, J. (2020). *Relational economics: A political economy.* Springer.

Williamson, O. E. (1995). *The economic institutions of capitalism.* Simon and Schuster.

World Commission on Environment and Development. (1987). *Our common future.* Oxford University Press.

Zadek, S. (2001). *The civil corporation: The new economy of corporate citizenship.* Earthscan.

Jacob Dahl Rendtorff is a professor of philosophy of management and business ethics at the Department of Business and Social Sciences, Roskilde University, Denmark. Rendtorff's research has a broad perspective on organization theory, management, responsibility, ethics and legitimacy of business firms and corporations, corporate social responsibility, business ethics, and philosophy of law.

Cooperative Economics and Management and Abolitionist Relationality

Jerome Nikolai Warren

Abstract This chapter explores Cooperative Economics and Management (CEM), connecting it with Relational Economics (RE) to highlight how both approaches contribute to understanding cooperation and cooperative enterprises. The paper aims to elucidate CEM's addition to RE by emphasizing three epistemological bases RE, moral economy, and abolitionism. These foundations are examined through their relevance to long-term stakeholder cooperation, the role of collective agency in social upheavals, and the abolition of unfree labor. The synthesis of these traditions fosters a humanist and community-oriented economic model, relevant to both the global cooperative movement and traditional enterprises. The paper details how CEM's narrower focus on relationality, democratic self-governance, and moral economy enhances cooperative enterprise analysis. It differentiates CEM from RE by its abolitionist stance, emphasizing voluntary cooperation over coercive relationships. The integration of these concepts produces a robust framework for understanding economic and organizational cooperation, particularly within cooperative enterprises. Methodological approaches such as innovative accounting, organizational democracy measures, and social network analysis (SNA) are discussed to capture the dynamics of cooperative enterprises. The paper concludes by underscoring the significance of CEM in advancing cooperative and sustainable business practices.

Keywords Cooperative economics · Relational Economics · Cooperative enterprise · Moral economy · Abolitionism · Democratic self-governance · Stakeholder cooperation · Innovative accounting · Social network analysis

---

J. N. Warren (✉)
Académie Royale des Sciences, des Lettres et des Beaux-Arts de Belgique, Brussels, Belgium
e-mail: jerome.warren@uclouvain.be

J. D. Rendtorff et al. (eds.), *Advances in Relational Economics*, Relational Economics and Organization Governance,
https://doi.org/10.1007/978-3-031-75725-9_6

1 Introduction

This chapter seeks to orient readers regarding numerous approaches derivative of "Cooperative Economics and Management" (CEM). Connecting scholarship on cooperation in general, especially including relational approaches as exemplified by Relational Economics (RE) with cooperative enterprise in particular, CEM connects existing research communities within economics, management, and adjacent disciplines studying cooperation and cooperative enterprise. Therefore, one of the goals of this chapter, which is largely a derivative explication of various main theses within Warren et al. (2024), is to help readers understand what CEM adds to RE by emphasizing three epistemological bases on which CEM research rests. In outlining these three bases, it hopes thereby to enlarge the "exoteric thought collective" (Fleck, 1994) that both approaches share, thereby hopefully stimulating and challenging further dialogue and debate.

The chapter argues that these three bases can be located at the intersection of three distinct research trends. Firstly, the domain of RE, with its focus on the prerequisites for long-term cooperation between different stakeholders in producing relational goods, transactions, contracts, and forms of management. Secondly, the tradition of the *moral economy*, originating with the historian E.P Thompson in his analysis of the role of groups in guiding social upheavals in eighteenth-century England and whose task is to locate agency in groups or collectives. Thirdly, an augmentation of these two research strands by connecting them with the tradition of Abolitionism, an intellectual and political movement whose formal origins date to the goal of abolishing slavery, but which also contains strands seeking to abolish any kind of unfree labor, including the traditional labor contract (Ellerman, 2021b). The chapter outlines how these three traditions in dialogue are producing—and will increasingly continue to produce—new knowledge that strengthens the impetus for an economic model in keeping with both humanist ambitions (Novković et al., 2023) and an extended notion of community that includes the "more-than-human" world (e.g., nature) (Raworth, 2017). It will conclude by pointing out the relevance of this synthesis especially for the global cooperative movement but will also emphasize the significance for "traditional" enterprises dealing with the challenges of the knowledge and information economy. It will do this especially by emphasizing the methodological distinctions entailed by research emanating from such a perspective.

The chapter proceeds as follows. In Sect. 2, it begins by summarizing the three main epistemological bases of CEM, beginning with reviewing key concepts of RE. After explaining how CEM requires a narrower notion of "relationality" in Sect. 3, it introduces the other two primary concepts: the tradition of Abolitionism in its problematization of the "insider–outsider" relationship and the "moral economy" in Sects. 4 and 5, respectively. Following this discussion, in Sect. 6, it summarizes the analytical implications of the preceding discussion, before reviewing numerous methodological approaches able to capture the demands of "abolitionist relationality" and "moral economy" in Sect. 7. Section 8 features a discussion, and Sect. 9 is a conclusion.

2 Relational Economics

Networks lie at the center of an extended notion of economics and are central to much of modern organizational science (Biggiero et al., 2022). Networks, emphasizing the structural dimensions of relationality (typically territorial and sectoral) between individuals, groups, and organizations, are especially important in contemporary supply chains, knowledge diffusion, and innovation clusters. Relationships between individuals are also mediated by networks. They are therefore vital to understanding cooperation in firms as well as between them. In many advanced economies, for instance, Belgium, it is not institutions but networks of individuals that reveal trajectories and horizons of possibility for investment, research and development, and similar domains (Tödtling & Kaufmann, 1999).

RE is a relatively new approach to economics, political economy, accounting, management, and related disciplines that emphasizes long-term cooperation in knowledge and network-based (network) economies (Biggiero et al., 2022). One of RE's aims is to move beyond so-called Transaction Cost Economics (TCE), a field quite close to mainstream economics which focuses on transaction costs as levers for economic (dis)advantage. TCE is exemplified by (Williamson, 2007). As opposed to this focus, RE attempts to look not only at the costs but also the *benefits* of cooperation. It does this by developing concepts such as "relational rent" and analyzing increasing *willingness, opportunities*, and *ability* for cooperation (Wieland, 2018).

Moreover, RE emphasizes the relational dimension as well in the intersection of logics, an approach analytically distinct but orthogonal to Polanyi's "embedding." In an RE interpretation, given by Wieland (2018), it isn't via re-embedding a social sphere into an economic one that one gets, for example, occupational health and safety regulations or corporate social responsibility (CSR) policies, but through stepwise processes of blending and mixing an economic metric of profits–losses with metrics like "common good–private interests" or "engagement–non-engagement" (Wieland, 2018, p. 93). According to RE, "modern value creation is achieved by interlinking the resources of stakeholders originating from multiple economic as well as social systems and organisations" (Biggiero et al., 2022, p. 10). For instance, an RE perspective on cooperatives would not argue that cooperative enterprises belong to a "third" or "non-profit" sector but instead would interpret them as enterprises specializing in a particular type of mixing and blending, one specifically combining the metric of "profits–losses" with a broadened notion of membership and a mandate for democratic governance of the enterprise.

The outcome of this process of mixing is an emerging epistemological view generating concepts such as relational goods, relational rents, relational contracts, and relational governance.

Relational goods are goods that, by their nature, necessitate a shift in perspective from "standard economics [, which] essentially shows us a purified 'thing-to-thing' world, in which there are no actor-to-actor relations" (Wieland, 2018, p. 35) to a perspective embracing moral goods, a term associated, among others, with Kenneth

Arrow. Relational goods cannot simply be reduced to instrumentality (Wieland, 2018). For instance, a relational good may arise due to intrinsic motivation, or by a "unit of difference between economic and moral coding." This means that relational goods are goods, but not commodities, meaning they have a value, but usually no price. An example described by Wieland is the atmosphere at a football match. Such events involve both issues of status (such as being a fan of a particular team) and esteem (perhaps the intensity of one's conviction, as measured in the percent of the body covered in the team's colors), which are notoriously difficult to attribute discrete value to (Brennan et al., 2004).

A relational rent refers to a jointly produced profit (i.e., a profit that could not have been generated in isolation). The idea merges the Ricardian notion of rent with the ability, opportunity, and willingness to cooperate. Transcultural skills or shared meanings in heterogeneous settings, for instance, contribute to such a rent (by generating new conditions for exploiting resources) (Schwengber & Kindlein, 2021, pp. 250). Meanwhile, relational contracts are thus "functional equivalents of formal contracts and hierarchy in a setting characterized by uncertainty" (pp. 43–44). They therefore include numerous "structural" dimensions, especially including informal dimensions for instance present in cooperative contracts (Fici et al., 2013; Warren, 2023).

Relational governance refers to the fact that, in governance relations, formal and informal mechanisms and logics interact and are not independent. Relational governance, as Josef Wieland emphasizes regarding this formal-informal distinction, does not refer to "self-enforcement." That is, the focus "lies in the mechanism of their enforcement" (Wieland, 2018, p. 43). In other words, relational governance consists of a "suitable proportioning of multiple governance forms" (Wieland, 2018, p. 43). This proportioning is necessary to ensure continued coöperation among a firm's stakeholders. Therefore, RE "is a constitutively process-oriented and interdisciplinary political economy [. . .] interested in the interaction of economic, legal, technical, political, cultural and moral events and language games, which constitute the process and success of economic transactions" (Biggiero et al., 2022, p. 12).

3 Moving Beyond Mere "Relationality"

In a way, one could say that Cooperative Economics and Management (CEM) is a more specific derivative of RE. Similar to RE, CEM also abandons the domain of "spot" transactions to emphasize the importance of relationships in analyzing and interpreting cooperation in economy and organization. It is also, similar to RE, invested in processes and relationships and is engaged in analyzing the role of networks in acting as facilitator or hindrance to cooperation.

However, some distinctions also exist between RE and CEM, which emerge from the more specific normative context of CEM. RE, for instance, is concerned with the notion of creating shared value, which it opposes to an analytically poorer concept, "shared value creation"; this is largely an epistemological shift that, while correct, does little to positively contribute to advancing a robust understanding of the suitable tools and processes that can best facilitate the creation of shared value, or in helping define value or "what counts." Meanwhile, CEM in general departs from an idea of the dignity of labor, which can lead to an instrumentalization of the idea of value-creation itself, for instance, among social cooperatives or as embodied in the Mondragon cooperatives' principle of seeing capital as an instrument (Warren, 2023). In other words, while RE is at its root relational, CEM is additionally also *abolitionist* (Ellerman, 2021b).[1]

Moreover, one could argue that concepts such as "relationality" are still too vague to generate a coherent research approach without further specification (for instance, of the type of relationship). Therefore, CEM scholarship is generally not satisfied with the term "relationality." While it is a useful starting point, CEM scholarship generally carries out theory-building and testing in the context of really-existing cooperative enterprises as an ideal-typical case of an abolitionist relationality.[2]

What does the distinction between "pure" and abolitionist relationality mean in practice? Recent contributions to CEM see the distinction as having two main implications (Warren et al., 2024). Firstly, abolitionist relationality problematizes the "insider"–"outsider" relationship that cooperative enterprise has historically posed. This extends naturally to the relationship between workers and the firm, the latter interpreted as a kind of social organism, with the worker cooperative standing as the cornerstone model of the cooperative enterprise (Ellerman, 2021a; Dow, 2018). Nevertheless, recent discussions on technology and automation reveal similar questions regarding the insider–outsider relationship with respect to online platforms with respect to their users, among other contexts (Bauwens & Kostakis, 2014; Schneider & Mannan, 2020).

This means that the "relational transactions" that RE speaks of take a distinct dimension in the context of cooperative enterprise. One even speaks of "patronage," "cooperative contracts," or "cooperative acts" (Fici et al., 2013; Warren, 2023). However, as multiple entries in the CEM literature point out, phenomena like multi-stakeholder cooperatives already signify relationships beyond "patronage" or a strict (even extended) insider–outsider dichotomy (Lund & Novkovic, 2023). These notions place much of CEM in a "transgressive" camp that goes beyond contractual or ownership relations (Sacchetti & Borzaga, 2020).

The second distinction between "pure" and abolitionist relationality is implicit in CEM's epistemological emphasis on group action, sometimes called "moral economy." This refers to the fact that cooperatives traditionally consist of self-managed groups of members. Therefore, the ideal cooperative must develop processes and mechanisms not only to manage the creation of shared value but must

[1] In the sense of promoting self-determination, autonomy, and self-management not only among members of existing cooperatives and their members, but in advocating for and disseminating the model broadly, as was the case for cooperative pioneers like Robert Owen Cole (1930).

[2] Vieta (2019) speaks of a process involving "struggle" in recuperating enterprises for workers in Argentina.

simultaneously balance the commercial needs of the company with the mandate of democratic management, which also makes the cooperative a community, as Draheim (1952) noted (Puusa & Hokkila, 2015).

In other words, while RE deals broadly with "relational governance," CEM constrains this notion further to refer to democratic or self-governance, which in the literature is also called self-management (Dolgoff, 1974; Vieta, 2019). This can mean different things in practice and should not be confused with the idea that cooperatives have no hierarchy and operate only on the basis of consensus (Dow, 2018). The question of moral economy immediately imposes the need for legitimacy and responsibility. It also raises the question of balancing the needs of members, both individually and collectively, with the needs of more or less broad notions of community outside the enterprise.

For instance, one can certainly speak of "relationality" in the Sicilian mafia. Indeed, when asking the question of how the mafia enforces cooperation among its members, the answer is that, in many ways, it does so similarly to how a cooperative, a church group, or a large company does so: by harnessing the power of networks. However, what in the case of the mafia, and some would argue in the traditional company (Ellerman, 2021b), is a coercive relationship that should at least theoretically be voluntary in a cooperative or church group. This means that not only are networks fundamentally important for both describing and explaining cooperation but also their differential structure, including practical relationships such as seniority, is important for distinguishing between different qualities or types of networks.

Therefore, as opposed to supporting the idea of a sort of essentialism, abolitionist relationality demands that all firms exist along a kind of spectrum. What distinguishes firms along the axis is the existence and intensity of a set of rules and constraints, in short, embodied relationships, in part manifested in cooperative principles, but also living practices, so-called "change rules" (Tilebein, 2006) and complex of connections between non-members and members, etc., that make a "difference that makes a difference" in terms of rendering management both reflective, of and responsive to, the groups comprising an organization.

4 Abolitionism, Cooperatives, and the "Insider–Outsider" Dichotomy

The history and practice of cooperative enterprises in itself gives the first specification over and against RE. The emergence of cooperative enterprise as a distinct "genotype" to the traditional factory system in the wake of the French Revolution (Cole, 1930, p. 55) has revived a discussion on "belonging" (membership) that has links to the abolitionist struggle to end slavery and that, in many ways, dates back at least to the Middle Ages, with roots in ancient practices, as legal historian Otto von Gierke has argued (von Gierke, 1868). This discussion, ongoing to the present day, problematizes the "inside–outside" relationship in organizations with respect to their members, which occurs within cooperative enterprises and which, as mentioned above, can be quite distinct from the notion of ownership.

In fact, the adherence of cooperatives to an abolitionist relationality can be seen in the following codex of seven principles promoted by the International Cooperative Alliance:

1. Voluntary and open membership;
2. Democratic member participation;
3. Member economic participation;
4. Autonomy and independence;
5. Education, training, and information;
6. Cooperation among cooperatives; and
7. Concern for community (ICA, 1995).

Similarly, the ten Mondragon principles, which in addition to the above seven also include principles like "participation in management," "wage solidarity," "sovereignty of labor," and "social transformation" (Altuna Gabilondo, 2008) even more clearly embody an abolitionist relationality.

Additionally, several philosophical traditions have historically promoted ethical and ontological perspectives that are closely related to an abolitionist sense of relationality. This arguably includes Hegel (Buck-Morss, 2009) and a tradition of thinkers influenced by him, including Marx, in concepts like alienation and emancipation, and Nietzsche, in concepts like the will to power.[3] Bringing such traditions into contact with biological theories has led to numerous theories suggesting cooperation as something that occurs quite naturally in human societies (Wilson & Wilson, 2007; De Waal, 2006). This synthesis saw and has seen cooperation as an evolutionarily progressive set of practices and behaviors that can be found at least in rudimentary forms in other species and which is influenced by human language and our capacity for abstraction, both with reference to relationships of time, but also with reference to what Cornelius Castoriadis called "the imaginary" (Castoriadis, 1987). It finds its early exponents in pioneers such as Robert Owen and Pyotr Kropotkin.

Robert Owen (1771–1858), a Welsh industrialist who founded several experimental productive communities, including in New Lanark and New Harmony, is frequently considered a patron saint of the cooperative movement. Owen, for his part, believed not only that "I can make manufacturing pay without reducing those whom I employ to misery and moral degradation" but also "went far beyond other employers who built up industrial villages centered round their works" in holding to a view of human nature "that man is a creature of his environment, and that,

[3]These traditions are too diverse and deep to fully summarize here. For the connection between Nietzsche and abolitionism, cf., for example, Deleuze and Guattari (2009). For connections between Marx and abolition, see, for example, the work of Jossa (2019) or Wolff (2012). For an attempt to connect the two, see Roberts (2019).

according as his material and moral surroundings are good or bad, so will his nature and character be good or bad" (Cole, 1930, pp. 14–15). Therefore, Owen invested particularly in educating the resident workers of his productive communities, including both adults and children (Cole, 1930; Davis & O'Hagan, 2014).

Pytor Kropotkin (1842–1921), a Russian nobleman and political radical, was both critical of Social Darwinism and interested in the reality and theory of cooperation, carrying out early ethnographic, ecological, and anthropological studies of cooperation in human, plant, and animal communities (Kropotkin, 1998; Kinna, 1992; Warren, 2022b) at the same time as he wrote a book on an evolutionary ethic based on established habits of cooperation (Kropotkin, 2021).

In later iterations, this line of thinking adopted clear influence from ecosystem science and computational science, e.g., in the work of Herbert Simon (Simon, 1990; Biggiero et al., 2022, p. 55). Nevertheless, Simon's work never truly extended beyond viewing firms as places of coordination, not cooperation (Simon, 1991).

Just as Kropotkin saw a dynamic, evolutionary cooperative ethic at work in communities during his ethnographic studies in Siberia, the cooperative form challenges fixed notions of so-called "stakeholder theory" as espoused for instance by (Friedman & Miles, 2006). Concepts such as "steward ownership" (Sanders, 2023) and legal innovations like the Employee Stock Ownership Plan (ESOP) (Ashford & Shakespeare, 1999), especially when combined with the cooperative legal form (Gonza et al., 2021), challenge practitioners and scientists to question the "natural order" of division into investor-owners and workers, signifying a model of the firm that incorporates workers into the firm and, potentially, is able to leverage future profits to increase ownership on the part of workers. Similarly, the notion of "collaborative enterprise" blurs the boundaries between capital and labor.[4]

4.1 Hierarchy

As emerges in particular from the work of Greg Dow, for example (Dow, 2003, 2018), a cooperative is not simply an enterprise without hierarchy. As Dow (2018) argues, any type of hierarchy possible for a firm owned or managed by investors is also replicable for a cooperative firm owned and managed by its workers. In fact, most cooperatives have some form of hierarchy. Therefore, distinguishing between cooperative and noncooperative businesses based on the existence or otherwise of hierarchy is an analytically poor practice.

Therefore, and in accordance with the interests of clear and sound theorizing, a more nuanced and analytically rigorous conceptual catalog is needed for dealing with the integration of democracy, self-management, and hierarchy that is generally present in cooperative enterprise. This includes the integration of numerous dimensions of an enterprise that go beyond the simple "market-hierarchy" dichotomy of

[4] See Kristjanson-Gural in Warren et al. (2024).

Oliver Williamson. This could include extending "market-hierarchy" by a third, distinct, pole of "cooperation," as Thibault Mirabel has done.[5] At the same time, it could involve extending and deepening the analysis of hierarchies, as Lucio Biggiero has argued for, taking into consideration degrees of extension in beneficial claimancy, stratification of authority, and inclusion in the selection of management in firms, among other indicators.[6]

Importantly, the literature also features discussions on distributed forms of leadership (Cousin & Audebrand, 2023) and on innovating beyond voting for decision-making in cooperatives, including in the selection of board members (Pek, 2019; Boeke, 1945). These processes clearly impinge on an enterprise, inter-firm network, or meta-organization's hierarchical structuring and are important dimensions in any nuanced and deep analysis of hierarchy in the cooperative enterprise, and more generally, in any enterprise adopting them, such as Alpha Innovations NV, a technology company in Wallonia, Belgium, which operates on the basis of decision circles.

These discussions reveal that a "cooperative" is not an *idée fixe*, a *telos,* or Kantian *Ding-an-sich*, but can be seen as a container for a type of evolving relationship that tends to privilege horizontality and mutualism, and which is prone to change and shift in its manifestations depending on a particular historical moment or economic context. This means that cooperative firms, which tend like other firms to operate in a changing environment, must continually challenge themselves to realize in practice the principles to which they at least formally subscribe, many of which directly impinge upon, constrain, and challenge traditional notions of hierarchy. As just one simple example, Mondragon's ten principles include both "wage solidarity" and "participation in management," which directly impinge upon and limit two formal aspects of hierarchy: wage differentials and uni-directionality in accountability (Altuna Gabilondo, 2008).

If the "cooperative" is not an obvious and self-evident phenomenon, but one end of a multidimensional spectrum based on varying degrees and intensities of abolitionist relationality, this raises the question of the vector space between the extremes of the cooperative and the corporation. Let's move on to the next category beyond the hierarchy that can define and serve to measure abolitionist relationality: that is, the concept of hybrid.

4.2 Hybrids

Directly related to the debate around hierarchy is the concept of a "hybrid." A hybrid can be defined as any firm that contains any mix of residual claimancy and leadership selection among multiple stakeholder classes such as workers and investors. For

[5] See Mirabel in Warren et al. (2024).

[6] See Biggiero in Warren et al. (2024).

instance, an investor-owned firm that engages in employee stock ownership or "co-determination" could be considered a hybrid (Jirjahn et al., 2011).

A growing number of hybrid organizations can be found around the world. This includes, for example, cooperatives selling investor shares to secure capital for investments (Bekkum & Bijman, 2006; Chaddad, 2012; Spear, 2021). These and similar developments, including the pluralism of enterprise types ranging from ESOPs (Kim & Ouimet, 2014), to employee ownership trusts (EOTs) (Nuttall, 2022; Warren, 2022a), to multi-stakeholder and "public" cooperatives (Lund & Novkovic, 2023), "purpose," "mission-oriented" and "steward" (Sanders, 2023) enterprises, etc., are calling into question the habit, on occasion practiced by various stakeholders within the cooperative sector, of "walling" the cooperative enterprise into a "third sector" (Defourny & Develtere, 2009), separated on the one hand from the private sector and on the other from the state one, very similar to genomic speciation in the natural world (Salamon & Sokolowski, 2016).

Instead of accepting a "walled garden" approach, fencing off cooperatives arbitrarily, perhaps together with foundations, non-profits, and other enterprises into a vague category of "third sector"—and returning again to engage with RE's epistemological approach of mixing and blending, one can interpret labor-managed, cooperative and investor-managed businesses as phenotypes along a multidimensional spectrum (Langton, 1989; Leydesdorff, 2021). Between the extremes at each pole, which one can interpret as Weberian "ideal types," are numerous hybrids, in essence, blends with varying degrees of control or ownership by investors, workers, community members, users, or other interested parties, along various axes.

As cooperatives continue selling minority shares to outside investors[7] and investor-owned firms like Renault sell shares to employees, the divisions will likely become increasingly blurred, and further analytical tools will be needed to add rigor and precision to similarities and distinctions. In a later section, I outline several strong candidates.

5 Moral Economy

The second distinction between RE and CEM is a more specific understanding of agency based on what historian E.P. Thompson called the "moral economy of the crowd" (Thompson, 1971) and which has since been simplified to the "moral economy" (Bowles, 2016; Vieta, 2019). This "moral economy" is based on attributing collective agency to groups of individuals. It has also been referred to as "structural individualism" (Biggiero et al., 2022, p. 44). Institutional economist John Commons identified this type of group agency as a "new universal right of collective action" (Commons, 1936, p. 247). Therefore, for Commons, Thompson, and others, the "moral economy" is a notion that presents opportunities of "how to give to

[7] See, for example, the chapter on "new cooperatives" in Elliott and Boland (2023).

collective action, in all its varieties, its due place throughout economic theory" (Commons, 1934, p. 5).

Fundamentally, the "moral economy" is a framework for meso-level theory and practice, as it focuses on the feedback effects between social and relational principles and practices, on the one hand, and emerging individual and collective agency on the other. This feedback includes its (group and individual) psychological, sociological, and anthropological dimensions. For example, consumer boycotts (Holcomb, 2016; Hawkins, 2010) and labor strikes (Posusney, 1993) could be considered examples of a "moral economy." Similarly, the moral economy describes the emergence of meta-organizations, business clusters, and cooperative federations (Ahrne & Brunsson, 2008), including in the global south.[8] Much of the modern economic research on the moral economy is derivative of Herbert Simon's approach to "bounded rationality," though Simon himself primarily dealt with coordination and not cooperation at a deeper level (Kyriazis & Metaxas, 2013).

It has been demonstrated that economic or organizational cooperation of the "moral economy" type, as opposed to mere instrumental coordination (Simon, 1991), is present at numerous levels and contexts throughout history. For example, Robert Owen's experimental approaches in New Lanark and New Harmony mixed productive relationships with "recreational" and "reproductive" ones (Cole, 1930; Davis & O'Hagan, 2014). Similar mixtures have been found in various religious communities throughout history (Backstrom, 1974). More recently, Avner Ben-Ner has shown that the reciprocal relationships comprising autonomous communities in Israel (*kibbutzim*) enable the long-term cohesion of such communities (Ben-Ner & Neuberger, 1982; Ben-Ner, 1987). In the same vein, Elinor Ostrom's work on commons and polycentric governance demonstrates that coordination beyond, on the one hand, markets utilizing bargaining over private property rights and, on the other hand, authority relations involving state actors is not only possible, but that a deep and broad domain of self-management in groups based on reciprocity can be observed across the world across history in the form of commonly-managed resources, commons or "common pool resources" (Ostrom, 1990).

It is to this manifestation of the moral economy we turn to next.

5.1 *Commons and Commoning*

Fundamentally connected to the notion of the moral economy is the concept of commons. The connection between the moral economy concept and the commons can again be seen by studying the work of E.P. Thompson, who developed the notion of "moral economy." However, at the same time as Thompson was deeply concerned with analyzing the emergent moral economy of crowds (groups) in various historical social movements, he connected the emergence of the English

[8] See Molefe in Warren et al. (2024).

working classes during industrialization to the process of the enclosure of the commons, which, according to Thompson, "entailed for the poor a radical sense of displacement" (Thompson, 2016).

Far from being relegated eventually to the historical dustbin as an analytical novelty, the study of commons has in fact flourished and grown since Thompson's book was written. For instance, the 2009 economics Nobel Prize was awarded to Ostrom, who had studied the governance of various commons across the world for decades.[9]

While "Ostrom's closeness to [...] new institutional economics is [...] an ambivalent fact" (Warren, 2022b, p. 61) and despite the fact that she considered mainly the governance of natural resources such as fisheries, pastures, irrigation canals, groundwater reserves, forests, etc., the notion of commons has subsequently been extended away from particular resources and towards a more general framing, including Benkler's (2003) notion of "commons-based peer-production," largely focused on the online domain, with Wikipedia and Linux serving as examples. Inspired by Benkler, such concepts as "open cooperativism" have been developed in recent years (Bauwens & Kostakis, 2014). Similar ideas have also been labeled "new cooperativism" (Vieta & Lionais, 2022).

Beyond "commons-based peer production" is Linebaugh (2009), De Angelis (2010), Bollier (2020) concept of "commoning." Commoning "turn[s] a noun into a verb" and departs from the idea that "there are no commons without incessant activities of commoning, of (re)producing in common" (De Angelis, 2010, p. 955). In addition to this, commoning involves "human deeds [...] embedded in a labor process [...,] is collective [...and,] being independent of the state, is independent also of the temporality of the law and state" (Linebaugh, 2009, pp. 44–45).

An economy based on bestowing agency to self-managed groups, as the moral economy envisions, therefore is closely tied to the role of commons and commoning activity.

5.2 Common Good

Also central to this CEM's concept of a "moral economy" and its embrace of commons and commoning activities is the concept of the "common good", being a concept inherited from classical philosophy, for example, Aristotle's *eudaemonia* (Aristotle, 2011). While the common good had been present in mainstream economics since its origins in moral philosophy, the notion largely disappeared after the rise of Benthamite utilitarianism, in favor of a mechanistic view that is embodied by Adam Smith's adage about "the butcher and the baker" (Mitchell, 1918; Etzioni, 2010; Brown, 2010). A moral economy approach meanwhile attempts to abandon

[9] Ostrom's work is being continued by numerous groups, including the International Association for the Study of the Commons (IASC), the Ostrom Workshop and ProSocial World among others.

the "neo-Hobbesian" world of neoclassical economics and is in outlook much closer to the perspective advocated for by RE proper, or also to the perspective represented by American pragmatist philosopher and pedagogue John Dewey, who distinguished between both public–private and social–individual axes (Dewey, 1954).

Dewey's multidimensional perspective and RE's discussion of relationalizing notions like individual benefit and common good within a firm are important milestones because the two dimensions allow for the disentangling of the notion of the common good from the public purse or state proper. According to a Deweyan democratic, process-based, relational approach, private organizations including firms can provide for social ends. In other words, it isn't just a Weberian bureaucratic state that is in a position to provide for the common good. Similarly, cooperative enterprise, as the literature confirms, defies the strictures and assumptions of the neoclassical model, since cooperatives do not, as neoclassical applications to cooperatives surmised, maximize member income, but also overlay member-driven benefits with a greater or lesser "concern for community," itself one of the seven canonical ICA cooperative principles (Ellerman, 2021a).

There are numerous other practical and theoretical examples of private firms providing for the common good. For example, Christian Felber has introduced both an engaging discussion of how firms can serve the common good, as well as presenting the Economy for the Common Good as an innovative, self-organized reporting scheme (Felber, 2019), which is in essence similar to the more recent French enterprises a mission (Segrestin et al., 2022).

6 Implications

Relational economics has to date been more concerned with the ontological and epistemological questions of why and how to shift the attention of researchers from the domain of "spot transactions" to focusing on relationships via concepts like relational transactions.[10] It is in connecting the moral economy perspective to an abolitionist framework problematizing the insider–outsider relationship that the power of the CEM approach is revealed. CEM intends to challenge organizations and societies, including cooperatives, municipalities, investor-owned firms, NGOs, and others to rethink various aspects of their economic and organizational games, including organizational learning, investment, value production, and entrepreneurialism.

This challenge must be met with suitable methodological approaches that are able to understand, measure, model, and simulate cooperation in organizations, including in cooperative enterprise, based on the collective agency of groups. Beyond this,

[10] See, for instance, the "Manifesto for a Relational Economics" in Biggiero et al. (2022), which argues that "modern value creation is achieved by interlinking the resources of stakeholders originating from multiple economic as well as social systems and organisations" (Biggiero et al. 2022, p. 10).

these approaches must furthermore be suitable to recognize the role of self-organization and consider the insider–outsider dichotomy dynamically. These requirements are therefore quite concrete.

7 Examples and Applications

Where CEM can augment the relational framework is by providing insights into suitable methodological approaches that emphasize relationality in a particular context. That is to say, it can help to concretize a research program based on the study of a particular phenotype, the cooperative enterprise, and in so doing, strengthen and feedback on RE proper and thereby provide tools for firms generally. In the following, I outline some examples from the forthcoming volume of Warren et al. (2024) that can help illustrate this potential.

7.1 Innovative Accounting Regimes

Derivative of CEM's abolitionist relationality is the ambition to develop more inclusive accounting schemes. Related to critical accounting's question of "who counts?", scholars taking a CEM approach have attempted to ask how firms may introduce accounting schemes that reflect the value firms have for stakeholders like workers or that platforms have for their users. Introducing such innovative accounting schemes would increase overall social welfare via what Sean Geobey calls the "trash-to-treasure" transformation, which entails the fact that "[a] firm that is making below market-rate returns for capital-providers might actually be providing above-market returns for other patrons." According to Geobey, "these firms are well-placed for an ownership transition from capital-based ownership structures to an alternative form" (Warren et al., 2024).

Beyond transitions to worker ownership, innovative accounting regimes could promote alternative ownership regimes: for instance, data cooperatives for owning and managing user data, versus the corporate model, with features like the "enshittification cycle."[11] Similar to the "trash-to-treasure" model for worker-converted firms, new accounting regimes could promote a "deshittification" of platforms by providing concrete verification of "who or what counts" for and in a particular platform (Hall et al., 2015).

Through such innovative accounting schemes, transformations of legacy firms into community-based enterprises or worker cooperatives could find strong analytical support (Schneider & Mannan, 2020). In an era where many firms are "offshoring," i.e., selling their local production facilities and relocating to cheaper

[11] See Doctorow (2023) or Warren et al. (2024).

markets overseas, providing community members, local authorities, and other stakeholders with concrete evidence of the value of retaining enterprises can promote more sustainable ecosystems. Such accounting regimes could be useful in promoting employee ownership transitions, such as have been promoted in the UK, Canada, Italy, Spain, and France (Mygind, 2023).

The bottom line of such innovative accounting schemes is always the question of value and valuation. Providing the means to account for such differential value is central to moving to a more pluralistic economy that provides resources where they are needed. This may in fact involve new currencies, as Martignoni (2018) has called for. However, realizing such innovative accounting schemes might mean moving beyond a purely object-based view of cooperation to embracing processes, including processes of "who counts." Such process-based accounting methods likely go beyond the foundations of double-entry bookkeeping and require new methodologies, whose results could then be included in company accounts (Pitkänen, 2013).

7.2 Process-Oriented Methodologies

Things become a bit trickier when moving beyond merely new dimensions or ways of accounting for value. If we are moving beyond mere binary exchanges of stocks and flows, which can be represented as states, and instead towards a discussion of complex processes of interactions, then a shift to process-oriented methodologies is necessary. RE proper deals with processes largely by focusing on relationalizing of logics in the commercial domain: transactions become acculturated in that they become ambiguous events of plurality: polylingualism, polycontextuality, and polycontexturality are all consequences of this relationalization (Wieland, 2018).

However, as stated at the outset of this contribution: the concern with a "pure" relationality is not necessarily conducive to a translation to suitable methodological approaches, as there aren't necessarily concrete measures or indicators for something so general as "relationalized logics." Therefore, CEM intends to specify an abolitionist relationality as an engaging object of study for contextualizing relationality.

Below, several approaches are outlined in their connection between process-orientation, abolitionist relationality, and organizational outcomes.

7.2.1 Organizational Democracy Measures

Derivative of the CEM approach is the question of organizational democracy. As numerous authors have argued, this is not a simple question to resolve.[12] Such measures are critical elements of CEM's abolitionist relationality, since they begin to offer measurable indicators of the degree to which an organization is accountable

[12] See, for example, Biggiero in Warren (2023) or Warren (2022b).

to various stakeholders, including workers. By offering a concrete methodological framework for measuring organizational democracy (ODM), the notion can move away from pure normative speculation and be introduced into firms' strategic policies, into countries' statutory regulatory frameworks and also be studied by workers interested in working in more responsive, inclusive workplaces (Cross et al., 2002).

However, one of the problems of past ODMs has been their reduction of complex, multidimensional data into simple (typically) quantitative measures. This is the case, for instance, for Ahmed et al. (2019).

Biggiero in Warren et al. (2024) offers two innovations over and against such approaches: firstly, grouping primarily relational indicators into three distinct dimensions: the first dimension, the economic-legal, includes indicators such as the overlap between (a) property and control, (b) employees and control, as well as the degree of property fragmentation. The second dimension consists of "typical organizational/industrial attributes," consisting in (a) an index measuring the variety of organizational goals and (b) one measuring entry and exit freedom. The third dimension refers to the structural dimensions of hierarchy, consisting in (a) the degree of dyadic hierarchy, which concerns "the direct relationship between two persons," (b) the degree of topological hierarchy, "which checks the hierarchical degree related to power concentration due to the topology of the whole structure" and (c) the democraticity of a firm's selection mechanism for its managers. The second innovation of Biggiero's ODM consists in applying an outranking algorithm in order to interpret these indicators without reducing their dimensionality and thereby removing degrees of complexity (Biggiero in Warren et al., 2024).

In addition to advancing theory by offering measurable indicators of the degree of relationality in and, it should also be said, between firms,[13] this type of ODM also begins to move theories of relationality away from broad, sweeping epistemological debates. In this way, it is an approach particularly representative of CEM's specification beyond a "pure relationality" and allows firms to measure the extent to which they are incorporating various groups and subgroups concretely into decision-making and reward in the firm's profits and ownership.

7.2.2 Path-Dependence Analysis

Another example of a relational methodology that can be manifested or embodied in a way that emphasizes both the collective decision-making involved in a moral economy framework, as well as the emancipatory ontology problematizing the "insider–outsider" relationship, is path-dependence analysis. Path-dependence analysis (PDA), a graphical methodology embedded in systems science, with roots in historical sociology, economics and economic history (Mahoney, 2000, p. 507), investigates "a dynamic process governed by its own history, characterised by self-

[13] Since dyadic and topological hierarchies, etc., also apply in inter-firm relationships.

reinforcing dynamics and positive feedback."[14] Positive feedback typically results from "irreversibility, uncertainty, unpredictability of results, self-reinforcing mechanisms and non-linear change" (Gigante, 2016, p. 14). Therefore, institutions and outcomes can be the result of singular local, regional, or national contexts.

Schreyögg & Sydow, 2011 have developed a scheme for applying PDA to organizations, termed organizational path dependence. Linda Bennison has applied organizational PDA to the historical isolation of cooperatives from the legal and institutional landscape in Australia and, following Schreyögg et al. (2011), distinguished three phases: "pre-formation, formation, and lock-in."[15] The point of such analyses is to emphasize the importance of relationships in hindering or facilitating an abolitionist relationality. In the case of organizational PDA, the relationships exist both "laterally," between events, between events and individuals, and "vertically," across time. It thereby embodies one attempt to introduce evolutionary methods into economics analysis (Mahoney, 2000).

Beyond this, organizational PDA is particularly sanguine to the moral economy framing because the conjunctive events it focuses on generally imply lock-in effects specifically due to the agency of groups of individuals (Economou & Kyriazis, 2019). The approach also connects directly to the "insider–outsider" framing via enabling questions on which stakeholders are included and which excluded in the promulgation of new policies. For instance, a more inclusive and consistent dialogue between cooperatives, policymakers, and governments, as was arguably the case in Italy (Warren, 2024), might have led to a different outcome in Australia, instead of one where "cooperatives have inadvertently been disadvantaged by multiple regulators and fragmented legislation" (Bennison in Warren et al., 2024).

7.2.3 Social Network Analysis

Social networks are networks of nodes connected by edges. The nodes represent agents, either individuals or firms, whereas the edges represent relationships. Since social networks "appear to fall between [the] two extremes" of anonymous (e.g., market) and group interactions (Scott & Carrington, 2011, p. 76), the study and analysis of social networks is one of the best examples of a relational methodology that can be naturally employed to fill current gaps in research methods for studying cooperation generally and cooperative enterprise specifically, especially when compared to reductivist or aggregative approaches like statistics (Biggiero et al., 2022). But social network analysis (SNA) also enables a framing open to an abolitionist relationality. By measuring elements like the degree of reciprocity of relationships in organizations, both researchers and functionaries of firms like managers can increase their understanding of possible feedback between particular configurations of relationships and organizational outcomes, including perceptions.

[14] Bennison in Warren et al. (2024).

[15] See Warren et al. (2024).

Warren (2024) points to examples like the study of the "viral" marketing campaign of the Italian dairy cooperative Granarolo in the post-WWII era, about which (Battilani & Bertagnoni, 2015, p. 44) write that "[t]estimonials [...] confirm the conquest of these dairy shops began by selling to 'friendly' shops, run by relatives of cooperative members and people who shared the same ideals." Such examples show how SNA can embody both a moral economy framing and the abolitionist "insider–outsider" framing that CEM advocates for. Similar studies such as Moretti (2017) and Hahn et al. (2008) demonstrate furthermore the connection between SNA and sustainability by underlining how important contact and regular communication are in establishing commonly shared epistemic frames upon which project-based collaboration can be founded.

7.2.4 Boolean Networks and NK Modeling

Boolean networks (BNs) were developed by Kauffman (1993). Similar to social networks, Boolean networks consist of nodes connected by edges. The main distinction between BNs and social networks is that BNs reduce relationships to simple binary "Boolean" operators, while a particular social network's structure depends on the relationships being depicted, for instance, business partnerships or neighborhood proximity (Borgatti et al., 2024, p. 16). Therefore, in BNs, "each node has a binary state (e.g., ON or OFF) [and c]hanges in the state of a node through time are governed by its programming, by its current state, and by the states of its neighbors (nodes directly linked to it by edges)" (Green et al., 2007, p. 403). BNs form a particular class of "NK" models, in which N refers to agents' attributes, while K refers to the independence of these attributes from another (Kauffman, 1993, p. 218; Tilebein, 2006, p. 1090). An increase in K "results in co-evolution when evolving agents affect each other."

NK modeling, and BNs in particular, can be usefully applied to understanding meso-level interactions between individual elements, whether individuals in groups, groups in firms, or firms in firm clusters. While the ability to emphasize "insider–outsider" relationships is likely not NK modeling's strength, the ability to decompose the analysis into two domains: fitness landscape (NK-FL) and network dynamics (NK-BN) allows the comparison of different aspects of firm networks. For instance, NK-FL models allow a researcher to compare what Kauffman (1993) refers to as "the fitness differences between adjacent genotypes" in a system (see also Biggiero, 2016, p. 72). In organizational contexts, this would involve comparing relative outcomes of "pure labor-managed firms (LMFs)" or "pure capital-managed firms (KMFs)" in differing environments, for instance, by comparing a situation where one segregates LMFs to interact with other LMFs in federations to another situation in which firms are relatively unencumbered by the environment as to whom they interact with.

At the same time, NK-BN models focus on "pure" Boolean network dynamics and assume "a topologically invariant system... that does not mutate[,] neither [in] its size nor [in] its links distribution" (Biggiero, 2016, p. 62). That is to say, while NK-FL models emphasize "adjacent genotypes," NK-BN models study "phenotypical" expressions, comparing these according to their relative fitness. Applied to enterprises, the NK-BN literature includes research on industrial clusters and organizational teams, an overview of which can be found in Biggiero (2016, p. 67). Given a particular cluster or team, a CEM application of NK-BN approaches might investigate the impact of a changing of the composition or interaction rules within teams or among member firms of a cluster, for instance, by increasing the number of meetings.

Authors like Tilebein (2006) have suggested introducing NK approaches into firms in the same manner as strategic management has been adopted as a general function of firms. At the same time, and closer to the domain of CEM, authors like Caio Silva have suggested the complex adaptive system as a suitable analytical framework for interpreting cooperative enterprise, specifically focused on its adaptability.[16]

7.2.5 Agent-Based Modeling

Agent-based modeling (ABM) provides a toolkit for simulating or modeling complex relationships in a network. ABM must be calibrated with the number of individuals (N), the number of generations (G), and the number of rounds per generation (K). Given these parameters and certain rules of interaction, ABM algorithmically coordinates interactions based on the inputs specified. This process is depicted in Fig. 1.

Generally speaking, "[b]ecause of the algorithmic structure of the models, [their] outcomes are nothing else than the implications (deductions) from the assumptions and the rules (mechanisms) according to which agents are supposed to behave" (Biggiero et al., 2022, p. 54). This characteristic has been labeled "generative explanation" (Epstein, 1999, 2012), meaning that a model that generates certain outcomes itself provides explanatory power (Valente, 2016).

Researchers engaged in ABM generally make use of software such as AnyLogic, NetLogo, GAMA Platform, or Repast (Abar et al., 2017). With this software, users are able to either process or generate large data sets that can be used to simulate different states and interactions between heterogeneous agents. There are as many different ABMs as there are heterogeneous attributes and interactions between individuals or groups embodying those attributes, which is to say there are likely infinite permutations (Axtell & Farmer, 2022, p. 5).

It is also important that ABM, like SNA, distinguishes itself via its ability to visualize network relations, including emerging patterns. Due to their complexity, these dynamics can often be understood phenomenologically, rather than by reducing them to their microscopic components. This is precisely why ABM is frequently

[16] See Silva in Warren et al. (2024).

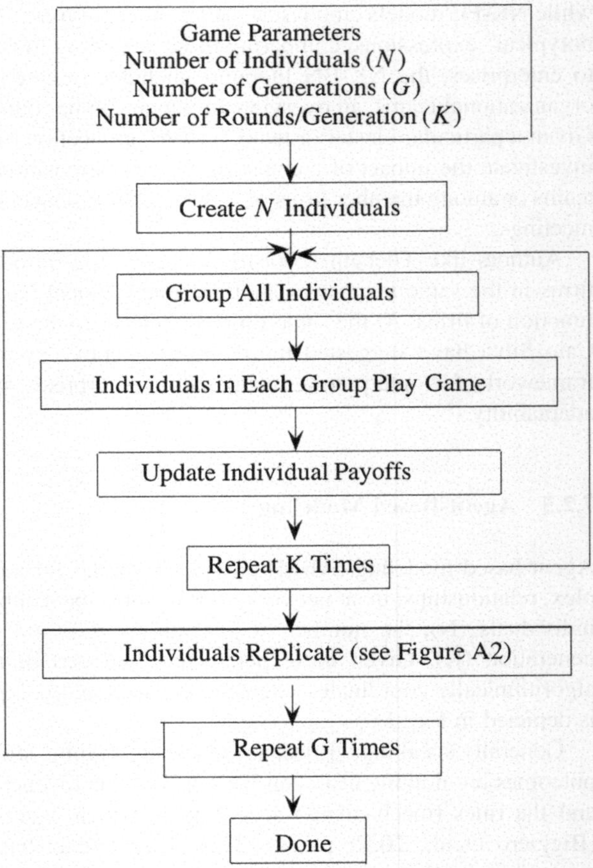

Fig. 1 A graphical representation of the algorithmic steps involved in calibrating and executing an AVM. (From Bowles and Gintis (2013, p. 202))

considered as part of the qualitative research toolkit (Pyka & Grebel, 2006; Yang & Gilbert, 2008).

8 Discussion

The importance of CEM's framing between economics and management includes building up a strong dialogue between economists and management scholars researching various dimensions of cooperation within economy and organization, especially as far as these various research practices embody an abolitionist relationality. The cooperative enterprise forms a cornerstone of this "thought style," since it ideally embodies the principles of being a member-based and member-driven collective and a collective of individual members. This has been referred to as a "dual nature" (Draheim, 1952) and is reflected in some jurisdictions, like the Basque region of Spain, within the legal framework as a distinct deviation from either "employment" or "self-employment" (Alkorta, 2021).

The common features of the CEM-derivative approaches outlined above are that they are meso-level oriented, facilitate insights into abolitionist relationality, and are embedded in a moral economy perspective.

They are meso-level in that each of these approaches facilitates feedback between different selection levels. For instance, innovative accountancy schemes provide new information for both public administrators, as well as to individual workers, about divergences in the appraisal of a firm's value depending on the perspective chosen. SNA, meanwhile, can reveal connections between structural aspects of the specific relationships of which a firm consists (for instance, seniority), both formally and informally, and individual outcomes (for instance, workers' motivation), or again outcomes at more aggregated levels (for example, total firm value-added). Similarly, an approach like ABM can help explain how organizations can either improve outcomes via cooperation, for instance, by modeling how the introduction of more cooperative agents affects a network, or can improve cooperation via processes or changes in policies, for instance, lowering the costs of monitoring or punishment of cheating behavior.

The approaches outlined above facilitate insight into abolitionist relationality because they give insight into, and help explain, the benefits of more inclusive hierarchies and more democratic firms. An organizational democracy measure an be an important parameter for (cooperative) firms, as well as their various stakeholders, including also investors, and can give concrete insight into the degrees of freedom in a particular organization or network and, importantly, can measure changes in these values over time.

Approaches like organizational PDA are embedded in a moral economy perspective because they connect certain contingent or conjunctural events to the collective activities of groups or organizations. Similarly, BN and NK models reveal emergent processes of self-organization in groups of individuals, even if the initial stage is relatively poorly organized (Kauffman, 1993).

Other elements of CEM's "methodological turn" could surely be summarized, including anthropological, communications, psychological, and sociological approaches dealing with abolitionist relationality or a moral economy framing.[17] However, in order to respect the limitations of this volume, I restrict myself to the above brief survey.

[17] For example, the work of Ferreras (2017). Several of these and related approaches are presented in the forthcoming Warren et al. (2024).

9 Conclusion

Cooperative Economics and Management (CEM) is in dialogue with Relational Economics (RE), participating together in the critical turn in both economics and management science away from "spot" transactions towards long-term relationships as an object of interest. Both approaches, RE and CEM, are responding to the rise of a network economy, where relationships "re-capture" and "re-embed" the economy, in the language of Karl Polanyi.

However, while RE can be criticized for remaining vague in further distinguishing among relationships beyond the concept of "relationality," frequently remaining on the level of epistemology, CEM departs from the notion of the dignity of labor, borrowed from classical political economy. It more narrowly restricts its focus to an abolitionist relationality, concerned with problematizing the "insider–outsider" relationship in firms with respect to membership.

It is also concerned with the role of a "moral economy" of self-organizing according to what John Commons referred to as the "new universal right of collective action" (Commons, 1936, p. 247). This domain of collective action, "new" in the economy, as represented by the rise of labor strikes and consumer boycotts in the past century, has its roots in the political domain and can be traced back to the notion of democracy, the quintessence of which the philosopher, economist and psychiatrist Cornelius Castoriadis referred to as "the extraordinary novelty of this conception of what constitutes the power of a human group" (Castoriadis, 2011, p. 136).

In the economic domain, the cooperative enterprise, and within that domain particularly the worker cooperative, could be considered an ideal type, maximizing both the distribution of ownership and residual claimancy across a broad membership. Using this "pure LMF" as one pole, CEM has developed, and will continue to develop, methodological approaches to measure and compare firms according to their democraticity, to analyze processes contributing to statutory regimes regulating firm activities, and to increase the degree of "thick" understanding ("Verstehen") of firms and their constituent groups across time. Much as "the magma of signification" (Castoriadis, 1987, p. 367) repeatedly settles and is brought to motion again through internal and external pressures, the suitable framework for CEM will evolve over time and is not final. It is hoped that works like Warren et al. (2024) will contribute to guiding the conversation.

References

Abar, S., Theodoropoulos, G. K., Lemarinier, P., & O'Hare, G. M. (2017). Agent based modelling and simulation tools: A review of the state-of-art software. *Computer Science Review, 24*, 13–33. https://doi.org/10.1016/j.cosrev.2017.03.001

Ahmed, K., Adeel, A., Ali, R., & Rehman, R. U. (2019). Organizational democracy and employee outcomes: The mediating role of organizational justice. *Business Strategy & Development, 2*(3), 204–219. https://doi.org/10.1002/bsd2.63

Ahrne, G., & Brunsson, N. (2008). *Meta-organizations*. Edward Elgar Publishing.
Alkorta, A. B. (2021). Employment in worker cooperatives in the framework of Spanish cooperative law. *International Journal of Cooperative Law, 2*, 72–87.
Altuna Gabilondo, L. (2008). *La experiencia cooperativa de Mondragon: una síntesis general*. Lanki.
Aristotle. (2011). *The Eudemian ethics*. Oxford University Press.
Ashford, R., & Shakespeare, R. (1999). *Binary economics: The new paradigm*. University Press of America.
Axtell, R. L., & Farmer, J. D. (2022). Agent-based modeling in economics and finance: Past, present, and future. *Journal of Economic Literature*, 1–101.
Backstrom, P. N. (1974). *Christian socialism and co-operation in Victorian England: Edward Vansittart Neale and the Co-operative Movement*. Taylor & Francis.
Battilani, P., & Bertagnoni, G. (2015). The use of social networks in marketing: The Italian co-operative experience. *Journal of Historical Research in Marketing, 7*(1), 31–57. https://doi.org/10.1108/JHRM-06-2013-0034
Bauwens, M., & Kostakis, V. (2014). From the communism of capital to capital for the commons: Towards an open co-operativism. *tripleC: Communication, Capitalism & Critique. Open Access Journal for a Global Sustainable Information Society, 12*(1), 356–361.
Benkler, Y. (2003). The political economy of commons. *Upgrade: The European Journal for the Informatics Professional, 4*(3), 6–9.
Ben-Ner, A. (1987). Preferences in a communal economic system. *Economica, 54*(213), 207–221.
Ben-Ner, A., & Neuberger, E. (1982). Israel: The kibbutz. In *The performance of labour-managed firms* (pp. 186–213). Macmillan.
Biggiero, L. (2016). NK simulation modeling. In *Relational methodologies and epistemology in economics and management sciences* (pp. 61–99). IGI Global.
Biggiero, L., De Jongh, D., Priddat, B., Wieland, J., Zicari, A., & Fischer, D. (2022). *Relational view of economics*. Springer.
Boeke, K. (1945). Sociocracy: Democracy as it might be. http://worldteacher.faithweb.com/sociocracy.htm
Bollier, D. (2020). Commoning as a transformative social paradigm. In *The new systems reader* (pp. 348–361). Routledge.
Borgatti, S. P., Everett, M. G., Johnson, J. C., & Agneessens, F. (2024). *Analyzing social networks*. SAGE.
Bowles, S. (2016). *The moral economy: Why good incentives are no substitute for good citizens*. Yale University Press.
Bowles, S., & Gintis, H. (2013). *A cooperative species: Human reciprocity and its evolution*. Princeton University Press.
Brennan, G., Pettit, P., et al. (2004). *The economy of esteem: An essay on civil and political society*. OUP Oxford.
Brown, M. T. (2010). *Civilizing the economy: A new economics of provision*. Cambridge University Press.
Buck-Morss, S. (2009). *Hegel, Haiti, and universal history*. University of Pittsburgh Press.
Castoriadis, C. (1987). *The imaginary institution of society*. MIT Press.
Castoriadis, C. (2011). Thucydide, la force et le droit. In *Ce qui fait la Grèce, 3: Séminaires 1984–1985. La création humaine IV*. Seuil.
Chaddad, F. (2012). Advancing the theory of the cooperative organization: The cooperative as a true hybrid. *Annals of Public and Cooperative Economics, 83*(4), 445–461. https://doi.org/10.1111/j.1467-8292.2012.00475.x
Cole, G. D. H. (1930). *The life of Robert Owen*. Macmillan London.
Commons, J. (1934). *Institutional economics, its place in political economy*. Macmillan.
Commons, J. R. (1936). Institutional economics. *The American Economic Review, 26*(1), 237–249.

Cousin, L., & Audebrand, L. K. (2023). *Cooperative associations: Frameworks of distributed leadership for collective digital innovation*. Innovating in Cooperative Governance. Governing Cooperative Innovation.
Cross, R., Borgatti, S. P., & Parker, A. (2002). Making invisible work visible: Using social network analysis to support strategic collaboration. *California Management Review, 44*(2), 25–46. https://doi.org/10.2307/41166121
Davis, R. A., & O'Hagan, F. (2014). *Robert Owen*. Bloomsbury Publishing.
De Angelis, M. (2010). The production of commons and the "explosion" of the middle class. *Antipode, 42*, 954–977.
De Waal, F. (2006). *Our inner ape: A leading primatologist explains why we are who we are*. Penguin.
Defourny, J., & Develtere, P. (2009). The social economy: The worldwide making of a third sector. In *The worldwide making of the social economy: Innovations and changes*. Acco.
Deleuze, G., & Guattari, F. (2009). *Anti-Oedipus: Capitalism and schizophrenia*. Penguin.
Dewey, J. (1954). *The public and its problems*. Ohio University Press.
Doctorow, C. (2023). *The 'enshittification' of TikTok*. Wired.
Dolgoff, S. (1974). *The anarchist collectives: Workers' self-management in the Spanish Revolution, 1936–1939*. Black Rose Books Ltd.
Dow, G. K. (2003). *Governing the firm: Workers' control in theory and practice*. Cambridge University Press.
Dow, G. K. (2018). *The labor-managed firm: Theoretical foundations*. Cambridge University Press.
Draheim, G. (1952). *Die Genossenschaft als Unternehmungstyp*. Vandenhoeck & Ruprecht.
Economou, E. M. N., & Kyriazis, N. C. (2019). *Democracy and economy: An inseparable relationship from ancient times to today*. Cambridge Scholars Publishing.
Ellerman, D. (2021a). *The democratic worker-owned firm: A new model for the East and West*. Routledge.
Ellerman, D. (2021b). *Neo-abolitionism: Abolishing human rentals in favor of workplace democracy*. Springer Nature.
Elliott, M. S., & Boland, M. A. (2023). *Handbook of research on cooperatives and mutuals*. Edward Elgar Publishing.
Epstein, J. M. (1999). Agent-based computational models and generative social science. *Complexity, 4*(5), 41–60.
Epstein, J. M. (2012). *Generative social science: Studies in agent-based computational modeling*. Princeton University Press.
Etzioni, A. (2010). *Moral dimension: Toward a new economics*. Simon and Schuster.
Felber, C. (2019). *Change everything: Creating an economy for the common good*. Zed Books Ltd.
Ferreras, I. (2017). *Firms as political entities: Saving democracy through economic bicameralism*. Cambridge University Press.
Fici, A., Cracogna, D., & Henry, H. (2013). *International handbook of cooperative law*. Springer.
Fleck, L. (1994). *Entstehung und Entwicklung einer wissenschaftlichen Tatsache: Einführung in die Lehre vom Denkstil und Denkkollektiv*. Suhrkamp.
Friedman, A. L., & Miles, S. (2006). *Stakeholders: Theory and practice*. OUP Oxford.
Gigante, A. A. (2016). *Reviewing path dependence theory in economics: Micro-foundations of endogenous change processes*. University of Salento.
Gonza, T., Ellerman, D., Berkopec, G., Zgank, T., & Siroka, T. (2021). Marcora for Europe: How worker-buyouts might help save jobs and build resilient businesses. *European State Aid Law Quarterly, 20*(1), 61–74.
Green, D. G., Leishman, T. G., & Sadedin, S. (2007). The emergence of social consensus in Boolean networks. In *2007 IEEE symposium on artificial life* (pp. 402–408). IEEE. https://doi.org/10.1109/ALIFE.2007.367792

Hahn, T., Schultz, L., Folke, C., & Olsson, P. (2008). Social networks as sources of resilience in social-ecological systems. In J. Norberg & G. S. Cumming (Eds.), *Complexity theory for a sustainable future* (pp. 119–148). Columbia University Press.

Hall, M., Millo, Y., & Barman, E. (2015). Who and what really counts? Stakeholder prioritization and accounting for social value. *Journal of Management Studies, 52*(7), 907–934. https://doi.org/10.1111/joms.12146

Hawkins, R. A. (2010). Boycotts, buycotts and consumer activism in a global context: An overview. *Management & Organizational History, 5*(2), 123–143. https://doi.org/10.1177/1744935909356236

Holcomb, J. L. (2016). *Moral commerce: Quakers and the transatlantic boycott of the slave labor economy*. Cornell University Press.

International Co-operative Alliance (ICA). (1995). *Statement on the co-operative identity*. International Co-operative Alliance.

Jirjahn, U., Mohrenweiser, J., & Backes-Gellner, U. (2011). Works councils and learning: On the dynamic dimension of codetermination. *Kyklos, 64*(3), 427–447. https://doi.org/10.1111/j.1467-6435.2011.00515.x

Jossa, B. (2019). *The political economy of cooperatives and socialism*. Routledge.

Kauffman, S. A. (1993). *The origins of order: Self-organization and selection in evolution*. Oxford University Press.

Kim, E. H., & Ouimet, P. (2014). Broad-based employee stock ownership: Motives and outcomes. *The Journal of Finance, 69*(3), 1273–1319. https://doi.org/10.1111/jofi.12136

Kinna, R. (1992). Kropotkin and Huxley. *Politics, 12*(2), 42–47. https://doi.org/10.1111/j.1467-9256.1992.tb00157.x

Kropotkin, P. (1998). *Mutual aid: A factor of evolution*. Freedom Press.

Kropotkin, K. (2021). *Ethics: Origins and development*. Black Rose Books Ltd.

Kyriazis, N., & Metaxas, T. (2013). *The emergence of democracy: A behavioural perspective*. Munich Personal RePEc Archive.

Langton, C. (1989). Artificial life. In C. G. Langton (Ed.), *Artificial life* (pp. 1–47). Addison-Wesley.

Leydesdorff, L. (2021). *The evolutionary dynamics of discursive knowledge: Communication-theoretical perspectives on an empirical philosophy of science*. Springer Nature.

Linebaugh, P. (2009). *The Magna Carta manifesto: Liberties and commons for all*. University of California Press.

Lund, M., & Novkovic, S. (2023). Multi-stakeholder cooperatives. In M. S. Elliott & M. A. Boland (Eds.), *Handbook of research on cooperatives and mutuals* (pp. 531–548). Edward Elgar Publishing.

Mahoney, J. (2000). Path dependence in historical sociology. *Theory and Society, 29*(4), 507–548. https://doi.org/10.1023/A:1007113830879

Martignoni, J. (2018). The district currency: A new currency design for managing the commons. *International Journal of Community Currency Research, 22*(2), 16–38. https://doi.org/10.15133/j.ijccr.2018.002

Mitchell, W. C. (1918). Bentham's felicific calculus. *Political Science Quarterly, 33*(2), 161–183. https://doi.org/10.2307/2141911

Moretti, A. (2017). *The network organization: A governance perspective on structure, dynamics and performance*. Springer.

Mygind, N. (2023). Overcoming barriers of employee ownership in France, Italy, Spain, the UK, and the US. *Journal of Participation and Employee Ownership, 6*(3), 230–263. https://doi.org/10.1108/JPEO-06-2023-0037

Novković, S., Miner, K., & McMahon, C. (2023). *Humanistic governance in democratic organizations: The cooperative difference*. Springer Nature.

Nuttall, G. (2022). Gandhi's theory of trusteeship and its influence on employee ownership in the twenty-first century. In *Gandhi's wisdom: Insights from the founding father of modern psychology in the east* (pp. 127–147). Springer International Publishing.

Ostrom, E. (1990). *Governing the commons: The evolution of institutions for collective action*. Cambridge University Press.
Pek, S. (2019). Drawing out democracy: The role of sortition in preventing and overcoming organizational degeneration in worker-owned firms. *Journal of Management Inquiry*. https://doi.org/10.1177/1056492619868030
Pitkänen, H. (2013). Theorizing formal and informal feedback practices in management accounting through three dimensions.
Posusney, M. P. (1993). Irrational workers: The moral economy of labor protest in Egypt. *World Politics, 46*(1), 83–120. https://doi.org/10.2307/2950660
Puusa, A., & Hokkila, K. (2015). Cooperative ideals versus practice. In *European conference on management, leadership & governance* (p. 360). Academic Conferences International Limited.
Pyka, A., & Grebel, T. (2006). Agent-based modelling – A methodology for the analysis of qualitative development processes. In T. Terano, H. Kita, & K. Takadama (Eds.), *Agent-based computational modelling: Applications in demography, social, economic and environmental sciences* (pp. 17–35). Springer. https://doi.org/10.1007/4-431-31882-3_2
Raworth, K. (2017). *Doughnut economics: Seven ways to think like a 21st-century economist*. Chelsea Green Publishing.
Roberts, M. J. (2019). Twilight of work: The labor question in Nietzsche and Marx. *Critical Sociology, 45*(2), 267–280. https://doi.org/10.1177/0896920517747190
Sacchetti, S., & Borzaga, C. (2020). The foundations of the "public organisation": Governance failure and the problem of external effects. *Journal of Management and Governance, 1–28*. https://doi.org/10.1007/s10997-020-09520-2
Salamon, L. M., & Sokolowski, S. W. (2016). Beyond nonprofits: Re-conceptualizing the third sector. *Voluntas: International Journal of Voluntary and Nonprofit Organizations, 27*, 1515–1545. https://doi.org/10.1007/s11266-016-9726-z
Sanders, A. (2023). Binding capital to free purpose: Steward ownership in Germany. *European Company and Financial Law Review, 19*(4), 622–653. https://doi.org/10.1515/ecfr-2022-0025
Schneider, N., & Mannan, M. (2020). Exit to community: Strategies for multi-stakeholder ownership in the platform economy. *Georgetown Law Technology Review, 5*, 1.
Schreyögg, G., & Sydow, J. (2011). Organizational path dependence: A process view. *Organization Studies, 32*(3), 321–335. https://doi.org/10.1177/0170840610397481
Schreyögg, G., Sydow, J., & Holtmann, P. (2011). How history matters in organisations: The case of path dependence. *Management & Organizational History, 6*(1), 81–100.
Schwengber, J. G., & Kindlein, B. B. (2021). Building bridges not silos: Organisational learning processes and the role of a shared lingua franca as an a priori requirement for transcultural cooperation. In F. Döring & T. Keller (Eds.), *Relational leadership – Case studies from Brazil* (pp. 243–264). Peter Lang. https://doi.org/10.3726/b18854
Scott, J., & Carrington, P. J. (Eds.). (2011). *The SAGE handbook of social network analysis*. SAGE.
Segrestin, B., Hatchuel, A., & Levillain, K. (2022). Rethinking the purpose of the corporation with the creative power of the enterprise. In G. B. Whittaker (Ed.), *The corporation: Rethinking the iconic form of business organization* (Vol. 78, pp. 191–207). Emerald Publishing Limited. https://doi.org/10.1108/S0742-332220220000078015
Simon, H. A. (1990). Bounded rationality. In J. Eatwell, M. Milgate, & P. Newman (Eds.), *Utility and probability* (pp. 15–18). Palgrave Macmillan. https://doi.org/10.1007/978-1-349-20568-4_6
Simon, H. A. (1991). Organizations and markets. *Journal of Economic Perspectives, 5*(2), 25–44. https://doi.org/10.1257/jep.5.2.25
Spear, R. (2021). Co-operative hybrids. *Review of International Co-operation, 12*, 70–92.
Thompson, E. P. (1971). The moral economy of the English crowd in the eighteenth century. *Past & Present, 50*, 76–136. https://doi.org/10.1093/past/50.1.76
Thompson, E. P. (2016). *The making of the English working class*. Open Road Media.
Tilebein, M. (2006). A complex adaptive systems approach to efficiency and innovation. *Kybernetes, 35*(7/8), 1087–1099. https://doi.org/10.1108/03684920610675123

Tödtling, F., & Kaufmann, A. (1999). Innovation systems in regions of Europe – A comparative perspective. *European Planning Studies, 7*(6), 699–717.
Valente, M. (2016). Agent-based simulation modeling: Definitions and a methodological proposal. In *Relational methodologies and epistemology in economics and management sciences* (pp. 128–139). IGI Global.
van Bekkum, O., & Bijman, J. (2006). Innovations in cooperative ownership: Converted and hybrid listed cooperatives. In *Business paper presented at the 7th international conference on management in AgriFood chains and networks* (Vol. 31, pp. 1–15).
Vieta, M. (2019). The emergence of Argentina's empresas recuperadas por sus trabajadores: From workers' lived experiences of crisis to autogestión. In *Workers' self-management in Argentina*. Brill.
Vieta, M., & Lionais, D. (2022). The new cooperativism, the commons, and the post-capitalist imaginary. *The Journal of Cooperative Studies, 55*(3), 9–24.
von Gierke, O. (1868). *Rechtsgeschichte der deutschen Genossenschaft* (Vol. 1). Weidmann.
Warren, J. (2022a). *Co-operative conversions & community development in the UK: An ecosystems perspective*. Centre for Learning, Social Economy & Work.
Warren, J. N. (2022b). *The cooperative economy: Towards a stakeholder-led democracy*. Doctoral dissertation.
Warren, J. (2023). Law, legislation, cooperation: Towards a general theory of cooperation. *International Journal of Cooperative Law, 5*, 55–94.
Warren, J. (2024). A path-dependence analysis of Italian social and community cooperatives. *Journal of Entrepreneurial and Organizational Diversity*. (forthcoming).
Warren, J. N., Hübner, J., Bigiero, L., & Oguyemi, K. (Eds.) (2024). *Routledge handbook of cooperative economics & management*. Taylor & Francis.
Wieland, J. (2018). *Relational economics: A political economy*. Springer.
Williamson, O. E. (2007). The economic institutions of capitalism. Firms, markets, relational contracting. In *Das Summa Summarum des Management* (pp. 61–75). Springer.
Wilson, D. S., & Wilson, E. O. (2007). Rethinking the theoretical foundation of sociobiology. *The Quarterly Review of Biology, 82*(4), 327–348.
Wolff, R. D. (2012). *Democracy at work: A cure for capitalism*. Haymarket Books.
Yang, L., & Gilbert, N. (2008). Getting away from numbers: Using qualitative observation for agent-based modeling. *Advances in Complex Systems, 11*(02), 175–185.

Jerome Nikolai Warren obtained an Advanced Diploma from the Alabama School of Mathematics and Science and subsequently studied Religious and Cultural Studies via New College at the University of Alabama. After this, he obtained a B.Sc. in Economics and an M.A. in Political Economy at the University of Siegen, before receiving his doctorate (magna cum laude) at the University of Cologne. Between 2022 and 2024, he was Chair SFPI at the Belgian Royal Academy of Sciences, Fine Arts and Letters, a position established by the Belgian sovereign wealth fund, SFPI, to advise on developing a sustainable view of the firm, encompassing both ecological and social dimensions. Beginning in early 2025, he will participate in an EU Horizon Innovation project, "BioFairNet," dedicated to providing solutions for regions attempting to move away from intensive agriculture and coalmining towards sustainable business practices. He is also the lead editor of the *Routledge Handbook of Cooperative Economics and Management* (2024) and its companion volume, *Global Cooperative Economics and Movements* (2025), and publishes on topics of economic democracy.

Understanding Barriers to Relational Contracting: Exploring Challenges and Solutions

Tim Cummins

Abstract Relational contracting emphasizes long-term partnerships, mutual benefits, and adaptive problem-solving, contrasting with traditional transactional contracting. Despite its advantages, implementing relational contracting faces significant barriers, including internal organizational challenges and external environmental factors. This chapter explores these barriers through theoretical frameworks and real-world case studies, offering strategies and solutions for organizations aiming to adopt relational contracting. It underscores the importance of organizational culture, leadership, and structural dynamics in fostering successful relational contracts. Furthermore, it discusses the potential of relational contracting to operate within broader relational networks, facilitating more resilient, equitable, and innovative economic ecosystems. The chapter concludes by advocating a balanced approach that integrates both relational and transactional models to navigate the complexities of modern business environments.

Keywords Relational contracting · Transactional contracting · Long-term partnerships · Mutual benefits · Adaptive problem-solving · Organizational culture · Trust-building · Collaborative decision-making · Sustainable business practices

1 Introduction

Relational contracting is a field of contract theory that saw its origins in the 1960s (Macneil, 1969), though drawing somewhat on earlier work on transaction cost economics (Coase, 1937). In contrast to these transactional approaches, relational contracting emphasizes long-term partnerships, mutual benefits, and adaptive problem-solving mechanisms.

In terms of behaviors, transactional contracting tends to be associated with a more adversarial approach where mutual benefit is not necessarily viewed as important.

T. Cummins (✉)
University of Leeds, Leeds, UK
e-mail: tcummins@worldcc.com

J. D. Rendtorff et al. (eds.), *Advances in Relational Economics*, Relational Economics and Organization Governance,
https://doi.org/10.1007/978-3-031-75725-9_7

Relational contracting is collaborative in nature and creates an environment for ongoing cooperation between the parties in a spirit of equity and fairness.

However, despite the potential advantages of a more collaborative style, the implementation of relational contracting has proven challenging. By examining both theoretical frameworks and real-world case studies, this chapter explores the barriers that organizations face in developing and maintaining effective relational agreements. It then discusses strategies and solutions to mitigate these barriers, offering recommendations for organizations and practitioners who seek to implement relational contracting in contemporary business environments.

2 Contracts Versus Contracting: What Is the Difference?

While the terms "relational contract" and "relational contracting" are often used interchangeably, there are real and substantive differences between them. A relational contract is the artifact itself, whereas relational contracting is the overall process through which a relational contract is formed and managed. In general, both theory and practice have tended to view relational contracts as a specific type of contract used exclusively for complex, long-term relationships where core elements cannot be fully defined at the outset. However, there is an alternative and much broader view of relational contracting, where it is seen as an approach that prioritizes long-term relationships and cooperation across all types of contracts.

These differing perspectives are important because many of the barriers we will explore are a consequence of the dominant transaction-based view. As Oliver Williamson identified in his 1981 paper, it is difficult for organizations to develop the capabilities needed to operate with a hybrid of transactional and relational contracting (Williamson, 1981). The effort to minimize transaction costs often leads to rigid structures and practices that can be counterproductive when flexibility and deeper relational engagement are required to support long-term collaboration.

3 The Growth of Interest in Relational Contracts

Relational theory is more than 60 years old, and the barriers to adoption are substantial, so why are we observing growing interest in this concept?

Firstly, the uncertainty inherent in contemporary business environments serves as a powerful impetus for the adoption of more structured collaborative relationships, such as relational contracting (Frydlinger, 2021). Organizations are operating in an era marked by rapid technological advances, geopolitical shifts, and volatile market conditions. Traditional transactional approaches often fall short in addressing the complexities and uncertainties that organizations face. Servitization[1] is one example of the resulting shift in trading relationships. For customers, this typically results in greater adaptability to market changes and reduced uncertainty through flexible service options and performance-based contracts tailored to their needs (Michalik et al., 2019). Relational contracting goes beyond this by offering a framework that allows parties to navigate uncertainty through mutually agreed mechanisms that introduce open communication, maintenance of shared goals, and joint governance. By emphasizing trust-building mechanisms and long-term commitments, relational contracts provide a foundation for parties to collaboratively manage risks, adapt to changing circumstances, and co-create value over time.

Secondly, relational frameworks have the potential to operate within the broader context of relational networks or ecosystems, in this context serving as an enabler of relational economics. Rather than viewing relationships in isolation, relational contracting acknowledges the interconnectedness between organizations, suppliers, customers, and other stakeholders within a networked ecosystem. By embracing a network perspective, relational contracts can leverage the collective resources, expertise, and capabilities of ecosystem partners by establishing shared standards that assist in greater resilience, more equitable sharing of risk, and an environment that encourages continuous improvement and innovation (Dyer & Singh, 1998).

In both situations, relational contracting takes us beyond transactional exchanges to an environment where collaboration can unlock new opportunities for growth and sustainability. As such, the integration of relational frameworks within relational networks could represent a particularly significant paradigm shift in economic thinking and offer a path toward more inclusive and sustainable forms of economic development.

4 Addressing the Barriers

4.1 Organizational Culture

The culture of an organization shapes the way it interacts with suppliers and customers, influencing values such as trust, collaboration, and ethical conduct. A cooperative, ethical culture typically encourages strong, mutually beneficial relationships, founded on a readiness to be more open and transparent in its dealings. A culture that is more driven by rapid growth and profit will often prioritize short-term gains over long-term partnerships and operate with a greater level of secrecy or reluctance to share information.

[1] "We regard servitization as an overarching concept that includes but goes beyond service infusion, where servitization is defined as the transformational process of shifting from a product-centric business model and logic to a service-centric approach" (Kowalkowski et al., 2017, p. 7).

These cultural attributes manifest themselves in a variety of ways, many of which are individual barriers to a relational approach and will therefore be addressed later in this chapter. They include things like attitudes to risk, incentive structures, and management systems. At this point, we will examine the role of leadership, since it is clear that an organization's leaders set the tone for its culture. In this context, there is no question that relational contracting depends upon visible leadership endorsement and support for its success. Even with that support, it can be difficult, perhaps impossible, to perform in accordance with a relational contract if the embedded organizational culture is transactional.

Research by World Commerce and Contracting has identified that, on average, 29% of an organization's workforce is somehow involved in the contracting process (WorldCC, 2023). Based on this, it becomes easy to understand how complicated it is to successfully implement relational behavior in an organization where this is not the norm. One approach is to limit initiatives to programs or projects which are relatively self-contained and therefore depend on a smaller group of individuals. Let's look at some case studies that demonstrate this approach.

Rolls-Royce assembled a dedicated group to collaborate closely with airline clients to tailor services precisely to their operational needs. This relational approach led to its TotalCare service, which not only ensured optimum engine performance and reduced downtime but also aligned cost with engine usage, creating shared value.

Microsoft and **Accenture** set up an initial collaboration based on the outsourcing of Microsoft's finance and accounting support. It hinged on a dedicated group of individuals who focused on aligning business objectives and technology strategies and led to the creation of an organization called Avanade. This team applies principles of relational contracting by ensuring continuous communication, mutual understanding of goals, and flexibility to adapt as project needs evolve.

A key success factor has been their ability to co-innovate and share risks and rewards equitably, treating each project not just as a transaction but as part of a strategic relationship. This synergy has led to high-quality services delivered to clients worldwide and illustrates how focused relational contracting can drive mutual growth and success.

The **Australian Department of Defence** (DoD) offers a further example, in this case, their sustainment contracts for various defense platforms, in particular, ship maintenance and repair. In each case, a relatively small core team from the DoD works closely with defense contractors and service providers under relational frameworks that establish stand-alone governance principles. These are designed to foster a collaborative environment where all parties are incentivized to focus on shared outcomes rather than fulfilling rigid transactional obligations.

The contracts often involve performance-based logistics (PBL), where compensation is tied to the achievement of agreed-upon outcomes, such as the availability and readiness rates of the vessels. This setup encourages all parties to innovate and find cost-effective solutions to sustainment challenges.

Finally, **ConocoPhillips**, a global energy corporation, provides an example of relational contracting in its thoughtful approach to managing complex and large-scale projects within the oil and gas sector. The company has emphasized the importance of forming strategic alliances with selected suppliers and contractors to enhance efficiency and innovation across its operations.

One such instance involves ConocoPhillips' use of relational contracting in its major projects, such as the development of oil fields and other energy infrastructure. A key aspect of their approach is integrating contractors and suppliers in project planning and design to optimize project execution plans. This integration is again facilitated by governance standards that encourage all parties to work toward common goals, such as reducing costs, improving safety standards, and meeting project timelines.

The success of this approach has been demonstrated by a high degree of efficiency and innovation, leading to cost savings, timely projects completion, and enhanced operational performance for all those involved.

4.2 *Organizational Structure*

It has been suggested that relational contracting is incompatible with hierarchical organizational structures. Yet when we consider the levels of collaboration traditionally achieved in hierarchical management models such as those of Japan, we must challenge this idea. The following brief article, examining this paradox, was prepared by the author, based on research with representatives of Japanese industry.

4.2.1 Unraveling the Paradox

This apparent paradox requires analysis and understanding of power and authority in Japanese society. Japanese organizational structures operate with clear lines of authority and respect for seniority. However, unlike in some Western contexts where hierarchy may impede collaboration and innovation, Japanese culture alters the power dynamic through an emphasis on relational bonds, consensus-building, and group harmony.

The research has led to several key concepts, the first of which is "uchi-soto," which refers to the distinction between insiders (uchi) and outsiders (soto). Within hierarchical organizational structures, there is a strong sense of loyalty and cohesion among insiders, who share common goals and values. This internal unity enables organizations to navigate complex social hierarchies and external challenges while fostering trust and cooperation among members. (I find this interesting because I recall a Japanese colleague expressing surprise that Western executives make themselves inaccessible by having corner offices with windows. He told me that in Japan, a "window person" is someone on the way out.)

Japanese culture also places a premium on "wa" (harmony) and "nemawashi" (consensus-building), which prioritize the collective good over individual interests. Together, these mean that hierarchical power structures are softened by relational norms that encourage consultation, collaboration, and mutual respect. Even within hierarchical organizations, decision-making processes often involve extensive discussions and consensus-building exercises to ensure buy-in and alignment among stakeholders.

Finally, there is the concept of "amae," which recognizes mutual dependency and the need for nurturing relationships. This underpins many interpersonal interactions in Japanese society. So, while an organization might be hierarchical, superiors are expected to provide guidance and support to subordinates, which fosters an environment of trust and reciprocity—which are the types of behavior that facilitate relational exchanges.

4.2.2 So, Is It the Structure, or Is It Us?

From this, we must conclude that it is not so much organizational structure that impacts the ability to collaborate, but rather the cultural and behavioral norms and expectations that operate within it. Hierarchical power structures can work fine if they are complemented by relational norms and values that promote collaboration, consensus-building, and group cohesion. (And it is worth noting that until Japan engaged more fully in the global economy, it did not need contracts at all: relationships were everything.)

4.3 Internal Barriers

There are a range of characteristics that impede the use of relational contracts or restrict relational contracting capabilities (Gibbons & Henderson, 2012). The most significant of these are discussed below.

4.3.1 Short-Term Focus

Many organizations operate with measurement and motivational systems that prioritize immediate gains over long-term value creation. This focus stands in the way of relational contracts, which require upfront investments of time and resources to support their approval and negotiation, as well as an implication of ongoing support.

4.3.2 Lack of Trust

In many organizations, the culture surrounding contracts is one of low trust. It is founded on a belief that external parties cannot be trusted to deliver on their commitments and that internal staff cannot be trusted to negotiate responsibly. Hence, as we know from WorldCC's regular studies of "The Most Negotiated

Terms," there is a strong focus on negative incentives and the protection of assets—liability, indemnity, liquidated damages, and intellectual property rights. Frequently driven by the Legal department, the contract is often the antithesis of the collaborative spirit and the open communication and shared vulnerability required for relational contracting. Without trust, parties are less likely to engage in the open exchange of information necessary for these types of agreements.

4.3.3 Risk Aversion

It is not only legal traditions that underlie risk aversion. Increasingly, the organizational response to growing regulation and market uncertainty is to reduce their risk appetite. Since they do not understand the relational model and its ability to better manage risk, they see it instead as "new and untested"—and therefore in itself risky. Organizations with a risk-averse culture may be reluctant to enter into contracts that require flexibility and adaptation over time. Since relational contracting involves adjusting to changing circumstances, it is often perceived as riskier than more defined transactional agreements, which are based on rigid control.

4.3.4 Silo-ed Departments

Silo-ed departments are a consequence of growing specialism and represent an internal contention system that is often risk-averse and resistant to change. Since relational contracts typically require input and cooperation from multiple parts of the organization, generating the necessary support is challenging. The silo-ed model is also typically reflected in enterprise systems deployment. This results in fragmented data and makes it difficult to support the coherent oversight and integrated communications that are required for relational contracting.

4.3.5 Command-and-Control Leadership

As previously explained, hierarchical structures do not in themselves prevent a relational approach. However, top-down decision-making structures can limit the autonomy of teams to make the collaborative decisions necessary for relational contracting. Experience has shown that relational approaches prove threatening to an organizational structure that was designed for transactional dealings and in such an environment, if relational contracting occurs at all, it is very much the exception and depends on sustained focus by an executive sponsor.

4.3.6 Transactional View of Relationships

Shifting from a transactional to a relational view requires fundamental change, as illustrated by the characteristics set out above. When an organization views business relationships purely through a transactional lens (which is often the case for the way that suppliers are handled), its people and systems are geared toward cost minimization and contract enforcement. It is a long journey to shift to a perspective that values mutual benefits and shared success.

5 A Transactional World

To understand and assess the potential for change, we must first understand and evaluate the forces that lie behind the dominance of today's transactional model. While the scene for this had been set in the 1980s (Williamson, 1981), the rapid adoption of this approach was influenced by several key factors that occurred over the last 30 years. These factors reflect broader economic, technological, and cultural changes that collectively reshaped business practices and priorities.

Globalization was perhaps the most visible and dynamic of these forces. As businesses expanded their operations internationally, they engaged with a diverse array of suppliers and customers. The opportunity for low-cost sourcing resulted in many traditional supply relationships being disrupted or discarded. "Loyalty" thus became a thing of the past (Gereffi et al., 2005). This expansion also necessitated a more standardized, scalable approach to manage numerous, often short-term, relationships efficiently. The development and use of contract templates surged, with clear, predefined terms and policies that sought to limit negotiation.

Just as technology fueled globalization, it also streamlined and standardized operations and business efficiency. The automation of procurement and supply chain processes made transactional relationships more manageable and appealing because they could be easily monitored, measured, and adjusted based on performance metrics. In addition, technology often removed the people on whom relationships had previously depended.

These forces also underpinned increasingly competitive and price-sensitive markets, leading companies to prioritize cost reduction and operational efficiency to maintain profit margins. A transactional approach, with its focus on clear deliverables and costs, allowed businesses to tightly control expenses and make quick adjustments as required so as to remain competitive.

At the same time, market and regulatory forces started to drive more frequent reporting and, as a consequence, a much shorter term focus on financial performance. The quarterly earnings cycle led businesses to favor transactional relationships that could quickly impact financial results, rather than investing in the slower yield of relational strategies.

This overall business environment led to shifting attitudes toward risk and risk allocation. Transactional relationships were seen as less risky in that they can be more easily dissolved or restructured in response to changing conditions, providing businesses with greater flexibility. At the same time, regulatory and compliance pressures resulted in a far greater focus on power and control, with contracts increasingly focused on imposing obligations and establishing rights of audit.

Taken together, these factors have created an environment where transactional relationships are often seen as more pragmatic and less risky, particularly in contexts demanding high agility and compliance. However, this shift has also led to challenges such as reduced loyalty and collaboration between parties, potentially stifling innovation and long-term sustainability. Organizations, both public and private sector, are left struggling with how best to respond.

6 Conclusion: The Way Ahead

Turbulent markets taught us the value of more robust, sustainable relationships. They demonstrated the fact that transactional agility works only when there is abundant supply. This means that there are compelling forces that should be driving a shift away from the dominant transactional model toward relational contracting.

Ironically, this shift is both enabled and driven by some of the same forces that took us to a transactional approach. Digital technologies underpin a more integrated operational model and the consolidated data flows that support greater adaptability. Dynamic market forces and a changing regulatory environment have made longer term, stable relationships more attractive and more necessary. Traditional transactional methods are increasingly inadequate in addressing the complexities and uncertainties of today's global markets. In contrast, relational contracting offers a robust framework for sustainable partnerships and collaborative problem-solving.

Among these forces, the advent of Environmental, Social, and Governance (ESG) standards is reshaping corporate priorities and approaches, although with some inconsistency across regions. For example, the European Union is taking the lead in proposing stringent regulations that demand greater openness and transparency, forcing businesses to reassess their operational and relational strategies. These regulations provide opportunities to innovate and embed sustainable practices that can lead to enhanced long-term value creation.

So, while the forces for change are increasingly evident, the embedded systems, structures, and practices of a transactional model are not easy to overcome. Indeed, the real point may be that transactional and relational models need to coexist; they are not mutually exclusive. Relationships operate across a spectrum. This requires business leaders to champion a shift toward a culture that appreciates the need for a balance between long-term benefits and short-term gains and cultivates trust and openness in both internal and external dealings. A key step in enabling this change will be a realignment of incentive structures to support collaborative efforts and innovative thinking, taking us beyond conventional metrics of success.

In conclusion, the evolution toward relational contracting is both an imperative and an opportunity. Success depends upon a readiness to challenge current approaches to contracts and relationships, understanding that they serve different purposes in different situations. As markets now require us to be more adaptive, we must also be more adaptive in our view of contracts and contracting. Rigid models will not serve us well, which is why relational contracting itself must be flexible in the form it takes.

For practitioners and theorists alike, our world currently offers fertile ground for innovation in how we conceptualize and execute contract relationships. In embracing these changes, we have the potential to create more resilient, responsive, and responsible trading relationships and business practices.

References

Coase, R. H. (1937). The nature of the firm. *Economica, 4*(16), 386–405.

Dyer, J. H., & Singh, H. (1998). The relational view: Cooperative strategy and sources of interorganizational competitive advantage. *The Academy of Management Review, 23*(4), 660–679.

Frydlinger, D. (2021). *Contracting in the new economy: Using relational contracts to boost trust and collaboration in strategic business relationships* (with K. Vitasek, J. Bergman, & T. Cummins). Springer International Publishing.

Gereffi, G., Humphrey, J., & Sturgeon, T. (2005). The governance of global value chains. *Review of International Political Economy, 12*(1), 78–104.

Gibbons, R., & Henderson, R. (2012). Relational contracts and organizational capabilities. *Organization Science, 23*(5), 1350–1364.

Kowalkowski, C., Gebauer, H., Kamp, B., & Parry, G. (2017). Servitization and deservitization: Overview, concepts, and definitions. *Industrial Marketing Management, 60*, 4–10.

Macneil, I. R. (1969). Whither contracts? *Journal of Legal Education, 21*, 403–420.

Michalik, A., Besenfelder, C., & Henke, M. (2019). Servitization of small- and medium-sized manufacturing enterprises: Facing barriers through the Dortmund management model. *IFAC-PapersOnLine, 52*(13), 2326–2331.

Williamson, O. E. (1981). The economics of organization: The transaction cost approach. *American Journal of Sociology, 87*(3), 548–577.

World Commerce & Contracting (Ed.). (2023). *CCM: The journey to operational excellence.* Benchmark report 2023 (with T. Cummins & S. Guyer).

Tim Cummins is President of World Commerce & Contracting and a former Professor in the School of Law at the University of Leeds. For 25 years, Tim has led research and the development of standards for the Commercial and Contract Management discipline, an achievement that was recognized by the Financial Times "Market Shaper of the Year" award in 2019.

Leadership as a Temporal Abstraction: A Conceptual Reflection

Willem Fourie

Abstract Integrating the temporal dimension of reality into the philosophical foundations of leadership theory remains a challenge. To address this challenge, this conceptual article uses the process-philosophical concept of the event to explore ways in which to reframe understanding of leadership by taking time seriously. It builds on existing work, particularly the research conducted by Ladkin and Wood, by highlighting two implications. Firstly, the process philosophy of the event makes it possible to conceive of leadership as a fluid phenomenon that essentially serves as an abstraction derived from concrete influential events. Secondly, and relatedly, leadership as a temporal abstraction is relational in at least three respects.

Keywords Leadership · Whitehead · Temporality · Leadership and time · Post-heroic leadership

1 Introduction

Numerous attempts have been made to incorporate the temporal dimension into conceptions of leadership. Recently, Kalish and Luria (2021) employed implicit leadership theories as a framework to investigate how leadership predictors change over time. In an earlier article, Alipour et al. (2017) explored how temporal individual differences could be productively included in both implicit leadership and followership theories.

When considering research that reflects on the integration of the temporal element at a conceptual level, the work conducted by Ladkin and Wood remains highly influential. Wood utilizes Whitehead's concept of the "event" to underscore the procedural components of leadership (Wood, 2005; Wood & Ladkin, 2008). Ladkin, in collaboration with Wood, further develops the concept of the leadership "moment."

W. Fourie (✉)
Department of Business Management, University of Pretoria, Pretoria, South Africa
e-mail: willemf@sun.ac.za

J. D. Rendtorff et al. (eds.), *Advances in Relational Economics*, Relational Economics and Organization Governance,
https://doi.org/10.1007/978-3-031-75725-9_8

According to Ladkin (2017, p. 394), the leadership moment allows us to perceive leadership as "a lived and dynamic experience" rather than an abstract set of traits or behaviors attributed to an individual. This perspective suggests that leadership emerges when the context, purpose, followers, and individuals willing to assume the leader role align in a particular manner. Ladkin shifts the focus to who determines what leadership is and when it emerges, asserting that it is not merely about how these factors align but rather how they are perceived by followers that truly determines who is accepted in the leader role (Ladkin, 2017, p. 394).

While Wood's work more explicitly concentrates on the temporal dimension of the leadership moment, Ladkin's use of the word "moment" does not necessarily imply a temporal dimension (Ladkin, 2020, pp. 25–27). Instead, it refers to the three types of phenomena delineated in phenomenology: wholes, parts, and moments. Framing leadership as a moment recognizes that it is "wholly dependent on the historical, social, and psychological context from which it arises" and can only be expressed "through particular localised conditions and the individuals who participate in both creating it and making sense of it" (Ladkin, 2020, p. 27).

The conceptual argument presented in this article builds upon the work of Wood and Ladkin and seeks to expand the conceptual reflection on integrating the temporal dimension into the theoretical basis of leadership studies. It does so by specifically focusing on the "event" in Whitehead's philosophy. It complements Wood's work on leadership and the event in Whitehead's philosophy by placing less emphasis on the procedural components and focusing more on how the event can be used as an analogy to understand leadership as an abstraction emanating from distinctive influential events.

2 Whitehead and the Event

Whitehead's philosophy of the event can be framed in terms of a more general philosophical problem also familiar to leadership scholars: while the world of scientific thought is "neat, trim, tidy and exact," reality, according to Whitehead, is "radically untidy" (Whitehead, 1917, p. 110). In fact, "the influence of language, moulded by science, which foists on us exact concepts as though they represented the immediate deliverances of experience" conceals the "disorderly character" of reality. The result is that we think we have "immediate experience of a world of perfectly defined objects implicated in perfectly defined events which, as known to us by the direct deliverance of our senses, happen at exact instants of time, in a space formed by exact points" (Whitehead, 1917, p. 110).

Whitehead's work is famously categorized as process philosophy, according to which he proposes "a vision of reality that opposes the notion of substance-stability and defends the relational nature of the world" (Matiz et al., 2021, p. 203). In terms of management research, this turn to temporality exemplified by process philosophy "demands [of] the researcher and the manager learning to see the world in its multiplicity and direct himself towards a constant becoming, focusing on the instability and dynamics of organizational life" (Matiz et al., 2021, p. 203).

Whitehead offers valuable insights to bring leadership studies closer to the complexity of reality, with his notion of an "event" as a valuable starting point. He does not employ or define "event" in the same manner as we do in everyday language. Instead, Whitehead regards events as the "fundamental facts of nature," interconnected through their "spatio-temporal relationships." In his earlier work, he maintains a conceptual distinction between space and time, where "spatial extensions are described by relationships between objects," and "temporal extensions are described by relationships between events." However, in his later thinking, he employs the concept of "space-time" to elucidate the relationship between events. In essence, events are not confined within time and space; rather, as Whitehead puts it, time and space are "inseparable from events" (MacKenzie, 1923, p. 235). Whitehead also describes space and time as "abstractions from events" (Whitehead, 1919, p. 63).

According to Whitehead, events "can contain (or extend over) other events which are part of them." In fact, "every event spans over other events that are constituent parts of itself, and every event is spanned over by other events of which it forms a part" (Whitehead, 1911, pp. 4, 61). Whitehead also characterizes events—extensions with space and time as properties between these extensions—as "components of actuality and elements of becomingness" (Whitehead, 1919, p. 61). In Whitehead's words:

> [An event] is what does become in nature. It can never happen again; for essentially it is just itself, there and then. An event is just what it is and is just how it is related, and it is nothing else. Any event, however similar, with different relations, is another event. There is no element of hypothesis in any actual event. (Whitehead, 1919, pp. 60–61)

While events themselves remain unchanged, change occurs through the relationships of an actual event to events that were not yet actual but become so in the creative evolution of nature (Whitehead, 1919, p. 62).

Figure 1 provides a visual representation of the event in Whitehead's philosophy, as well as the closely related topic of occasions. As shown in the figure, the temporal dimension is a constitutive component of this conceptual structure. As additional context, it is useful to note that, in some of his works, Whitehead conceptualizes an event as a meeting point of "actual occasions." Actual occasions, as used in this context, are

> drops of experience or particles of instantaneous point-flashes. Actual occasions are not readily perceptible because they fade in and out instantaneously. What remains perceptible are the events, which manifest themselves by things. (Matiz et al., 2021, p. 205)

Radically, objects should be understood as qualities of events, and events as relations between objects (Whitehead, 1919, p. 60). Practically, this implies that the same object can be linked to different events (Whitehead, 1919, p. 63). It also signifies that objects and events enter into our experience in distinct ways. Events are "lived through," extending around us as "the medium within which our physical

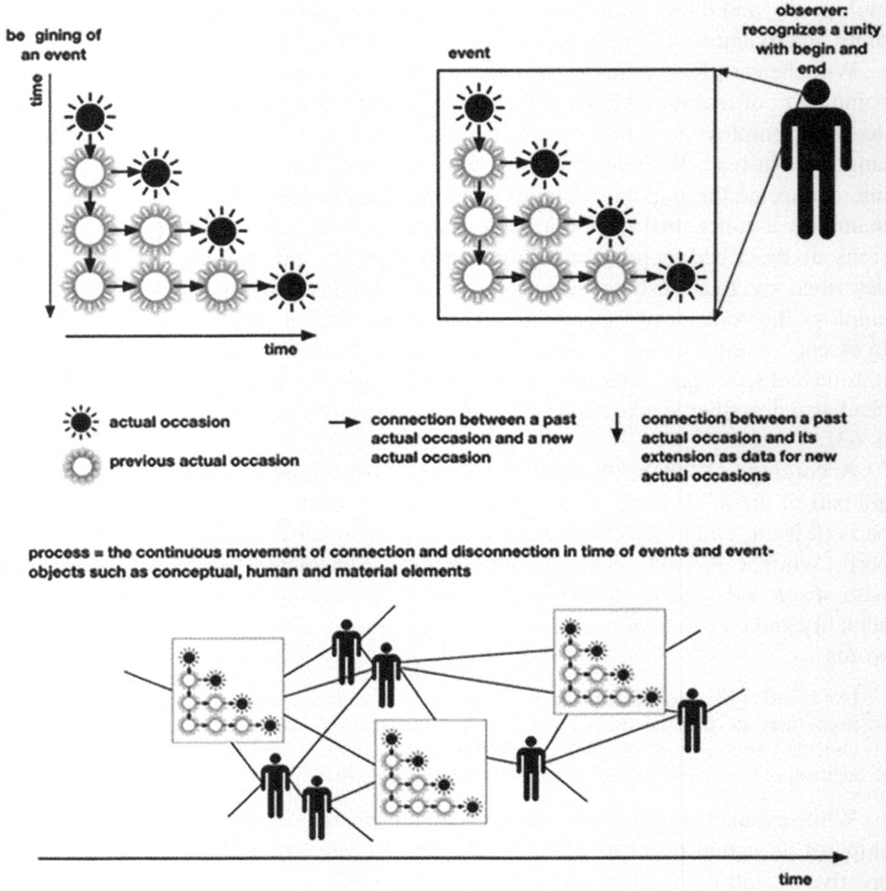

Fig. 1 Actual occasions and events according to Whitehead's conception of the process (Matiz et al., 2021, p. 206)

experience unfolds," and "they are themselves the development of that experience" (Whitehead, 1919, p. 63).

Objects, on the other hand, enter our experience through what Whitehead terms the "intellectuality of recognition." Since the present is not "instantaneous" but "a duration" or "a stretch of time," we perceive an object as "constancy amid the partial events of the present duration" (Whitehead, 1919, p. 64). Objects make rational thought, defined as the "comparison of event with event," possible.

Whitehead's concept of the event of course does more than merely raise awareness of the temporal aspect of reality. In a fundamental sense, it amplifies the definitiveness, tangibility, and distinctiveness of the occurrences that constitute reality. It also reshapes our perception of reality, portraying it not as a collection of instantaneous moments but as extended durations or episodes. Additionally, it redefines our understanding of time and space as relative concepts. According to Whitehead's philosophy, space and time can only be understood in relation to the events that become actual within the perception of a particular observer.

While Whitehead's work addresses ontological and epistemological questions largely outside the scope of leadership studies, it provides stimuli and conceptual frameworks that could help incorporate the temporal dimension of reality into the philosophical underpinnings of leadership theory. As will be discussed in more detail in the next section, he does so by offering insights into the conceiving of leadership in terms of concrete episodes. When we consider leadership in terms of concrete episodes or occurrences, we come closer to the intricacies of reality.

3 The Fluidity of Leadership

Day and Antonakis' view, synthesizing much of the past decades' research on leadership, that leadership is in essence about "an influencing process that occurs between a leadership and followers" and "how this influencing process is explained" (2012, p. 5), remains generally accepted. The consequence of this influencing process is typically a change in how followers behave, think, or believe.

Yet the actual process of influence is of course complex. As has been researched extensively, factors related to individual leaders, such as their personality (e.g., Kwok et al., 2018; Deinert et al., 2015) and even their mood (Joseph et al., 2015; Jin et al., 2016), play a role. Yet followers and other group-level factors play a much more active role in the granting of influence to leaders than often simplified approaches to leader influence would assume (e.g., Fourie & Mystris, 2021).

Even though it is now over a decade old, the analysis by Day and Antonakis, as shown in Fig. 2, of trends in research on leadership serves to illustrate the complexity

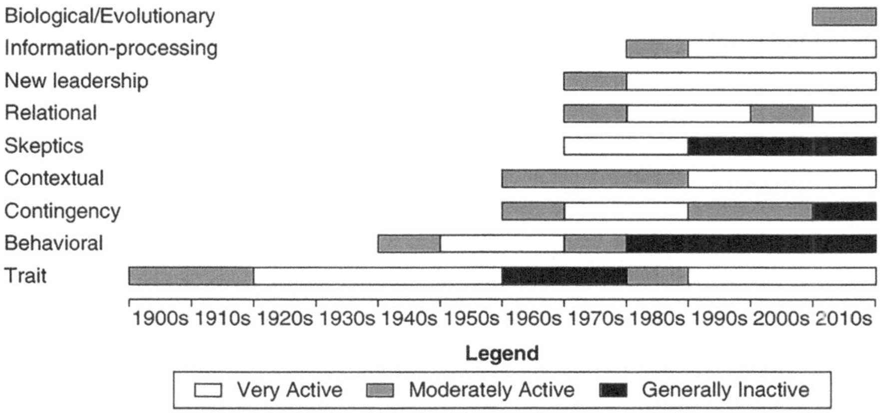

Fig. 2 Approaches to leadership (Day & Antonakis, 2012, p. 7)

also inherent in the influence process. The ebb and flow of, say, trait-based approaches to leadership at least partly reflects differing views on where to place the origin of influence. Contextual and contingency approaches have a much stronger substantive inclusion of the context, whereas biological and evolutionary perspectives look to natural processes to some extent beyond the control of an individual and beyond the "reach" of the context.

Drawing inspiration from Whitehead and relying on the definition of leadership provided by Day and Antonakis, it seems possible, conceptually at least, to dissect the act of leading in a specific context into distinct yet interconnected influence processes or events. A change in behavior, thought, or belief brought about by the symbol of a leader and the accompanying bestowal of influence by followers could be viewed as a single episode, or, in the context of this chapter, an event, following Whitehead's terminology. This influence event is inherently complex, as it extends over other influence events that constitute its components while being extended over by other events in which it plays a part.

More dramatically, and analogously to how Whitehead describes space-time as abstractions from events, we are faced with the question of whether leadership should not be viewed as the constituting component of an influence event but as an abstraction thereof. Put differently, if we continue to assume that leadership is about influence, and if we thus take an influence process—simplified as a change in behavior, thought, or belief—as the starting point and the defining characteristic of the influence event, it becomes possible to view leadership as a function of the event.

This implies that identifying leaders and followers within a particular setting is not a straightforward or observational task; rather, it involves making inferences based on a multitude of overlapping influence processes in that environment. In practical terms, this means that the roles of leaders and followers can shift at any given moment.

4 Steering Clear of Randomness

Does this mean that leadership is left to be a random shifting of roles over time? Our experience of reality seems to indicate otherwise. One way of making sense of the temporal fluidity of leadership is through the perhaps surprising reference to elements from social identity theory.

A starting point is the reality that followers find themselves simultaneously subject to multiple and overlapping influence processes. This is because followers belong to multiple groups concurrently.

A group, in the sense that I use it here, follows minimalist definitions according to which a group is any collection of people that share an attribute (Blau, 1977, p. 7; Stangor, 2004, p. 24; Asch, 1952, p. 265). Consequently, a vast array of groups exists, varying in numerous aspects, including size, cohesion, member commitment, permanence, purpose, communication patterns, structure, decision-making processes, membership stability, resources, and many other factors.

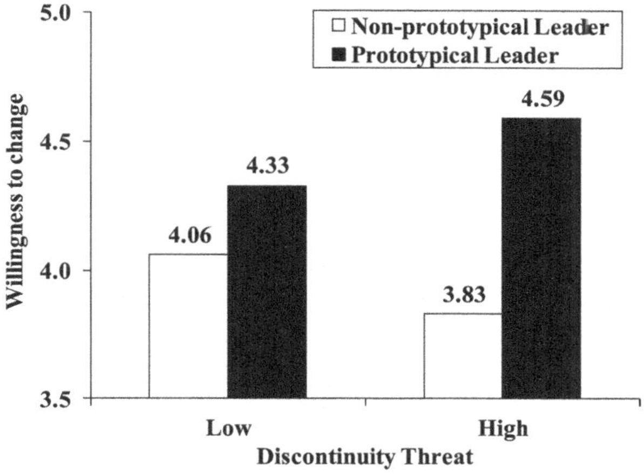

Fig. 3 Willingness to change as a function of leader group prototypicality and discontinuity (Hogg et al., 2012, p. 276)

In each group, as has been argued by social identity leadership theorists (e.g., Hogg, 2001 and more recently Steffens et al., 2021), the perception that some group members are more prototypical than others contributes significantly to these prototypical leaders becoming leaders. Although this may not hold for all leaders in all groups and under all circumstances, it generally aligns with reality. Leaders in a group setting symbolize who the group fundamentally aspires to be at its core. In doing so, they effectively influence other members, often through the mechanism of social attraction.

The concept of leader prototypicality has been shown to have various effects related to leader-follower and group dynamics. Highly prototypical leaders have been found, for example, to have great influence when it comes to motivating change among followers, as illustrated in Fig. 3.

However, it is evident that not all group members, or followers, will be equally influenced by the leader as a symbol of influence within their respective groups. Simultaneously, they are members of multiple groups, and, through these groups, multiple influence processes occur concurrently. The decision of a group member to grant one leader influence in a particular influence process results from the negotiation of multiple memberships and influence processes at a specific moment. Several factors come into play when members, or followers, make this calculation, including group cohesion, their commitment to the group, their level of identification with the group, and clarity of the group's identity, among others (Fourie & Mystris, 2021).

Overlapping group memberships and the resulting differences in the influence that could be exerted by leaders in any particular moment can be visualized in various ways. One useful approach is using the methodologies championed by social network analysis research. As shown in Fig. 4, using these methods, group memberships overlap and intersect in various ways, while group characteristics and the relative distance between groups differ.

When considering leadership and followership as abstractions derived from interconnected yet distinct influence processes and when keeping in mind followers'

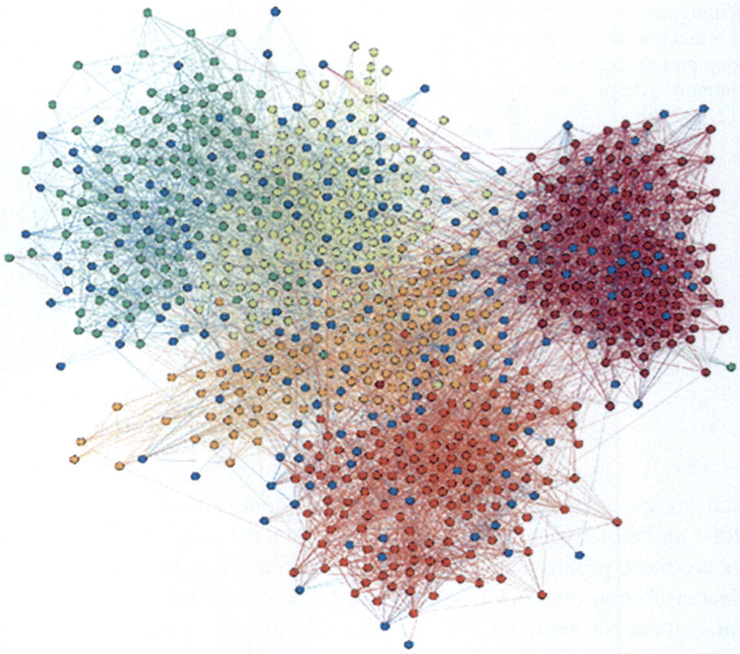

Fig. 4 Social network visualization (Crnovrsanin et al., 2014)

multiple commitments and their agency in interpreting these commitments within each influence process, it becomes conceivable why I argue that leader and follower roles remain fluid. There are few assurances that a particular leader will exert the same level of influence across various events or leadership moments. Ultimately, factors specific to each influence process determine the extent to which followers are willing and able to confer influence upon leaders.

5 The Polyvalence of Influence Events

Thinking of leadership in terms of concrete episodes or moments also highlights the polyvalence of these influence events—here used descriptively to signify the numerous relational dimensions at play in any moment of influence.

Firstly, from the followers' standpoint, an influence event is polycontextual. At the heart of an influence process lies the followers' multiple and overlapping group memberships. These memberships must be navigated, or more precisely, negotiated to ultimately determine how and to what extent they will grant influence in a given event.

In this context, it is essential to acknowledge that group memberships, and consequently, other spheres of influence, can shift depending on the nature of the specific influence event. This is almost certainly the case even within the same organizational context.

Secondly, within a given organizational setting, the defining characteristics of the groups to which a follower belongs at any given moment are intertwined and interconnected. This applies to the ensuing structures, behavioral patterns, and explanations thereof that emerge from these defining attributes. It is therefore inaccurate to discuss the functioning of groups and their internal influence processes as if they operate in isolation from other groups in their environment. Analogous to how Whitehead describes events, groups are also nested within other groups and overlap in various ways.

When one considers the minimal definition of groups that is used in this chapter, namely, that a group is any collection of people who share a common attribute, the group is the most fundamental level at which this interconnectedness occurs—at least as I use it in this chapter. This attribute gives birth to group-level structures and underlying values and worldviews. And attributes themselves stand in a particular relationship to each other. One is never, for example, only a football player. One is always a football player of a specific gender, or a specific sex, with specific cultural and political group memberships.

Thirdly, the act of influence is inherently polylingual. As followers navigate the various spheres of influence to which they are simultaneously subjected—being members of multiple groups—they have no choice but to translate the languages used within these groups to make informed decisions. Monolingualism, or focusing solely on the language of one group, is simply not an option.

6 Concluding Thoughts

The overarching aim of this conceptual chapter was to reflect on how Whitehead's philosophy of the event can enrich our understanding of leadership and the act of leading by incorporating the temporal dimension. Utilizing Whitehead's philosophy of the event, I argue that it is possible to dissect the act of leading in a specific context into distinct, yet interconnected, influence processes. Each of these influence processes can be linked to events in the Whiteheadian sense. When assuming that leadership is in essence about influence, it becomes possible to view both leadership and followership not as inherent components of each influencing process but as abstractions derived from tangible influence processes. This approach highlights the idea that leadership and followership are attributes of specific influence processes and should not be assumed to apply uniformly across all influence processes.

As discussed, it appears that leadership shifts between these influence events. This is primarily because each influencing event demands followers to bestow influence, and this act of granting influence necessitates intricate polyvalent cognitive processes on the part of followers. In practical terms, this implies that followers must negotiate their multiple group memberships and the inherent spheres of influence they encounter in each specific influence event.

By doing so, I reinforce the point made by critical leadership scholars: leadership is not a universal trait or characteristic of an individual, but rather an outcome of influence processes that occur in specific moments or episodes within a given context. These influence processes are embedded within the complex web of relationships, group memberships, and competing commitments that followers navigate.

This perspective challenges us to depart from static notions of leadership and instead embrace the complexity of leadership as it evolves in diverse and ever-changing contexts. It also encourages us to consider the role of followers and their agency in determining when and how they grant influence to leaders.

References

Alipour, K. K., Mohammed, S., & Martinez, P. N. (2017). Incorporating temporality into implicit leadership and followership theories: Exploring inconsistencies between time-based expectations and actual behaviors. *The Leadership Quarterly, 28*(3), 300–316.

Asch, S. E. (1952). *Social psychology*. Prentice-Hall.

Blau, P. M. (1977). *Inequality and heterogeneity: A primitive theory of social structure*. Free Press.

Crnovrsanin, T., Muelder, C. W., Faris, R., Felmlee, D., & Ma, K. (2014). Visualization techniques for categorical analysis of social networks with multiple edge sets. *Social Networks, 37*, 54–64.

Day, D. V., & Antonakis, J. (Eds.). (2012). *The nature of leadership*. Sage Publications.

Deinert, A., Homan, A. C., Boer, D., Voelpel, S. C., & Gutermann, D. (2015). Transformational leadership sub-dimensions and their link to leaders' personality and performance. *The Leadership Quarterly, 26*(6), 1095–1120.

Fourie, W., & Mystris, D. (2021). Leader influence beyond the individual leader: Group-level and member-level factors that affect leader influence. *European Management Review, 18*(1), 115–124.

Hogg, M. A. (2001). A social identity theory of leadership. *Personality and Social Psychology Review, 5*(3), 184–200.

Hogg, M. A., Van Knippenberg, D., & Rast, D. E., III. (2012). The social identity theory of leadership: Theoretical origins, research findings, and conceptual developments. *European Review of Social Psychology, 23*(1), 258–304.

Jin, S., Seo, M., & Shapiro, D. L. (2016). Do happy leaders lead better? Affective and attitudinal antecedents of transformational leadership. *The Leadership Quarterly, 27*(1), 64–84.

Joseph, D. L., Dhanani, L. Y., Shen, W., McHugh, B. C., & McCord, M. A. (2015). Is a happy leader a good leader? A meta-analytic investigation of leader trait affect and leadership. *The Leadership Quarterly, 26*(4), 558–577.

Kalish, Y., & Luria, G. (2021). Traits and time in leadership emergence: A longitudinal study. *The Leadership Quarterly, 32*(2), 101443.

Kwok, N., Hanig, S., Brown, D. J., & Shen, W. (2018). How leader role identity influences the process of leader emergence: A social network analysis. *The Leadership Quarterly, 29*(6), 648–662.

Ladkin, D. (2017). How did that happen? Making sense of the 2016 US presidential election result through the lens of the 'leadership moment'. *Leadership, 13*(4), 393–412.

Ladkin, D. (2020). Why are there so many different theories of leadership? In D. Ladkin (Ed.), *Rethinking leadership: A new look at old questions* (2nd ed., pp. 14–32). Edward Elgar Publishing.

MacKenzie, W. L. (1923). What does Dr. Whitehead mean by 'event'? *Proceedings of the Aristotelian Society, 23*, 229–244.

Matiz, Q. R. S., Chaerki, K. F., & Charki, S. F. (2021). Theorizing relations between past, present, and future: Interactions between process and historical organizational studies through Whitehead's process philosophy. *Philosophy of Management, 20*(2), 201–217.

Stangor, C. (2004). *Social groups in action and interaction*. Psychology Press.

Steffens, N. K., Munt, K. A., Van Knippenberg, D., Platow, M. J., & Haslam, S. A. (2021). Advancing the social identity theory of leadership: A meta-analytic review of leader group prototypicality. *Organizational Psychology Review, 11*(1), 35–72.

Whitehead, A. N. (1911). *An introduction to mathematics*. Henry Holt and Company.

Whitehead, A. N. (1917). The organization of thought. In *The organization of thought: Educational and scientific*. Williams and Norgate.

Whitehead, A. N. (1919). *An enquiry concerning the principles of natural knowledge*. Cambridge University Press.

Wood, M. (2005). The fallacy of misplaced leadership. *Journal of Management Studies*, 42(6).

Wood, M., & Ladkin, D. (2008). The event's the thing: Brief encounters with the leaderful moment. In K. T. James & J. Collins (Eds.), *Leadership perspectives*. Palgrave Macmillan. https://doi.org/10.1057/9780230584068_2

Willem Fourie is an Associate Professor at Stellenbosch University's School for Data Science and Computational Thinking. His research and public engagement focus on the human and technological enablers of policy innovation. His approach to leadership is informed by post-heroic leadership theories, as illustrated in his monograph *Why Leaders Fail and What it Teaches Us About Leadership*, published by Routledge in 2023.

Part III
Relational Philosophy

Relational Process Atomism: Epistemological and Methodological Considerations on the Metaphysics of Transactions

Michael Schramm

Abstract "Relational Economics" places the category of *relation* at the center of its conception. This fact requires consideration of how the category of relation relates to other conceptual pillars of "Relational Economics," namely, the (distinct) *transactions* and the category of *event* or *process* ("Relational Economics" draws on Whitehead's "Process Philosophy"). On the basis of a "Business Metaphysics," which is dedicated to the question of "how the economic world works (in general)," the chapter analyses the *epistemological* and *methodological* implications of this theoretical strategy and summarizes the result with the heading "Relational Process Atomism." The chapter argues that only a *realistic* epistemology is suitable to adequately address the controversy between different types of metaphysics. Thus, logically the usefulness of our theories—including our metaphysical theory, how the world works, or our economic theory, how the economic world works—depends on whether they sufficiently represent the "way the world really is." Whitehead's cosmology and Commons' economics now specify these metaphysical implications to the effect that they argue for a "Relational Process Atomism" that assumes "*events*" as "*atoms*" ("actual occasions" or "transactions" as ultimate units) with *internal relations*, which are then referred to as "relational transactions" in "Relational Economics." *Methodologically*, research into the functioning of these "relational transactions" can only proceed through a step-by-step "tinkering" (Popper), which is illustrated by Whitehead with the image of a repeated take-off and landing of an airplane.

Keywords Event · Ultimate unit · Atom · Ontology · External relations · Internal relations · Epistemology · Methodology · Metaphysics · Theory of Relativity · Quantum Physics · Process Philosophy · Social Ontology · Transactions

---

M. Schramm (✉)
University of Hohenheim, Hohenheim, Germany
e-mail: schramm@uni-hohenheim.de

J. D. Rendtorff et al. (eds.), *Advances in Relational Economics*, Relational Economics and Organization Governance,
https://doi.org/10.1007/978-3-031-75725-9_9

1 Introduction: The Lego Universe

Denmark is best known for one product in particular—and that is Lego.[1] Lego is probably the most famous and popular product from Denmark. Each and every one of us played with Lego in childhood and loved it (more or less). Therefore, I will start with some ontological remarks about the Lego universe. Unfortunately, the metaphysical thesis of my chapter will state that the "universe" of modern economics does *not* work like the Lego universe. But nevertheless—or precisely because of this—these notes on the Lego universe are hopefully useful.

If we analyze the Lego universe ontologically, three points can be noted: (1) First of all, the Lego universe consists of bricks. The classic Lego brick is the two-by-four (2×4) brick. But as everyone knows, there are even smaller bricks in the classic Lego universe, and the real basic unit is the one-by-one (1×1) brick.[2]

So there are basic building blocks in the classic Lego universe: ultimate units. These basic units cannot be divided any further. Ontologically, these building blocks are the "atoms" (gr. ἄτομος = "uncuttable," "indivisible") of the classic Lego universe. (2) Secondly, it must be noted that these are pre-fabricated, unchangeable building blocks. They do not change, nor can they be changed without damaging them. They are—to use Isaac Newtons's words—"solid, massy, hard, impenetrable, moveable Particles," which—themselves unchangeable—can form all possible "may compose Bodies of one and the same Nature and Texture in all Ages".[3] Ontologically, it is thus to be stated that there are no processes at all in the ultimate (basic) units of the Lego universe. The building blocks remain substantially unchanged. They do not exist as events, but as ready-made "substances." (3) And finally, they have only external relations, no internal relations. "Internally," such a brick remains the same. If I put two bricks together (= external relation) and then take them apart again, then it is still exactly the same building block which has no internal relations. The relation to other building blocks does not change our brick "internally." So, external relations only.

In the following, I would like to develop the metaphysical concept of a "Relational Process Atomism," which describes the reality in our *real* universe much better than the ontology of the Lego universe. I will also discuss the epistemological and methodological implications of this concept, which leads to a metaphysics of the transaction. Terminologically, "*ontology*" refers to the discipline that is dedicated to

[1] Lego was invented in 1949 by Ole Kirk Christiansen (*1891; †1958) in Billund. The original Lego bricks from 1949 were hollow on the inside, while the classic bricks, for which a patent was applied for in 1958, had inner tubes that made them considerably more stable and also allowed the bricks to be put together in a laterally staggered manner.

[2] Meanwhile there is a myriad of other hybrid bricks that complicate everything enormously. But let's stay with the classic Lego universe for the sake of illustration.

[3] See the first quote in Sect. 2.

the question of what kinds of things exist in our universe.[4] "*Epistemology*," on the other hand, deals with the question of how we acquire our knowledge.[5] "*Methodology*" (from ὁδός = "way") is about the "way to something," i.e., about the approach or the scientific tools on the way to knowledge. After all, the term "*metaphysics*"—I use the word strictly in the sense of the philosophy of science—refers to the philosophical discipline that is dedicated to the question of "how the world works in general".[6] Our way of working out the concept of a "Relational Process Atomism" first leads us to physics, then to metaphysics and epistemology, and finally to economics and methodology.

2 Newton or Heisenberg & Co.? Lego Metaphysics Versus Event Metaphysics

If we now turn from the Lego universe to our real universe, we realize that the real universe was initially imagined to be like the Lego universe. The relevant theory here is the classical physics of Sir Isaac Newton. The universe of Newton's mechanical universe is a Lego universe. Namely, he assumed that the real world consists of unchanging building blocks:

> [I]t seems probable to me, that God in the Beginning form'd Matter in solid, massy, hard, impenetrable, moveable Particles [...]; even so very hard, as never to wear or break in pieces; no ordinary Power being able to divide what God himself made one in the first Creation. While the Particles continue entire, they may compose Bodies of one and the same Nature and Texture in all Ages. (Newton, 1730, pp. 375f)

The ontological analysis of Newton mechanistic clockwork universe shows three points: (1) Newton's universe also consists of "ultimate units," namely, his "solid, massy, hard, impenetrable, moveable particles." These "billiard balls" are Newton's "atoms" (gr. ἄτομος = "uncuttable," "indivisible"). (2) Newton's "billiard balls" are solid, hard, and unchangeable. Like the bricks of the Lego universe, they are not "events." (3) And finally, these "particles" have only external relations. The relation to other building blocks in "composing Bodies" of all kinds does not change the particle "internally".[7]

---

[4] In a nutshell, John Searle (1998/1999, p. 5) defines: "ontology (what exists)". Traditionally three groups of things are distinguished ontologically: firstly, physical things (stones, bodies, etc.), secondly, mental things (thoughts, feelings, etc.) and abstract things (such as numbers). Searle himself has added a fourth group, which he describes as "social ontology" (see Searle, 2010/2011).

[5] Again Searle (1998/1999, p. 5) defines: "epistemology (how we know)".

[6] See Schramm (2016, 2017, 2022, 2023, 2024).

[7] This way of thinking is still widespread today. For example, the philosopher John R. Searle writes of a "universe that consists entirely of mindless, meaningless, unfree, nonrational, brute physical particles" (Searle, 2004/2007, p. 5).

But then, at the beginning of the twentieth century, two revolutions in modern physics took place: the two Theories of Relativity and quantum physics. First Albert Einstein and later Niels Bohr and Werner Heisenberg came along and said, that there are no "solid [...] Particles," no unchanging "billiard balls": "The elementary particles are not [...] unchangeable, indivisible, basic building blocks of matter."[8] Instead, a new picture has now emerged: it is *energy* that is the basic stuff of the world, because mass or matter is actually energy (see Einstein's formula $E = mc^2$), so that energy is the substance from which all things are made. "Energy is in fact the substance from which all elementary particles, all atoms and therefore all things are made" (Heisenberg, 1958, p. 63). At the same time, energy occurs only in energy droplets, only in "discrete *quanta* of energy" (Heisenberg, 1958, p. 31; emphasis M. S.). So, if energy is the basic stuff of the world and if this energy exists only in droplets, then—because energy is something active—"quantum *events*" (Rovelli, 2014/2016, p. 112; own emphasis) are the ultimate units of which the world is made up.

The ontological analysis of modern quantum physics again provides three characteristics:[9] (1) Still, the quantum universe consists of "ultimate units": the "quantum events" (Rovelli, 2014/2016, p. 112) are the "atoms" of modern physics. (2) But these "atoms" are no "billiard balls" or inert "things." They are dynamic occasions, processes, undetermined actualities (events that "act"), in short: "The World is Made of Events, not Things" (Rovelli, 2017/2018, p. 85). (3) And finally, these events are no "substances" with only accidental relationships. Rather, they are relational through and through:

> The [...] formula: 'every elementary particle consists of all other elementary particles' seems to give a good description of the paradoxical situation we are confronted with in the experiments.[10]

Physically this means that in the process of becoming and perishing of elementary events the energy of other elementary events flows into the new elementary event. So, it's a relational universe we're living in. Relationships are essential for all concrete things (not accidental).[11]

---

[8]Heisenberg (1963), S. 3 (author's own translation). The original German version: "Die Elementarteilchen sind nicht, wie man früher etwa angenommen hätte, unveränderliche, unteilbare Grundbausteine der Materie."

[9]See for example Rovelli (2014/2016), pp. 91–121: "granularity, indeterminism and relationality".

[10]Heisenberg (1967), S. 2 (author's own translation.). The original German Version: "Die bekannte Formel: "jedes Elementarteilchen besteht aus allen anderen Elementarteilchen'scheint eine gute Beschreibung der paradoxen Situation zu geben, mit der wir in den Experimenten konfrontiert werden."

[11]Carlo Rovelli even advocates a strictly relational interpretation of quantum physics: the so-called "Relational Quantum Mechanics" and explains in this sense: "Reality is relational [...] Reality is reduced to relation." (Rovelli, 2014/2016, p. 115) I am not completely satisfied with this radical relationist interpretation, because it reduces reality to mathematical points. But an elementary event is not an extensionless mathematical point, which consists exclusively of relations. Because that would mean: it is nothing! I come back to this point later.

If we end up asking ourselves "how the world works in general"—after all, that is the question of "metaphysics"—then there's an overwhelming probability, that—compared to Newton's Lego metaphysics—an "*event* metaphysics" is true. And that leads us to epistemological questions.

3 The Cloudy Mountain Peak: Realistic Epistemology and Truth

I turn now to epistemology ("how we know"), to our ways of finding out, and our ways of getting knowledge. As already stated, the topic of "epistemology" is about "how we know" (Searle, 1998/1999, p. 5). How can we discover how the world really works, including the world of business?

1. According to historian Yuval Noah Harari, modernity began with the general discovery that in principle we do *not* know:

   > The Discovery of Ignorance [...] Modern science is based on the [...] injunction [...] 'we do not know'. It assumes that we don't know everything. Even more critically, it accepts that the things that we think we know could be proven wrong.[12]

2. This modern discovery of *not knowing* is also the basis of the epistemology developed by the theorist of science Karl R. Popper, which culminates in the short sentence: "We do not know: we can only guess."[13] Popper illustrates the matter with the example of the many white swans and the one black swan: we see swans and notice that they are all white. At some point, we logically come to the conclusion: "All swans are white!" This is an induction conclusion, where we infer general assertions from various empirical observations. But then we discover a black swan. Thus the original inductive conclusion (our conjecture that "All swans are white!") is—presumably—refuted, falsified. We can never be sure that our "guesses" are actually true. Nevertheless, despite the fact that we can only achieve conjectural knowledge, with Popper, it is possible and also necessary to always *search* for the truth!
3. This possibility of searching for truth is disputed by the U.S. philosopher Richard Rorty. He gave a radical, completely dismissive answer to the epistemological

[12] Harari (2011/2014), p. 279. In explanation he writes: "Premodern traditions of knowledge such as Islam, Christianity, Buddhism and Confucianism asserted that everything that is important to know about the world was already known. The great gods, or the one almighty God, or the wise people of the past possessed all-encompassing wisdom, which they revealed to us in scriptures and oral traditions. Ordinary mortals gained knowledge by delving into these ancient texts and traditions and understanding them properly. It was inconceivable that the Bible, the Qur'an or the Vedas were missing out on a crucial secret of the universe—a secret that might yet be discovered by flesh-and-blood creatures." (Harari, 2011/2014, p. 279 f.)

[13] Popper (1934/2002), p. 278 (emphasis removed, M.S.). The original German version: "Wir wissen nicht, sondern wir raten." (Popper 1934/2005, S. 266; emphasis removed, M.S.)

question "how we can know" anything at all: "[T]here is no way to know our distance from truth, nor even whether we are closer to it than our ancestors were" (Rorty, 1998, p. 3 f.). His argument runs as follows: (a) If we—as Popper has explained, too—cannot be sure that any of our scientific theories or hypotheses are true, then we cannot claim that any hypothesis is closer to the truth than any other hypothesis. And that means: we cannot prefer any hypothesis to another hypothesis, because no hypothesis is more likely to be true than another hypothesis. In the end, this means: "There is no way to find out any objective truth!" Or to put it this way: "We can't know anything (objectively)!" In short, he writes: "[T]ruth is not a goal of inquiry" (Rorty, 1998, p. 3). After this first step, it may seem that Rorty may want to search for the truth, but that a search for the objective truth is unfortunately impossible. But Rorty makes a second step: (b) He dissolves the epistemological idea of objective truth—that there would be something to recognize, how things really are—pragmatically. And he does this in two ways: (b1) First he abandons truth as such: according to Rorty the situation "requires one to abandon the idea that there is one way the world really is" (Rorty, 2000: min. 17:12). For if there is no way to compare the (possible) truth of one hypothesis with another anyway, one might as well throw the whole epistemological idea of objective truth overboard. (b2) The criterion he proposes instead of the epistemological criterion of truth is: *utility* for us humans. If one cannot compare the different hypotheses on the basis of their truth content, then we can, says Rorty, only choose that description of the world which increases the benefit of the people the most. He says:

> "[T]he sole virtue of any descriptive vocabulary is its utility. It can't have a further virtue called getting things right. [. . .] [T]here is no such thing as the search for truth, if that search is conceived of a something distinct from the search for greater human happiness." So, "pragmatists" like Rorty "deny that truth is a matter of correspondence to the way things are—independent of our needs".[14]

4. In my view, Popper's metaphor of the clouded mountain peak is epistemologically helpful to see where Rorty is right and where he goes wrong (in my view):

> The status of truth, in the objective sense, as correspondence to the facts and its role as a regulative principle, may be compared to that of a mountain peak usually wrapped in clouds. A climber may not merely have difficulties in getting there—he may not know when he gets there, because he may be unable to distinguish, in the clouds, between the main summit and a subsidiary peak. Yet this does not affect the objective existence of the summit; and if the climber tells us 'I doubt whether I reached the actual summit', then he does, by implication, recognize the objective existence of the summit. The very idea of error or of doubt (in its normal straightforward sense) implies the idea of an objective truth which we may fail to reach. Though it may be impossible for the climber ever to make sure that he has reached the summit, it will often be easy for him to realize that he has not reached it (or not yet reached it); for example, when he is turned back by an overhanging wall. (Popper, 1963/1985, p. 226)

[14] Both quotes Rorty (2000), min: 18.19 and 20.44.

The crucial point of this metaphor for epistemology is the following: although the hiker never knows if he has reached the main summit of the mountain, "this does not affect the objective existence of the summit." The mountain peak is—as John Searle would say—"ontologically objective" and therefore "epistemologically objective" too. "We do not know." But because of this epistemological objectivity, "we can only guess," which is objectively true!

So, on the one hand, I agree with Rorty that "there is no way to know our distance from truth"—just as it is "impossible for the climber ever to make sure that he has reached the summit" (Popper). But on the other hand, that doesn't mean "abandoning the idea that there is one way the world really is" (Rorty). Our epistemological uncertainty does "not affect the objective existence of the summit" (Popper), and does not affect the objective truth.

And I would like to address this important fact, namely, that it is useful to search for the truth, using the example of time in modern physics. (1) Newton advocated the (everyday) concept of an "absolute time": "[T]ime, space, place, and motion are very familiar to everyone [...] Absolute, true, and mathematical time [...] flows uniformly" (Newton, 1687/1999), p. 408). Everywhere in the universe, we have the same time, absolutely the same time.[15] (2) But then Einstein came along and realized that Newton's metaphysics of time cannot be true. According to Einstein's Theories of Relativity, time is relative to speed ("Special Theory of Relativity." 1905) and gravity ("General Theory of Relativity." 1915), so that "the concept of time had to be relativized by giving to each inertial system its special time."[16] Let's illustrate this astonishing fact with a device that we use every day in our smartphones or cars: the "Global Positioning System" (GPS).

It takes four satellites (theoretically only three, but practically four) to locate a car or smartphone accurately. The localization of a car (or a smartphone) is done by the satellites constantly sending signals to the car. The distances between the car and the satellites are measured by time measurements, by measuring how long the signal takes to travel from the satellite to the car (distance measurement by time measurement). So, it is crucial that this time measurement (of the length of the signal path to accurately determine the location of the car) is quite precise. But here's the problem: unfortunately, time does not pass equally fast everywhere in the universe. Newton's view, that "[a]bsolute [...] time [...] flows uniformly" is therefore wrong. Rather time passes differently—on the one hand relative to the *speed* of an object (according to the "Special Theory of Relativity") and on the other relative to *gravity* (according to the "General Theory of Relativity"). This means the following for the GPS: (a) On

[15] By the way: Newton's idea of an "absolute, true and mathematical time" is not a result of empirical observations, but a metaphysical hypothesis.

[16] Einstein (1934/2005), S. 147 (author's own translation). The original German version: "[...] daß der Zeitbe-griff relativiert werden mußte, indem jedem Inertialsystem seine besondere Zeit gegeben werden mußte." Again: Einstein's insight was of theoretical nature, because he came to this conclusion before one could measure with sufficiently exact clocks that time passes at different speeds at different places. However, in the meantime these differences have been proved empirically many times.

the one hand, the satellites, which are in a geostationary position, have a longer path when the earth rotates. So, the (geostationary) satellites have a higher speed than the car. And according to Einstein's "Special Theory of Relativity" from 1905 this means that time passes a little *slower* on the satellites than down on Earth in the car. (b) On the other hand, the satellite is further away from the gravitational center of the earth, so that the attractive or gravitational force is lower than on the surface of the earth. And according to Einstein's "General Theory of Relativity" from 1915, this has the consequence that time passes significantly *faster* in the satellites than down on Earth. (c) If both time effects are taken together, the result is that time passes *faster* in the satellites than on Earth. So, the engineers of a GPS system have to slow down the clocks of the satellites, namely, 38 microseconds per day. If this (seemingly tiny) *time* deviation is now converted into the corresponding length determination, then the following errors in *position* determination would result, if the engineers of the GPS system would not consider both Einstein's Theories of Relativity: about 13 centimetres after every second of measuring time, almost 500 metres after an hour and about 11.4 kilometres after a day.

Now back to epistemology: with respect to time we have two different hypotheses, namely, Newton versus Einstein. If we ask ourselves which of the two theories is (probably) closer to truth, then we must indeed concede that we have no idea what the exact distance is (a) between Newton's absolute theory on time and our epistemological goal (objective truth) or (b) between Einstein's relativistic theories of time and the objective truth (= the knowledge how the world really is) (Fig. 1).

But: the crucial point is that it is not necessary "to know the distance from truth" (Rorty). The only relevant question is: what's more likely, Newton or Einstein? Furthermore, Rorty's turn to the criterion of utility—he replaces "the search for truth" by "the search for greater human happiness"—also goes nowhere: the (presumably greater) truth of Einstein's theory of relativity does not depend on the question whether GPS is useful or not. Logically, it's the other way round: GPS is useful *because* it is true.[17] Therefore, it is important to know how the world (probably) works!

There is also an evolutionary argument for a realistic epistemology, formulated by the paleontologist George Gaylord Simpson this way:

> To put it crudely but graphically, the monkey who did not have a realistic perception of the tree branch he jumped for was soon a dead monkey—and therefore did not become one of our ancestors. (Simpson, 1963, p. 84)

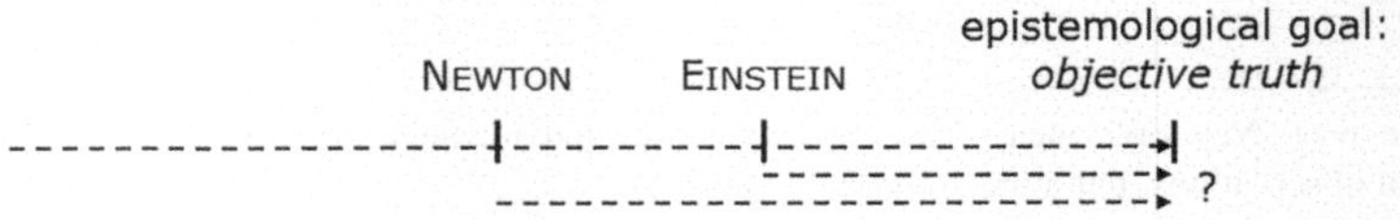

Fig. 1 Theories and objective truth

[17] In terms of scientific theory, the sentence should read: GPS is useful because it is (sufficiently) true—probably.

It *is* important if our epistemology is sufficiently realistic or not! Logically the usefulness of our theories—including our metaphysical theory, how the world works, or our economic theory, how the economic world works—depends on whether they *sufficiently* represent the "way the world really is." So, according to this realistic epistemology, we should have a (sufficiently) realistic ontology to know how the world works ("metaphysics").

4 Relational Process Atoms I: "Actual Occasions" in Whitehead's Metaphysics

The mathematician, physicist, and philosopher Alfred North Whitehead (*1861; †1947) created a very complex philosophy, usually called "Process Philosophy," but named by himself as "The Philosophy of Organism," which integrated natural sciences, aesthetics, ethics, and religion. In his metaphysical cosmology "process" and "creativity" are the fundamental or ultimate notions:

The first fundamental "metaphysical [...] principle is that the very essence of real actuality [...] is *process*. [...] There is no halt".[18] "In the philosophy of organism this ultimate is termed 'creativity'" (Whitehead, 1929/1979, p. 7).

1. The physical quanta of energy he transformed metaphysically into "actual occasions," also called "actual entities": "'Actual entities'—also termed 'actual occasions'—are the final real things of which the world is made up" (Whitehead, 1929/1979, p. 18).
2. All the more permanent things that the evolutionary process generates (atoms etc.) are "societies" of these elementary events: "The real actual things that endure are all societies. They are not actual occasions" (Whitehead, 1933/1967, p. 204).
3. If we now do our usual ontological analysis, again three characteristics emerge:

   (3.1) Whitehead's cosmos also consists of "ultimate units," and the "actual occasions" are the "atoms" of this universe:"[A]ctuality is incurably atomic" (Whitehead, 1929/1979, p. 61). But "atomism does not exclude complexity and universal relativity. Each atom is a system of all things." (Whitehead, 1929/1979, p. 36)

   (3.2) As already stated, Whitehead's "atoms" are "actual *occasions*." That means they are processes or "events." "[T]he ultimate facts of nature [...] are events" (Whitehead, 1919/1925/2011, p. 4).

   (3.3) And finally, these events have not only external (accidental) relationships, but internally they are genetically *related*: "In other words, it belongs to the nature of a 'being' that it is a potential for every 'becoming.' This is the 'principle of relativity'" (Whitehead, 1929/1979, p. 22). Like in physics

[18] Whitehead (1933/1967), p. 274; Whitehead (1929/1979), p. 22; Whitehead (1926/2007), p. 112; Whitehead (1938/1968), p. 140.

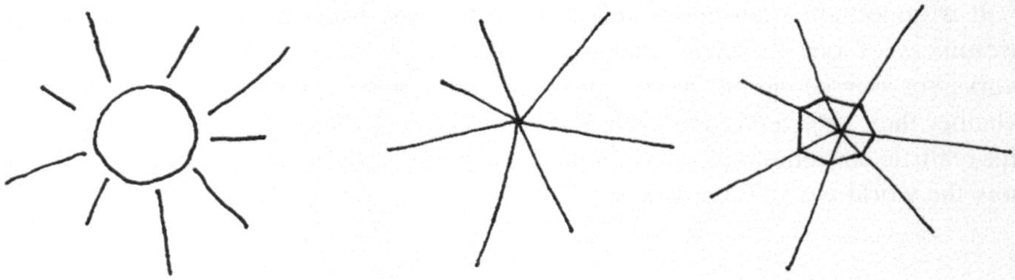

Fig. 2 Three metaphysical models of ultimate actualities

"actual occasions" have *internal* relations. In the process of becoming and perishing elementary events, the energy (or in Whitehead: the "creativity") of other elementary events flows into the new elementary event and influences its becoming.[19] And it's the network of all these relational events that creates the world, including space and time.[20]

If we graph the three metaphysical models of ultimate actualities discussed so far then the following picture emerges (Fig. 2):

(a) The model on the left shows the metaphysical idea of Newton's clockwork universe: a "solid, massy, hard, impenetrable, moveable Particle" with only external or accidental relations.[21] This model has been falsified by modern physics.

(b) The model in the center shows a *strictly relational* interpretation of quantum physics, for example, the "Relational Quantum Mechanics" by Carlo Rovelli in which an actuality is nothing but its relations, in which "[r]eality is reduced to relation" (Rovelli, 2014/2016, p. 115). But that would mean that reality is reduced to mathematical points which have no extension, neither in space nor in time. But that in turn would mean that the ultimate actuality is nothing! But from a *metaphysical* point of view, this radical relationalist view is *not* convincing because an elementary event is not an extensionless mathematical point which consists *exclusively* of relations. Sure, the ultimate units of modern physics do have internal relations and insofar are relational beings. But at the same time, they are entities, quanta of energy, "atoms," not just extensionless mathematical points.

(c) Finally, the model on the right depicts Whitehead's metaphysical idea of the ultimate entities in this universe: the "actual occasions" or "events" mentioned above. His "events" *are* relational beings (as described in his "principle of relativity"), but they are not just extensionless mathematical points, but "actual *entities*." If the world were made up of mathematical points only (from

[19] In the sense, Whitehead (1929/1979, p. 21) stated famously: "The many become one, and are increased by one."

[20] "Time and space [...] express relations between events." (Whitehead, 1919/1925/2011, p. 61).

[21] The illustration can also be applied to the so-called "metaphysics of substance".

"nothings"), then the whole actuality would be nothing. But it is the network of all these relational occasions or events that creates the world of our cosmos, including space and time.

5 Relational Process Atoms II: Economic Transactions

I now turn to the ultimate units or events of the economic world and economics. Before I can do that, there is a fundamental question to consider: what do the events of the *economic* world have to do with the events of the *physical* world? And the answer is: the universe in which we live in is exactly one.[22]

With regard to this question, some insights from the theory of so-called "social ontology" by philosopher John R. Searle are useful.[23]

1. Firstly, the whole "world" of our modern economy—as well as the "world" of politics, etc.—exists only because it has been *invented* by humans: "we are inventing a reality out of nothing" (Searle, 2010/2011, p. 105). So, "*social* ontology" is not natural ontology, but a human invention of a *social* reality. It was not nature ("*natural* ontology") that created banknotes or corporations, but human society ("*social* ontology").[24]

But although certain events are "*social*-ontological" in nature (e.g., payment transactions or management decisions), they can nevertheless only gain *concrete actuality* as physical and therefore "*natural*-ontological" events. For it belongs to the characteristics of the one world we're living in, that there can be no *concrete* realities without *physical* concretions.[25] For example: "[M]oney has to exist in some physical form or other. [. . .] Institutional facts exist, so to speak, on top of brute physical facts" (Searle, 1995/1996, p. 34 f.) or "basic facts" (Searle, 2010/2011, p. 108 f.). Therefore the "social ontology" of the economic system can only be realized in physically concrete transaction processes, in "some physical realization" (Searle, 1995/1996, p. 35).[26] Everything, so to speak, "has to reach a rock bottom" (Searle, 1995/1996, p. 56) in order to become concrete or actual. An event of the economic world, a transaction, has to become physical to be real. And this in turn shows that

---

[22] "We live in exactly one world, not two or three or seventeen." (Searle, 1995/1996, p. xi).

[23] See Searle, John R. (2010/2011). Searle considers his "social ontology" as a part of "the metaphysics of [...] social relations." (Searle, 1995/1996, p. 3)

[24] The same is true for political offices, soccer matches, market competition, democracy, marriage or companies. "God can create light by saying 'Let there be light!' Well, we cannot create light but we have a similar remarkable capacity. We can create [. . .] corporations by saying [...] 'Let there be a corporation!'" (Searle, 2010/2011, p. 100)

[25] However, there are other *ontologically objective* "things" besides the *concrete* realities, because there are also *abstract* entities like numbers or the possibilities (which are called "eternal objects" by Whitehead).

[26] Even if it's just a digital transfer of money, for example, there has to be some physical substrate for it to become a real transaction.

the metaphysical question of how the world works in general is of fundamental relevance for economic theory. According to realist epistemology, we should have a (sufficiently) realistic ontology of transactions to know how the economic world works ("Business Metaphysics").

For the ontological analysis of a transaction, I am guided by the transaction economics of John R. Commons. (1) Again, the economic world consists of "*ultimate units*" and therefore of economic "atoms," which are the "transactions":

> Thus the ultimate unit of activity which correlates law, economics and ethics must contain in itself the three principles of conflict, mutuality, and order. This unit is a transaction. A transaction, with its participants, is the smallest unit of institutional economics. (Commons, 1932/1996, p. 454; also Commons, 1934/2009, p. 58)

Transactions are the "steps" by which the economy moves forward. At the same time, the transaction must be a whole. (Just like when walking: you can't take a half step, to move forward, you have to take whole steps.) So, there are no half transactions. This fits the fact that Commons declared a corporation to be a "*going* concern."[27] A corporation re-produces itself step by step by generating a network of transactions: "[A] corporation [. . .] now became an economic going concern existing in its transactions" (Commons, 1934/2009, p. 53).

2. Secondly, Commons describes transactions as "*events*": "These [...] transactions are to economics what Whitehead's [...] 'event*[s]*' are to physics" (Commons, 1934/2009, p. 96). And the nature of the whole economy is "process" because the events keep the whole thing going.

Here we have a fundamental difference to neoclassical economics, in which the stasis of an equilibrium is described as the "natural" tendency of the economy. Innovations must be treated here as "exogenous" shocks that briefly throw the economy into turmoil (deform it) until a new equilibrium is reached again. But that's not the way the (economic) world works.[28] The computer scientist John Henry Holland puts it this way: "In fact, if the system ever does reach equilibrium, it isn't just stable. It's dead."[29] What Carlo Rovelli says about the "quantum events," i.e., the ultimate units of the physical world, also applies to the world of economics: the economic world is also made of events, not things.

---

[27] He even gives a German translation of his term "going concern": "gutgehendes Geschäft" (Commons, 1934/2009, p. 69, fn. 102). With both "going" and "gutgehen", you have to take whole steps. Complete transactions are therefore required as "ultimate units".

[28] For a more in-depth critique of this neoclassical equilibrium thinking see Beinhocker (2006), pp. 21–75.

[29] John Henry Holland, quoted in: Waldrop (1992), p. 147.

3. And thirdly, the nature of "transactions" is "*relational.*" Terminologically, only some occasional hints can be found in Commons, but in terms of content, however, Commons clearly advocates a relational ontology of transactions.[30] For a more detailed elaboration of the relational aspect we can turn to "Relational Economics":

> "[T]he basic paradigmatic unit of relational economics is the transaction as relation, that is, the transaction as an attractor of polyvalent contexts, decision logics and sources of value creation" (Wieland, 2018/2020, p. 21). "The relational transaction is the basic unit of relational economics (here the connection between this definition and Whitehead's process philosophy, which is characterized by the primacy of relation and the concept of the relational constitution of everything in existence, is self-evident. [...])." (Wieland, 2018/2020, p. 46)

The analysis of the relational ontology of transactions shows that the world of business is a continuously generated network of transactions, with the legacy of previous transactions flowing into the new transaction. That's the more Whiteheadian aspect of a transaction's ontology, because—as already mentioned—Whitehead's "principle of relativity" is meant *genetically*: every past event is a potential for every becoming event. The decisive hinge for Josef Wieland's conception, however, is the fact that each transaction works as an "attractor" for stakeholders and their polyvalent resources.[31] If you take the two perspectives (Whitehead and Wieland) together, the result is that the legacy of previous transactions and new resources of the stakeholders (economy; society) flow into the new transaction and thus drive the evolution of the dynamic network of transactions.

5.1 "Tinkering"Methodological Consequences

The conceptual outline of a micro-analytical description of polydimensional transactions in the modern economy and the pragmatic governance of their networking has methodological consequences. From the outset, the approach of "Relational Economics" is not designed to offer blissful "Geisteshostien" ("consecrated spirit hosts")[32] to the educated public. Rather, Wieland's theory is quite pragmatic about

[30] See Commons (1934/2009), pp. 386 ff: "relativity"; Commons (1950/1956), pp. 117 ff: "relativities".

[31] "Every stakeholder invests specific resources in a firm, which are required for the completion of a transaction and/or the theoretically infinite continuation of the firm's existence." (Wieland, 2018/2020, p. 71). In this sense, Commons spoke somewhere about the transaction as a "meeting point". However, I have not been able to verify the quote.

[32] I take the term "Geisteshostie" from the book "Alte Meister" ("Old Masters") by the Austrian writer Thomas Bernhard, in which he describes the attitudes of the German philosopher Martin Heidegger in a very amusing way. Commenting on a famous interview by the editor of the magazine *DER SPIEGEL*, Rudolf Augstein, with Heidegger, Bernhard writes (in the German original): "Selbst ein berühmter und gefürchteter norddeutscher Zeit-schriftenherausgeber kniete andachtsvoll vor ihm mit offenem Mund, als erwartete er in der untergehenden Sonne von dem auf

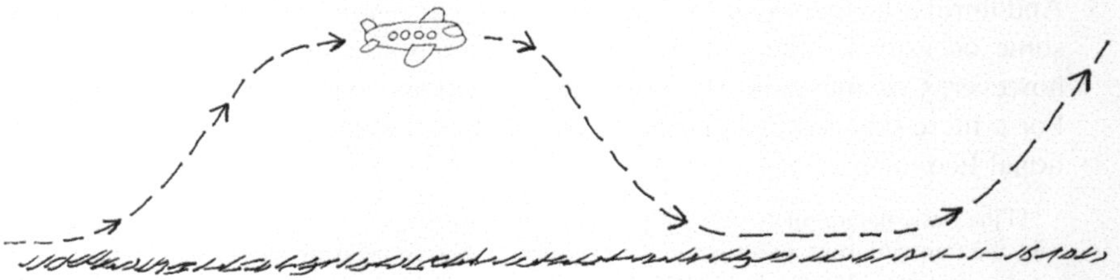

Fig. 3 Whitehead's methodology ("The Flight of the Aeroplane")

how polyvalent transactions should be built appropriately. It's about learning from our experiences, generating ideas from these experiences, and then using these ideas to make new experiences and learning from them in order to improve things step by step.

1. Wieland's methodology therefore corresponds to that of Whitehead (Fig. 3). In *Process and Reality*, Whitehead illustrated the scientific method with a repeated take-off and landing of an airplane:

> The true method of discovery is like the flight of an aeroplane. It starts from the ground of particular observation *[or: the ground of a problem; M.S.]*; it makes a flight in the thin air of imaginative generalization; and it again lands for renewed observation rendered acute by rational interpretation. (Whitehead, 1929/1979, p. 5)

The logic behind this method is as follows: (i) You have to look for empirical evidence ("particular observations"). (ii) Then you have to start your "flight," i.e., you come up with creative hypotheses or theories with which you try to explain how the world works ("imaginative generalizations"). These are Popper's "guesses." (iii) After your "theory flight" you land back on earth and check to what extent the hypothesis works or not ("renewed observations"). In this way, you are trying to learn from your mistakes. Then you start the next flight, i.e., you think up improved hypotheses. And so on and so on ... In short: If you want to know how the world works you have to look what works! And what works is useful because it is (sufficiently) true—probably.[33]

seiner Hausbank sitzenden Heidegger sozusagen die Geisteshostie" (Bernhard, 1985/1988, S. 94). My translation: "Even a famous and much-feared North German publisher of periodicals kneeled before him devotionally and open-mouthed, as though he was expecting, sitting there under the setting sun, in a manner of speaking, the consecrated spirit host from Heidegger on his bench before his house." The interview, conducted in 1966, was published after Heidegger's death in 1976 under the title "Nur noch ein Gott kann uns retten" (cf. Heidegger, 1976).

[33] As said above: the (presumably greater) truth of Einstein's theory of relativity does not depend on the question whether GPS is useful or not. Logically, it's the other way round: GPS is useful because it is sufficiently or probably true.

2. Theorist of science Karl R. Popper has aptly expressed this methodical approach—especially with reference to the social sciences (such as economics)—by the beautiful German words "Herumbasteln" ("piecemeal tinkering") und "Fortwursteln" ("muddling through").

> "The characteristic approach of the piecemeal engineer is this. Even though he may perhaps cherish some ideals which concern society 'as a whole'—its general welfare, perhaps—he does not believe in the method of re-designing it as a whole. Whatever his ends, he tries to achieve them by small adjustments and re-adjustments which can be continually improved upon. [. . .] The piecemeal engineer knows, like Socrates, how little he knows. He knows that we can learn only from our mistakes. Accordingly, he will make his way, step by step, carefully comparing the results expected with the results achieved".[34] Sure, some people may be "dissatisfied with 'piecemeal tinkering' and 'muddling through.'" (Popper, 1944–45/1957/1961, p. 74)

But that's the way (ὁδός = "way") "in the social as well as in the natural sciences" (Popper, 1944–45/1957/1961, p. 58). It is the methodology which fits ontologically to the metaphysics of "Relational Process Atomism." And modernity has done well with this method so far.

References

Beinhocker, E. D. (2006). *The origin of wealth: The radical remaking of economics and what it means for business and society*. Harvard Business School Press.

Bernhard, T. (1985/1988). *Alte Meister: Komödie*. Suhrkamp.

Commons, J. R. (1932/1996). The problem of correlating law, economics, and ethics. In M. Rutherford & W. J. Samuels (Eds.), *Selected essays* (Vol. 2, pp. 453–473). Routledge. (Original work published 1932 in Wisconsin law review, 8, 3–26)

Commons, J. R. (1934/2009). *Institutional economics: Its place in political economy* (Vol. 1 & 2, 3rd ed.). Transaction Publishers.

Commons, J. R. (1950/1956). *The economics of collective action* (3rd ed.). Macmillan.

Einstein, A. (1934/2005). In C. Seelig (Ed.), *Mein weltbild* (29th ed.). Ullstein.

Harari, Y. N. (2011/2014). *Sapiens: A brief history of humankind*. Vintage.

Heidegger, M. (1976). Nur noch ein Gott kann uns retten [Interview 1966]. *Der Spiegel, 23*, 193–219.

Heisenberg, W. (1958). *Physics and philosophy: The revolution in modern science*. Harper & Brothers.

Heisenberg, W. (1963). Die Entwicklung der einheitlichen Feldtheorie der Elementarteilchen. *Die Naturwissenschaften, 50*(1), 3–7.

Heisenberg, W. (1967). *Einführung in die einheitliche Feldtheorie der Elementarteilchen*. Hirzel.

Newton, I. (1687/1999). *The principia: Mathematical principles of natural philosophy* (I. B. Cohen & A. Whitman, Trans.). University of California Press.

Newton, I. (1730). *Opticks: Or, a treatise of the reflexions, refractions, inflexions and colours of light* (4th ed.). William Innys.

Popper, K. R. (1934\2002). *The logic of scientific discovery*. Routledge.

Popper, K. R. (1934\2005). *Logik der Forschung* (11th ed.). Mohr Siebeck.

Popper, K. R. (1944–45/1957/1961). *The poverty of historicism*. Harper & Row.

Popper, K. R. (1944–45/1957/2003). *Das Elend des Historizismus*. Mohr Siebeck.

[34] Popper (1944–45/1957/1961), p. 66 f. In the original German version: "'Herumbasteln' und 'Fortwursteln'" (Popper, 1944–45/1957/2003, S. 66).

Popper, K. R. (1963/1985). *Conjectures and refutations: The growth of scientific knowledge* (4th ed.). Routledge & Kegan Paul.
Rorty, R. (1998). *Truth and progress* (Philosophical papers, Vol. 3). Cambridge University Press.
Rorty, R. (2000). *Is there a conflict between religion and science?* [Guest lecture]. West Valley College. https://www.youtube.com/watch?v=fn2F2BWLZ0Q
Rovelli, C. (2014/2016). *Reality is not what it seems: The journey to quantum gravity*. Allen Lane (Penguin).
Rovelli, C. (2017/2018). *The order of time*. Allen Lane (Penguin).
Schramm, M. (2016). Wie funktioniert die Geschäftswelt wirklich? Business Metaphysics und Theorie der Firma. *Ethica, 24*(4), 311–360.
Schramm, M. (2017). How the (business) world really works: Business metaphysics and "creating shared value". In J. Wieland (Ed.), *Creating shared value: Concepts, experience, criticism* (pp. 81–117). Springer.
Schramm, M. (2022). Relational processes in Whitehead's metaphysics and commons' economics: The relevance of cosmology for economic theory. In L. Biggiero, D. de Jongh, B. Priddat, J. Wieland, A. Zicari, & D. Fischer (Eds.), *The relational view of economics: A new research agenda for the study of relational transactions* (pp. 249–275). Springer Nature Switzerland.
Schramm, M. (2023). Dilemma und Kontingenz: Die Interaktionsökonomik aus Sicht der Business Metaphysics. Zeitschrift für Wirtschafts- und Unternehmensethik (zfwu)/Journal for Business. *Economics & Ethics, 24*(1), 53–74.
Schramm, M. (2024). Value dimensions of the transaction: A proposal of business metaphysics for relational economics. In J. Wieland, S. Linder, J. G. Schwengber, & A. Zicari (Eds.), *Cooperation in value-creating networks: Relational perspectives on governing social and economic value creation in the 21st century* (pp. 187–216). Springer Nature Switzerland.
Searle, J. R. (1995/1996). *The construction of social reality*. The Free Press.
Searle, J. R. (1998/1999). *Mind, language and society*. Basic Books.
Searle, J. R. (2004/2007). *Freedom and neurobiology: Reflections on free will, language, and political power*. Columbia University Press.
Searle, J. R. (2010/2011). *Making the social world: The structure of human civilization*. Oxford University Press.
Simpson, G. G. (1963). Biology and the nature of science. *Science, 139*(3550), 81–88.
Waldrop, M. M. (1992). *Complexity: The emerging science at the edge of order and chaos*. Touchstone.
Whitehead, A. N. (1919/1925/2011). *An enquiry concerning the principles of natural knowledge* (2nd ed.). Cambridge University Press.
Whitehead, A. N. (1926/2007). *Religion in the making: Lowell lectures, 1926* (5th ed.). Fordham University Press.
Whitehead, A. N. (1929/1979). *Process and reality: An essay in cosmology* (D. R. Griffin & D. W. Sherburne (Eds.), Corrected ed.). Free Press.
Whitehead, A. N. (1933/1967). *Adventures of ideas*. The Free Press.
Whitehead, A. N. (1938/1968). *Modes of thought*. The Free Press.
Wieland, J. (2018/2020). *Relational economics: A political economy (relational economics and organization governance)*. Springer.

Michael Schramm is a Professor of Catholic Theology and Business Ethics at the Faculty of Business, Economics, and Social Sciences (University of Hohenheim) since 2001. He was Chair of the Association for Social Ethics (2006–2009) and is a member of the German Economic Association and the German Whitehead Society. His main research topics include business metaphysics, transaction ethics, and process theology.

A Dynamic Relational Ontology and Its Implications for Epistemology

Gil Santos

Abstract This chapter proposes a dynamic relational ontology (DRO) within a critical realist framework and a theory of ontological emergence and downward causation. The proposed DRO does not subscribe to the idea that relations are the sole constituents of reality. Instead, it argues that the existence and identity of every entity must be addressed and explained in terms of three co-relative and interdependent ontological categories: relations, relata, and relational systems. In the second part of this chapter, I will clarify and illustrate the most important epistemological implications of the proposed ontology. Specifically, I will show how ontological emergence and downward-structural causation require the development of interlevel integrative models of explanation, substituting those underpinning traditional reductionist approaches. I will conclude by briefly analyzing a case study specifically related to the domain of the social and human sciences. In particular, I will consider the problem of the emergence of mind and the domain of social relations, with a special focus on the interdisciplinary field called social neuroscience.

Keywords Relational ontology · Emergence · Downward causation · Integrative explanation · Social neuroscience

1 Science, Ontology, and Philosophy

Every science is defined by three core components: its material domain, its conceptual domain, and its methodological procedures. The material domain refers to the set of objects that a science studies (e.g., numbers, quantum systems, living organisms, political states). The conceptual domain refers to the ordered set of concepts, models, and theories that any science elaborates about its objects.

G. Santos (✉)
Departamento de História e Filosofia das Ciências, Faculdade de Ciências da Universidade de Lisboa, Lisbon, Portugal

J. D. Rendtorff et al. (eds.), *Advances in Relational Economics*, Relational Economics and Organization Governance,
https://doi.org/10.1007/978-3-031-75725-9_10

The challenge of defining or redefining a science's material domain exemplifies the inherent link between science and ontology. In physics, for instance, what fundamental entities—elementary particles, fields, strings, or loops—must constitute its core subject matter? Should all be included, or is a selective approach necessary? Further questions arise regarding the nature of dependency or fundamentality among the chosen entities. Similarly, in economics, the selection of fundamental entities—individuals, social classes, organizations, or institutions—raises ontological questions. The same goes for the determination of the fundamental economic relations—production, distribution, exchange, consumption, institutional, organizational, technological, etc. What entities and relations should be seen as the basic building blocks? And how should their dependencies or interdependencies be established? (Chang, 2014, pp. 109–169).

A science's ontology is fundamentally shaped by how it defines and conceptualizes its material domain, or by how specific formalisms, such as those in quantum mechanics, are interpreted. In this sense, no science can do without explicitly acknowledging and critically examining its ontological commitments. The history of any science, in fact, reveals the ongoing interaction and coevolution of its material domain, conceptual domain, and methodology. These interactions can lead to various challenges. Sometimes, the issue lies in redefining existing concepts, such as time, space, or mass, to better represent the phenomena being studied. On other occasions, the existence of certain entities themselves is called into question, as with phlogiston and the classical aether in the past, or quantum strings in contemporary physics. More frequently, the focus is not on an entity's existence but on its explanatory power. Identifying the fundamental entities within a particular domain often coincides with identifying the fundamental units of explanation for that domain.

There is a fundamental distinction, however, between the ontology of a specific science and the ontological research conducted in philosophy. Scientific ontologies are inherently "regional" or domain-specific. Limited to particular material domains of research (e.g., the physical, the biological, the social), they focus on entities and structures within those domains. In contrast, philosophical ontology is inherently general, given that its object of inquiry is the broader concept of being, existence, or reality itself (Bunge, 1977, p. 2).

Philosophical ontology, however, comes in various forms. One extreme view sees it as entirely independent of, and preceding, any scientific inquiry. This approach risks reducing ontology to a mere product of armchair philosophy or pure scholasticism. The other extreme view positions ontology as a science itself, though of a sui generis kind. This perspective has the tendency to define ontology as purely a priori conceptual analysis, typically driven by purely formal theories, such as quantified logic, mereology, or set theory. An alternative approach, the one I favor, views philosophical ontology as a science-informed intellectual inquiry. However, the fact that reality is inherently multidimensional and multilayered, as evidenced by the vast array of scientific disciplines devoted to its study, presents a significant challenge. If the concept of rationality that underlies both scientific and philosophical inquiry arguably implies the intelligibility of reality in terms of its own structure (see Weil,

1982, pp. 23–57, 1992, p. 501), and if the intelligibility of this structure implies the existence of an order and unity underlying the many different modes of existence through which reality manifests itself to us, then all partial scientific accounts should be able to cohere into a comprehensive picture of reality (Bunge, 1977, p. 5).

From a scientifically informed perspective, philosophical ontology should thus move beyond the abstract question of "What is Being?" avoiding treating "being" as a pure logical abstraction, as Parmenides did, or a supreme genus, as Plato did. As Éric Weil has noted, referring to Aristotle's philosophy, "it is the everyday reality, the natural, historical, and political reality, that must be grasped in itself, not by reference to another, merely alleged, transcendent reality," and it is from our experience of that reality that human reason must find "its springboard to launch itself towards the construction of a discourse that organizes the experience and thus the world as a coherent unity" (1992, p. 504).

From a science-informed viewpoint, philosophical ontology should therefore begin by asking, "What are the most general common features among the entities studied by the various sciences, as well as their most significant differences?"

1.1 On the Possibility of Ontology: Realism

However, it is important to acknowledge that ontology, like any other theory, is a semiotic system developed by human thought. Therefore, we must recognize the need for some realist epistemological view to ground the possibility of ontology. After all, there is no unmediated access to reality nor a purely intuitive grasp of its essence. While a full defense of realism is beyond the scope of this discussion, it is worth noting that realism can find support in two independent lines of argument and in a large body of empirical research.

The first argument is known as the no-miracle abductive argument for scientific realism: "the positive argument for realism is that it is the only philosophy that doesn't make the success of science a miracle" (Putnam, 1975, p. 73). In other words, the practical success of science would be simply miraculous if some scientific theories were not, at least, approximately true (see Niiniluoto, 1999, 2018; Psillos, 1999, 2009).

According to Niiniluoto, the following two theses differentiate critical realism from naïve realism and skepticism: (1) "Truth is not easily accessible or recognizable, and even our best theories can fail to be true. Nevertheless, it is possible to approach the truth, and to make rational assessments of such cognitive progress"; and (2) "The best explanation for the practical success of science is the assumption that scientific theories in fact are approximately true or sufficiently close to the truth in the relevant respects. Hence, it is rational to believe that the use of the self-corrective methods of science in the long run has been, and will be, progressive in the cognitive sense" (1999, p. 10). From a critical realist viewpoint, combined with fallibilism (as a via media between dogmatism and skepticism), "truthlikeness" or "verisimilitude" is the best naturalist explanation of the practical success of science (Niiniluoto, 1999, pp. 185–198, 2018, pp. 165–163).

The second argument draws support from a comprehensive body of research in biology, neuroscience, and cognitive psychology. These studies delve into the human brain and nervous system, particularly focusing on how their structure, functioning, and development contribute to the formation of mental representations. The first type of studies suggests a relation of structural similarity, correspondence, or isomorphy between mental images, neural maps, sensory patterns, and real-world objects, particularly when it comes to the preservation of spatial relations, such as distances, sizes, orientations, and shapes (Denis, 1979, pp. 137–151, 1991, pp. 34–66; see also Jeannerod, 2002, p. 10; Strasser, 2012; Shea, 2018). In this context, it is worth noting that the recognition of a specific mental format of depictive representations alongside a language-like or propositional format of descriptive representations corresponds to the distinction between two basic types of sign and modes of signification, namely, icons, by means of a natural, analogic resemblance (in terms of quasi-pictorial structural mappings), and symbols, which convey meaning by means of an arbitrary conventional relationship (Kosslyn, 1984, pp. 105–107, 1994; Kosslyn et al. 2001, 2006, pp. 3–59; Changeux, 2004, pp. 69–70; Neves, 2011).

While there is evidence for structural similarity between mental representations and the world, it's important to acknowledge that mental representations are not passive copies of reality. Their construction always involves interaction between organisms and external objects. Furthermore, this interaction often requires an active assimilation-accommodation process on the part of the subject (Piaget, 1977). Despite this, our minds possess the remarkable ability "to 'depict' and 'resemble' the objects and events that the sensory channels of vision and hearing or touch manage to detect and describe" (Damásio, 2018, p. 76; see also 2010, pp. 64, 70, 2018, pp. 186, 239, 2021, p. 39).

Damásio aptly refers to the human brain as a "born cartographer": "Whatever sits outside the brain—the body proper, of course, from the skin to the entrails, as well as the world around (...)—is mimicked inside the brain's networks" (2010, p. 64). As Damásio further clarifies, when "the brain makes a map of an object with the shape of an X, it activates neurons along two linear rows that intersect at the appropriate point and angle. The result is a neural map of an X. The lines in brain maps represent the configuration of an object, its sensory features or movements or location in space. The representation does not need to be 'photographic', although it can be. It is essential, however, that it preserve the internal relations among the parts of an entity such as angles between components, superpositions, and so forth" (2018, pp. 74–75).

A second type of study finds direct support in brain studies. While the brain has a genetic basis, it demonstrably defies the notion of a "rigid automaton." In fact, the very "architecture of the brain's cellular and molecular network and the activities that occur within this network" are demonstrably modified by developmental dynamics, particularly through interactions with the external world (Changeux, 2004). Experience and learning, therefore, induce physiological (functional) and anatomic (structural) changes in chemical synapses, including pruning of preexisting synapses and growth of new synaptic connections (e.g., Kandel et al., 2021).

The fact that the brain's structure and functioning are significantly shaped by its interactions with the external environment means that reality plays a crucial role in shaping the neural connectivity that underlies cognition. This concept aligns with the theory of the "epigenesis of neuronal networks by selective stabilization of synapses" during development and with the hypothesis of a "selective stabilization of semantic knowledge by means of cognitive games operating on variable neuronal networks" (Changeux, 2004, pp. 48–70).

In this view, the brain selectively stabilizes the most suitable synaptic connections and neural schemas (as "preliminary categories" or "pre-representations") based on the nature of signals received from the external world (Changeux, 2004, pp. 58–61). The "first test of truth" comes with the empirical "trial-and-error" testing of such neural schemas when a child "tries to recognize, identify, and categorize objects and phenomena of the world around" (2004, p. 60). Environmental feedback thus serves as a test of the agreement, congruence, or adequacy between thought and reality (2004, p. 61). Therefore, Changeux acknowledges the human brain's success in "accurately and objectively representing the world" and its capacity to "test the truthfulness of the knowledge it has acquired" (2004, pp. 9, 34, 69–70).

A third type of study draws on the biophysical origins and biochemical structure of brains and nervous systems. This approach supports the basic tenets of epistemological realism by highlighting the phylogenetic evidence that nervous systems and brains are products of the very same reality that human reason and science strive to know. Research in the field of psychogenesis, developmental cognitive psychology, and developmental epistemology provides compelling evidence that the logico-mathematical operational structures (which form the foundation of scientific knowledge) "are prepared by trial and error and their regulation at the level of pre-operational representation"; that the latter find "their starting point, at the behavioral level, in the sensory-motor operations"; that these operations are "rooted in the general co-ordination of subjects' actions (order, interlocking, correspondence, etc.)"; and that these actions, in turn, "depend on nervous and finally organic [and morphogenetic] coordinations," which means that our logico-mathematical operational structures can be seen as ultimately rooted in the "laws of molecular biology" and "biophysics." In this sense, they are "expressions of the entire physical reality, although filtered through internal bio-neuro-psychological processes" (Piaget, 1967a, p. 578, 1970a, pp. 73–74).

Through a series of regressions, it is thus possible to rediscover the biophysical reality within the subject itself: "between the structures of the organism and those of the physico-chemical universe there is an original relationship of descent or very primitive interactions" (1967b, p. 766). From this perspective, "the solidarity between the psychogenesis and the biogenesis of our cognitive tools seems to offer an almost binding solution" to the problem of the relationship between the knowing subject and external reality. Furthermore, this perspective also explains "the surprising agreement between the logico-mathematical operations, experience and physical causality." If the organism with its constructive operations "constitutes the starting point of the epistemic subject, it remains a physico-chemical object among the others, therefore being subject to the same laws even though adding new ones." Crucially, "the connection between the structures of the subject and those of material reality is established from within the organism itself" (Piaget 1970a, p. 74). In this sense, "at the origins of knowledge, there may then be a biophysical reality that ensures an agreement between the organism and physical structures, according to a harmony that is not 'pre-established', but rather 'established, and even very gradually, by a process that begins in its biological roots'" (1967a, p. 589, 1970a, p. 75, 1970b, pp. 37–44; see also Hooker, 1995, pp. 225–285). This means that the ultimate conditions of possibility for human knowledge are to be found not only in human reason but in reality itself.

The convergence of the three types of study we have just outlined suggests the validity of at least a minimal form of realism. Furthermore, this view can be strengthened by a new abductive argument—the no-miracle argument for biological persistence. This argument posits that only a certain degree of compatibility between living organisms and physical reality can explain their very persistence. As Bertalanffy aptly noted, "the fact that animals and human beings are still in existence, proves that their forms of experience correspond, to some degree, with reality" (1955, p. 257). Regardless of the specific evolutionary theory one adheres to, the very fact that all living organisms only exist and persist by coexisting and interacting with diverse environments indicates the necessity of a baseline level of cognitive adequacy to those same environments. How else could they persist? What other natural fact could explain their persistence? Different evolutionary theories may differ in how this minimal adequacy evolved, but none disputes that minimal adequacy as a biological fact and requisite.

In this sense, "the categories of perception as determined by the bio-physiological organization [of every living organism] cannot be completely 'wrong', fortuitous, and arbitrary. Rather they must, in a certain way and to a certain extent, correspond to 'reality'" (Bertalanffy, 1955, p. 256). Of course, this "does not mean that our general categories of experience fully correspond to the real universe, and even less that they represent it completely"—"it is sufficient that a certain degree of isomorphism exists between the experienced world and the 'real' world, so that experience can guide the organism in such way as to preserve its existence" (1955, p. 257).

As George Gaylord Simpson famously put it: "To put it crudely but graphically, the monkey who did not have a realistic perception of the tree branch he jumped for was soon a dead monkey—and therefore did not become one of our ancestors" (1963, p. 84). Building on Simpson's point, François Jacob emphasized: "if the image a bird forms of the insects it must provide as food for its offspring did not reflect at least some aspects of reality, there would be no more young birds" (1981, p. 109). In essence, "regardless of how an organism explores its environment, the perception it draws from it must necessarily reflect reality or, more specifically, those aspects of reality that are directly related to its behavior" (1981, p. 110).

Taken together, all these elements provide a strong basis for critical realism, thereby allowing for the possibility of an ontological thinking and discourse about objective reality—that is, the reality that exists outside and independent of thought and language.

2 A Dynamic Relational Ontology

While philosophical ontology inherently strives for generality, every particular philosophical ontology is ultimately driven by specific ontological questions. Of course, multiple ontological positions can be supported, depending on the ontological questions one prioritizes. The ontological view that I will propose here is no exception.

My ontological approach rests on two core assumptions grounded on the evidence stemming from various sciences. First, I posit that reality consists of ontically discontinuous entities, even if spatially contiguous or partially overlapping. Secondly, I assume that all entities necessarily interact through various relations (spatial, temporal, causal, organizational), and that through these interactions, entities form different kinds of systems or mereological complexes. In essence, (i) against absolute monism, I assume ontological pluralism, and (ii) against mereological nihilism or flat ontologies, I assume the existence of different levels of organization defined by part-whole (system-subsystem) relationships.

The dynamic relational ontology (DRO) that I will now propose focuses on what I consider to be the fundamental ontological categories that underpin scientific explanation, namely, (i) the conditions of existence and (ii) the nature of identity of any particular being or entity (Santos, 2015, pp. 439–442, 2024, pp. 235–236; Santos et al., 2020, pp. 8693–8697).

DRO goes beyond one-category ontologies, which struggle to adequately capture the rich diversity of phenomena investigated by science. Instead, it recognizes multiple ontological kinds or categories of being. DRO's main concern is the nature of existence and identity for any type of entity, however categorizable (e.g., object, property, process, event). DRO's main claim is that the existence and identity of every entity must always be addressed and explained in relational terms. More specifically, every entity owes its identity and persistence to a specific relationship between its endogenous and exogenous relations, including as a proper part of higher-level relational systems.

In this way, DRO stands in opposition to both the individualist essentialism of metaphysical atomism and extreme holistic views. First, DRO rejects the view that reality can be explained in terms of a number of self-sufficient entities whose essential identities are taken to be previous to, and independent of, any relations with the outside world. In other words, DRO denies that the qualitative identity of any particular entity is completely determined by a set of absolutely intrinsic (or context-independent) properties. Secondly, DRO also disagrees with views that see particular systems or wholes as self-sufficient or self-subsistent entities whose existence and essential identity are independent of their parts' relations and of their exogenous relations to other entities. DRO thus stands for both the ontological and epistemological primacy of a relational viewpoint. In fact, explaining something always involves relating it to other things through certain determining factors or interdependencies. In this sense, the main goal of scientific explanation is to reproduce the ontological unity of reality by bringing together the diverse elements of our world in our thought.

Against the atomistic view of qualitatively immutable individuals and the holistic notion of wholes as self-imposed totalities, DRO argues that the identity of any particular entity, as well as its existence conditions, can only be fully explained as constructed and transformable by its endogenous and exogenous relations. Therefore, the existence and identity of every entity can only be explained in terms of specific systems of organizational and transformative dynamic relations. By identity, I mean both the actual and potential identity, that is, both the properties and causal behaviors that an entity manifests in act, as well as all its potentialities—that is, all properties or behaviors that it *may* actualize.

DRO thus proposes that every particular entity is always and necessarily causally related to all other entities, either directly or indirectly, even though "indirect causal relations are always based on direct ones" (Blanshard, 1962, p. 473). This does not mean that every relation changes or makes a difference to its relata in an equal manner (1962, pp. 472–473, 475, 486). As Brand Blanshard pertinently argued, "[e] very character counts, but not all characters count equally" (1962, p. 482). We must admit, of course, different scales of intensity and degrees of relevance (1962, p. 485). For instance, some causal relations might only cause quantitative changes to the already possessed properties of the entities involved. If these changes fall below a certain threshold, the entities won't undergo any qualitative changes. Furthermore, it is important to recognize that any system can instantiate some properties which are produced by some organization of properties which its parts instantiate independently of the relations that structure that very system. This means that even though some properties seem intrinsic to an entity, while other properties seem dependent on relations, this distinction can only make sense depending on the particular system or part-whole context that is being considered. An entity can indeed instantiate properties independently of its relations within a particular higher-level system. However, this doesn't mean that these properties are absolutely intrinsic, in the sense of being completely independent of any other relations. Therefore, DRO acknowledges the existence of both extrinsic relational and intrinsic-like properties depending on the particular systems or part-whole contexts we are considering. In DRO's view, there is no room for absolutely intrinsic properties, that is, for properties which entities instantiate completely independently of the outside world. From this point of view, there are only endogenous and exogenous relational properties.

Finally, to say that all things are internally related in a way that renders them interdependent is compatible, as Schaffer has argued, "with the existence of external relations, so long as there are also internal relations pervasive enough to connect all things" (2010, p. 372).

2.1 An Ontological Triad: Relations, Relata, and Relational Systems

DRO is a multicategory ontology for two key reasons. First, DRO argues that relations are not the sole constituents of reality. Instead, it proposes a triad of co-relative and interdependent categories, with no inherent hierarchy: relations, relata, and relational systems. Secondly, this ontological triad is not meant to eliminate or reduce all other categories of being, such as objects, processes, or events. To put it bluntly, DRO rejects any metaphysical theory of being, in the sense of taking this or that ontological category as a reified absolute.

Let us start by examining the first reason in more detail. According to DRO, any particular entity must be seen as being, at the same time but in different respects, a relation, a relatum, and a relational system:

1. A relational system in the sense that every entity is constituted by a number of material parts or properties, or conceptual elements, and their relations. As a matter of fact, while elementary physical particles are not composed of further particles, their existence and identity still depend on specific relations between their various measurable properties like energy, spin, charge, or mass.
2. A relation in the sense that the existence and identity of any entity is always grounded in a specific relational organization between its constitutive parts or relata.
3. A relatum in the sense that every particular entity is related to exogenous entities as its co-relata.

Relations, relata, and relational systems always come together as three co-relative and interdependent ontological categories. This becomes clear when we consider that, unless abstraction is involved, (i) no relatum exists without being related to something, (ii) no relation exists without being a relation between some relata, and (iii) every relation between two or more relata immediately forms a whole, or system, of which those relata are parts.

From this vantage point, assigning absolute ontological or chronological priority to relata, relations, or the systems they constitute makes no sense. From a realistic temporal perspective, reality is seen as the continuous generation of new relational systems from prior changes in other systems and relations and the ongoing transformation of entities both as relata and as relational systems. Moreover, wouldn't it be paradoxical, if not self-contradictory, for a theory based on a relational view of reality to elevate the concept of "relation" to an absolute or self-sufficient, that is, nonrelational, category of being?

From a DRO perspective, objects, processes, events, and even relations are themselves relata, relating to or interacting with each other spatially, temporally, causally, etc. Relations relate to each other forming relational structures. The existence of many relations depends on the specific relata and other existing relations. For instance, gravitational interaction only exists because of masses (as relata) and relations of spatial distance.

This relational approach extends to properties as well. Unless taken as primitive, that is, nondefinable, every property is characterized in relation to other properties. Any dictionary or encyclopedia illustrates this point. For example, energy is defined by its relationship with work and a system able to perform it; work is defined by its relation to energy, the application of force along a displacement, and a moving system; momentum is defined by its relation to mass and velocity; velocity is defined by its relation to the rate of change of time, the position of a system, and a frame of reference; and inertial mass is defined by its relation to acceleration, the resistance of a system, and an applied external force. These examples demonstrate how properties themselves consist of relations with other properties as relata, forming interconnected relational systems.

In this respect as well, there is no room for unilateral reductions. Relations don't reduce to relata nor relata reduce to relations. As a matter of fact, every relational property is just a one-sided view of a polyadic relation. To say that "Martha is mother of Hellen" is the same as saying that "there is a directed relationship of motherhood between Martha and Hellen."

The same goes for laws. Any law consists of a relation (causal or not) between two or more properties, as its relata, together forming a relational system. On the other hand, any law is also a relatum given that the pattern of behavior that it expresses is always affected by external conditions and other laws. This explains why most, if not all, scientific laws are ceteris paribus or conditional. For example, the law that hydrogen atoms behave according to Schrödinger's equation with the Coulomb potential only holds true in the absence of magnetic or electric fields. Newton's law of gravitation only describes the behavior of heavy bodies if there are no charges or electromagnetic fields. As Jean Ullmo has observed, every law "describes a specific type of interaction in which an object may be involved, abstraction made of all interactions that take place simultaneously, and which one assumes, or makes sure to be, negligible" (1958, p. 156). In this sense, all laws are "conditioned," and "it is [their] implicit conditions that ensure their validity" (1958, p. 54).

As anticipated at the beginning of the section, the fact that DRO establishes relations, relata, and relational systems as its fundamental ontological categories does not mean it aims to abolish or replace other classical categories, such as object, process, event, or even substance. It rather proposes that all these categories ought to be reconceptualized in relational terms. For example, from the point of view of DRO, there is room for both objectual and processual relational systems. An object is a three-extensional enduring relational system, whose constitutive relata are further objectual systems. A process is a four-extensional perduring relational system, that is, an entity whose internal structure includes the temporal dimension as a fourth type of extension, and whose constitutive relata are therefore different temporal stages, phases, or steps of development (each capable of being conceptualized as events).

Importantly, DRO doesn't view objects and processes as conflicting categories. It all depends on the scale and purpose of the analysis. A living organism is both an enduring dynamic system, whose diachronic identity can ultimately be explained in terms of the preservation of its specific ("sortal") identity, and an organized system of multiple processes, whose ensemble constitutes its biography or trajectory in its "state space" (see Lowe, 2007; Wiggins, 2016).

The same goes for events and processes. Processes are typically viewed as causal sequences (and therefore relations) of events. On the other hand, no process takes place and evolves in time independently of its relations with the outside world. However, a process itself can be seen as an event-like point in time when considered in its entire unfolding (i.e., as a whole) in relation to other processes or events. Yet, no real-world event can be taken literally as a spatiotemporal atom or mathematical point event. Real-world events always consist of causal relation-based changes in the properties of enduring or perduring entities, such as a particle collision or a new act in a play or opera. In this sense, every process or event is both a relational entity, in the sense that it always consists in a relation between other entities, and a relatum, in the sense that no process or event occurs or evolves as an independent entity.

Finally, if relationality is the fundamental principle of all beings, it must also apply to relations themselves. This means that DRO must reject atomist relationalism. Relations do not come one by one, acting separately from the others, as independent atomic entities. It is within the framework of this relational approach that the notions of ontological emergence and downward causation will be formulated in the next two sections.

3 Ontological Emergence

The classical notion of ontological emergence is defined by the view that there are certain real-world entities—systems, properties, or laws—that are necessarily generated from and/or constituted by other entities but not fully reducible to them. Emergence is thus a relation in which an entity—the "emergent"—is not fully determined or predetermined by the entities with respect to which it is said to be emergent—the so-called "emergence base." In terms of part-whole relations, the emergent entity is a system or some of its properties, relations, or laws, and the emergent basis is constituted by the proper parts of the system, with their own micro-laws, individual properties and inter-individual relations. In this sense, systemic emergence is opposed to lower-level, whole-to-part or micro-reductionism. Systemic emergence indicates that the micro level of a system—that is, the set of all its parts—does not completely determine or produce the system. To say that x does not completely determine or produce y is the same as to say that x provides the necessary but not the sufficient conditions for the determination or production of y (Bishop et al., 2022, pp. 27, 94; Santos, 2021b, 2024, p. 238).

The main issue regarding the divide between emergence and micro-reduction is whether all levels of organization of reality can be reduced level by level (at least, in principle) to the basic properties, relations, and laws of the ultimate physical domain, or whether certain levels of organization, while being necessarily dependent on underlying or historically prior levels, have a relative degree of autonomy. As Kim once put it:

> How are the characteristic properties of a given level related to the properties at the adjacent levels—in particular, to those at the lower levels? How are biological ("vital") properties related to physicochemical properties? How are consciousness and intentionality related to biological/physical properties? How are social phenomena, phenomena characteristic of social groups, related to phenomena involving individual members? (Kim, 1998, p. 16)

From the point of view of part-whole relations, there are only two possible absolutely asymmetrical or unidirectional relations of reduction. Either we completely reduce the properties and relations of a system to the intrinsic or system-independent properties and respective relations of its proper parts, or we completely reduce the properties and respective relations of the parts of a system to the properties and relations only instantiated by that system. In other words, either we opt for the atomistic or individualist view of a complete micro-determinism and therefore micro-reduction, or we opt for a holist view of a complete macro-determinism and therefore macro-reduction.

From a DRO viewpoint, an epistemologically consequential notion of emergence must be able to reject atomism and micro-reduction without resorting to mysterious holisms. Building on the DRO principle that the identity of every entity is constructed and transformable by the interplay of its endogenous and exogenous relations, I propose the following naturalistic account of ontological emergence. This account recognizes two kinds or degrees of systemic emergence.

3.1 Organizational Emergence

The first kind of systemic emergence arises from the well-established fact that some composed entities exhibit properties that are determined by a specific macro-relational organization of their individual components. In these cases, the composed entity, as a unified system, can be considered the real bearer of some of its properties and relations, and therefore the real causal agent regarding the causal powers associated with such properties. In sum, this notion of emergence means that a system can be seen as a genuinely new individual, because its identity is based on a specific *macro*-relational organization, which means that it is fundamentally different from both its individual parts and any arbitrary composition or assemblage of them. Some wholes can therefore be considered to be more than, or different from, the mere sum of their parts because their identity and existence are fundamentally grounded in a specific organization of their parts.

This does not mean, however, that the organization of the system, and the properties associated with it, cannot be fully determined by the intrinsic properties and respective laws of the parts of that system. Micro-determinism and micro-reductionism can coexist with ontological emergence because these reductions reduce but do not eliminate the macro-organizations (see Santos, 2021, 2024, pp. 238–239).

3.2 Relational-Transformational Emergence

Ontological emergence only implies the in-principle failure of micro-determination and micro-reductionism when a systemic organization is not fully determined by the system-independent or intrinsic-like properties and laws of the lower-level entities that compose it (Santos, 2021a; 2024, pp. 238–239).

This corresponds to a different kind of emergence, which can be characterized as follows. A property P of a system s is emergent if and only if:

(i) P is a property of a specific global organization (R) of the proper parts of s.
(ii) R and consequently P are not completely determined by (thereby not being fully explainable or reducible in terms of) the intrinsic or system-independent properties, and respective relations and laws, of the proper parts of s.

This means that the existence and explanation of property P depend on some *system-dependent relational properties* of the parts of system s—that is, properties which the lower-level entities only have or manifest by virtue of being parts of system s, or by virtue of being relata within the specifically organized system of relations called s. This dependence typically includes some relationships that the system has with its external environment, including as a part of a higher-level system. The essential dependence of emergence processes on contextual or background conditions was appropriately highlighted and thoroughly analyzed in Bishop et al. (2022).

Only this kind of relational-transformational emergence (RTE) entails the in-principle failure of micro-determination and micro-reductionism (Santos, 2015, 2021a, 2024). Indeed, how completely micro-determined and therefore micro-reducible can the property of a system be if some of the properties of the parts that contribute to its production are only instantiated by virtue of the integration of the parts within that very system?

RTE is thus crucially defined by a transformation of the actual identity of lower-level entities as parts of some systems or as constitutive relata of some systems of relations. By a change in the actual identity of an entity, I mean a change in the set of properties or behaviors that an entity actually possesses or manifests, even though by gaining and losing some of those properties, the entity will also change in terms of its potential identity, that is, in terms of the powers or capacities associated with those properties.

The fundamental difference between simple organizational emergence and RTE is that, in the former, relations and organizations are only determinant for the construction of the system as a whole, whereas in the latter, they also determine the identity, if not the very existence, of the parts of the system. This is the reason why, in cases of RTE, there are no literal unilateral or asymmetrical reductions of systems to their parts, or vice versa, but rather a reciprocal and partial determination between the lower and higher levels (see Santos, 2024, pp. 237–240).

4 Downward-Structural Causation and Interlevel Integrative Explanations

Properly understood, the notion of downward causation helps us explain how parts can be conditioned or transformed by their systems.

The notion of whole-to-part causation should not be seen in terms of relations whereby a whole, taken as a set of parts and their respective relations, causally interacts with, thereby affecting the subset of its parts. Their causal relations should neither be thought of as relations between two object-like things: the whole as an object vs. its parts as a plurality of objects. From a truly relational perspective, any whole is simply the "relational context" in which different entities are embedded, as parts or relata. Therefore, an organized system is nothing but a specifically organized or structured set of relations between different entities as relata of those relations.

From a DRO viewpoint, it is a specifically organized or structured set of relations of a system that may be said to exert top-down or downward causation, by affecting the behavior of each of the system's parts, as relata of those relations. That is why I have called it downward-structural causation (DSC) (Santos, 2024, pp. 244–246). As Tony Lawson pointed out, it is the "organizing relational structure" of a composite whole, rather than the whole-as-a-whole, that may be said to exert top-down or downward causation (2013, p. 287, 2016, pp. 431–432, 2019, pp. 38, 74 n. 9, 87–88, 199–200, 214–219).

Now, these specifically organized sets of relations can causally influence their embedded parts or relata in two ways: (i) by changing the properties and behaviors that parts actually exhibit, or (ii) by changing the set of powers, capacities, or potential behaviors that they may manifest. I have proposed the term "downward-structural causal transformation" for the first type of change, and "downward-structural causal conditioning" for the second type. Finally, since parts may be changed by acquiring or losing powers, they may be subject to downward-structural causal conditioning, either in empowering or in constraining terms (Santos, 2024, p. 241).

DSC is typically observed not in "aggregative" or "component systems" but in "integrated systems" (Bechtel & Richardson, 2010, pp. 26–27). Integrated systems are defined by interdependent parts, meaning their behaviors are also interdependent. This makes their parts "minimally decomposable"; independent properties or causal roles cannot be ascribed to them (Bechtel & Richardson, 2010, pp. 27, 31). Furthermore, the interdependence between parts follows specific system-level modes of organization, which means that the parts' behaviors and interactions are not dependent on each other in a purely haphazard or arbitrary way (Santos 2021a, pp. 8698–8705, 2024, pp. 238, 243–244).

In sum, DSC refers to the set of conditionings or transformations that a specifically structured set of interdependent relations exerts on each of their relata as lower-level parts of that system. The concept of DSC thus implies the existence of second- or even higher-order structuring relations beyond the domain of the first-order or inter-individual relations between the systems' parts. These higher-order relations structure and organize the ways in which the parts interact with each other causally, spatially, and temporally. In this sense, they represent inheritable modes of organization whose existence can only be explained as the result of previous historical processes—physical, chemical, biological, social, etc. (see Santos, 2024, pp. 243–246, 256–258).

Finally, since DSC is a type of causal relation, it must necessarily be viewed as a diachronic process. At any given point in time, the relational structure of a system causally affects the behaviors that the parts of that system will or may instantiate at a later time. To say that part x of system s is conditioned by s at time t is to say that x can only act this way or that way at any time after t, thereby fixing the set of its possible future behaviors. Likewise, to say that system's part x has lost a given power P at time t is to say that x cannot act in a P-way from that moment on, that is, after t. At any time t, every entity is just acting given the possibilities that were set by a given relational structure before t. This applies both for downward causal transformation of actual properties and for downward causal conditioning of powers or potentialities (Santos, 2024, pp. 240–241).

The same is true of upward causation. Since, at any given time, the relational structure of a system causally affects, but never completely determines, the behavior of each of its parts, the actions and interactions of each part also causally contribute to the maintenance or modification of the collective behaviors of its system, thereby contributing to the "reproduction" or "transformation" of the system's relational structure (Archer, 1995; Lawson, 2019).

Metaphysical individualisms, despite acknowledging the importance of relations, cannot, of course, accept the notion of DSC. Their relationalism is limited to mere inter-individual interactions. In this "flat" ontological view, reality lacks the layered structure proposed by DRO. As Donati and Archer argue, "networks remain linkages between nodes instead of networks of relations" (Donati & Archer, 2015, p. 22), "despite there being no such thing as context-less action" (2015, p. i). In light of this atomist relationalism, social explanations should only involve "interpersonal relations (the individualist concept of 'social structure')" (Archer, 1995, p. 36, 34). Indeed, "structure becomes epiphenomenal in classic statements of methodological individualism because the social context is defined as made up of nothing more than other people" (Archer, 1995, p. 84).

In this way, methodological individualism "mistakes situated individuals for bare individuals and overlooks the causal feedback that society has on individuals." In particular, it "forgets that citizens are not Hobbesian men mushrooming from the earth; even in their most self-centered mode, they have internalized much social relation and conditioning, so that social concepts have been built into their characterization" (Auyang, 1999, p. 121). As Wimsatt observed, the "common reductionistic heuristics" typically obey the following strategy:

> Describe a relational property as if it were monadic (. . .). Thus, e.g., describe fitness as if it were a property of phenotypes or genes, ignoring the fact that it is a relation between organism and environment. (This strategy may be justified/facilitated [and its strong assumptions hidden] by fixing the environment, thus making it artificially disappear as a variable.) (. . .) Many context dependencies are hidden in this fashion. (2007, pp. 347, 82)

As Auyang pointed out, "[a]lmost all explanations in terms of concrete individuals involve social predicates. Thus, social concepts have not been eliminated as demanded by methodological individualism; they have only been swept under the rug" (1999, p. 357, n.1). This is why "many so called individualist explanations are really individualist only in name" (Kincaid, 2012, p. 149). And this is also why RTE and DSC contradict both micro- and macro-reductive explanations. Instead, they require interlevel integrative explanations through an "enrichment-reciprocal assimilation" dual process between theories working at different levels of organization (see Santos, 2024, pp. 250–260).

To be more precise, RTE and DSC demand an adequate integration of upward and downward explanations; that is, what we need is to be able to explain:

1. Why do lower-level systems behave the way they do as constitutive relata of certain higher-level systems of relations. This task must require the identification of all system-dependent relational properties of the system's parts, that is, all properties that parts only acquire or manifest by virtue of being relata within specifically organized systems of relations or interactions.
2. How some systems and their systemic properties result from specifically organized systems of relations between their constitutive parts, or between the precursor entities of those parts. This task must require the discovery of (2.1.) the specific laws of organization and transformation on the basis of which those systems were formed and evolve the way they do, as well as (2.2.) the relations which those systems have with other systems in their environments, including as parts of yet higher-level systems.

All things considered, the critical question is to explain how the different levels of organization of reality relate to each other, partially determining each other's existence and identity.

As I have previously provided a systematic account of the interlevel integrative model of explanation (see Santos, 2024, 250–260) and have already presented detailed analyses of some concrete examples of RTE and DSC, mostly taken from Developmental Biology, in previous works (see Santos 2021a, pp. 8703–8705; Santos et al., 2020; Vecchi & Santos, 2023; Santos, 2024, pp. 246–250), I will now conclude by briefly analyzing a new case study specifically related to the domain of the social and human sciences. More precisely, I will consider the problem of the emergence of mind and the domain of social relations, with a particular emphasis on the interdisciplinary field called social neuroscience.

4.1 The Emergence of Mind and Meaning

The material domain of the social and human sciences comprises the set of properties, activities, and relations that came into existence with the emergence of mind or, better, minded brains, at a certain stage of biological evolution.

According to neuroscience, mind is what the brain does, or, better, what the brain does by virtue of its interactions with the entire nervous, endocrine and immune systems, and many other non-neural parts of the body (for instance, even the brain is constituted by important non-neural cells, like glial cells) (e.g., Angevine, 2002; Bunge, 2010; Damásio, 2010). Yet, this does not mean that the mind is reducible to biochemistry. Whatever happens in the mind happens in the brain, but the "biochemical" and the "mental" constitute two qualitatively distinct dimensions. These dimensions are formed by two different sets of properties and relations instantiated by the same brain system.

At the biochemical level, neural activation patterns or circuit configurations take center stage. In contrast, the mental domain is characterized by mental representations or signs, such as mental images (interoceptive, proprioceptive, and exteroceptive; visual, auditory, olfactory, gustatory, visceral, and tactile), as well as concepts and categories (including human values—e.g., ethical, aesthetic). The biochemical level is governed by causal and topological relations between cells and molecules. At the mental level of analysis, in contrast, we find semiotic, logical, and mathematical relations between mental signs. The classical distinction between *causes* and *reasons* aptly captures this difference.

The emergence of minded brains thus corresponds to the emergence of two different domains:

1. The semiotic domain: This encompasses different kinds of mental representations or signs, such as indexes, icons, and symbols (either in the sense defined by linguistics or anthropology), with their respective modes of signification, signified meanings, and (where applicable) referents.
2. The domain of "meaningful" relations between those signs: This is the domain of discursive thought (intra-propositional or inter-propositional) with its respective set of logical and mathematical principles and laws.

Mind-as-mind is thus meaningful, and semiotically, logically, and mathematically productive, even though it lacks causal efficacy. In contrast, nonminded matter has causal efficacy but is semiotically empty and therefore devoid of inherent meanings or values—except, of course, the ones minded brains ascribe to it, such as when we interpret causal relations (e.g., dark clouds → imminent rain) as semiotic ones (e.g., dark clouds are index signs of imminent rain) (see Nöth, 1990, p. 86).

This perspective aligns with the rejection of interactionist substance dualism: minds and brain-body systems do not causally interact with each other. Therefore, the only consistent way to make sense of the notion of mental causation is to assume that "mental states have a causal effect on behavior by the very fact that they are at the same time brain states" (Jeannerod, 2001, p. 266; Jeannerod, 2002, pp. 29, 189; Damásio, 2010, p. 316). Minded brain states can thus cause other minded brain states, either within each individual or through inter-individual and social interactions.

Given the practical impossibility of reducing mental properties and relations to biochemical ones, as well as the naturalist rejection of substance dualism, the best option seems to be to assume a dimensional parallelism—by a "principle of prudence and greatest reduction of hypotheses" (Piaget, 1950, p. 161)—"between the physical substance of the brain and the mental processes it supports" (Johnson & de Haan, 2015, p. 2). In light of these considerations, the most reasonable expectation might be to find some isomorphic relationships between the organization and functioning of conscious mental phenomena and their biochemical concomitants (Piaget, 1968, pp. 186–190).

Be that as it may, the mere coexistence of the biochemical and the mental as two qualitatively different and irreducible dimensions of brain's activity warrants the disciplinary autonomy of not only cognitive and affective psychology, but also the studies carried out in the anthropology of the symbolic, imaginary, and human culture in general (e.g., Cassirer, 1944, 2021; Durand, 1999). The evolutionary process has shaped the nervous systems and brains of human beings in a particular way, determining the nature of both their individual and social lives as gregarious animals. This is reflected in the meaning content of their brain states. Mythical, religious, social, political, economic, ethical, and aesthetic concepts and values all coevolve with the various forms of human interaction and the historical products of those interactions. As Cassirer observed, the emergence of "a meaning, which is not detached from the physical but is embodied by it and in it, is the factor common to all those contents that we denote by the term *culture*" (2000, p. 43).

If the biochemical and the mental are constituted by two different sets of qualitatively distinct properties and relations, and therefore structures, principles, and laws—the first essentially dependent on systems of causal relations, and the latter essentially dependent on systems of meaningful relations—, then they will also require different modes of analysis, interpretation, and explanation (Piaget, 1950, pp. 137 ff., 1967c, pp. 1179 ff., 1970c, d; Cassirer, 2000, pp. 56–86).

4.2 Social Neuroscience

If mind is brain activity, but not all brain activity has a mental dimension, then the existence of mind requires more than the mere occurrence of some bioelectrochemical processes in the brain. Furthermore, if mind is essentially a *meaning-making* activity, then the emergence of mind must require the emergence of some degree of *consciousness* through the occurrence of more systemic brain processes (e.g., Dehaene, 2014), including their relations to the rest of the body. From this point of view, mental properties are *brain-body system-dependent relational properties* of neural circuit patterns or states. However, even this organismic level is not sufficient because every organism is also shaped by its social, economic, and cultural environments. Research in the field of social neuroscience has provided support for this idea by emphasizing the need for "multilevel, integrative analyses" that allow social, cognitive, behavioral, and developmental psychology and neuroscience to be linked in light of the principles of multiple, nonadditive, and reciprocal determination (Cacioppo & Berntson, 1992).

Social neuroscience investigates the complex interplay between three key domains:

1. The domain of the social and socio-economic structures of relations
2. The cognitive and affective dimensions of behavior
3. The cellular and neural domains at the level of the brain and nervous system

The third level includes both intercellular and intracellular interactions. Intercellular interactions encompass the brain's structure, functioning, and development (e.g., Sirin, 2005; Hackman et al., 2010; Noble et al., 2015; Brito et al., 2017). Intracellular interactions concern epigenetic modifications within brain cells, such as DNA methylation or histone acetylation (e.g., Weaver et al., 2004; Hackman et al., 2010; Szyf, 2021). For example, research has shown that social relationships, particularly stress, in animals can directly influence their brains and nervous systems, even at the level of epigenetic modifications, and that this can have lasting effects on behavior and cognition (e.g., Weaver et al., 2004; Szyf, 2011; Szyf & Bick, 2013).

One particular phenomenon gaining recent attention is socio-economic status (SES). SES is a multidimensional construct that "describes an individual's or a family's ranking on a hierarchy according to access to, or control over, some combination of valued commodities such as wealth, power, and social status" (Sirin, 2005, p. 418). In other words, it refers to "an individual's access to economic and social resources, as well as the benefits and social standing that come from these resources" (Brito & Noble, 2014, p. 2). SES is linked to various factors that can influence health and well-being, including differences in quality of nutrition; stress levels; type of parenting (cognitive stimulation); availability of physical, cognitive, and social resources; neighborhood characteristics and environmental factors impacting health; educational attainment; subjective social status (one's perceived position in the social hierarchy); and community values and expectations (e.g., Farah, 2017; Troller-Renfree et al., 2022).

While a detailed analysis of this relatively new and constantly developing field of research is beyond the scope of this chapter, it is noteworthy that given the established influence of SES on brain development and behavior, one of the main questions guiding social neuroscience research may be expressed in terms of the notion of *downward causation*: "How does SES relate to brain development, and what are the mechanisms by which SES might exert its influence?" (Hackman & Farah, 2009).

Numerous studies consistently highlight the causal impact of SES factors on cognitive and emotional abilities, including "executive functions" like attention, planning, decision-making, language, and working memory. The underlying assumption, as Thomas and Coecke note, is that "differences in socioeconomic status correlate both with differences in cognitive development and in brain structure," and that "associations between SES and brain measures such as cortical surface area and cortical thickness mediate differences in cognitive skills such as executive function and language" (2023, p. 1). For example, the largest study to date relating SES and brain structure, measuring, in particular, the cortical surface area has shown that the strongest effects of SES on brain structure were found in regions supporting language, reading, executive functions, memory, and spatial skills (Noble et al., 2015).

However, given the complexity of SES, it is crucial to understand how SES "distal" causes can affect neuro-cognitive development (both prenatally and postnatally), through more direct or "proximal" causal pathways. These proximal factors include stress levels, linguistic and cognitive stimulation, parenting styles, prenatal care, exposure to toxins, and nutrition (Brito & Noble, 2014; Brito et al., 2017; Farah, 2017; Thomas & Coecke, 2023).

Researchers have employed various methods to evaluate the influence of SES factors on brain development. These methods include standardized cognitive tests assessing vocabulary, reading, working memory, and selective attention. Additionally, researchers compare school achievement data and utilize brain imaging techniques such as structural and functional magnetic resonance imaging, electroencephalography, and magnetoencephalography. Even neuro-computational models of cognitive development are being explored in this field (see Thomas & Coecke, 2023).

The first randomized controlled trial of poverty reduction in children's cognitive, emotional, and brain development was conducted in the United States in 2018. According to the authors, this research has offered evidence on the "correlation vs. causation debate by showing that an intervention designed to reduce poverty appeared to cause changes in children's brain functioning in ways that have been linked to subsequent higher cognitive skills" (Troller-Renfree et al., 2022, p. 5). In particular, electroencephalographic analysis has shown that the frontal and central regions of the brain, which support the development of thinking, learning, and social-emotional control, suffer a crucial impact from environmental factors, such as socio-economic conditions and family stress (Troller-Renfree et al., 2022).

Building on this concept, social neuroscience has also been investigating the impact of socio-economic factors on decision-making processes, a critical concept in both neoclassical micro-economics and current neuro-economics (Chang, 2014, pp. 164–166). Research in this area demonstrates that individuals facing chronic stress from managing scarce resources, such as those with low incomes, experience negative consequences on attention, cognitive resources, and, ultimately, decision-making abilities (Shafir, 2017). As Sheehy-Skeffington (2020) has recently shown, there is strong evidence for the relationship between SES and the psychological, social, and cultural processes that underpin decision-making. In particular, "low income contexts present socio-ecological cues concerning resource scarcity, environmental instability, and low subjective social status, which trigger a regulatory shift towards the present and the tuning of cognitive skills and focus to address immediate needs" (2020, p. 183). As expected, these shifts in psychological processes result in decisions that may hinder the achievement of more distal long-term goals.

These studies collectively support the idea that the brain, and consequently mind and behavior, can be causally affected by social relations, as clearly illustrated by the well-known phenomenon of brain and neural plasticity (Bavelier & Neville, 2002).

This view is further supported by neuroconstructivism, according to which brain and cognitive development (and especially the formation of neural patterns underlying mental representations) is shaped by multiple interacting constraints at different levels, ranging from genes and cells to the brain, the whole body, and the physical and social environments (Westermann et al., 2007; Mareschal et al., 2007; Thomas & Baughman, 2014; Karmiloff-Smith et al., 2018).

As Lisa Barrett has noted, "the social world profoundly shapes the physical reality of the brain's wiring," through mechanisms like tuning and pruning of neural connections (2020, pp. 57, 47–63). This underscores the importance of an "integrated" perspective on developmental cognitive neuroscience, as advocated by Johnson and de Haan (2015, pp. 240–249).

All these studies highlight the shortcomings of any reductionist program that attempts to explain the human mind and behavior solely, or primarily, through the lens of the brain's neural and biochemical processes. In this context, the most problematic issue lies in trying to explain system-dependent relational properties, such as social behaviors or value-based decisions, within already socio-economically structured societies solely, or primarily, based on lower-level phenomena like an individual brain's structure and activity. As neuroscience itself demonstrates, higher-level social and socio-economic factors have a demonstrable impact on the structure, function, and development of the human brain, thereby influencing cognitive and emotional performance and development.

Mental states and human behavior are system-dependent relational properties of individuals. This means that they are fundamentally shaped by interactions within different kinds of environments, including in the context of different higher-level structures of relations (e.g., social, economic, cultural). In essence, this is what finally undermines the micro-reductive approaches by ontological and methodological individualisms (informed by agent-based models, rational choice theory, decision and game theory, etc.) that permeate social and human sciences (see Fullbrook, 2004; Kincaid, 2012, 2018; Lawson, 2019, pp. 197–222).

In conclusion, the proposed DRO compels us to rethink the way we approach scientific explanation. By acknowledging the existence of relational-transformational processes of systemic emergence, as well as the complex interplay between upward and downward-structural causation, the proposed DRO dismantles the illusion of one-level and unidimensional accounts and advocates, as an alternative approach, the development of interlevel integrative forms of explanation and understanding of our world.

Acknowledgments This work was funded by national funds through FCT—Fundação para a Ciência e a Tecnologia, I.P., within the scope of the R&D Unit Centre for Philosophy of Science of the University of Lisbon (CFCUL), a strategic project with the references FCT I.P. UIDB/00678/2020 and UIDP/00678/2020, and the DOI https://doi.org/10.54499/UIDB/00678/2020 and https://doi.org/10.54499/UIDP/00678/2020. I acknowledge the financial support of FCT, "Fundação para a Ciência e a Tecnologia, I.P." (Stimulus of Scientific Employment, Individual Support 2017: CEECIND/03316/2017). I would also like to express my gratitude to the organizers of the Conference "The Relational View on Economics 2023" held in Roskilde University, as well as to the conference participants for their valuable feedback.

References

Angevine, J. B. (2002). Nervous system, organization of. In V. S. Ramachandran (Ed.), *Encyclopedia of the human brain* (pp. 313–371). Academic.

Archer, M. (1995). *Realist social theory: The morphogenetic approach*. Cambridge University Press.

Auyang, S. (1999). *Foundations of complex-system theories – In economics, evolutionary biology, and statistical physics*. Cambridge University Press.

Barrett, L. F. (2020). *Seven and a half lessons about the brain*. Houghton Mifflin Harcourt.

Bavelier, D., & Neville, H. (2002). Neuroplasticity, developmental. In V. S. Ramachandran (Ed.), *Encyclopedia of the human brain* (pp. 561–578). Academic.

Bechtel, W., & Richardson, R. (2010). *Discovering complexity: Decomposition and localization as strategies in scientific research*. The MIT Press.

Bertalanffy, L. V. (1955). An essay on the relativity of categories. *Philosophy of Science, 22*(4), 243–263.

Bishop, R. C., Silberstein, M., & Pexton, M. (2022). *Emergence in context. A treatise in twenty-century natural philosophy*. Oxford University Press.

Blanshard, B. (1962). *Reason and analysis*. George Allen & Unwin Ltd.

Brito, N. H., & Noble, K. G. (2014). Socioeconomic status and structural brain development. *Frontiers in Neuroscience, 2014*(8), 276.

Brito, N. H., Piccolo, L. R., & Noble, K. G. (2017). Associations between cortical thickness and neurocognitive skills during childhood vary by family socioeconomic factors. *Brain and Cognition, 116*, 54–62.

Bunge, M. (1977). *Treatise on basic philosophy. Vol. III: The furniture of the world*. Reidel.

Bunge, M. (2010). *Matter and mind. A philosophical inquiry*. Springer.

Cacioppo, J. T., & Berntson, G. G. (1992). Social psychological contributions to the decade of the brain: Doctrine of multilevel analysis. *American Psychologist, 47*(8), 1019–1028.

Cassirer, E. (1944). *An essay on man*. Yale University Press.

Cassirer, E. (2000). *The logic of the cultural sciences*. Yale University Press.

Cassirer, E. (2021). *The philosophy of symbolic forms (three volume set)*. Routledge.

Chang, H.-J. (2014). *Economics: The User's guide*. Penguin Books/Pelican.

Changeux, J. P. (2004). *The physiology of truth. Neuroscience and human knowledge*. Harvard University Press.

Damasio, A. (2010). *Self comes to mind: Constructing the conscious brain*. Pantheon/Random House.

Damásio, A. (2018). *The strange order of things: Life, feeling, and the making of cultures*. Pantheon.

Damasio, A. (2021). *Feeling and knowing: Making minds conscious*. Pantheon.

Dehaene, S. (2014). *Consciousness and the brain: Deciphering how the brain codes our thoughts*. Viking Press.

Denis, M. (1979). *Les images mentales*. PUF.

Denis, M. (1991). *Image and cognition*. Harvester Wheatsheaf.

Donati, P., & Archer, M. (2015). *The relational subject*. Cambridge University Press.

Durand, G. (1999). *The anthropological structures of the imaginary*. Boombana Publications.

Farah, M. (2017). The neuroscience of socioeconomic status: Correlates, causes, and consequences. *Neuron, 96*, 56–71.

Fullbrook. (2004). Descartes' legacy. In *Elgar companion to economics and philosophy* (pp. 403–422). Elgar.

Hackman, D. A., & Farah, M. J. (2009). Socioeconomic status and the developing brain. *Trends in Cognitive Sciences., 13*(2), 65–73.

Hackman, D. A., Farah, M. J., & Meaney, M. J. (2010). (2010). Socioeconomic status and the brain: Mechanistic insights from human and animal research. *Nature Reviews Neuroscience, 11*(9), 651–659.

Hooker, C. A. (1995). *Reason, regulation, and realism: Towards a regulatory systems theory of reason and evolutionary epistemology*. State University of New York Press.
Jacob, F. (1981). *Le Jeu des Possibles*. Fayard.
Jeannerod, M. (2001). Y a-t-il des limites à la naturalisation des états mentaux? In A. Ehrenberg & A. M. Lovell (Eds.), *La maladie mentale en mutation: psychiatrie et société* (pp. 266–278). Odile Jacob.
Jeannerod, M. (2002). *La Nature de l'Esprit*. Odile Jacob.
Johnson, M. H., & de Haan, M. (2015). *Developmental cognitive neuroscience: An introduction*. Wiley.
Kandel, E. R., Schwartz, J. H., & Jessell, T. M. (2021). *Principles of neural science*. McGraw-Hill.
Karmiloff-Smith, A., Thomas, M. S. C., & Johnson, M. H. (Eds.). (2018). *Thinking developmentally from constructivism to neuroconstructivism: Selected works of Annette Karmiloff-Smith*. Routledge.
Kim, J. (1998). *Mind in a physical world*. The MIT Press.
Kincaid, H. (2012). Some issues concerning the nature of economic explanation. In U. Mäki, D. Gabbay, P. Thagard, & J. Woods (Eds.), *Handbook for the philosophy of science: Philosophy of economics* (pp. 137–159). Elsevier.
Kincaid, H. (2018). Individualism versus holism. In S. Durlauf & L. Blume (Eds.), *The new Palgrave dictionary of economics* (pp. 6311–6317). Palgrave Macmillan.
Kosslyn, S. M. (1984). Mental representations. In J. R. Anderson & S. M. Kosslyn (Eds.), *Tutorials in learning and memory: Essays in honor of Gordon bower* (pp. 91–117). Freeman.
Kosslyn, S. M. (1994). *Image and brain. The resolution of the imagery debate*. The MIT Press.
Kosslyn, S. M., Ganis, G., & Thompson, W. L. (2001). Neural foundations of imagery. *Nature Reviews. Neuroscience, 2*(9), 635–642.
Kosslyn, S. M., Thompson, W. L., & Ganis, G. (2006). *The case for mental imagery*. Oxford University Press.
Lawson, T. (2013). Emergence and social causation. In R. Groff & G. Greco (Eds.), *Powers and capacities in philosophy: The new Aristotelianism* (pp. 61–84). Routledge.
Lawson, T. (2016). Some critical issues in social ontology: Reply to John Searle. *Journal for the Theory of Social Behaviour, 46*(4), 426–437.
Lawson, T. (2019). *The nature of social reality. Issues in social ontology*. Routledge.
Lowe, E. J. (2007). Sortals and the individuation of objects. *Mind & Language, 22*(5), 514–533.
Mareschal, D., Johnson, M., Sirois, S., Spratling, M., Thomas, M. S. C., & Westermann, G. (2007). *Neuroconstructivism: How the brain constructs cognition*. Oxford University Press.
Neves, R. S. (2011). *Psychologie cognitive*. Armand Colin.
Niiniluoto, I. (1999). *Critical Scientific Realism*. Oxford University Press.
Niiniluoto, I. (2018). *Truth-seeking by abduction*. Springer.
Noble, K. G., et al. (2015). Family income, parental education and brain structure in children and adolescents. *Nature Neuroscience, 18*(5), 773–778.
Nöth, W. (1990). *Handbook of semiotics*. Indiana University Press.
Piaget, J. (1950). *Introduction à l'Épistémologie Génétique. Vol. 3: La pensée biologique, la pensée psychologique et la pensée sociologique*. PUF.
Piaget, J. (1967a). Les problèmes principaux de l'épistémologie des mathématiques. In J. Piaget (Ed.), *Logique et Connaissance Scientifique* (pp. 554–596). Gallimard.
Piaget, J. (1967b). Les relations entre le sujet et l'objet dans la connaissance physique. In J. Piaget (Ed.), *Logique et Connaissance Scientifique* (pp. 754–778). Gallimard.
Piaget, J. (1967c). Classification des sciences et principaux courants épistémologiques contemporains. In J. Piaget (Ed.), *Logique et Connaissance Scientifique* (pp. 1151–1271). Gallimard.
Piaget, J. (1968). Explanation in psychology and psychophysiological parallelism. In J. Piaget, P. Fraisse, & M. Reuchlin (Eds.), *Experimental psychology: Its scope and method. Vol. I: History and method*. Routledge and Kegan Paul.
Piaget, J. (1970a). *L'Épistémologie Génétique*. PUF.

Piaget, J. (1970b). *Structuralism*. Routledge & Kegan.

Piaget, J. (1970c). Introduction: The place of the sciences of man in the system of sciences. In *Main trends of research in the social and human sciences. Part 1: Social sciences* (pp. 1–57). Mouton/UNESCO.

Piaget, J. (1970d). General problems of interdisciplinary research and common mechanisms. In *Main trends of research in the social and human sciences. Part one: Social sciences* (pp. 467–528). Mouton/UNESCO.

Piaget, J. (1977). *The development of thought: Equilibration of cognitive structures*. The Viking Press.

Psillos, S. (1999). *Scientific realism: How science tracks truth*. Routledge.

Psillos, S. (2009). *Knowing the structure of nature: Essays on realism and explanation*. Palgrave Macmillan.

Putnam, H. (1975). *Mathematics, matter and method: Philosophical papers* (Vol. 1). Cambridge University Press.

Santos, G. (2015). Ontological emergence: How is that possible? Towards a new relational ontology. *Foundations of Science, 20*(4), 429–446.

Santos, G. (2021a). Integrated-structure emergence and its mechanistic explanation. *Synthese, 198*, 8687–8711.

Santos, G. (2021b). Emergentism. In V. P. Glăveanu (Ed.), *The Palgrave encyclopedia of the possible* (pp. 1–8). Palgrave Macmillan.

Santos, G. (2024). Emergence, downward causation, and interlevel integrative explanations. In J. L. Cordovil, G. Santos, & D. Vecchi (Eds.), *New mechanism. Explanation, emergence and reduction* (History, philosophy and theory of the life sciences) (Vol. 35, pp. 235–265). Springer.

Santos, G., Vallejos, G., & Vecchi, D. (2020). A relational-constructionist account of protein macrostructure and function. *Foundations of Chemistry, 22*, 363–382.

Schaffer, J. (2010). The internal relatedness of all things. *Mind, 119*, 341–376.

Shafir, E. (2017). Decisions in poverty contexts. *Current Opinion in Psychology, 18*, 131–136.

Shea, N. (2018). *Representation in cognitive science*. Oxford University Press.

Sheehy-Skeffington, J. (2020). The effects of low socioeconomic status on decision-making processes. *Current Opinion in Psychology, 2020*(33), 183–188.

Simpson, G. G. (1963). Biology and the nature of science. *Science, 139*(3550), 81–88.

Sirin, S. R. (2005). Socioeconomic status and academic achievement: A meta-analytic review of research. *Review of Educational Research, 75*(3), 417–453.

Strasser, A. (2012). Mental representations. In N. M. Seel (Ed.), *Encyclopedia of the sciences of learning*. Springer. https://doi.org/10.1007/978-1-4419-1428-6_1884

Szyf, M. (2011). The early life social environment and DNA methylation: DNA methylation mediating the long-term impact of social environments early in life. *Epigenetics, 6*(8), 971–978.

Szyf, M. (2021). Perinatal stress and epigenetics. In D. F. Swaab, F. Kreier, P. J. Lucassen, A. Salehi, & R. M. Buijs (Eds.), *Handbook of clinical neurology* (Vol. 8, pp. 125–148). Elsevier.

Szyf, M., & Bick, J. (2013). DNA methylation: A mechanism for embedding early life experiences in the genome. *Child Development., 84*(1), 49–57.

Thomas, M. S. C., & Baughman, F. D. (2014). Neuroconstructivisme: comprendre les trajectoires développementales typiques et atypiques. *Enfance, 3*(3), 205–236.

Thomas, M. S. C., & Coecke, S. (2023). Associations between socioeconomic status, cognition and brain structure: Evaluating potential causal pathways through mechanistic models of development. *Cognitive Science, 47*, e13217.

Troller-Renfree, S. V., Costanzo, M. A., Duncan, G. J., Magnuson, K. A., Gennetian, L. A., Yoshikawa, H., Fox, N. A., Halpern-Meekin, S., & Noble, K. G. (2022). The impact of a poverty reduction intervention on infant brain activity. *Proceedings of the National Academies of Sciences USA, 119*(5), e2115649119.

Ullmo, J. (1958). *La Pensée Scientifique Moderne*. Flammarion.

Vecchi, D., & Santos, G. (2023). The multi-causal basis of developmental potential construction. *Acta Biotheoretica, 71*(6). https://doi.org/10.1007/s10441-023-09456-8

Weaver, I. C., Cervoni, N., Champagne, F. A., D'Alessio, A. C., Sharma, S., Seckl, J. R., Dymov, S., Szyf, M., & Meaney, M. J. (2004). Epigenetic programming by maternal behavior. *Nature Neuroscience, 7*(8), 847–854. https://doi.org/10.1038/nn1276

Weil, E. (1982). *Philosophie et Réalité*. Beauchesne.

Weil, E. (1992). *Raison. Encyclopædia Universalis. Corpus* (Vol. 19, pp. 501–509). Encyclopædia Universalis France S.A.

Westermann, G., Mareschal, D., Johnson, M. H., Sirois, S., Spratling, M. W., & Thomas, M. S. C. (2007). Neuroconstructivism. *Developmental Science, 10*, 75–83.

Wiggins, D. (2016). *Continuants: Their activity, their being, and their identity*. Oxford University Press.

Wimsatt, W. (2007). *Re-engineering philosophy for limited beings: Piecewise approximations to reality*. Harvard University Press.

Gil Santos obtained his Ph.D. in philosophy at the NOVA University Lisbon. He currently works as a researcher at the Faculty of Sciences of the University of Lisbon. His main areas of research include philosophy of science, relational ontology, theory of emergence, interlevel causation, and models of integrative explanation.

Relational and Transactional Rationalities in Chinese Thought and Social Practice

Matthias Niedenführ

Abstract Both relational and transactional rationalities are central concepts in Chinese thought and social practice. Historical and philosophical foundations of these rationalities are examined, focusing on diverse influential schools such as Confucianism, Daoism, and Legism, and their respective impact on Chinese business culture and economic history. The chapter highlights the evolution of traditional business ethics, also in response to Western influences, and the resurgence of relational approaches in contemporary entrepreneurship. By analysing the flexibility and application of both rationalities in modern society, this chapter underscores the importance of applying a relational perspective in managing a guanxi network while also integrating a transactional perspective to navigate the complexities of global business environments.

Keywords Relational rationality · Transactional rationality · Confucianism · Chinese business culture · Guanxi network · Chinese economic history

1 Introduction

In the field of economics, which originated in the West, there is an implicit assumption that the modernisation and development of market economies are not only tied to the specific historical, cultural, and geographic characteristics of Europe, North America, South America, and Oceania, but are also the model for modernisation that all other economies, cultures, and civilisations must follow in their efforts to catch up to the West. A key aspect of the modernisation experience—and subsequent global success—of the West is the gradual shift from economic exchanges focused on relational rationality to one focused on transactional rationality. The former is considered typical of a backward and less-developed economy,

---

M. Niedenführ (✉)
Zeppelin University, Friedrichshafen, Germany
e-mail: Matthias.Niedenfuehr@zu.de

J. D. Rendtorff et al. (eds.), *Advances in Relational Economics*, Relational Economics and Organization Governance,
https://doi.org/10.1007/978-3-031-75725-9_11

while the latter is considered a key aspect of a modern economy with a well-functioning market.

Transactional and relational rationalities refer to how individuals and groups in a society interact in business and social situations with the goal of ensuring their own or their group's survival, success, and well-being. In social structures, economic capital represents one's economic standing based on the accumulation of wealth, while social capital represents one's social standing based on the accumulation of reputation. Exchanges allow for the extraction of economic capital (resources gained through transactions) or social capital (resources gained through social relations). Sociologist Lin Nan argues that transactional rationality considers relationships as part of gain-loss calculations, while relational rationality views transactions as part of cost-benefit calculations. Relational rationality prioritises the maintenance and promotion of relationships even when the transactions in this relationship are not optimal, since it is oriented on the costs and benefits of maintaining relationships over time. Transactional rationality prioritises the optimal outcome of transactions and even allows specific relationships to be terminated when these optimal outcomes cannot be met (Lin, 2009, pp. 84–86). This difference becomes clearer when we use the terminology of "Relational Economics": Then, transactional rationality operates with dyadic exchanges between merely two parties or stakeholders, whereas relational rationality allows for multiple relations to be considered. The first refers to discrete, that is separate and distinct, instances, while the latter allows for continuity, that is a continued series of interactions over time (Wieland, 2020, pp. 17, 29–34).

From a theoretical point of view, considering relational rationality as indicative of a less-developed market implies that any sacrifice of transactional gain due to imperfect information reflects an imperfect market. Hence, social organisations and networks serve as necessary constraints due to such imperfections (Lin, 2009, pp. 95–97).

The traditional Western view of economics has often been used to explain the success of the West and the widespread adoption of Western science, technology, democracy, and capitalism around the world. However, this view is increasingly being challenged by the economic success of East Asian countries such as Japan, the "four tigers" (South Korea, Hong Kong, Taiwan, and Singapore), and mainland China, as well as Southeast Asian nations like Malaysia, Indonesia, and Vietnam over the last five decades. These economies, heavily influenced by Chinese culture and its relational rationality, have raised questions about the global dominance of the West and its ideas going forward.

This chapter explores the Chinese economic experience to demonstrate how relational rationality can be just as important as Western transactional rationality in a thriving modern economy. It delves into ancient Chinese philosophies that developed both relational and transactional rationalities, examines how these philosophies influenced the establishment of a relational society and economic order in the past, and looks at how social interactions and business practices in contemporary China operate within an area of tension of competing relational and transactional logics.

2 Influential Philosophical Schools in China

To understand the philosophical underpinnings of social practices, business behaviour, and governance concepts in China, we will look at Chinese cosmology and how successive generations have situated themselves within it. Subsequently, we will delve into various schools of thought that have, to varying degrees, shaped the ways in which individuals and groups interact, the values that guide their actions, and their approaches to conducting business, managing companies, and governing political entities up to the present day.

2.1 Chinese Cosmology and the Legitimacy of Dynastic Rule

In ancient China, there was a rich tradition of philosophers contemplating governance, resource management, and proper education. The most productive phase for ingenious philosophy and political thought in Chinese history was a phase of constant military strife and upheaval over two millennia ago.

When the Zhou dynasty (1046–256 BCE) came to power in the area now known as China, they introduced the concept of "heaven" (tian) as a depersonalised notion of a god. This replaced the deity of the previous Shang dynasty as the source of legitimacy for their rule. The Zhou rulers gave themselves the title "Son of Heaven" to emphasise their claim to rule over "all under heaven" (tianxia) and their role as mediators between heaven and humanity (Ebrey, 1986, p. 179). Since then, in Chinese cosmology, humanity has been seen as standing between heaven and earth, both of which watch over their fate as "father and mother". A "heavenly mandate" justified the rule of the dynastic leader, but it could also change, morally justifying the overthrow of a dynasty with a change of this mandate.

In the latter part of the Zhou period, the role of the Son of Heaven had diminished to a purely ceremonial function. Numerous smaller feudal states, resembling duchies or kingdoms and governed by influential families, vied for supremacy. Despite the decline of the old order, this period, which encompassed the spring and autumn period (722–481 BCE) and the subsequent Warring States period (475–221 BCE), is widely regarded as one of the most intellectually fertile eras in Chinese history. It witnessed the emergence of various competing schools of thought, collectively called the "Hundred Schools". These schools presented divergent views on governance, social order, and military strategy (Chan, 1969, Bauer, 2001).

In the competition for supremacy over the empire, the originally peripheral state of Qin (9th c.–207 BCE) prevailed and subjugated all competitors. The first emperor introduced standardisations that simplified the efficiency of the infrastructure and the basis of trade throughout the empire. This included standardising currencies, measures, weights, and writing systems and unifying administrative structures and laws over an area that covers about a third of today's China (Bodde, 1986, pp. 52–64).

The success of this dynasty exemplifies a profound clash between two competing philosophies: Confucian thinkers, who advocated for the education of people to follow the government willingly, were marginalised and persecuted by their Legist rivals. Legalism promoted a strong central rule of the state and proved effective in building a powerful military. The Han dynasty (202 BCE–220 CE), which followed the Qin after a lengthy civil war, favoured a civilian government to end the militarisation of society that had facilitated their ascent, thus endorsing Confucianism. I mention this shift in state philosophies to highlight the diverse spectrum of thoughts Chinese philosophy offers that may influence people's actions.

2.2 *Confucianism*

Regarded as the most influential thinker in China, Confucius (551–479 BCE) significantly impacted philosophy, political science, and social doctrine in China and East Asia. During the earlier Han period, Confucianism became the dominant tradition, serving as the state philosophy and eventually emerging as the "most powerful intellectual belief" (Tu, 2010, p. 37). Its development can be categorised into a "creative age" until the first century BCE, when a coherent tradition evolved, and an "interpretive age" extending to the present day (Fung, 1958). Despite later challenges from Daoism and Buddhism to its centrality, Confucianism thrived throughout the entire imperial period (Yu, 1959).

Confucius served as an advisor to the rulers of the state of Lu and endeavoured to impart his ideas on virtue ethics, albeit with limited success. In response to the observed decline in morals and customs of his time, Confucius drew inspiration from older writings, such as the "Five Classics", which depict a "golden age" of virtuous leaders (Yao, 2000, pp. 57–62). Although his students compiled his ideas in the "Analects of Confucius" (Lunyu), he did not view himself as a founding figure but rather as a teacher who transmitted pre-existing wisdom.

Confucianism places significant emphasis on cultivating moral virtues as the ultimate aspiration for individuals, who are encouraged to embody a person of "all-encompassing virtues" (Fung, 1947, p. 69). Individuals' societal roles and positions are viewed as interconnected (Lai, 1995, p. 259). Confucian philosophy focuses on the practice of ethical virtues within social relationships, emphasising mutual responsibilities and obligations. The concept of the "five constant relationships" reflects family values and maintains a hierarchical structure: ruler and subject, husband and wife, parents and children, older and younger siblings, and friends. The family is a fundamental element of the hierarchical order, with the empire and the ruler at the apex, symbolising a benevolent patriarch caring for his subjects (Niedenführ & Hennig, 2020).

One of the fundamental virtues in this philosophy is "ren", translated as "humanity" (Chan, 1969, p. 788) or "human-heartedness" (Fung, 1947, p. 68). It represents the "highest human achievement of self-cultivation" (Tu, 1979, p. 7). Ren should not be equated with "universal love" in the European-Christian context. Instead, it is practised within concentric circles around the individual, family, and clan, with decreasing intensity extending outward (Fei, 1947, p. 63). The ideal human is the "noble person" (junzi), who fully realises their moral potential, while the "common person" (xiaoren) does not. Alongside "ren", the other cardinal virtues of the "five constants" include righteousness, morality, wisdom, and trustworthiness (Liu, 2018, p. 88).

During a period of significant upheaval, subsequent advocates of Confucianism, notably Mencius (372–289 BCE) and Xunzi (313–238 BCE), further developed this ethical framework. While many rulers of the time sought the counsel of military strategists advocating centralised rule to bolster the state, Mencius envisioned an ideal of a "benevolent and humane government" (renzheng), in which the personal example set by the ruler would lead to the well-being of the people (Chan, 1963, p. 61). The effectiveness of this leadership model would manifest in the loyalty of the populace and the migration of people from neighbouring states to resettle. Mencius believed in the innate "good nature" of people, which could be cultivated towards virtue through education and incentives. In contrast, Xunzi posited that human nature was inherently bad and emphasised the necessity of stringent laws to guide the population. These contrasting conceptions of human nature gave rise to distinct perspectives on the roles of government, business, and desirable social virtues.

In Confucian philosophy, there was strong scepticism towards the pursuit of profit and self-interest, significantly shaping the image of merchants in ancient China. The Lunyu states that "exemplary persons cherish their (moral) excellence", while "petty persons cherish the thought of gain" (Ames & Rosemont, 2010, p. 91). Confucius himself did not harbour prejudice against merchants; rather, he merely prioritised morality over profit. In fact, he commended his student Zigong who "made money by exchanging goods at the right time" (Wang, 2019).

Mencius, in contrast, strongly opposed profit-seeking. He emphasised the importance of prioritising moral excellence over self-interest when the two came into conflict (Lau, 1970, pp. xxi–xxii). Additionally, he expressed concern that competition could foster negative character traits, potentially leading individuals to become "despicable fellows" (Yu, 2016a, p. 233). He cautioned rulers and officials against leveraging their privileged positions for personal business gain, highlighting the potentially drastic consequences, such as the erosion of morality within the state.

Xunzi's philosophical perspective follows a similar path. He outlined a hierarchy of virtues, emphasising that justice is more important than profit and is essential for maintaining societal order. According to him, reversing this hierarchy would lead to widespread chaos. Xunzi believed that the pursuit of profit mainly concerns the lower social classes, and although merchants play a crucial role within the community, he thought that leaders engaging in profiteering raise moral concerns (Hutton, 2016, p. 304).

Scholar Cheng Chung-ying criticises the scientific rationalisation of humanity in Western rationalism as dehumanising. An overemphasis on science and technology fails to acknowledge the entirety of human beings, including intuition, imagination, memory, and feelings (Cheng, 1994, pp. 4–5). Tu Wei-ming developed the notion of "spiritual humanism", which refers to the ancient concept of a "unity of heaven and humanity". In this Confucian concept, "being attuned to the changing patterns in nature is essential for harmonising human relationships, formulating family ethics, and establishing a responsive and responsible government" (Tu, 2001, pp. 261–262). These cosmological notions of Chinese thought are ingrained with relational considerations.

Confucians are encouraged to explore the mutual relationship between themselves and the community to understand that their individual success is connected to the people around them. These mutual relationships require people to develop a sense of responsibility and, through this, "learn to become proper human beings". Individuals are to engage in constant moral reflection and "self-cultivation" (xiuji) and then focus on "establishing oneself while establishing others" (chengji chengren). According to Tu, the Confucian worldview argues in favour of avoiding anthropocentrism, disregarding the needs and interests of fellow living beings (ibid.).

As we can see from this deliberation, Confucianism is grounded in a form of relational rationality. It focuses on interpreting the correct moral behaviour of individuals in relation to specific groups, social settings, social hierarchy, and circumstances (Hermann-Pillath, 2011). These guiding principles for individuals are applied to larger social units, such as the family, the firm, the village, the nation. While Western moral philosophers, such as Immanuel Kant, emphasise the rationality of human behaviour based on principles and categorical notions, Chinese moral philosophy adopts a holistic approach, eschews strict categorisations, and instead considers the relative circumstances of a given moral choice (Fig. 1).

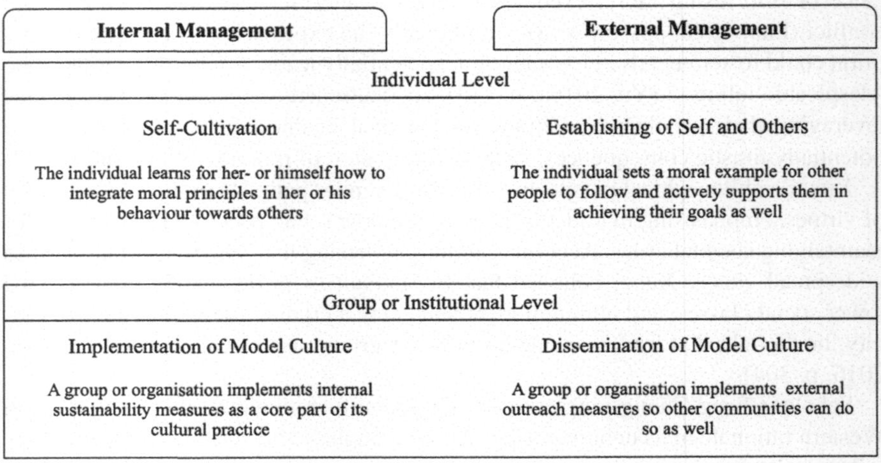

Fig. 1 Confucian application of the "Inner Sage and Outer King" – principle. (Own illustration)

2.3 Daoism

Along with the humanistic Confucian doctrine, the naturalistic ideas of the Daoist Laozi were the "predominant cultural forces" in China, profoundly shaping Chinese thought, social norms, and political concepts (de Bettignies et al., 2011, p. 625). Laozi (dates unknown) and Zhuangzi (365–290 BCE) are considered the most influential thinkers of Daoism. The classics attributed to these two thinkers share concepts but differ in terms of purpose, core message, and style (Hansen, 2000) and are associated with different phases of the school's development (Fung, 1958). The Daoist school was first introduced as a form of political ideology, offering guidance on governing in times of war (Creel, 1970). It elevated the concept of the Dao (way) to a leitmotif and focused on understanding the organisation of nature and the cosmos, which had to be incorporated into political strategy (Moeller, 2004, Hennig & Niedenführ, 2020).

The Daodejing, traditionally attributed to Laozi, aims to guide rulers in restoring order and outlines the concept of a "wise ruler" who embodies the principles of being "a sage inward and a king outward" (neisheng waiwang). This concept emphasises personal morality, maintaining order within the kingdom, and managing relationships with neighbouring states (Bell, 2011). Additionally, the text uses water as a metaphor to illustrate the Dao's characteristics: life-giving, overcoming the hardest substances, and finding the most stable position (Granet, 1985) (Fig. 2).

Chinese philosophy was strongly influenced by the rural way of life, which revolved around the cyclical nature of the seasons (Bauer, 2001). This conceptualisation of time and the cosmos gave rise to a way of thinking that demands the submission of rulers to nature and its rhythms (Liu, 2001). The concepts of "nature" and "non-action" (wuwei) play a central role (Gerstner, 2011). Acceptance

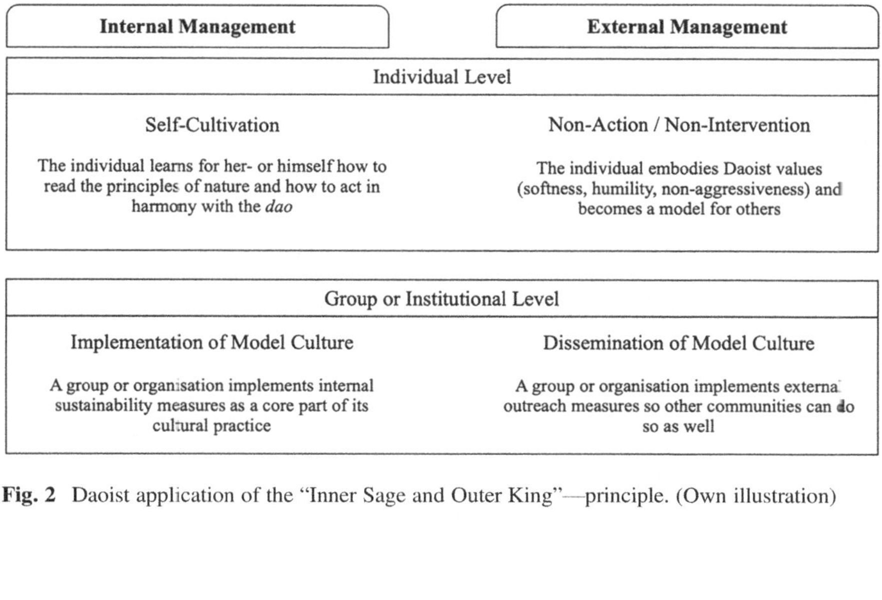

Fig. 2 Daoist application of the "Inner Sage and Outer King"—principle. (Own illustration)

of nature's limits and spontaneity flows into restrained action, which is seen as necessary to avoid disruptions to the Dao (Miller, 2006).

The Daoists criticised the pursuit of profit, not because of moral considerations but primarily because they feared that people could be consumed by their ambitions and physical needs, causing them to lose their true selves. However, Zhuangzi believed that the professions of farmer and merchant were well suited to the "common people" (Legge, 1891).

In Daoist thought, relational rationality is crucial. However, unlike Confucianism, the relational aspects of Daoism are not based on specific social requirements. Instead, they are rooted in the idea that human beings and their behaviour are part of a larger system. Relational rationality, in this context, means the need to respect and consider this system's nature and guiding principles when making decisions or moral choices. The principle of wuwei—that is non-intervention in natural processes—emphasises the importance of being aware of the limitations of one's understanding and avoiding hasty decisions to maintain the balance in the system. According to Cheng, Chinese philosophy offers a way to understand reality that can be used to develop the concept of the entire system. The Dao then represents the process of the entire system, including all living beings, inanimate matter, and the universe, while the Great Ultimate (taiji) encompasses the aspect of the structure of the system's creation (Cheng, 1994, pp. 15–16). Contemporary Chinese philosophers refer to these concepts when discussing corporate social responsibility and ecological sustainability and offer a Chinese perspective to this global discourse.

2.4 Legalism

Between the late Warring States period and the early imperial age, a group of thinkers with shared ideas emerged, known today as "Legalism" or "Legism",[1] but it was only in the Han period that it finally was understood as a coherent system of thought when the historian Sima Qian recognised it in the "Records of the Historian" (Shiji). Legalism emphasises the importance of laws and is known for influential leaders such as Shang Yang (d. 338 BCE) and Han Feizi (280–233 BCE) (Creel 1974). Like Xunzi, a teacher to Han Feizi, Legalism assumes that human nature tends towards selfishness.

While Xunzi believed education could help nurture human nature towards goodness, the Legalists thought it was inherently egoistic and tended towards immoral behaviour. Han Feizi posited that morality was an unreliable tool and relied on people's interest-driven nature to steer them towards the state's objectives (Chan & Lee, 2014, pp. 4–5). So, instead of education, they preferred to use incentives and punishments to guide the people towards social goals (Nivison, 1999, p. 807).

[1] These translations do not fully capture the breadth of meaning that the term fa has in Chinese, as it also refers to "method" or "standards" (Pines, 2018).

The Legalists delivered by far the most severe criticism of the merchant profession. They pursued a physiocratic economic thinking in which peasant and military professions were given priority because they would help to "enrich the state and strengthen the military". They were suspicious of travelling merchants because these were "unproductive" and lived off the farmers' products. Their uncontrolled accumulation of wealth and the danger of cooperating with enemy states further increased Legalist reservations against them (Pines, 2018). Although Legalism supports industry and trade, it only does so with strict state regulations (Hermann-Pillath, 2011).

The Legalists believed that moral principles should not be used actively. This made them incompatible with other schools of thought (Chan, 1963, p. 251). However, despite strong criticism from other schools, Legalism is considered one of the most realistic schools of thought in China because it deals with the world as it is, not as it should be (Pines, 2018).

Legalist thinkers played a significant role in forming the first imperial dynasty because their statesmanship strengthened the Qin economically and militarily. The shift towards Confucian orthodoxy as the base of state ideology in subsequent dynasties from the Han onwards until the end of Chinese imperialism in the early twentieth century remained a reason for the official marginalisation of Legalism for over two millennia. Yet when natural disasters or military uprisings ushered in a dynastic decline and opened opportunities for potential dynastic successors to fill the power vacuum, Legalist political ideology again proved instrumental in guiding the founding figures of new dynasties.

The emphasis on strong relational rationality that we observed in Confucian and Daoist thought is much less prominent in Legalism. Instead, Legalism focuses heavily on laws and the rational application of incentives and disincentives to motivate subjects to align their actions with the state's objectives. This rational approach fosters an emotionally detached perspective, allowing individuals to act with transactional logic to achieve a specific objective while disregarding the long-term consequences of their actions for the individuals or groups affected.

2.5 *School of Military Strategists*

While Mencius advocated peaceful means of strengthening the state to make an attack by competitors unlikely, the "School of Military Strategists" consisted of advisors who prepared rulers for the eventuality of war. In doing so, they had to rely on capable generals as advisors.

The most renowned representative of this school is "Master Sun" or Sunzi (dates unknown), but other philosophers are also counted among the "Military Classics". Sunzi was an ancient military strategist, a philosopher, and an author of "The Art of War" (Sunzi bingfa), a seminal work on military strategy and tactics. It is arguably the most renowned military classic from ancient China, providing a strategic philosophy for effectively managing conflicts and achieving victory (Gawlikowski &

Loewe, 1993). By the Song period (960–1277 CE), this work was East Asia's most influential military classic. Until today, it is widely regarded as a masterpiece of strategy and is frequently referenced by military experts. The author was long believed to be Sun Wu, who lived during the Eastern Zhou period. However, historical details about his life are unclear, and some scholars debate his existence (Theobald, 2019). Sunzi maintains that warfare is essential for the survival of a state since, once defeated, a feudal state is unlikely to regain its former position.

"The Art of War" emphasises the importance of strategy and planning. Sunzi argued that war should be conducted with careful thought and calculation, avoiding unnecessary conflict and maximising the chances of success. He advocated deception and intelligence gathering to mislead and confuse the enemy, believing that understanding the enemy's plans and intentions was crucial. Sunzi also emphasised the need for adaptability and flexibility in military operations, arguing that effective commanders should be able to adjust their strategies and tactics based on changing circumstances on the battlefield. Furthermore, he believed that wars should be conducted with moral and ethical considerations, urging restraint and fairness and avoiding unnecessary harm to civilians and infrastructure (McNeilly, 2015). Consequently, achieving victory without combat is portrayed as the ideal method of warfare (Ames, 1993).

This school says little about the social function of merchants, but its strategic thinking remains an important orientation for the leadership thinking of business people in East Asia. In terms of relational and transactional logic, this school allows for both, depending on the objective. The use of tactics to achieve victory over an opponent is clearly based on transactional logic. However, this logic is tempered by relational considerations, such as the reminder to avoid excessive negative impacts on the civilian population or on infrastructure in enemy territory.

2.6 Forms of Leadership in Chinese Philosophy

The four schools mentioned above—Confucianism, Daoism, Legalism, and the School of Military Strategists—have had a profound influence on moral values, notions of leadership and hierarchy, and community and group coordination in the areas of social norms, business culture, and governance ideologies in contemporary China. When we focus on leadership theories, they can be categorised into the locus of leadership, from individual, dyadic, to institutional. Each of the respective schools has a different focus on these levels.

2.6.1 Confucian Leadership Principles

Confucian leadership prioritises the individual's capacity to govern and manage themselves. This is manifested in the practice of self-reflection, commonly called "self-cultivation", to attain a higher level of personal moral excellence. Within the hierarchical structure of superiors and subordinates, the emphasis lies on leading by moral example, rather than employing coercion to achieve collective objectives. Educating and guiding individuals within one's sphere of influence are favoured over enforcing compliance, thereby promoting a nurturing and morally driven leadership approach. Confucian thinking prefers individual and dyadic leadership for "socialisation and enculturation", favouring these over institutional forms of leadership (Chan & Lee, 2014, pp. 11–12).

2.6.2 Daoist Leadership Principles

Daoist leadership principles also revolve around the individual leader's ability to implement "self-cultivation" effectively. However, this involves a departure from the Confucian benchmark, as Daoist leadership does not emphasise moral virtues. Instead, it focuses on embodying "non-action" or "non-intervention" and displaying spontaneous and "natural" behaviour in alignment with the Dao (Chan & Lee, 2014, pp. 11–12; Hennig & Niedenführ, 2020, p. 858). In the dyadic leadership realm, Daoist principles underscore the importance of values such as "non-competition", softness, and modesty. The principle of "non-interference" is implemented in non-aggressiveness and a supportive and empowering attitude towards others. An inward-outward leadership approach (neisheng waiwang) in Daoist terms lies in the ability to exercise inward restraint while cultivating a positive atmosphere of enabling cooperation externally, fostering mutual appreciation, and embodying all-encompassing respect for all parties involved (ibid.).

2.6.3 Legist Leadership Principles

The Legist School, unlike Confucianism and Daoism, emphasises institutional over individual and dyadic forms of leadership. It focuses on creating the right conditions for people to act in the state's interest through incentives and disincentives (Chan & Lee, 2014, pp. 11, 13). Initially designed for a feudal state, these leadership principles can also be applied to other forms of organisation and institution, such as businesses, political parties, and interest groups. Based on a rational understanding of human behaviour as being primarily driven by self-interest, Legist leadership prioritises strategic use of incentives and disincentives, meaning that desired behaviour is supported and rewarded, while undesirable behaviour is punished. Since the state's resources are limited and cannot sustain lavish rewards for compliance indefinitely, strict punitive measures are seen as necessary to complement this leadership approach in a sustainable way. The state does not expect moral or loyal behaviour of subjects, as it is seen as unattainable; instead, compliant behaviour is coopted and/or enforced (ibid.) (Fig. 3).

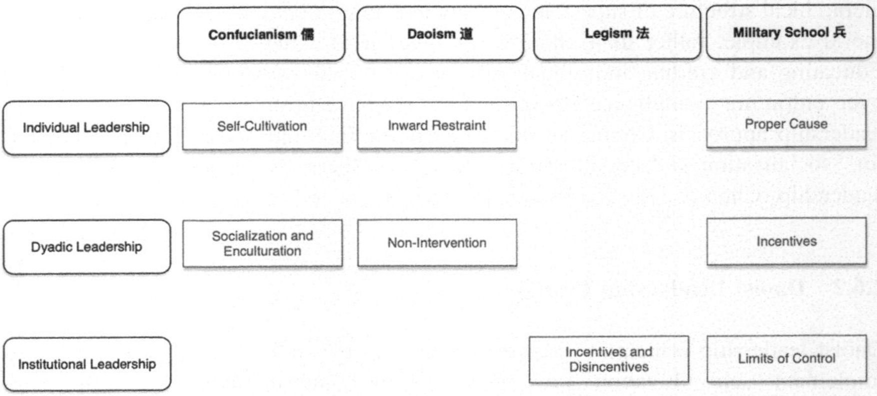

Fig. 3 Forms of leadership by school of thought. (Own illustration)

2.6.4 Leadership Principles of the School of Military Strategists

Conclusively, the School of Military Strategists combines these leadership aspects and approaches of Confucianism, Daoism, and Legalism. Sunzi integrates situational flexibility by utilising different, sometimes contradictory, leadership notions and concepts to achieve his goals. This enables him to deceive and surprise his opponents, making his actions less predictable (Theobald, 2019).

For example, on the level of self-leadership, Sunzi follows Confucian notions of morality by requiring leaders to pursue higher purposes in waging war beyond mere self-interest. They are expected to conduct war with moral considerations in mind, minimising the impact on their troops and populace and limiting damage to people and infrastructure in enemy territory. However, on the level of dyadic leadership, his approach to motivating soldiers to fight does not rely on appeals to morality but on the Legist approach, providing incentives for soldiers to support the war effort and risk their lives.

Lastly, on the level of institutional leadership, Sunzi incorporates the Daoist notion that many success factors are beyond the individual leader's control, thus requiring strategic flexibility from a shrewd military commander to read the changes on the battlefield, like the way a Daoist observes the principles of nature and water (Chan & Lee, 2014, pp. 12–13).

The "Art of War" is a text that draws on various Chinese schools of thought, making it relevant to various circumstances where a leader must adapt to ever-changing conditions in a competitive setting. This flexibility has led to its widespread use as a reference for military leaders, businesspeople, politicians, and other group leaders. It offers insights for effectively managing an organisation or group of people and making challenging decisions on a day-to-day basis. The Daoist principle of being mindful of one's limitations and embracing sudden changes resonates strongly with modern management theories (Hennig & Niedenführ, 2020).

After this philosophical excursion into Chinese schools of thought in which we addressed their respective points of departure, leadership foci, and the question of their relational and transactional rationalities, we will now delve into how these philosophies affected the economic history, as well as the business culture and social practices, in the past and present in China.

3 Relational Rationality in Traditional Business Culture

3.1 Confucian Relational Thinking and Chinese Economic History

The schools mentioned above and their economic philosophical ideas shaped business culture in China in different ways. The social image of merchants was different, positive or negative, at different times, depending on which school was dominant or how consistently effective their positions were in everyday life. The thinkers of the classical period were clear that pursuing one's own advantage is a deeply rooted motivation. The Shiji states that self-interest does not need to be taught (Watson, 1968, p. 491), and Xunzi also had to admit that even the cultural heroes of the Golden Past could not get rid of the profit-seeking of ordinary people (Hutton, 2016, p. 304). The different schools come to very different conclusions as to the extent to which profit-oriented thinking can have socially negative consequences, whether people can be trained not to do this, or whether it might even be desirable in the interests of society.

Although trade and commerce flourished, the philosophical criticism of the pursuit of profit and mercantile activities created an environment in which the standing of merchants suffered. Nevertheless, the chapter "Biographies of Wealthy Merchants" in the Shiji is a positive treatise on merchants and people who strive for wealth, in contrast to the "exemplary people" who choose the "way" (Ruan 1996, p. 8). However, the social status of merchants was largely ignored in later historiography (L'Haridon, 2015, p. 172).

The ideal of social stratification emerged, the "four occupations" (simin), a hierarchy with the educated officials at the top, followed by farmers and artisans. Traders and merchants formed the lowest rank, which reflected social prejudices against them. The thin layer of officials held power and provided ethical guidance; the agrarian population was important for supplies and filled the state treasury, while artisans produced various secondary products (Hansson, 1996, pp. 20–21). However, merchants always played a crucial role in society by providing necessary services. The literate officials viewed them with suspicion and saw them as a potential threat to social peace, as they could concentrate considerable land holdings, income, and political influence (Kuhn, 1988, p. 20).

The bureaucratic elite had early replaced the nobility as the highest layer of society. They were recruited through the meritocratic system of civil service examinations. This restricted hereditary positions and transformed the state into an extraordinarily stable patrimonial order (Ertman, 2017, pp. 10–12). While peasants' sons could rise to high offices, the official scholars tried to deny merchants access to these examinations to limit the social mobility of wealthy competitors (Yu, 2016a, p. 293).

While this demarcation of occupational groups was still relatively strict until the Tang (617/18–907 CE), the group boundaries gradually became more blurred from the Song onwards as Chinese society became more commercialised (Yu, 1987, So, 2000). The merchants began to cooperate with the class of official scholars. Some officials used middlemen when participating in trade so as not to damage their reputation. Since the government had nationalised key industries such as salt production or mining with strict state monopolies, these state-owned enterprises were run like large commercial enterprises with responsible officials (Gernet, 1962, p. 77).

In the middle of the Song, economic reforms aimed to improve government spending and taxation of peasants. Favourable loans to peasants were intended to make them less dependent on the arbitrary decisions of the landowners and more resilient to poor harvests (Tillman, 2004, p. 127). After the political failure of these reforms, officials debated whether they were still on the correct path, as outlined by the classics. On the one hand, Zhu Xi (1139–1193) and his followers called for a return to a strict interpretation of the classics, especially in rejecting the pursuit of profit. Their opponents, such as Lu Xiangshan (1130–1200) and later Wang Yangming (1472–1529), integrated Daoist and Buddhist ideas and believed that people had an innate sense of morality (Gernet, 1962, pp. 68–69). They saw positive social effects through the actions of responsible merchants (Tillman, 2004, pp. 128–130; Ming, 2016).

Confucianism was reinterpreted during this period when Zhu compiled the so-called "Four Books" from the canon of existing classics and demanded a rigid moral orthodoxy. The Zhu-Cheng school became popular among scholars, eventually becoming state doctrine and the mainstream in examinations until the end of the imperial period. The Lu-Wang school, on the other hand, which was better positioned in economic thought and commercial pragmatism, was marginalised officially but flourished among entrepreneurs (Tillman, 2004, p. 139).

Imperial Chinese economic history portrayed here gives us a glimpse into the continued influence of competing philosophical concepts. Confucian orthodoxy, focusing on rigid morality, continuously promoted relational awareness of social obligations and responsibilities.

3.2 Permeability Between Social Classes

During the Ming and Qing dynasties, the boundaries between the social classes of scholar-bureaucrats and merchants became blurred. Two social trends emerged fusing Confucianism and trade: the downward mobility of scholars and the upward mobility of merchants. Population growth led to increased competition for official positions, with disappointed exam candidates turning to commercial careers, which conflicted with their traditional values. Educated merchants, in turn, sought social recognition by combining business acumen with Confucian ideals. As a result, a new hybrid class emerged known as "Confucian traders" (rugu) or "Confucian merchants" (rushang) (Ming, 2016, pp. 21–23). A mingling of these groups, contradicting orthodox ideas, irritated conservative scholars who demanded strict class separation. Yet, this separation was more an ideal than a lived practice (Yu, 2016a, p. 252).

During this period, merchant groups (shangbang) with distinct properties emerged in various regions, especially in the Anhui, Shaanxi, and Zhejiang provinces. They developed an informal code of conduct that governed business relationships, earning them a reputation for conducting business with good faith, trustworthiness, and honour (RCCCE, 2008). For instance, Anhui merchants were known for adhering to Confucian teachings by supporting their local communities. They engaged in charitable work, such as providing low-interest loans, offering aid during natural disasters, or selling stored grain at reasonable prices (Lufrano, 1997, pp. 60–61). Additionally, these "scholar merchants" financed and organised community projects such as building irrigation systems, repairing essential infrastructure, and establishing local schools, thus addressing the gaps in the regional economy resulting from the lack of government investment (Brook, 1998, pp. 90–93, Ming, 2015). By the end of the Ming period, the boundary between scholar-officials and merchants had become so permeable that the official family histories of the literati no longer concealed the fact that they had merchant ancestors (Yu, 2016a, p. 252). To earn social status, they needed a relational understanding of their profession, demanding moral requirements and a long-term perspective to support community goals. This relational rationale goes beyond transactional logic.

A century ago, Max Weber studied how religions affect economic behaviour in societies dominated by a particular religion (Weber, 2016, p. 151). He examined the socio-economic foundations of Chinese society and found that early developments led to traditionalism rather than capitalism (Kaesler, 2015, p. 139). Recent research criticises this perspective as a Eurocentric devaluation of non-Western societies (Amelung & Schefold, 2021, p. 298). Weber's view that capitalism did not develop in classical China has been countered, with China being able to produce a very advanced market economy on her own (Yu, 2016b, pp. 208–219). It is, hence, more useful to view Chinese economic thinking as an "economic style or mentality" (Hermann-Pillath, 2016).

4 Relational Rationality in a Transforming Contemporary Business Culture

4.1 *Western Challenges to the Traditional Relational Order*

During the late Qing period, the adoption of Western business norms began due to the Westernisation movement and the rise of modern commerce, bringing significant changes to society. The intellectual elite advised the necessity of modernisation and discussed which business ethics approach to adopt during the process (Zhu, 2006, p. 24). The influx of Western technology and ideas not only challenged the established Confucian order but also spurred entrepreneurial activity. Officials and private entrepreneurs merged Chinese values with Western technology to establish state-owned production facilities and private businesses, embodying the concept of "entrepreneur-official". Similarly, in Meiji-era Japan, Shibusawa Ei'ichi (1840–1931), the "father of Japanese capitalism", integrated Confucian ethics with modern business practices (Shibuzawa, 1998, pp. 18–19).

In China, two factions emerged with differing views on the central question of property rights. The conservative faction (wangupai) prioritised "agriculture over commerce" and "righteousness over profit" (Yu, 2016a, pp. 249, 261–262), believing that "the people form the foundation of the nation" and fearing that modern industry would harm the agrarian economy and lead to people losing their livelihoods (Zhu, 2006, p. 24). The Westernisation faction (yangwupai) believed that industrialisation and commerce were essential for the country's growth and development.

The traditional emphasis on valuing agriculture has some parallels to Western physiocracy. The conservatives believed the country's strength lay in traditional virtues rather than equipment. Therefore, they aimed to reverse early attempts to adopt ideas like science, technology, and democracy. Additionally, they wanted to curb the development of a Western-style commercial economy that was already taking shape in China.

The debate between these factions centred on whether the country should modernise by adopting Western techniques while retaining its traditional system. Both sides believed in the superiority of Chinese thinking and social values over Western science and technology. Most intellectuals were against too much foreign influence.

The Westernisers believed in combining Chinese systems with Western technology to "defend the nation" while preserving the country's moral teachings. Some scholars justified adopting industries such as railways and factories to create a prosperous society and strengthen the nation (Zhu, 2006, p. 25). This was a shift in Chinese economic thought, moving away from prioritising agriculture to valuing commerce for national prosperity (Institute for Early Modern History of China, 2000, p. 6).

Government officials effectively controlled commerce and key industries during early industrialisation, creating a hierarchical relationship. They acted as guardians of commerce, expecting favours in return. This allowed the government to control property rights and retain monopolies (Zhu, 2006, p. 25). Confucian-trained scholars traditionally rejected competition due to concerns about a negative impact on social morals (Yuan, 1998).

Like the conservatives, the Westernisation faction also aimed at "building up the country" while preserving the "people first" tradition, but they wanted to do so by introducing capitalism. Both reformists and revolutionaries among them thought that improving people's income was the key motivation for refashioning the economy. Scholars began to question the maxim of separating "righteousness and benefits" and adopted de Mandeville's notion of "private vices as a public virtue" supporting private self-interest as a valuable force in the market economy. Republican leader Sun Yat-sen (1866–1925) demanded an end to officials intervening in market processes. They supported the independence of property rights and free competition (Zhu, 2006, pp. 25–26).

The economic liberalism they advocated aimed to promote individual rights and establish rules that applied equally to all market participants. This approach sought to eliminate many traditional business practices that focused on personal relationships. Unlike the Chinese business model, the Western approach was more focused on transactions and establishing transparent rules and regulations to facilitate smooth market interactions without relying on personal connections with bureaucrats, business networks, or family.

4.2 *Transformations in the Late Qing and Early Republican Periods*

After the abolishment of the imperial system during the revolution of 1911, China underwent significant changes. This period witnessed the introduction of a Republican system, the end of the traditional examination system, and the erosion of the traditional Confucian social system. Additionally, Western capitalist principles gradually replaced traditional business ethics to promote modern industry and commerce. Both traditional culture and private entrepreneurship faced criticism, and the influence of Confucianism on society began to decline. Subsequent modernisation movements further weakened traditional beliefs and social norms. With its relational approach to business, Chinese-style entrepreneurship faced challenges following the founding of the People's Republic in 1949.

During the Republican era, the development of capitalism on a national level faced many obstacles. The modernising industrial system suffered from internal conflicts and external aggression, which affected the process of industrialisation and modernisation until the founding of the People's Republic. The subsequent Communist nationalisation policies targeted private entrepreneurs, leading to their mass exodus to Hong Kong and Taiwan. Mao Zedong's anti-traditional campaigns, particularly the Cultural Revolution (1966–1976), eradicated traditional cultural institutions and persecuted their supporters. As Levenson argued, "Confucianism was uprooted and relegated to the museum" (Billioud 2018, p. 2). Consequently, the elements of Chinese entrepreneurship—relational awareness, traditional morals, and private entrepreneurship—lost their foothold in China.

The changes in traditional business practices posed challenges in both Mainland China and Taiwan. On the mainland, traditional societal norms and values were eliminated, making it hard to maintain traditional business ethics based on relationships. Traditional business ethics in China favour public property rights over the private sector. This preference persisted through socialist reforms, disenfranchising landowners and business owners (Long & Chi, 2021). Although the Nationalist government in Taiwan encouraged the market, there was government intervention until 1975 due to martial law. However, the islanders had greater opportunities to modernise traditional business ethics than the mainland.

4.3 Cultural Revival and the Return of Entrepreneurship

After 1978, there were more opportunities to start businesses as markets and private property were gradually reintroduced through the "Reform and Opening" policy. These changes improved living standards, but also caused social friction due to the dismantling of state enterprises and the shift of many people to the market economy.

While the liberalisation was mainly limited to the economic sphere, there was a tentative relaxation of Communist anti-traditionalism in academia and society. The rejection of tradition by the Communist government created a void in society. When restrictions were reduced, Confucianism saw a revival, with the establishment of research institutions and academic journals and a "Culture fever" in the 1980s (Makeham, 2011, p. 15; Billioud, 2010, p. 220). Scholars, business networks, and religious institutions from Taiwan, Hong Kong, and the diaspora joined mainland actors in promoting traditional culture (Ji, 2018, p. 61). They emphasised the need for new generations to learn about their heritage so as to assert a Chinese identity. While many were interested in learning from the developed West, there was also a growing interest in the neglected roots of Chinese culture. In the 1990s, the "National Studies" (guoxue) movement proposed classical teaching to revitalise traditional Chinese culture (Tang, 2015, p. 4). This led to the emergence of unofficial learning institutions promoting the reading of classics as an alternative form of education. This bottom-up phenomenon triggered a top-down cooptation of traditional thinking, with the state increasingly advocating nationalism and tradition as useful for reinforcing patriotism. This change in state ideology resulted in a campaign to establish "Confucius Institutes" worldwide from 2004 onwards and the promotion of conservative moral norms as "Chinese values", which were presented as being equal to or superior to Western individualism.

4.4 Transformation of Traditional Business Ethics

The multifaceted revival of Confucianism in the 1990s serves as a backdrop for a return to Chinese-style entrepreneurship, which had survived outside the mainland among entrepreneurs in "Cultural China" (Tu, 1991), which includes Taiwan and Hong Kong, the Chinese diaspora, as well as Korea and Japan. Ethnic Chinese (huaren) in the Southeast Asian diaspora, who maintain their heritage, were among the first to invest in China. They brought capital and skills and reimported a Confucian entrepreneurial spirit. Business leaders such as Inamori Kazuo (Japan) and Li Ka-Shing (Hong Kong), whose management styles reflect traditional values, have also influenced followers in China.

The government received external assistance from the diaspora to jumpstart the economy. One of the contributors was the "China Merchants Group" in Hong Kong, which provided expertise on the private property system (Chan, 2019). At the same time, a strong local identity re-emerged among a new generation of entrepreneurs in China, who looked to their indigenous predecessors as role models. Regions with a rich entrepreneurial culture in the past once again became home to contemporary business success stories, such as in Zhejiang, Jiangsu, and Guangdong (RCCCE, 2008). The models of the past sometimes influence their philanthropic efforts.

Local entrepreneurs, often self-taught in management due to a lack of formal training, hired educated professionals to assist them. This created a need for them to catch up in terms of education. As a result, there was a rise in executive degrees from business schools that offered Western management training. Additionally, prestigious universities began offering tailor-made courses in leadership (Niedenführ, 2021b). While for some entrepreneurs, participation was merely a superficial interest in tradition to gain social recognition and networking opportunities (Yao, 2011), for others, it was part of an intrinsically motivated attempt to become "Confucian businesspeople" (Billioud, 2010, p. 204). They aimed to implement cultural knowledge in developing a corporate culture which combined modern management and "China studies" in a "Chinese-Western hybrid" (zhongxi hebi).

Chinese-style management promotes traditional notions of family and community and heavily emphasises "Chineseness". It aims to implement humanistic management to address social stability issues on a meso level in Chinese society (Niedenführ, 2021b). Some Western scholars have criticised this commodification of tradition as "a sign of its final demise" (Dirlik, 1995, p. 273), arguing that Confucianism is manipulated to support any given agenda, a mere "chameleon" to underscore Chinese uniqueness (Kam, 2011, pp. 77–78).

The success of economic reforms depended on clearly defined property rights, a separation between government and businesses, and the transformation of business enterprises into competitive market-based entities. To legitimise private property rights, a legal system for ownership had to be established in China to ensure equal treatment of citizens versus the government- and state-owned enterprises. These reforms aimed to establish rights based on equality and coexistence of the "public" and the "private", challenging traditional business ethics. However, the process of transforming traditional business ethics concerning property rights into modern market-oriented business ethics is still incomplete (Zhu, 2006, pp. 27–28).

The Confucian entrepreneurship phenomenon mentioned above reflects the discomfort of many Chinese businesspeople and blue-collar workers with transactional Western management approaches. These approaches are at odds with China's traditional order and societal values (Niedenführ, 2021b). This can be viewed as a deliberate effort to reinforce relational rationality in Chinese business ethics.

5 Relational Rationality in Social Practice

The previous sections discussed the deep influence of relational rationality in Chinese philosophy. They showed how this influence was prevalent in Chinese social and business practices for the past 2000 years, brought about by the interplay of government priorities and social formations. However, the rise of Western global dominance in science, technology, culture, and economic systems has caused disruptions in the traditional Chinese Confucian order. This has led to debates on how to incorporate modern Western ideas while preserving Chinese cultural identity and values in social and business contexts, shaping political, economic, and social developments in China over the last 150 years.

It is important to note that previous discussions have mainly focused on the "great tradition" perspective, which emphasises the universalised collective heritage and knowledge in China, while overlooking the "little tradition" of localised heritage and knowledge. The final section of this chapter examines anthropological insights into how relational rationality characterises Chinese "communities of practice" (CoP).

5.1 Group Affiliation in China

Fei Xiaotong (1910–2005), a sociologist and anthropologist at Peking University, conducted groundbreaking research on China's ethnic groups. His work in the late 1930s established the foundation for sociological and anthropological studies in China and helped introduce Chinese social and cultural phenomena to the world. Fei argued that Chinese society is primarily based on family ties, with family bonds being more important than other social loyalties (Fei, 1947, p. 63). He explained that social relations are like concentric circles around individuals, with family and close relatives being the most trusted and emotionally connected, relations to acquaintances being both emotional and practical, and strangers receiving the least trust and having relations with them being mainly instrumental. In other words, the aspect of focusing on relational logic is strongest with people or groups close to the centre of everyone's network and weakest at the periphery (Fig. 4).

Fei coined the term "groupism" (tuanti zhuyi) to compare Western and Chinese approaches to social interaction. For him, the Western idea of group membership is based on abstract categories, where all individuals have an equal relationship to it regardless of social contact. In contrast, Chinese social interaction is dominated by "circles" (quanzi), which are open and inclusive and shaped by actual social relationships in context (Hermann-Pillath, 2016, p. 100) (Fig. 5).

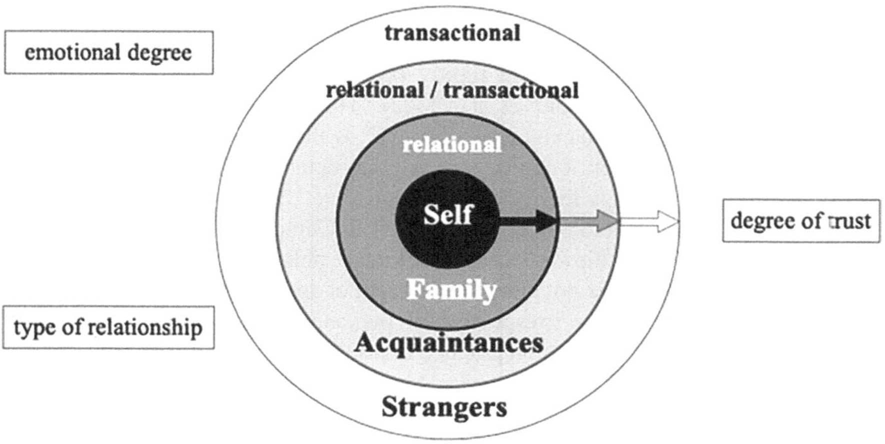

Fig. 4 Relationality in Chinese social context. (Own illustration)

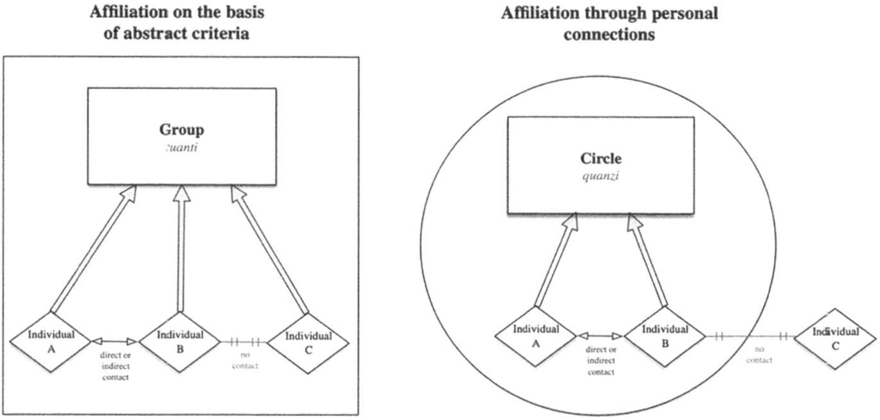

Fig. 5 Group affiliation in China and the West according to Fei Xiaotong. (Own illustration)

5.2 Guanxi *and Relationship Building*

The concept of guanxi ("relationship") is used in Chinese culture to describe an individual's social network of mutually beneficial personal and business relationships.[2] In Western media, pinyin romanisation is more widely used because translations such as "connections" or "relationships" do not capture the significance of a person's guanxi network to most personal and business dealings in China. Unlike in the West, these relationships are rarely established purely through formal meetings,

[2]The character "guan" means "closed" and "caring," while "xi" means "system." Together, the term refers to a closed, caring system of relationships.

but they must also include spending time getting to know each other. Essentially, guanxi requires a personal bond before any business relationship can develop. As a result, relationships are often more tightly bound than relationships in Western personal social networks (Gold et al., 2002). The concept of guanxi is often oversimplified in Western management literature as merely exploiting connections to those in power. However, it can be a socially acceptable practice if it is based on ethical principles, as seen in the previous sections.

Therefore, navigating and positioning oneself in Chinese society heavily rely on managing social relationships effectively. Chinese philosophy—with the notable exception of Mohism—does not know the concept of applying moral considerations equally to all human beings irrespective of personal significance, proximity, or hierarchy. As a result, it is common practice to prioritise family or personal connections in business dealings and to value stable, long-term relationships over short-term transactional gain.

We can apply the circular concept of social relationships mentioned above to a guanxi network, consisting of individuals with varying degrees of relatedness. We can observe that the intensity of relationships is very strong with family and friends, somewhat strong with acquaintances, limited with strangers, and non-existent with outsiders (Zhang, 2001). The proximity along the degree of relatedness facilitates cooperation potential, which can be illustrated by the overlap between the circles representing the respective individuals. In Chinese society, guanxi management is a continuous process of reasserting relationships through mutual trust building (Fig. 6).

Managing a guanxi network in China is a social practice that prioritises relational rationality over transactional rationality. It is supported by considerations of personal utility, such as social recognition, as well as social and moral expectations of the community. In enduring relationships where transactions are not symmetric, even in the long run, unequal transactions can occur without requiring balance. Social credits and debts are crucial for maintaining such relationships. The provider gains visibility and a positive reputation by acknowledging and accepting transactional losses to sustain the well-being of others (Lin, 2009, pp. 87–88). Persistent relationships play a vital role in spreading recognition through social connections. The larger and more persistent the social network, the greater the impact on recognition and reputation.

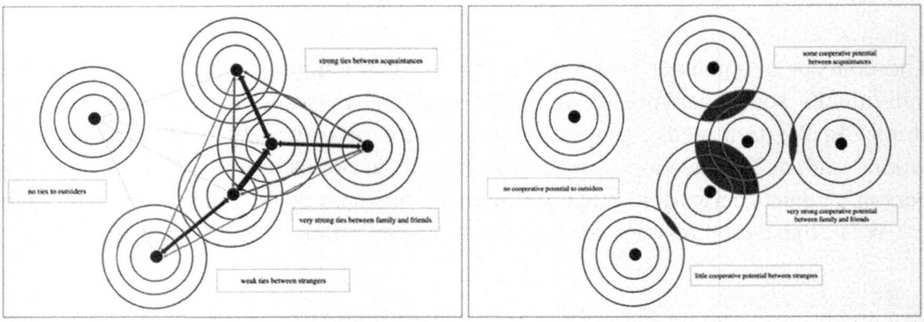

Fig. 6 Intensity of relations and collaboration potentials in a guanxi network. (Own illustration)

Individuals depend on their social circles to sustain and promote their social standing. Even those with lower social standing can benefit from active participation in social networks. While transactional rationality can be seen on an individual level, where partners in exchanges are interchangeable as long as they fulfil the requirements of the transactional utility, relational rationality relies on the group. The more resources are integrated within the networks, and the stronger the connections, the more significant the collective benefit to the group and the relative benefit to each actor in it (Lin, 2009, p. 92).

Guanxi involves the willingness to maintain social relations, which is viewed as an expression and practice of higher-order moral and ethical obligations to other human beings. An individual's social reputation and standing—"face" (mianzi) in Chinese culture—are central, while transactions are considered of secondary importance. Sacrificing relationships for transactional gain is seen as immoral, inhuman, and unethical. Negative recognition within the network is a serious issue. When a debtor perceives a returned favour as insufficient and begins to spread negative feedback, it not only tarnishes the individual's reputation in the direct relationship but also within the broader network. In response, the creditor may opt to increase future favours, alter their perception of the debtor, or terminate the relationship entirely (ibid., pp. 98–99). However, reciprocity within the network does not necessarily need to be immediate or evenly balanced since the balancing of gains and losses is considered to happen from a long-term perspective. The security for everybody involved in the community is another vital consideration here (Hermann-Pillath, 2011).

5.3 *Trust Building in a Relational Society*

According to political scientist Francis Fukuyama, trust relationships in China are primarily based on kinship ties. For him, this results in a "low-trust culture" outside of family conglomerates, which may lead to the proliferation of small family businesses while bringing challenges in institutionalising the corporate form of organisation (Fukuyama, 1998, p. 133). This lack of trust among economic agents who are unrelated or unfamiliar with one another can increase economic transaction costs (Fukuyama, 1995, p. 74; Marsh, 2019, p. 211). However, some scholars argue that trust in the Chinese social setting is merely limited to insiders rather than there being a general lack of social trust (Kwok & White, 2004, p. 72).

Whether or not we agree with the concept of a "low-trust culture", interpersonal trust in Chinese firms plays a central role. Chinese entrepreneurs and managers address this by turning the company into a familial structure, which provides the necessary legitimacy for its members to build trust with superiors, other organisational units, team members, and subordinates (Chan & Lee, 2014; Niedenführ, 2021b). The predominance of relational rationality in Chinese society, as opposed to the transactional rationality prevalent in Western society, is an important concept for this study.

As we've seen in Fei Xiaotong's circular model, relational rationality is particularly dominant in interactions with family and kin, decreases in interactions with acquaintances, and is least evident in interactions with strangers. In Chinese business culture, decision-makers generally prefer to interact with individuals who are already part of their guanxi network before engaging in business. Alternatively, decision-makers aim to establish indirect and, eventually, direct introductions. At the same time, to some scholars, Chinese business people have a strong sense of autonomy which is a subjective force directing them to favour self-management as a way of market participation, whereas relational rationality—that is relying upon the relations among family members and friends—is the objective force determining whether the necessary social resources can be obtained (Wang, 2006).

One important aspect that differentiates this relational approach built upon transactional rationality is the role and understanding of the individual vis-à-vis the others and the scope of time involved. "Relational rationality factors in future expectations and demands, as well as future expected benefits deriving from the relation". These are not extremely relevant in transactional rationality. In a transactional view, the business relationship is focused on the mutual exchange of information prior to the business deal and the conclusion of the exchange of payments, goods, or services upon reaching a contract.

5.4 The Role of Affective Relations

In Chinese business culture, relational rationality dominates decision-making. This means that the long-term impact of a decision on the relationship with business partners and one's reputation within the guanxi network significantly influences business calculations. As a result, the boundary between private and business matters, as well as family and community, is not as distinct as it is in non-Chinese business contexts.

The presence of "affective relations" (renqing) in business and politics in China is crucial in understanding the role of guanxi. Tillman's research on the Song dynasty as the first heyday of the market economy in Chinese economic history demonstrates that "affective relationships" among intellectuals, politicians, and businesspeople facilitated cooperation on social and political matters and allowed for sociopolitical activism with networking going beyond mere friendship (Tillman, 2004, pp. 121–125, 131). In the past and present, businesspeople who rely on Confucian values in the field of business are accomplished networkers who comprehend emotional ties. Their business dealings are frequently dependent on obtaining support from family members and a diverse array of individuals (ibid, p. 136), (see also Niedenführ 2021a).

Any attempt to define a distinct Chinese form of relational rationality needs to (a) consider the role of the individual in relation to the community, especially in terms of social benefits and obligations (guanxi), and (b) to factor the dominant aspect of affection in business dealings in Chinese business culture.

5.5 Flexible Application of Relational and Transactional Logic

The previous discussions do not imply that Chinese people only focus on relationships in their social interactions or business dealings. Similarly, suggesting that people in Western societies are solely motivated by transactional considerations would be inaccurate. In contemporary societies, including China, Japan, Italy, and much of East Asia, and economically competitive societies like the United States, Britain, Germany, and France, relationships remain a significant factor in economic transactions. This indicates that the importance of relationships in exchanges thrives in diverse contemporary societies (Lin, 2009, p. 95).

In every culture, both relational and transactional rationalities exist, but to a different degree. It is also incorrect to argue that only one type is rational, while the other is merely irrational. However, historical factors have favoured one over the other as a preferred institution. Transactional rationality recommends prioritising transactional gains over relationships and suggests ending a relationship if better options are available. This often requires choosing between transactional rationality and relational rationality. Both rationalities are fundamentally different in terms of what time frame is involved, how decisions are made, and what standards of fairness, ethics, and modes of communication are applied (Table 1).

Chinese business decision-makers must navigate both domestic and East Asian business environments using a networked mode of interaction, especially in their dealings with the government. Simultaneously, they face external pressure to adhere to the global economic and financial system established by Western powers. The ability to apply competing and sometimes conflicting logic is a characteristic of

Table 1 Comparison of transactional and relational rationalities (own illustration)

	Transactional rationality	Relational rationality
Time frame	Short-term/medium-term	Medium-term/long term
Decision making	Based on current information	Based on experience and expectations
Standard of fairness	Transactional ethics	Relational ethics
Rationality	Reduced risk by using contractual clarity	Reduced risk by employing trust and mutual interest building
Cultural complexity	Communication failures difficult to address due to the short time of interaction	Communication failures addressed through long-term interaction and transcultural learning
Moral hazard	Abusing incomplete information as a one-sided advantage	Nepotism, price and quality compromises due to expectation of leniency
Contingency of unfair behaviour	Cheating addressed through contractional fines	Cheating addressed through contractional fines and collapse of relationship
View of the individual	Atomistic view	Interrelated, quantum view

ancient Chinese philosophy and contemporary social reality. In China, developing and maintaining a guanxi network is socially necessary, providing ample opportunities to contemplate relational rationality. Therefore, Chinese decision-makers may be well equipped to adopt a flexible approach that employs relational and transactional logic based on specific circumstances.

6 Relational Rationality and the Tianxia Debate

In Chinese Contemporary philosophical and political discourse, the dominant role of Western individualism is critiqued as having a negative effect on Western societies and social cohesion and a similar effect on Chinese society. Chinese scholars define "Relational rationality" using the relationship between individuals as the foundation for understanding the meaning of human existence. It emphasises the value of mutual recognition, respect, dependence, and harmonious coexistence. This concept realises the negation and transcendence of both objective and subjective rationality (Deng & Du, 2020). They suggest that there is a contradiction between "subjective rationality" and a genuine sense of "commonality". They argue that it is not helpful to operate solely with an "objective rationality" based on an abstract "community" on the one hand and a "subjective rationality" relying on abstract "individuals" on the other. Instead, they propose a "relational rationality" that transcends both, allowing for the establishment of the concept of "subjectivity for others" (He, 2015).

Philosopher Zhao Tingyang has referred to ancient governance ideals of pre-imperial China, particularly the concept of tianxia ("All under Heaven"), and updated it to fit the contemporary global situation (Zhao, 2005, 2009a). In this thinking, tianxia is—first and for all—understood as a set of civilisational principles with a corresponding institutional system, and not an empire. In today's world, where Western and Chinese values and political systems compete for global dominance, Zhao suggests "an ontology of coexistence for the 21st Century" (Zhao, 2009b). His proposal envisions a world order where states are no longer the most important political entities shaping global politics. Instead, the new system would be based on the equality of all states and individuals being equal, embracing the world's diversity of cultures and religions (Zhao, 2016). This new tianxia system would integrate the outside world, transforming adversaries into allies and establishing an anti-imperial framework aimed at achieving universal peace and security. It would underscore the idea that an individual's advancement is contingent upon the collective improvement of conditions. Universalist principles and values would underpin this model. The concept of "relational rationality" is crucial for this system, fostering a social order that prioritises common interests and underscores the notion that cooperation outweighs competition (Zhao, 2019).

Historian Ge Zhaoguang heavily criticises this domestic discourse, arguing that it describes an ancient Chinese utopia of an "all the world is one family" in both the "ethical" and the "political science" sense. Ge rejects the notion that in any phase of Chinese history did tianxia form a geographical and political body offering equality for people and religions, since it always distinguished between "inside" and "outside", "Chinese" and "barbarians", as well as between "superiors" and "inferiors" (Ge, 2015; Duke and Chiu-Duke, 2020). Hence, the notions of a new tianxia may better be understood as a way forward for China to escape the traps of excessive national pride and geopolitical competition. For Zhao, the value of the concept lies in the fact that "an attempt was made to think of the whole world as such, including all the nations and all the peoples that exist under heaven" (Kahn-Ackermann, 2020).

Although Zhao rejects the competition of imperial powers, many Chinese scholars tend to link discussions of modernity with the belief in the potential superiority of the Chinese political and cultural system. For them, the rediscovery of the idea of tianxia was mainly a product of China's rise, aiming to establish a "Chinese moment" in the twenty-first century, following the idea that the nineteenth century was dominated by the British and the twentieth century by the Americans.

Historian Xu Jinlin warns against excessive nationalism and suggests that a "new universalism, 'a kind of axial civilization wisdom that comes from ancient traditions and is reinterpreted in a modern way', was necessary to counteract the national consciousness". This new spatial imaginary and political system does not position China in its centre since when China was great in the past, it was an open country, not a closed one. If China wishes to be great again, it must adopt the same posture because civilisations, by definition, must be universal (Xu, 2015; McConaghy et al., 2018).

7 Conclusion

This chapter examined relational and transactional rationalities in business and social interaction in East Asia, especially in China, with the aim to illuminate the factors in Chinese philosophy and economic history that guide people's behaviour in contemporary social and business practice.

Different historical experiences, geographical conditions, and political and moral considerations have had a lasting impact on societies in the West and China. Over time, a cultural identity shaped by individualism, freedom, and competition has emerged in the West because of political and economic events, technological advancements, and successful resource acquisitions. This ideology forms the bedrock of people's identity, influencing their beliefs, institutions, and behaviour. In contrast, relational rationality has deep historical roots in the East, particularly in China. Over time, Confucian scholars defined the meaning and importance of relational rationality as institutions and empires promoted the ideology and put it into practice in forming bureaucracies and local organisations. Hence, in China, individuals are expected to prioritise reputation as their guide in behaviour and social interactions (Lin, 2009, pp. 103–104).

It would be incorrect to argue that transactional rationality was superior while discarding relational rationality. It is also incorrect to argue that only one type is rational. Both types of rationality are present in every culture. However, history has a significant and decisive role in elevating one type of rationality over the other as a favoured institution (ibid., pp. 102–103).

When conducting business in China as an outsider, or vice versa, it can be challenging to understand what behaviours are considered fair and morally acceptable. This difficulty arises from a lack of social experience, as well as historical and cultural knowledge, to serve as references. Gaining transcultural competencies may empower Western people to navigate the intricacies of Eastern cultures and learn how to apply relational logic appropriately and successfully.

Chinese scholars believe that it is important to give equal importance to relational and transactional rationalities in intellectual discussions as a first step in tackling this issue. Placing the discussion within the framework of cultural identity could be a useful perspective in addressing this challenge. Similar to how transactional rationality benefited from the industrial advancement of the West, relational rationality may also gain prominence as China and industrialising economies in the East further develop (ibid., pp. 103–104).

In the past 20 years, Chinese scholars have been exploring the idea of expanding Chinese concepts of relational rationality from interactions within families, guanxi networks, businesses, and entire societies to a global level. They propose embracing the ancient notion of tianxia as a new vision for global cooperation based on relational rationality. However, this discussion is affected by unique issues, including the politicisation of academic discourse in China. Despite these challenges, further research on the relevance of this concept for discussions on relational governance is definitely warranted.

References

Amelung, I., & Schefold, B. (2021). Towards a systematic comparison of different forms of economic thought. In I. Amelung & B. Schefold (Eds.), *European and Chinese histories of economic thought: Theories and images of good governance* (Routledge studies in the history of economics, pp. 277–302). Routledge.

Ames, R. T. (1993). *Sun-tzu: The art of warfare: The first English translation incorporating the recently discovered Yin-ch'üeh-shan texts*. Ballantine Books.

Ames, R. T., & Rosemont, H., Jr. (2010). *The analects of Confucius: A philosophical translation*. Ballantine Books.

Bauer, W. (2001). *History of Chinese philosophy: Confucianism, Daoism, Buddhism*. C.H. Beck.

Bell, D. A. (2011). Introduction. In X. Yan (Ed.), *Ancient Chinese thought, modern Chinese power* (pp. 1–18). London School of Economics and Social Sciences.

Billioud, S. (2010). Carrying the Confucian torch to the masses: The challenge of structuring the Confucian revival in the People's Republic of China. *Oriens Extremum, 49*, 201–221.

Billioud, S. (2018). *The varieties of Confucian experience: Documenting a grassroots revival of tradition*. Brill.

Bodde, D. (1986). The state and empire of Ch'in. In D. Twitchett & M. Loewe (Eds.), *The Ch'in and Han empires, 221 BC–AD* (Vol. 220 (Vol. 1, pp. 20–102). Cambridge University Press.

Brook, T. (1998). *The confusions of pleasure: Commerce and culture in Ming China*. University of California Press.

Chan, Y. K. (2019, June 6). *China's economic system: From where? To where? Lecture at China Centre Tübingen*. University of Tübingen.
Chan, C.-C., & Lee, Y.-T. (2014). *Leadership and management in China: Philosophies, theories, and practices* (2nd ed.). Cambridge University Press.
Chan, W.-t. (1963). *The way of Lao Tzu*. Bobbs-Merrill.
Chan, W.-t. (1969). *A source book in Chinese philosophy*. Princeton University Press.
Cheng, C.-Y. (1994). The "C" theory: A Chinese philosophical approach to management and decision-making. *Sun Yat-sen Management Review, 2*(4), 1–20.
Creel, H. G. (1970). *What is Taoism? And other studies in Chinese cultural history*. University of Chicago Press.
Creel, H. G. (1974). *Shen Pu-hai: A Chinese political philosopher of the fourth century BC*. University of Chicago Press.
De Bettignies, H.-C., Ip, P.-K., Bai, X., Habisch, A., & Lenssen, G. (2011). Practical wisdom for management from the Chinese classical traditions. *Journal of Management Development, 30*(7/8), 623–628.
Deng, S., & Du, S. (2020). Research on building the Chinese nation community from the perspective of relational rationality. *Guangxi Ethnic Studies, 2*(152), 11–18.
Dirlik, A. (1995). Confucius in the borderlands: Global capitalism and the reinvention of Confucianism. *Boundary 2, 22*(3), 229–273.
Duke, M. S., & Chiu-Duke, J. (2020). Ge Zhaoguang, "Tianxia and Utopia." *Reading the China Dream*. Retrieved February 2, 2024, from www.readingthechinadream.com/ge-zhaoguang-tianxia-and-utopia.html
Ebrey, P. B. (1986). Economic and social history of later Han. In D. Twitchett & M. Loewe (Eds.), *The Ch'in and Han empires, 221 BC–AD 220* (Vol. 1, pp. 608–648). Cambridge University Press.
Ertman, T. (Ed.). (2017). *Max Weber's economic ethic of the world religions: An analysis*. Cambridge University Press.
Fei, X. (1947). *From the soil: The foundations of Chinese society* (G. G. Hamilton & W. Zheng, Trans.). University of California Press.
Fukuyama, F. (1995). *Trust: Social virtues and the creation of prosperity*. Simon & Schuster.
Fukuyama, F. (1998). *Trust: Social virtues and the creation of prosperity*. Far East Publishers.
Fung, Y.-L. (1947). *A short history of Chinese philosophy*. Tianjin Academy of Social Sciences Press.
Fung, Y.-L. (1958). *A short history of Chinese philosophy*. Macmillan.
Gawlikowski, K., & Loewe, M. (1993). Sun Tzu ping Fa. In M. Loewe (Ed.), *Early Chinese texts: A bibliographical guide* (Early China special monograph series 2, pp. 446–455). University of California Press.
Ge, Z. (2015). Imagining 'all under heaven:' The political, intellectual and academic background of a new utopia. *Reflections, 29*. Retrieved February 2, 2024, from www.aisixiang.com/data/92884.html
Gernet, J. (1962). *Daily life in China on the eve of the Mongol invasion, 1250–1276*. Stanford University Press.
Gerstner, A. (2011). Leadership and organizational patterns in the Daodejing. *Journal of Management Development, 30*(7/8), 675–684.
Gold, T., Guthrie, D., & Wank, D. (Eds.). (2002). *Social connections in China: Institutions, culture, and the changing nature of guanxi*. Cambridge University Press.
Granet, M. (1985). *The Chinese thinking* (M. Porkert, Trans.). Suhrkamp.
Hansen, C. (2000). *A Daoist theory of Chinese thought: A philosophical interpretation*. Oxford University Press.
Hansson, A. (1996). *Chinese outcasts: Discrimination and emancipation in late Imperial China*. Brill.
He, L. (2015). Relational rationality and real community. *Social Sciences in China, 6*(22–44), 205–220.

Hennig, A., & Niedenführ, M. (2020). Daoism and ethics in management. In C. Neesham & S. Segal (Eds.), *Handbook of philosophy of management* (pp. 851–861). Springer.
Hermann-Pillath, C. (2011). *A "third culture" in economics? An essay on smith, Confucius and the rise of China*. (Frankfurt School of Finance & Management Working Paper Series, p. 119). https://hdl.handle.net/10419/45025
Hermann-Pillath, C. (2016). *China's economic culture: The ritual order of state and markets*. Routledge.
Hutton, E. L. (2016). *Xunzi: The complete text*. Princeton University Press.
Institute for Early Modern History of China. (2000). *Westernization movement (Yangwu Yundong)*. Shanghai People's Press.
Ji, Z. (2018). Making a virtue of piety: Dizigui and the discursive practice of Jinkong's network. In S. Billioud (Ed.), *The sage and the people: The Confucian revival in China* (pp. 60–89). Oxford University Press.
Kaesler, D. (2015). *Max Weber – Prussian, thinker, mother's boy: A biography*. C.H. Beck.
Kahn-Ackermann, M. (2020). Introduction. In T. Zhao (Ed.), *All under heaven: Past and future of world order*. Suhrkamp.
Kam, L. (2011). Confucius the chameleon: Dubious envoy for 'Brand China'. *Boundary 2, 38*(1), 77–100.
Kuhn, D. (1988). Textile technology: Spinning and reeling. In J. Needham (Ed.), *Science and civilisation in China* (Vol. 9). Cambridge University Press.
Kwok, L., & White, S. (2004). *Handbook of Asian management*. Springer Science & Business Media.
Lai, K. L. (1995). Confucian moral thinking. *Philosophy East and West, 45*(2), 249–272.
Lau, D. C. (Trans.). (2004). *Mencius*. Penguin Classics. (Original work published 1970).
Legge, J. (Trans.). (1891). *The writings of Chuang Tzu*. Oxford University Press.
L'Haridon, B. (2015). The merchants in Shiji: An interpretation in the light of later debates. In H. van Ess, O. Lomová, & D. Schaab-Hank (Eds.), *Views from within and beyond: Approaches to the Shiji as an early work of historiography* (pp. 171–192). Harrasowitz.
Lin, N. (2009). The relational and transactional rationality: Exploring eastern and Western bases of exchanges. *Taiwan Journal of East Asian Studies, 6*(2), 71–109.
Liu, X. (2001). Non-action and the environment today. In N. J. Giradot, J. Miller, & X. Liu (Eds.), *Daoism and ecology: Ways within a cosmic landscape* (pp. 315–339). Harvard University Press.
Liu, H. (2018). *Chinese business – Landscapes and strategies* (2nd ed.). Routledge.
Long, D., & Chi, X. (2021). Outline of the institutions for land transactions in traditional China. In I. Amelung & B. Schefold (Eds.), *European and Chinese histories of economic thought: Theories and images of good governance* (pp. 49–62). Routledge.
Lufrano, R. (1997). *Honorable merchants: Commerce and self-cultivation in late imperial China*. University of Hawai'i Press.
Makeham, J. (2011). The revival of Guoxue. China. *Perspectives, 1*, 14–21.
Marsh, R. (2019). Social trust in Japan and Taiwan: A test of Fukuyama's thesis. In M. Sasaki (Ed.), *Trust in contemporary society* (pp. 210–229). Brill.
McConaghy, M., Tang, X., & Ownby, D. (2018, February 2). Xu Jilin, "The New Tianxia". *Reading the China Dream*. https://www.readingthechinadream.com/xu-jilin-the-new-tianxia.html
McNeilly, M. R. (2015). *Sun Tzu and the art of modern warfare*. Oxford University Press.
Miller, J. (2006). Daoism and nature. In R. S. Gottlieb (Ed.), *Handbook of religion and ecology* (pp. 220–235). Oxford University Press.
Ming, X. (2015). The theory of the change from the roots to Confucian entrepreneurship. *China Philanthropist, 6*. http://www.shanda960.com/shandaguan/article/4069
Ming, X. (2016). Attitude and will: The emergence of the concept of "Confucian Merchants" during the Ming dynasty. Hua Mulan Wenhua Chubanshe.
Moeller, H. G. (2004). *Daoism explained: From the dream of the butterfly to the fishnet allegory*. Open Court Publishing.

Niedenführ, M. (2021a). Confucian entrepreneurship and moral guidelines for business in China. In I. Amelung & B. Schefold (Eds.), *European and Chinese histories of economic thought: Theories and images of good governance* (pp. 259–274). Routledge.
Niedenführ, M. (2021b). Humanistic management with a Confucian twist – The case of FOTILE. In E. von Kimakowitz, C. Dierksmeier, C. Largacha-Martinéz, & H. Schirovsky (Eds.), *Humanistic management in practice* (Vol. 2, pp. 217–238). Palgrave Macmillan.
Niedenführ, M., & Hennig, A. (2020). Confucianism and ethics in management. In C. Neesham & S. Segal (Eds.), *Handbook of philosophy of management* (pp. 837–849). Springer.
Nivison, D. S. (1999). The classical philosophical writings. In M. Loewe & E. L. Shaughnessy (Eds.), *The Cambridge history of ancient China – From the origins of civilization to 221 BC* (pp. 745–812). Cambridge University Press.
Pines, Y. (2018). Legalism in Chinese philosophy. In E. N. Zalta (Ed.), *The Stanford encyclopedia of philosophy* (winter 2018 ed.). Stanford University. http://plato.stanford.edu/archives/win2018/entries/chinese-legalism
Research Centre for the Culture of Confucian Entrepreneurs (RCCCE). (2008). *Overview of Confucian entrepreneurs* (Rushang renwu pian). http://www.pku-rswh.com/personae.asp (retr. 10.11.2016).
Ruan, Z. (1996). Engaging in trade and propriety and righteousness – Analysis of "biographies of merchants in the Records of the Grand Historian". *Taida Lishi xuebao, 19*, 1–49.
Shibuzawa, E. (1998). *The analects and the abacus*. Kadokawa Bunkō.
So, B. (2000). *Prosperity, region, and institutions in maritime China*. Harvard University Press.
Tang, Y. (2015). *Confucianism, Buddhism, Daoism, Christianity and Chinese culture*. Springer.
Theobald, U. (2019). *Sunzi Bingfa*. http://www.chinaknowledge.de/Literature/Diverse/sunzibingfa.html
Tillman, H. C. (2004). Selected Confucian networks and values in society and the economy. In D. A. Bell & H. C. Ark (Eds.), *The politics of affective relations: East Asia and beyond* (pp. 121–147). Lexington.
Tu, W. (1979). *Humanity and self-cultivation: Essays in Confucian thought*. Asian Humanities.
Tu, W. (1991). Cultural China: The periphery as the center. *Daedalus, 120*(2), 1–32.
Tu, W. (2001). The ecological turn in new Confucian humanism: Implications for China and the world. *Daedalus, 130*(4), 243–264.
Tu, W. (2010). *The global significance of concrete humanity – Essays on the Confucian discourse in cultural China*. Centre for Studies in Civilizations.
Wang, H. (2006). Self-action and self-management: Understanding why the Chinese people regard self-management as their first choice in market practice. *Chinese Journal of Sociology, 26*(3), 24–45.
Wang, J. (2019). *The Confucian entrepreneur: Model of a new business civilization* (M. Niedenführ, Trans.). Academy Association of Confucianism of Germany 2019 conference proceedings (pp. 1–17).
Watson, B. (1968). *Records of the grand historian of China* (Vol. 1–2, 3rd ed.). Columbia University Press.
Weber, M. (2016). *Max Weber study edition – Economy and society*. Mohr & Siebeck.
Wieland, J. (2020). Relational economics – A political economy. In *Relational economics and organization governance*. Springer.
Xu, J. (2015). The new Tianxia: Rebuilding China's internal and external order. In J. Xu & Q. Liu (Eds.), *New Tianxia* (Intellectuals series) (Vol. 13). Shanghai People's Publishing.
Yao, X. (2000). *An introduction to Confucianism*. Cambridge University Press.
Yao, M. (2011, December 13). Businessmen seek Confucian chic. *Shanghai Daily*. http://archive.shine.cn/feature/Businessmen-seek-Confucian-chic/shdaily.shtml
Yu, Y. (1959). New self-awareness and new thoughts of scholars between the Han- and Jin-dynasties. *Yinya Journal of Chinese Studies, 4*(1), 25–144.
Yu, Y. (1987). *Religious ethics and business spirit in modern China*. Lianjing.

Yu, Y. (2016a). Toward a study of the evolution of merchant culture in Chinese history. In Y. Yu, J. Chiu-Duke, & M. S. Duke (Eds.), *Chinese history and culture: Sixth century BCE to seventeenth century* (Vol. 1, pp. 222–272). Columbia University Press.
Yu, Y. (2016b). Confucian ethics and capitalism. In Y. Yu, J. Chiu-Duke, & M. S. Duke (Eds.), *Chinese history and culture: Sixth century BCE to seventeenth century* (Vol. 1, pp. 208–221). Columbia University Press.
Yuan, S. (Ed.). (1998). *Zhang Zhidong's complete works*. Hebei Renmin Chubanshe.
Zhang, X. (2001). Practicing kinship. In S. Franklin & S. McKinnon (Eds.), *Relative values: Reconfiguring kinship studies* (pp. 224–245). Duke University Press.
Zhao, T. (2005). *The Tianxia system: An introduction to the philosophy of world institutions*. Jiangsu Educational Publishing.
Zhao, T. (2009a). A political world philosophy in terms of all-under-heaven. *Diogenes, 56*(1), 5–18.
Zhao, T. (2009b). Ontology of coexistence. *Diogenes, 228*(4), 35–49.
Zhao, T. (2016). *Redefining a philosophy for world governance*. Palgrave Pivot.
Zhao, T. (2019). *What exactly is the world? – A response to Salvatore Barbonas' "American world"*. Bergruen Institute. https://www.berggruen.org.cn/article/zhao-ting-yang-what-is-the-world
Zhu, Y. (2006). On China's traditional business ethics and its modern transformation. In X. Lu & G. Enderle (Eds.), *Developing business ethics in China* (pp. 23–34). Palgrave Macmillan.

Matthias Niedenführ is a Senior Research Fellow at the Leadership Excellence Institute Zeppelin. He is a sinologist and business ethicist, having spent over a decade researching and working in China, Japan, and Taiwan. His research focus is on leadership, corporate culture, and sustainability in companies in East Asia. He completed a junior professorship in "Business Culture and Ethics in China" at the University of Tübingen and established the China Centre Tübingen as its Vice Director.

The manufacturer's authorised representative in the EU is Springer Nature Customer Service Centre GmbH, Europaplatz 3, 69115 Heidelberg, Germany. If you have any concerns regarding our products, please contact ProductSafety@springernature.com

Printed and bound by CPI Group (UK) Ltd, Croydon, CR0 4YY
01/10/2026
02225934-0007